1001

Things Everyone Should Know About

The South

Happy Birthday to a real
Southern Gentleman, from
his Virginian Mother

Love for 44 yrs
Mom

10/14/012

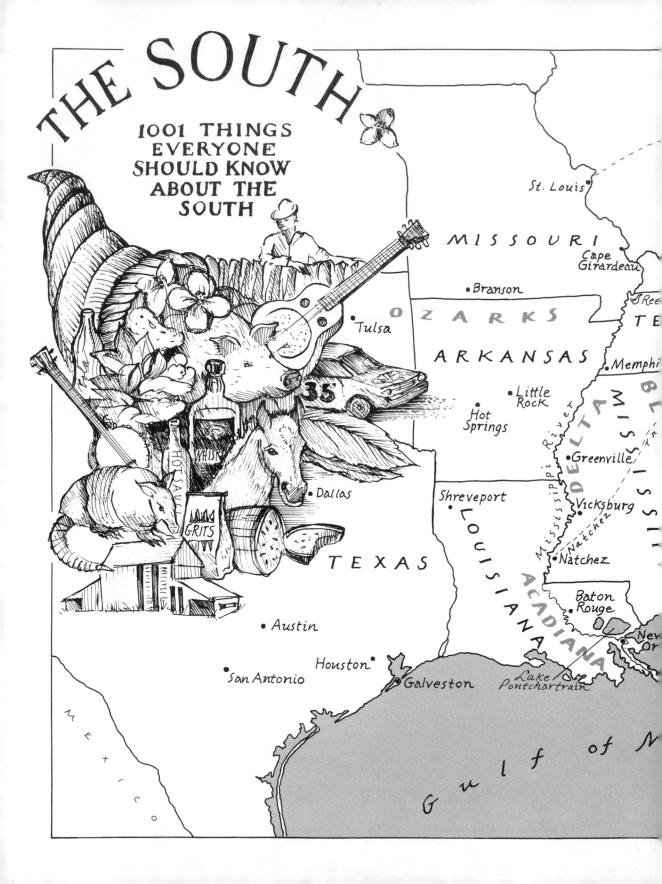

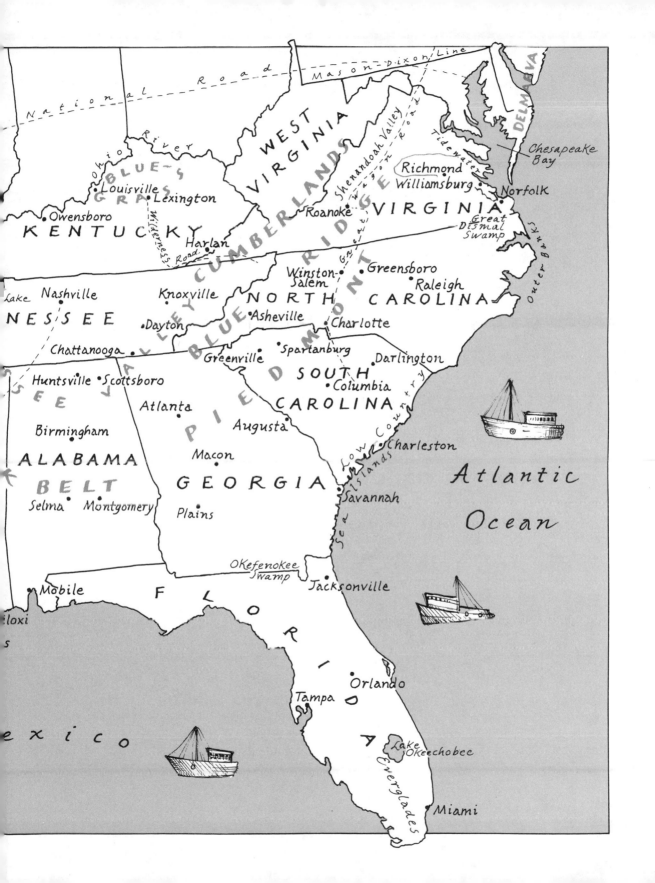

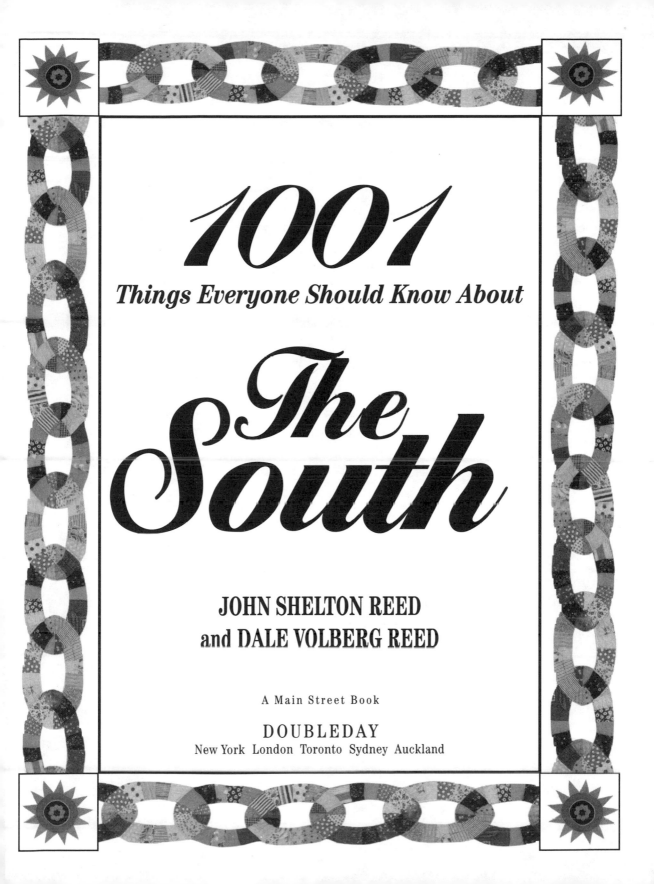

1001
Things Everyone Should Know About

The South

JOHN SHELTON REED
and DALE VOLBERG REED

A Main Street Book

DOUBLEDAY
New York London Toronto Sydney Auckland

A MAIN STREET BOOK

PUBLISHED BY DOUBLEDAY

a division of Bantam Doubleday Dell Publishing Group, Inc.

1540 Broadway, New York, New York 10036

MAIN STREET BOOKS, DOUBLEDAY, and the portrayal of a building

with a tree are trademarks of Doubleday,

a division of Bantam Doubleday Dell Publishing Group, Inc.

Book design by Bonni Leon-Berman

Map designed by Martie Holmer

1001 Things Everyone Should Know About the South was originally

published in hardcover by Doubleday. The Main Street Books edition is published by

arrangement with Doubleday.

The Library of Congress has cataloged the Doubleday edition as follows:

Reed, John Shelton.

1001 things everyone should know about the South / John Shelton

Reed and Dale Volberg Reed.

p.   cm.

Includes index.

1. Southern States—Miscellanea.   2. Southern States—History—

Miscellanea.   I. Reed, Dale Volberg.   II. Title.

F209.R43   1996

975—dc20   95–41854

CIP

Contents

Introduction   ix

1. **The Southland:** Geography and Environment   1
2. **Southern Culture(s):** Origins and Folkways   23
3. **Boom and Bust:** Agriculture, Commerce, and Industry   47
4. **The Southern Nation:** The Confederacy and Its Legacy   73
5. **The Central Theme:** Race and Politics   101
6. **Grit Lit:** Writers and Literature   129
7. **Picking and Singing:** Music and Dance   159
8. **Eating and Drinking:** Southern Cuisine   189
9. **Paintings and Porticoes:** Architecture and Art   209
10. **Preaching and Teaching:** Religion and Higher Education   235
11. **Kicking Back:** Sports and Tourism   251
12. **The Mythic South:** The South of the Mind   271

Acknowledgments   295
Index   297

$\mathcal{Introduction}$

No lie, the average Yankee knows about as much about the South as a

hog knows about the Lord's plan for salvation.

—WILLIAM PRICE FOX

LET'S GET IT STRAIGHT up front: these are *a* thousand and one things everyone should know about the South, not *the* thousand and one, okay? We were just getting started when we had to quit. And they're *our* thousand and one. If you don't like our list, make your own.

But, seriously, we had a hard time choosing. What you've got here are 1001 paragraphs dealing with subjects we think are important, or interesting, or even both. Many are things you've probably heard of but don't exactly *know*. We haven't mentioned some things we assume everybody *does* know, and, frankly, some things we left out because they're boring.

Maybe we didn't leave out *everything* boring (we have to live with our consciences), but this doesn't pretend to be a reference book or a comprehensive overview. There are plenty of both, and we've drawn freely on them, but this is our own idiosyncratic catalog of Southern people, places, and—well, "things" that we wish everybody knew, but suspect they don't.

The people may be overrepresented. A third or so of these items are about them, and a good many more are about groups or organizations. Even some of the places and things are excuses to talk about people. But it is Southern people, after all, who've made the South *the South*—that is, something more than just the southeastern United States. And there'd be even more people in here if we knew who invented pork barbecue and the shimmy.

This format inevitably suggests that we think our 1001 things are of roughly equal importance. All we can do is deny it (while recognizing that equal billing for Robert E. Lee, Martin Luther King, and the Moon Pie should offend just about everybody). We haven't even been consistent from chapter to chapter. When it comes to sports and music, we've treated only the really major—original or world-class—figures. For religion and business we've mostly gone with the colorful or odd. For Confederate statesmen and soldiers and Southern literary folk, it's a mixture: some are important, some just amusing. Surely everybody knows that there have been notable Southern musicians, writers, athletes, soldiers—even entrepreneurs—so we've just given a few representative or peculiar or truly great examples. But many people *don't* know that there are Southern artists worth knowing, so there we dug deeper. Perhaps we should have done the same for areas like education, science, and medicine—but see our next book, *1001 MORE Things Everyone Should Know About the South*.

In general, we've focused on things that make the South different from the rest of America. After all, the American South is a complex modern society, just a little bit less complicated than the nation as a whole, and we needed a principle of selection. But we violated that rule whenever it seemed like a good idea, examining how the South is *not different*, when that's surprising or insufficiently appreciated.

Our "things" may be too historical for some tastes, but our own view is the Southern one (see **475**) that (as Faulkner wrote, famously) "the past is never dead. It's not even past." So many "Southern things" are rooted in the region's history, so much of that history colors the present, that half the time we don't know which is which. We've tried to strike a balance, to include a good deal of history without turning this into a book about Southern history. But, although we start with Spanish Florida (**82**) and Captain John Smith (**442**), we tend to believe that the South didn't really become The South until the sectional crisis of the 1830s, so we haven't said much about the earlier period.

At the same time, we've also gone easy on the current scene. Maybe Southerners like R.E.M. and Hootie and the Blowfish should be in our music chapter, for instance, but, then again, maybe they'll go the way of earlier groups like John Fred and His Playboy Band ("Judy in Disguise") and the Swingin' Medallions ("Double Shot of My Baby's Love"). Time will tell. Meanwhile, we'll stick with Bessie Smith (**589**) and Johnny Mercer (**604**).

As for our definition of "the South"—well, that's partly what chapter 1 is about. We've included the easy ones: the Carolinas, Tennessee, Georgia, Alabama, Mississippi, and Arkansas. Also Louisiana, although it complicates our discussion of everything from food to religion. Virginia for historical reasons, if nothing else. And the rest of the former Confederacy: the states of Texas and Florida and the territory of Oklahoma. (In many ways they don't look Southern these days and in some ways they never did, and putting them in made our job a lot harder, but damned if we'll let them go without a fight.) Kentucky's in here, too. A state known for fast horses, bourbon whiskey, and fried chicken just can't be left out of the South. Besides, it had a star in the Confederate flag, even if that was mostly wishful thinking. Missouri had a star, too, but that's more of a stretch. We've treated the Show-Me State the same way we've handled Maryland and West Virginia: it's Southern when it suits us and not when it doesn't—which is, in fact, pretty much the way the citizens of those states seem to feel about it.

And who's a Southerner? Well, Southern birth and residence will usually do it, as far as we're concerned. But it would be perverse to exclude Southerners who made careers in the North: that's often where the careers were, especially in the arts, and show business, and sports. We're inclined to claim folks who spent their formative years in Dixie (certainly if they ever spoke of themselves as Southerners), but we've generally omitted those who left at an early age, like Nat "King" Cole (b. Montgomery but raised in Chicago) or Jim Henson (b. Leland, Mississippi, but raised in D.C.). On the other hand, we've included many from elsewhere who made their lives in the South and contributed to it.

Finally, there's one *Northern* characteristic that we have to mention. Faulkner's character Gavin Stevens talks about Yankees' "volitionless, almost helpless capacity and eagerness to believe anything about the South not even provided it be derogatory but merely bizarre enough and strange enough." If you run across any blatant falsehoods in this book, consider the possibility that we put them in on purpose, to test that proposition.

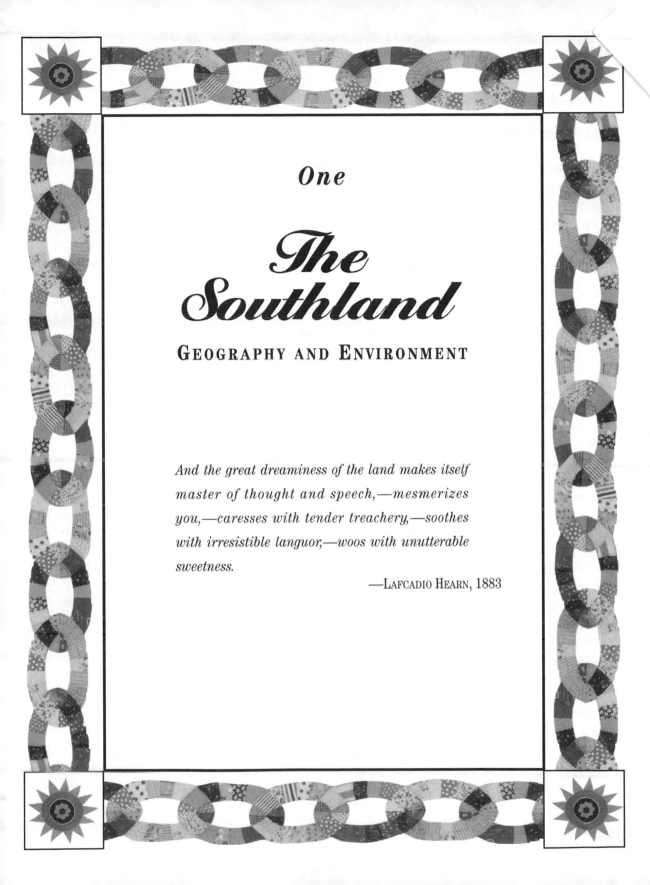

One

The Southland

GEOGRAPHY AND ENVIRONMENT

And the great dreaminess of the land makes itself master of thought and speech,—mesmerizes you,—caresses with tender treachery,—soothes with irresistible languor,—woos with unutterable sweetness.

—LAFCADIO HEARN, 1883

Definitions of the South

In 1787 Charles Pinckney said, "When I say Southern, I mean Maryland, and the states to the southward of her." But it's not that simple now, if it ever was. Here are three of the most common definitions, and what's wrong with them.

1. **Below the Mason-Dixon Line** once meant south of the Pennsylvania-Maryland boundary, surveyed in the 1760s by two Englishmen, Charles Mason and Jeremiah Dixon. The line gained significance in the nineteenth century when all of the states north of it had abolished slavery. "Below the Mason-Dixon Line" came to mean "in the South," and it has kept that meaning in innumerable popular and country songs as well as in common speech. But the only recent definition of the South that uses the real Mason-Dixon line as a boundary is—

2. **The Bureau of the Census definition.** The Census Bureau's South includes West Virginia, Maryland, Delaware, and the District of Columbia, as well as Oklahoma and twelve less questionable states. (But it doesn't simply include all of the 1860 slave states and territories: Missouri's not in it.) Few other definitions of the South are

The Census South.

that inclusive. These days most stop at the Potomac, and even the southern suburbs of Washington are known in some circles as "occupied Virginia." Generally speaking, the "Census South" is more urban, richer, and better educated than the actual South. It also has more armed robbery, AIDS, and lawyers.

3. **The Confederate States** sounds like a simple definition, but unfortunately it's not. Kentucky and Missouri both had stars in the Confederate flag and representatives in Richmond as well as in Washington. And the Confederacy never recognized West Virginia's "secession from secession." Oklahoma's Cherokees signed a treaty with the Confederacy and many fought in its army: Oklahoma wasn't a state, but was it Confederate? The Stars and Bars flew briefly over Santa Fe, New Mexico: does that count?

Maybe the best definition is just—

4. **Where people think they're in the South.** You want to tell them they're wrong? A study of business and organization names in metropolitan phone books compared the number of

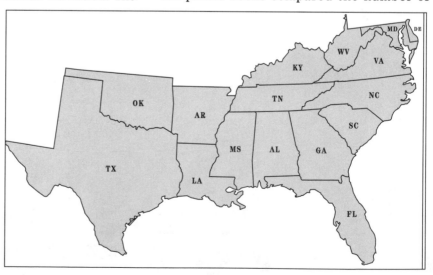

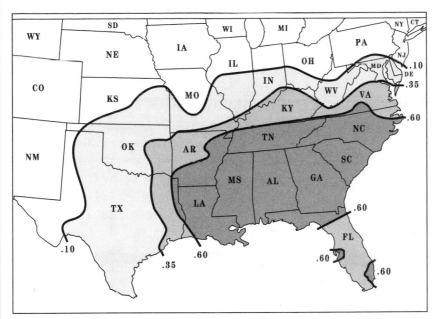

Ratio of "Southern" to "American" phone book entries.
Social Forces/University of North Carolina Press

country." It did. But by 1970 the word was used in business names mostly in the Deep South and on the Dixie Highway in Tennessee and Kentucky; now Dixie as a business name persists strongly only in Mississippi and parts of Georgia outside Atlanta. Even in Alabama—still "the Heart of Dixie" on its license plates—the word seems to be going out of style.

6. **The Cotton Kingdom** referred essentially to the part of the United States with more than twenty-three inches of rain and two hundred frost free days a year,

"Southern" entries to the number of "American" entries, and gave a map that makes pretty good sense: a solid core from the Carolinas to Louisiana; some shakiness in Florida, Arkansas, Kentucky, and Virginia; and a sphere of influence along the border from Delaware to Missouri. Texas and Oklahoma are marginal but show an east-to-west gradient that will not surprise natives.

THE SOUTH A/K/A

THE SOUTH HAS BEEN called many things, for many reasons.

5. **Dixie**'s origins are lost in obscurity (let's not get into it), but it was a song title (**325**) before it meant the South as a whole. One Confederate wrote in 1861, "We shall be fortunate if [the song] does not impose its very name on our

"Dixie" persists in *some* business names. DixiePix

The Cotton Kingdom in 1870. *The Great South* (1875)

which made cotton cultivation possible and, for a time, profitable—in other words, to the *Deep South* (**14**). By the 1850s Southern cotton was the nation's chief export; Europe's dependence on it led South Carolina's Senator James Hammond to declare that "cotton is king." "No power on earth dares to make war upon it," he boasted. (He was wrong about that.) When the boll weevil (**72**) appeared in Texas in the 1890s, King Cotton's days were numbered.

7. **The New South,** a phrase popularized by Henry Grady (**997**) in 1886, referred to an ideal South rebuilt by outside investment and industry, and free of "sectional controversies." (White supremacy and the continuation of planter rule were simply assumed.) The growth and progress of Atlanta, its heart, would be an example for the rest of the region. This ideal still has charms for Southern Chambers of Commerce and Northern investors, but the phrase "New South" long ago lost its precision and is now invariably applied to whatever the South seems to be about to become.

8. **The Sahara of the Bozart** (beaux arts) was journalist H. L. Mencken's label for the South in his 1917 essay with that title. It condemned the modern South as "almost as sterile, artistically, intellectually, culturally, as the Sahara Desert," a fact Mencken attributed to the destruction of the region's aristocracy in the Civil War. That the Southern Renaissance (**488**) in literature began almost immediately after Mencken's essay may not be accidental.

9. **The Bible Belt** was another of Mencken's contemptuous labels for a region he saw as "a cesspool of Baptists, a miasma of Methodism, snake-charmers, . . . and syphilitic evangelists." Most Southerners, however, would probably accept the designation with pride; most are in fact evangelical Protestants who adhere to Bible-believing churches (**794**).

10. **Below the Smith and Wesson Line,** a phrase apparently first used in print by sociologist Rupert Vance in 1930, refers to the South's homicide rate, historically twice that of other U.S. regions. The gap has narrowed since 1970 (the South's rate has not decreased, but those of other regions have increased faster), but this regrettable statistic can still be used to map the South.

11. **The Solid South** referred to the South's consistent Democratic voting after Reconstruction. (The phrase appears to date from the election of 1876 [**411**].) Although there were cracks in the Solid South as early as 1920, it was only after the Dixiecrat revolt in 1948 (**413**) that the South really began to move to a two-party system in presidential elections, and more recently

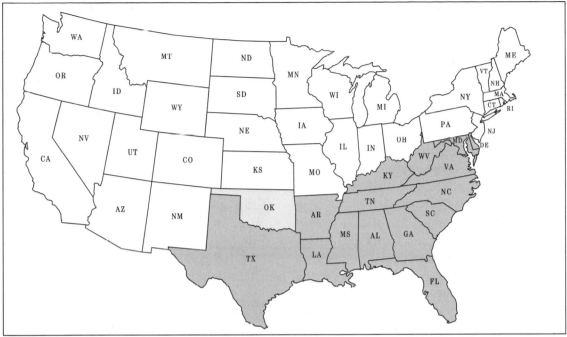

The Solid South in 1904: states for Parker (Dem.) over Roosevelt (Rep.).

still that Republicans began to win many state and local offices.

12. The Sunbelt was journalist Kevin Phillips's term (in 1969) for the Southern and Western states increasing in population, wealth, and political influence. The 1976 presidential campaign (**416**) focused media attention on these trends and popularized Phillips's label. Geographers and many Southerners scoffed at the idea of a resemblance between Southern California and the South—Texas and Florida, maybe, but (as one Southern politician put it) there was "a lot of shade in the Sunbelt." The concept soon went out of fashion, and the word is seldom used these days, except ironically.

13. The Southeast can be a useful descriptive term for the part of the South to the east of Greater Texas; it recognizes, for instance, that the regional economy centered on Atlanta does not include the Texas metropolises and their dependencies. In many respects, however, this increasingly widespread term denotes a geographical gelding, a mere quadrant, with none of the South's rich heritage. No one speaks of Southeastern cooking, religion, music, accents, or history—because "the Southeast" has none of these things. The word should usually be avoided.

Subregions

THE BIG THREE

TEXAS AND FLORIDA ASIDE, the South has three major subregions, and the boundaries of most Southern states have been laid over some combination of the three. Each state's character, politics, and economy have been largely determined by what its mix has been.

14. **The Deep South** is roughly coextensive with the old cotton belt, a long arc extending from eastern North Carolina through South Carolina, west into east Texas, with extensions north and south along the Mississippi. This area can still be defined by locating rural counties with populations more than 25 percent black. South Carolina, Georgia, Alabama, Mississippi, and Louisiana are commonly considered the Deep South states, although parts of these states don't meet the criteria, and parts of adjoining states do. Many things thought of as Southern, from alligators (**63**) and Spanish moss (**74**) to peculiar voting in 1948 (**413**) and 1964 (**414**), are found in their most concentrated form (sometimes only) here.

15. **Piedmont** means "foothills," and that's what the foothills of the Appalachians are called in the Carolinas and Georgia. They're the Cumberland plateau when they fishhook around to take in middle Tennessee, but they're similar physiographically and economically. Wedged between the Appalachians and the Deep South, this subregion's marginality to the plantation system and abundant water power gave it a leg up on industrialization and made it the heartland of the original New South. Today it includes the Southeast's urban core: Richmond, Charlotte, Greenville-Spartanburg, Atlanta, Birmingham, Nashville.

16. **The Southern highlands** have been the mother lode of such "Southern" things as family feuds, stock car racing (**851**), moonshine whiskey (**660**), country music (**557**), and snake-handling religion (**813**). In the Appalachians (pronounced *appa-LATCH-ians,* please) and

the Ozarks (**24**), plantation agriculture didn't pay, and not much of anything else did either. Consequently, these areas were settled by small farmers, nearly all white, who were unreliable Confederates in 1861–65 and have tended to be Republicans to this day. The South's twentieth-century economic development largely bypassed the highlands (except for the coalfields, but most of that money left the region). Ironically, this now makes them an attractive tourist and retirement destination for Floridians (in the Appalachians) and Midwesterners (in the Ozarks).

THREE BIG EXCEPTIONS

SOUTHERN FOR SOME PURPOSES but not for others, these three subregions provide the major exceptions to many generalizations about the South.

17. **The (eastern) Southwest.** Most of Texas, parts of Arkansas, and nearly all of Oklahoma long since went their own way economically, and their identification with the South is a sometime thing. But they were settled by Southerners and retain Southern ways in religion, speech, and music. Frank Vandiver, historian and president of Texas A&M: "Look at Southwesterners closely and traces of the South can be glimpsed clearly: a sense of honor, a code of courtesy, a feeling for place, a belief that people are more important than things or ideas." Byron Price, director of the Cowboy Hall of Fame, concurs: "To these may be added an attachment to the soil, a simple way of life, a respect for women, and an unyielding pride." Someone should write a book about the South's influence on the entire West. In fact, someone has: *The Virginian,* America's first western novel, by Owen Wister, grandson of Fanny Kemble (**451**).

18. **South Florida** begins somewhere south of Daytona Beach, and it's very different—ecologically, economically, ethnically, however you want to look at it—from other parts of the South, including north Florida. It's an urban place, increasingly so, with an economy based on tourism, retirement, and drugs. Well over half of its residents weren't born in the South, much less in Florida, and many were born outside the United States. It would be tempting to exclude it from the South altogether, if there were anywhere else to put it.

19. **South Louisiana** is Southern, sure enough, but with a Gallic twist that has caused us all kinds of headaches in this book. New Orleans is—well, something else. And then there's "Acadiana," twenty-two parishes officially recognized by the state government as the homeland of the Cajuns (**101**). The center of Cajun cultural life is the town of Lafayette, home of the Ragin' Cajuns of the University of Southwestern Louisiana (Université des Acadiens).

Jackson Square, French Quarter, New Orleans. *Library of Southern Literature* (1907)

Graves of Kentucky thoroughbreds. Caufield & Shook Collection, Photographic Archives, University of Louisville

SOME MINI- AND MICROREGIONS

GEOGRAPHER TERRY JORDAN HAS identified twenty-nine "vernacular regions" in Texas alone. In every state, piney woods and wire grass and sandhills regions enjoy their distinctiveness; nearly every river valley seems to have not just a name but an identity. What all these tiny subregions are isn't something "everyone should know about the South," but everyone should know that they exist and that they're important to their citizens. Some are important beyond their borders, among them:

20. **The Black Belt** properly refers to a roughly twenty-five-mile-wide band of dark soil extending some three hundred miles through Alabama into Mississippi and Tennessee, a rich cotton region until the coming of the boll weevil. Less precisely, the phrase often refers to African-American population rather than calcareous soil; in that sense, it's roughly equivalent to "Deep South."

21. **The Bluegrass country** of northern Kentucky sits atop a limestone plain that furnishes

the material for its distinctive rock walls. The eponymous grass makes good eating for the great horses this area has produced since antebellum times.

22. **The Mississippi Delta** is the rich bottomland between the Yazoo and Mississippi rivers, extending by one well-known reckoning from Vicksburg to the lobby of the Peabody Hotel in Memphis. This has been called "the most Southern place on earth," and in some respects—for example, cotton agriculture, black population, rural poverty, oppressive race relations—it has been. The recent importance of catfish farming hasn't made a great deal of difference. Reclaimed from primeval forest relatively late, by 1900 this was the heart of the Cotton Kingdom and the home of the blues.

23. **The Cumberlands** are the mountains of eastern Kentucky, a southwestward extension of the Alleghenies of Pennsylvania and West Virginia. Site of John Fox's local-color novels and, latterly, of extensive coal-mining operations, this is the heart of Appalachia. The Cumberland Plateau, an area of valleys and rolling uplands, extends southward through Tennessee into northern Alabama.

24. **The Ozarks** bestride much of northern Arkansas and southern Missouri. In many respects they're a sort of vest-pocket version of the Appalachians: once offering a hardscrabble living for a sparse native population, they now offer caves and lakes and hillbilly villages and folk festivals for tourists and retirees (**905**). The most notable recent development is the emergence of Branson, Missouri, as a major country-music center.

25. **The Gulf Coast,** from western Florida almost to the Mexican border (interrupted by French Louisiana), has been called, to the distress of its Chambers of Commerce, the Redneck Riviera. Always a popular tourist destination for Southerners, it's increasingly popular with other North Americans, including some drawn by Mississippi's new enthusiasm for casino gambling.

26. **The Delmarva Peninsula** (from *Del*-aware, *Mar*-yland, and *Va.)* includes Delaware and the "eastern shores" of Virginia and Maryland. Settled in the seventeenth century, the peninsula was isolated for many years and even tried to incorporate as a separate state in the early nineteenth century. Improved transportation now links it to Washington, Baltimore, and Philadelphia. It's increasingly a dependency of those metropolises and decreasingly "Southern," but its economy still rests on tourism, chickens, and seafood.

27. **The Outer Banks** are the chain of narrow barrier islands that stretch along the North Carolina coast, separating Albemarle and Pamlico sounds from the Atlantic. Formerly the haunt of pirates, fishermen, and Ohio bicycle mechanics (the Wright brothers), they were always sparsely populated, and remain so: much of the Outer Banks has been preserved in its natural state as parkland.

28. **The Sea Islands** of Georgia and South Carolina were formerly the site of large cotton plantations, but what the Civil War didn't wipe out, hurricanes did. The Gullah (**95**) population at midtwentieth century lived by fishing and subsistence farming, supplemented by small-scale

vegetable production, mostly for local markets. They're still there, but their future's uncertain. In 1886 rich Yankees bought Jekyll Island for a hunting preserve, and they've been buying ever since. The Sea Islands are increasingly a chain of resorts and vacation-home developments, of which the best known is probably Hilton Head. The U.S. Marines also have a presence, at Parris Island.

29. **Little Dixie** is a phrase applied to a number of border areas, notably in Missouri, Illinois, and Oklahoma. (Former Oklahoma congressman and Speaker of the House Carl Albert was known as the Little Giant from Little Dixie.) These are usually areas settled from the South and retaining at least some Southern cultural traits, especially in food, religion, speech, and politics.

Eponymous Cities and Towns

THE NAMES OF MANY Southern towns have come to stand for something, evoke some image, *mean* something. One thing, for each.

30. **Appomattox** (Virginia) witnessed the surrender of Robert E. Lee to Ulysses Grant on April 9, 1865. Other Rebel commanders surrendered later, but this marked the effective end of the Confederate cause. Nothing much had happened there before, and nothing much has happened since (the site's now a National Park), but that one event put Appomattox in our vocabulary as a word like "Pearl Harbor": shorthand for the end of an era and the beginning of another.

The Surrender of General Lee to General Grant at Appomattox, April 9, 1865 (1867), by Louis Guillaume. Appomattox Court House National Historical Park, National Park Service

Lulu White's doorway, Storyville. Historic New Orleans Collection, acc. no. 1980.2.2

31. Storyville, New Orleans's turn-of-the-century red-light district, existed only from 1897, when alderman Sidney Story's ordinance restricted prostitution to that area, until 1917, when it was abolished under pressure from Secretary of the Navy Josephus Daniels (of North Carolina), who feared it would corrupt his sailors. During that time, however, its opulent brothels nurtured many famous jazz musicians **(555).**

32. Dayton (Tennessee) hosted the 1925 "monkey trial" of John Scopes for violating a state law against teaching about evolution. With Clarence Darrow for the defense, William Jen-

nings Bryan assisting the prosecution, and H. L. Mencken reporting, it received national attention. (The Vanderbilt Agrarians [**922**] later cited the ridicule as one of the reasons for their manifesto *I'll Take My Stand.*) In a circuslike atmosphere, Scopes was convicted and fined $100. (The conviction was subsequently reversed on a technicality.) The play and motion picture *Inherit the Wind* did not mention that local businessmen had induced Scopes to stand trial in a misbegotten attempt to gain publicity for their town or that Scopes later denied that he had ever actually taught the proscribed doctrine.

33. Gastonia (North Carolina) was the scene of a violent textile strike mounted by the National Textile Workers Union in 1929. First, an exchange of gunfire killed the local police chief, then antiunion vigilantes killed Ella May Wiggins, a young mother whose songs had rallied the strikers. The presence of Communists among the union's leaders was an issue: seven strike leaders charged with murder jumped bail and sought asylum in the Soviet Union. Although the strike was broken within two weeks, in left-wing circles "Gastonia" came to stand for workers' struggle and bosses' brutality.

34. Harlan (Kentucky)—more precisely, Harlan County—got the name Bloody Harlan in 1931 when the United Mine Workers' organizing efforts met resistance from the coal operators and their private "deputy sheriffs." Thirteen people died in the ensuing strife. Theodore Dreiser and John Dos Passos covered Harlan, and Robert La Follette investigated it, making the name another symbol of ruthless opposition to unionization.

Clarence Darrow for the defense. Courtesy Chicago Historical Society/*Dictionary of American Portraits* (Dover, 1967)

35. Scottsboro (Alabama) is identified with another left-wing cause, that of nine black teenagers accused in 1931 of raping two white women hoboing on a freight train. After eight of the nine were sentenced to death, the legal arm of the Communist Party undertook their defense. Marches, rallies, and letter-writing campaigns brought international attention, but the prosecution persisted through innumerable appeals and retrials. Even though one of the women changed her story and declared that no rape had occurred, five of the "Scottsboro boys" were eventually sentenced to prison terms.

36. Darlington (South Carolina) has been since the 1930s synonymous with the Southern 500, or, in its current incarnation, the Mountain Dew Southern 500 NASCAR Winston Cup Series Race. As "Stroker Ace" put it in *Stand on It,* Darlington is "the cradle of Southern stockcar racing [**851**]. First of the big tracks in the Southland, the granddaddy of them all. The land of racing heroes." Daytona might dispute the title, but Daytona has some other things going. Darlington doesn't.

Wernher von Braun, Alabamian. *U.S. News & World Report*/Library of Congress U9-317-B-7

At the Darlington Raceway. DixiePix

37. Huntsville (Alabama) was an unassuming county seat and textile mill center when the U.S. Army built its Redstone Arsenal, a missile research facility that houses the George C. Marshall Space Flight Center. This development made former German missile expert Wernher von Braun an Alabamian almost as well known as Bear Bryant (**872**), George Wallace (**428**), and Hank Williams (**602**), and made Huntsville an eponym for rocket science.

38. Augusta (Georgia) is known to the sporting world for one thing: the annual Masters Tournament on the splendid links of the Augusta National Country Club—"the only tournament with class," in Gene Sarazen's informed opinion. Although many of the club's members are from outside the South, its architecture, flowering shrubs and trees, and general ambience convey an image of Southern gentility, and have done so ever since Bobby Jones (**878**) organized it. As a symbol of the new, affluent, suburban South, this isn't bad. It sure beats nearby Tobacco Road (**48**).

39. Plains (Georgia) enjoyed a brief moment in the spotlight as a local habitation of down-home virtues during and immediately after the presidential campaign of native son Jimmy Carter (**440**). Brother Billy's filling station, Cousin Hugh's store, and the family's peanut warehouse became as familiar to television viewers as the landmarks of Hazzard County, home of Bo and Luke Duke (**994**). As the electorate's infatuation with President Carter ebbed, so did interest in his hometown, and Plains has now subsided into a becoming obscurity. Sixteen years later, Bill Clinton tried to orchestrate a similar association, billing himself as "the man from Hope" (an Arkansas town previously known mostly for large watermelons [**674**]), but it didn't work, perhaps because Clinton's actual boyhood home was Hot Springs.

Streets and Roads

EVEN THE NAMES OF Southern highways are evocative.

40. The Great Wagon Road ran from eastern Pennsylvania down Virginia's Shenandoah Valley to western North Carolina. Originally an Indian "warrior's path," by the mideighteenth century it was the route to the Southern interior for thousands of Scotch-Irish (**98**) and German (**103**) settlers. After 1760 an extension led through South Carolina to Augusta, Georgia; after 1775 a link to the Wilderness Road led to Kentucky and Tennessee. It was once the most heavily traveled road in the American colonies.

41. The Wilderness Road was the name of several routes on the eighteenth-century Southern frontier, the best known of which was the trail blazed by Daniel Boone in 1775 from present-day Kingsport, Tennessee, north and west

through the Cumberland Gap to Boonesborough, in "Transylvania" (Kentucky). Widened to a wagon road, it opened up Kentucky for settlement. Tolls were imposed in 1797.

42. The Trail of Tears refers to the thousand-mile route along which some thirteen thousand Cherokees were driven by federal troops in the winter of 1838–39. Thousands died from starvation, exposure, and disease as members of the Five Civilized Tribes (**88**) were "removed" from the Southeast to Oklahoma. Today part of the trail is a historic route maintained by the state of Tennessee.

43. The Natchez Trace runs from the Mississippi River at Natchez to the vicinity of Nashville. Once an Indian trail traveled by Hernando De Soto and French explorers, it became a major thoroughfare in the early nineteenth century when flatboatmen used it to go home after selling their products and their boats (for lumber) in New Orleans. It was abandoned after the advent of steamboats capable of going upstream, but in 1934 the federal government began a survey of the old route, and the Natchez Trace Parkway now allows tourists to retrace it in their automobiles.

44. The National Road was built in the early decades of the nineteenth century near present-day Interstate 70 through Ohio, Indiana, and Illinois. It roughly separated areas to the south settled from Virginia and areas to the north settled by upstate New Yorkers of New England stock. Geographer Wilbur Zelinsky has shown that well into this century this affected such practices as farming with mules (Southern) or horses (Northern) and painting barns (Northern) or not (Southern), and the distinction is still evident in religious affiliations and speech patterns. During the Civil War the southern parts of these states were centers of Copperhead (**401**) sentiment, and in 1993 a team from southern Illinois even won the Memphis in May International Barbecue Competition.

45. **Beale Street** became in the 1880s the main street of Negro Memphis and a shopping and entertainment center for blacks from miles around. Renowned for its rowdy nightlife, it nurtured scores of musicians, from W. C. Handy (**590**) to B. B. King (**608**) to the young Elvis Presley (**606**) (who bought his fancy clothes at Lansky's store). Like many black business districts in the South, it was killed by urban renewal and the end of segregation, but it has come back in recent years as a sort of blues theme park, with clubs and restaurants catering to the (mostly white) tourist trade.

46. **Bourbon Street** has long been the main street for nightlife in New Orleans's French Quarter (**800**). Its name these days evokes images of low-rent tourist bait like tired Dixieland jazz (**555–56**), seedy strip joints, and potent alcoholic concoctions called hurricanes, but somehow in New Orleans the combination of transvestites and drunken fraternity boys is more fun than it sounds.

47. **Highway 61** runs from New Orleans through the Mississippi Delta (**22**) and Memphis to the urban Midwest. In the Great Migration (**368**) during and after World War I it was celebrated as the way out for countless black Mississippians (and some white ones, too). Bill Ferris, director of the Center for the Study of Southern Culture (**844**), named his Saturday night Mississippi Public Radio blues program for this road.

The Old Method of Getting Tobacco to Market.

A tobacco road. *The Great South* (1875)

48. **Tobacco Road,** located near Augusta, Georgia, was the fictional address of Jeeter Lester and his degenerate kinfolks in Erskine Caldwell's scandalous 1932 novel. Caldwell's *Tobacco Road,* the long-running Broadway play, and the sanitized John Ford movie have made the phrase synonymous with white-trash (**941**) depravity, but originally "tobacco roads" were just the trails made by rolling hogsheads of tobacco from plantation to waterway. After the soil was exhausted, the roads remained, populated by poor farmers.

49. **The Blue Ridge Parkway** is one of the best known of the South's many Depression-era federal public works. The Blue Ridge runs down the eastern side of Virginia's Shenandoah Valley through North Carolina, and the parkway runs down the top of the Blue Ridge for 470 miles from Front Royal, Virginia, to near Asheville, North Carolina. Opened in 1933, it provides access to scenic vistas and mountain crafts, paralleling the Appalachian Trail (for hikers).

50. **Thunder Road** is the title of what critic Leonard Maltin has called "the definitive moonshine picture," made in 1958 and still playing drive-ins today. The title song was also a hit record for the movie's star, Robert Mitchum. The road traveled by the bootlegger-hero as he runs illegal whiskey and battles both revenue officers and the mob is in the vicinity of Knoxville, Tennessee.

51. **Peachtree Street,** a major artery in Atlanta, may be coming to stand for Atlanta and the modern South more generally, as in songs by Emmy Lou Harris and Charlie Daniels and expressions like "from Tobacco Road to Peachtree Street." Many visitors to Atlanta have discovered too late that West Peachtree Street is a parallel route, not the western end of Peachtree.

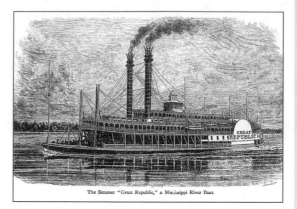

The Steamer "Great Republic," a Mississippi River Boat.

A common sight in the 1870s. *The Great South* (1875)

Atlanta skyline. DixiePix

Waterways and Wetlands

THE SOUTH IS WET—even soggy. Some of the more important bodies of water:

52. **The Mighty Mississippi,** the Father of Waters, the Big Muddy. What would the South be without steamboats and levees and mud to beat our feet on? Would there be a Memphis or a New Orleans—would it have mattered who held Vicksburg (**313**)—if the Mississippi didn't just keep rolling along? The part that rolls through the South is often a mile wide and can still come up with a pretty good flood despite the efforts of the Corps of Engineers. More or less parallel to the river's course are oxbow lakes, crescent-shaped sections of what was once the river's winding main channel, cut off when Old Man River took a shortcut.

53. **The Great Dismal Swamp** was named in 1728 by William Byrd (**443**), who apparently didn't care for it. George Washington later formed a company to drain this wetland; he and others have shrunk it from 2,200 square miles to about 750. Located on the eastern North Carolina/Virginia border, what's left is a tangle of juniper and cypress trees, vines, and brambles, populated by bears, bobcats, otters, scores of species of birds, ninety-one kinds of butterflies, and three of the four species of poisonous snakes found in the United States. In the middle is Lake Drummond, with water the color of tea, thanks to vast peat deposits. (The water was once taken aboard sailing ships, because it

Lake Drummond, in the Dismal Swamp. Porte Crayon (**452**), "The Dismal Swamp" (1856)

Okeechobee means "big water," and the lake *is* big (730 square miles in south-central Florida), if only wading depth. Its overflow feeds the 'Glades, which are basically a river fifty to seventy-five miles wide and a few inches deep, running about one hundred miles to the southern tip of Florida. Early in this century a government program of dikes, levees, and canals stopped the lake from flooding adjacent settlements, diverted water to irrigate vegetables and sugarcane (**172**), and "reclaimed" over 4 million acres of swamp. What's left is mostly saw-grass marsh, mangroves, and hammocks, with vegetation essentially the same as that of the West Indies. The Seminole Indian Reservation is at its western end. The 1.4-million-acre National Park is popular with alligators, mosquitoes, tourists, and many other species, including the rare American crocodile.

stayed fresh for so long.) In 1828 a twenty-two-mile canal was built through the swamp to connect Albemarle Sound and the Chesapeake Bay.

54. **The Okefenokee Swamp** is technically a bog, not a swamp—but never mind. This seven-hundred-square-mile natural dish straddles the Florida line near Waycross, Georgia, offering a mix of hammocks (thicketed islands), marsh, cypress swamp, and open water. The name means "shaky ground": jumping on the spongy peat can cause large trees to sway. Hernando De Soto came across it in the 1530s and quickly moved on; since then it has served as a refuge for Indians, fugitive slaves, Confederate deserters, outlaws, and (since 1937) federally protected wildlife. Its best-known resident mammal is Pogo Possum, whose creator is honored with an exhibit at the Okefenokee Heritage Center.

55. **Lake Okeechobee and the Everglades.**

56. **Lake Pontchartrain** is the largest of Louisiana's several saltwater lakes (actually lagoons—i.e., enclosed tidal bays): roughly twenty-five by forty miles, with an average depth of under sixteen feet. Explored by the French in 1699, its shores have housed popular resorts since antebellum days, especially the pine-scented "Ozone Belt" around Covington and the mineral wells at Abita Springs. The "lake" is connected to the Gulf of Mexico by natural channels and to the Mississippi River by a canal, and it's now traversed by a causeway between New Orleans and Covington.

57. **Reelfoot Lake,** in Tennessee's northwest corner, was formed by the violent New Madrid earthquake of 1811, which also turned northeastern Arkansas into a swamp. Deceptively peaceful today, this thirteen-thousand-acre lake is home to cypress, water lilies, and bald eagles.

TVA dam at Chickamauga. Farm Security
Administration/Library of Congress USF34-15619

58. TVA lakes are found, not surprisingly, behind the thirty-two dams of the Tennessee Valley Authority. Although the rationale for TVA
had to do with flood control, river traffic, and
hydroelectric power, the fishing and boating
provided by the lakes have been a delightful by-
product. In fact, the authors of this book had
their first date waterskiing on Boone Lake in
east Tennessee.

59. Bayous are bodies of water, and beyond that
it's hard to generalize, thanks to French explor-

ers who took an Indian word that meant "sluggish stream" and casually applied it to everything from saltwater bays to glorified puddles.
These days the word most often identifies south
Louisiana's multitude of sluggish streams drain-
ing eventually into the Gulf of Mexico, including
such Cajun (**101**) thoroughfares as the Bayou
Teche and Bayou Lafourche.

Other Aspects of the Landscape

60. Red clay covers much of the upland South.
Orange to near purple, slick and sticky when
wet, hard as rock when dry, it erodes easily
(**187**) and doesn't support much in the way of
agriculture. Consequently, it has come to be associated with yeoman farmers rather than
planters. "The ground of our being," as one
Charlotte newspaperman called it, has lent its
name to such Piedmont (**15**) enterprises as the
periodical *Red Clay Reader* of Charlotte and the
musical Red Clay Ramblers of Chapel Hill.

61. Levees are simply earthen embankments
built for flood control, especially those on the
Mississippi River from Cape Girardeau, Mis-

Up the bayou. Russell Lee, Farm Security
Administration/Library of Congress USF33-11856

Working on a levee, Louisiana, 1935. Ben Shahn, Farm
Security Administration/Library of Congress USF33-06113-M4

souri, south to the Gulf. Originally built and maintained by landowners, then by state and local governments and commissions, they are now largely the responsibility of the U.S. Army Corps of Engineers. As prominent features of the landscape, they have been celebrated in song and story (e.g., William Alexander Percy's *Lanterns on the Levee*).

62. **Caves** abound in the upper South. Three-fourths of all caves in the United States are found there. Kentucky, Virginia, Tennessee, and Missouri have over a thousand each, and they've attracted both natives and tourists since before the days of Tom Sawyer. Along old U.S. 11 in Virginia are a number of commercially developed ones, among them Luray, Skyline, Dixie, Endless, and Shenandoah Caverns. But the most impressive single hole in the ground is Kentucky's Mammoth Cave system, with more than three hundred miles of passages charted. The world's attention was focused on a nearby Kentucky cave in 1925, when Floyd Collins was trapped and died there.

Wildlife

THE SOUTH IS HOSPITABLE to life. *All* life: some useful, some decorative, some we could do without. A few of the wild things more or less identified with the region:

63. **The alligator** is found in the more picturesque parts of the coastal South from the Carolinas to Texas and has had a special fascination for visitors since the eighteenth century. Alligator wrestling was developed for their amusement. Gators have been the subject of humorous postcards and country songs and a

A carnival attraction. DixiePix

source of potions, charms, and portents. Their meat feeds poor folk and is sometimes served as a novelty to tourists and Southern yuppies. Hunting (originally for sport, then for hides) put the alligator on the endangered species list in the 1970s, but the population was quickly restored, and when alligators allegedly threatened dogs and children and began to interfere with golf, the selling of hides was made legal again.

64. **The possum**—that is, the Virginia opossum—was originally unique to the region. Captain John Smith (**442**) described the female thus: "An oppossum hath a head like a Swine, and a taile like a Rat, and is of the bigness of a Cat. Under her belly she hath a bagge wherein she lodgeth, carrieth, and sucketh her young." When frightened, the animal "plays possum" (goes into a catatonic state and looks dead), but most of the possums lying on Southern highways really *are* dead. Possum hunting for sport and food is a popular nocturnal pastime in the rural South. The possum has a rustic image in Indian folktales, Uncle Remus stories, fiddle tunes like "Possum up a Gum Tree," and Walt Kelly's *Pogo* comic strip, but like the raccoon, it has made the transition to the modern South just fine,

Possum.

and it's now a pest in many suburban neighborhoods.

65. The armadillo, or "possum on the half shell," has become for Texas what the possum is for the rest of the South—potent cultural symbol and ubiquitous roadkill. Found in all of the Gulf Coast states and throughout Central America, this armored mammal became a Texas totem only in the 1960s, when it was adopted by the Austin counterculture and linked to good times, marijuana, and antiwar politics. During the seventies Armadillo World Headquarters in Austin was a center of Southern rock (**567**) music.

The armadillo as icon. DixiePix

66. The mockingbird is about the only Southern bird other than the chicken (**665**) with any cultural significance. It figures in the title of Harper Lee's *To Kill a Mockingbird* (**524**) (a sin), appears in the lyrics of songs including the state song of Louisiana, and is the official bird of five other Southern states. Unfortunately, its beautiful singing disguises a foul disposition and obnoxious habits.

SOME OF THE LOWER forms of wildlife have ways of demanding attention, too.

67. Hookworm is spread (to be blunt) by walking barefoot in human excrement. Larvae enter through the foot and eventually lodge in the intestine, causing lethargy and anemia. At the turn of the century as many as 2 million people were infected by the "laziness germ" in parts of the South where shoes and privies were luxuries. This revolting parasite is now rare (though not endangered) thanks to the philanthropy of John D. Rockefeller and state public-health efforts.

68. Chiggers or (in the lower South) redbugs are the tiny larvae of mites, whose bites cause itching and redness. Mentioned in a sixth-century Chinese medical treatise, they're widespread in East Asia, and the word itself is either African or Caribbean Indian. But they like warm, moist weather and scrub vegetation, so they're regrettably well known to native Southerners and an unpleasant surprise for visitors. Contrary to popular belief, chiggers don't burrow into the skin; they take leisurely bites and then drop off. The resulting red spots are localized allergic reactions, so folk remedies like nail polish to suffocate the bugs are based on a misconception (although they may help the itching).

69. **Mosquitoes** aren't uniquely Southern by any means, but Southern mosquitoes have been uniquely deadly. They were responsible for frequent epidemics of yellow fever (the "saffron scourge"), including one that killed 10 percent of the residents of New Orleans in 1853 and another in the Gulf states and Mississippi valley that killed twenty thousand in 1878. (In 1853 painter T. Addison Richards [**754**] complained in *Harper's* about the South's "mosquitos and Miasmas.") As late as the 1930s an estimated 2 million people were infected annually with mosquito-borne malaria, reducing Southern industrial output by one-third. Now, however, thanks to bug-zappers, mosquitoes furnish harmless entertainment on summer nights.

70. **Ticks and black widow spiders** lack cultural significance, but we mention them because the South has more than its share of tick-borne Rocky Mountain spotted fever and poisonous spider bites. North Carolina usually leads the nation in both. The spiders are reportedly fond of nesting underneath the seats of privies and biting the unwary on the unmentionable.

71. **Fire ants** entered the United States early in this century through Mobile, as stowaways from Brazil. They have since spread to cover most of the lower South, where their venomous bites hospitalize about 25,000 people a year. They have killed dozens of people as well as a good deal of livestock and wildlife. They also suck eggs, destroy beehives, and chew up air-conditioner wiring, transformers, and telephone lines. A single hill can house a half million, and they are virtually indestructible. (Folk wisdom says ants will eat uncooked grits [**650**] and explode when the grits expand, but scientists deny

this.) Making the best of it, Marshall, Texas, celebrates an annual Fire Ant Festival.

72. **Boll weevils** are also unwanted immigrants. First observed in Mexico in 1843, they crossed the border near Brownsville, Texas, in the 1890s, and by 1915 had moved through the South's cotton fields to the Atlantic Coast. Amazingly destructive, they inadvertently encouraged migration from the cotton belt, diversification of Southern agriculture, and the growth of government agricultural research and extension programs. The citizens of Enterprise, Alabama, wryly erected a statue of the weevil in gratitude. It's still U.S. agriculture's most costly pest, and efforts at control and eradication continue.

Enterprise, Alabama, thanks the boll weevil. *Enterprise Ledger*

Vegetation

PLANTLIFE ABOUNDS AS WELL, and some wild or ornamental forms have acquired totemic significance. (We'll talk about crops later.)

73. **The Southern magnolia** *(M. grandiflora)* is an evergreen tree with large glossy leaves and huge fragrant white flowers. Native to the coastal plain, it's now found throughout the region. Especially identified with the Deep South (Mississippi is the Magnolia State), it's linked to the romantic myth of the Old South (**912–17**) —as in "moonlight and magnolias." Historian Charles Wilson notes that the blossom (sweet, white, and soft) is like the Southern lady, an identification made explicit in the phrase "steel magnolias" (**945**).

A cypress tree, with Spanish moss. Standard Oil (New Jersey) Collection, Photographic Archives, University of Louisville

A magnolia blossom. DixiePix

74. **Spanish moss** doesn't look like moss, and isn't. It doesn't look like a member of the pineapple family either, but it is. Its long gray-green strands hang from hardwood trees in the coastal plain from southern Virginia to Texas, using the trees for support but drawing nutrients from the humid air. It has been used as packing material, as mattress stuffing, as Christmas decoration (by Cajuns [**101**]), even for clothing (by Indians), but mostly it's just a decorative element in the landscape, lending an air of mystery to whatever's going on.

75. **Cypress and live oak** are both popular hosts for Spanish moss. The live oak (so called because it's an evergreen) grows near the coast, while cypress is found chiefly in Southern swamps and wetlands, providing spooky silhouettes when its branches are bare (its "knees" rise from the principal roots). Both were widely used in shipbuilding, and cypress is still used for houses, barrels, and fencing, but the live oak is

now almost entirely ornamental: it's the state tree of Georgia and has given its name to towns in Florida, Louisiana, and Texas.

76. The dogwood isn't unique to the South—the native *Cornus florida* ranges as far north as Maine—but the wild white ones ornament Southern forests in springtime, the blossom's the state flower of Virginia and North Carolina, and selling "Legend of the Dogwood" postcards to tourists seems to be a major source of hard currency in some parts.

77. Palm trees were part of the stage set for the Paris production of Erskine Caldwell's *Tobacco Road* (**48**), but Jeeter Lester would never have seen one except maybe on a postcard from Florida, where a score of native and imported varieties are practically clichés. Proper palm

Iron Palmetto in the State-House Yard at Columbia.

The Great South (1875)

trees are found mostly in the Sunshine State, on the Gulf Coast, and in south Texas, but the cabbage palmetto (so called because its heart can be eaten like cabbage) grows as far north as North Carolina. Even in the Palmetto State of South Carolina, however, only a few sorry specimens cling to life as far inland as the state capital of Columbia.

78. Ginseng, or "sang," can still be found in the Southern mountains, where Indians and frontiersmen once used its mildly stimulating leaves and roots for medicinal purposes. Some mountaineers now supplement their incomes by gathering wild ginseng roots. They're sold mostly to the Orient, where they're thought to be aphrodisiac and can bring hundreds of dollars an ounce.

79. Carnivorous plants are a unique feature of bogs and wetlands in much of the coastal South, but you don't have to worry that they'll take a bite out of *you:* the Venus flytrap and various

Pitcher plant, or flytrap. DixiePix

pitcher plants attract, capture, and digest small insects.

80. **Kudzu** is a leafy vine, perennial in the South, introduced in 1876 from Japan. Planted extensively for forage and erosion control, like some other newcomers it's now a nuisance: the *Economist* calls it "a horrible, triffid-like plant"; James Dickey (**515**), "a vegetable form of cancer." Growing up to a foot a day, it covers, shades, and eventually kills trees, and it now infests hundreds of thousands of acres of Southern forests. Although it has medicinal and dietary uses in Asia and research suggests that an extract may be useful in treating alcoholism, Southerners tend to see the "miracle vine" as hyperactive, feckless, and vaguely amusing. This import is now so identified with the South that its name has been used for a James Dickey poem, an Atlanta rock group, a Doug Marlette comic strip, a Birmingham alternative newspaper, a jelly ("It grows on you"), and a regional book service (motto: "We cover the South").

81. **Camellias and azaleas** are flowering evergreen shrubs, grown throughout the South. Camellias have long been identified with the region (although the most common variety is *japonica).* They're usually thought of as aristocratic: the Knights of the White Camellia were one of the many Klan-like groups (**358**) active during Reconstruction. Azaleas have been thought of as Southern only since gardens (**881**) were developed as tourist attractions after 1900, but the flowering of these Asian imports now evokes festivals from Wilmington, North Carolina, to Lafayette, Louisiana. Equally striking are the impromptu displays put on by wild, deciduous azaleas (which, like their relative the rhododendron, are natives) in the South's mountains and swamps.

Kudzu gonna get you. DixiePix

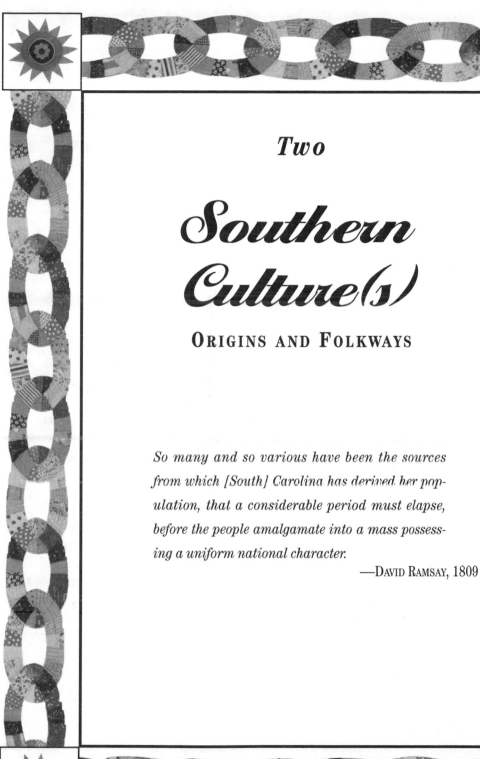

Two

Southern Culture(s)

ORIGINS AND FOLKWAYS

*So many and so various have been the sources
from which [South] Carolina has derived her population, that a considerable period must elapse,
before the people amalgamate into a mass possessing a uniform national character.*

—DAVID RAMSAY, 1809

"Culture Hearths"

HERE'S WHERE EUROPEANS AND Africans moved into what was to become the South.

82. **Florida** was first settled in 1565 when the Spanish expelled some French intruders from their colony and established St. Augustine (**883**), the oldest European settlement in what would become the United States. Spain's influence extended at times as far north as South Carolina, but Florida's Europeans were mostly soldiers and missionary priests, not families. Florida was ceded to the United States in 1819.

83. **Roanoke Island** was the site of the ill-starred first English settlement in America. In 1587, 108 colonists came to land (now in North Carolina) granted to Sir Walter Raleigh. Shortly after the birth of Virginia Dare, the first English child born in North America, the colony's leader, John White, went back to England. His return to Roanoke was delayed by war with the Spanish until 1591; by then the Lost Colony (**903**) had disappeared.

84. **The Chesapeake region** attracted English colonists beginning with the establishment of Jamestown (**884**) in 1607. From there, settlement spread along the rivers and estuaries and north onto Virginia's Eastern Shore and to Maryland. By 1700 some seventy thousand settlers made Virginia the largest colony in North America.

85. **The Carolina Low Country** saw two unsuccessful settlements in the sixteenth century: the Spanish founded a mission, then French Huguenots settled at Port Royal. The arrival of

English colonists in 1670 established the first permanent European and African presence. Within ten years "Charles Town" (Charleston) (**739, 889**) was founded. Soon the Low Country, linked to it by inland waterways, was settled, too, at first primarily by immigrants from Barbados, then by French Huguenots (**99**), and finally by Dissenters from New England and miscellaneous other folks. Black slaves from the West Indies and Africa were a majority of the population by 1708.

86. **Louisiana** was nothing but isolated French trading posts and forts until the founding of New Orleans (**741, 890**) in 1718. The city's reputation was so bad that it was populated in part with inmates of French jails. (A few Germans settled in the countryside.) When France ceded it to England and Spain in 1763, the population was only a few thousand. Ironically, when French-speaking farmers—the Cajuns (**101**)—did begin to arrive, they came to a Spanish colony, although it remained culturally French and reverted to French ownership in 1803, just in time to be sold to the United States.

87. **Texas** was largely neglected by the rulers of New Spain until the French started sniffing around in the late 1600s. The Spanish then set up a string of missions, forts, and settlements from present-day Robeline, Louisiana, west to the San Antonio River. In 1718 the mission later known as the Alamo was built, and ten families settled in what became San Antonio, the capital of Spanish Texas after 1773. Texas became part of independent Mexico in 1821, an independent republic itself in 1836, and one of the United States nine years later.

The Multicultural South

WE DON'T USUALLY THINK of ethnic diversity as characteristic of the South, but there has been more than you might suppose.

INDIANS AND MIXED-RACE POPULATIONS

88. **Indians in Oklahoma** were mostly put there by the federal government. The Five Civilized Tribes were the Cherokees, Choctaws, Creeks, Chickasaws, and Seminoles (former Creeks who moved south to settle Florida). They were called civilized because they'd adopted such white ways as Christianity, farming, and slaveholding. But that didn't matter when gold was discovered on Cherokee land and the Creek and Choctaw territories turned out to be prime cotton country. Sixty thousand or so were deported

Sequoyah and his Cherokee alphabet. Library of Congress USZ62-1292

to what would become Oklahoma (**42**); one in six died on the way. The Cherokees were by far the largest group (and remain that today). After the Civil War the government seized the western part of the Civilized Tribes' territory and used it to dump Indians from the Great Lakes region, defeated Plains Indians, and difficult Apaches and Modocs from the West. As late as the 1970s there were thirty-nine distinct groups in the state. The Indian population of Oklahoma is over 250,000, nearly half of the U.S. total.

89. **The Lumbees,** formerly known as the Croatans or simply "the Indians of Robeson County" (North Carolina), are by far the largest of the Southeast's recognized Indian populations. Most have lived near Pembroke, North Carolina, since the 1730s. Fanciful theories of their origins abound (one says that they're descended from the Lost Colony). There's no evidence that they've ever spoken anything but English, and they're apparently of mixed-race ancestry, but they've long insisted on their Indian identity. Under segregation they had their own school system, and they still have their own Baptist Association. The Lumbees are an exception to the apparent rule that mixed-race groups are being assimilated into the larger black and white communities: their status as Indians now seems secure, and their numbers are growing rapidly. Nearly a third are named Oxendine or Locklear.

90. **Other Indians in the Southeast** numbered some 150,000 in the seventeenth century, but disease, warfare, and especially the removal to Oklahoma reduced the population to under 10,000 (not counting the Lumbees). Although the numbers have since increased, they're still nowhere near their earlier level. The largest group is the Eastern Band of Cherokees, de-

scended from those who avoided removal. Living on a reservation in southwestern North Carolina (**904**), most are Baptists and perhaps half speak Cherokee at home. Catawbas in South Carolina (nearly all Mormons), Seminoles in Florida, and Choctaws in Mississippi number a few thousand apiece, and there are smaller groups in Georgia, Alabama, and Florida.

91. **"Little races"** are isolated bi- or triracial groups found throughout the eastern United States, but especially in the South. Every Southern state except Arkansas and Oklahoma has at least one group like the Melungeons (Tennessee), the Red Bones (Louisiana and Texas), the Turks and Brass Ankles (South Carolina), the Issues (Virginia), the Haliwa (North Carolina), or the Cajans (Alabama). The 1950 census identified over twenty such populations, numbering from a few hundred to a few thousand. Often isolated in swamps or mountain coves, these groups are almost certainly descended from some mixture of recalcitrant Indians, renegade whites, and freed or fugitive slaves. Denied entry to white society and unwilling to be grouped with blacks, they withdrew into their own communities, with separate schools, churches, and other institutions. Usually stereotyped as inbred, violent, and degenerate (Louisiana's mixed-race Creoles [**96**] are an exception), most of these groups are disappearing, as increased mobility and the end of legal segregation have let individuals escape the stigma of belonging to them.

AFRICAN-AMERICANS

92. **Africans** were in the South before the Pilgrims were in New England. By 1807 over a half million had been brought (some via the

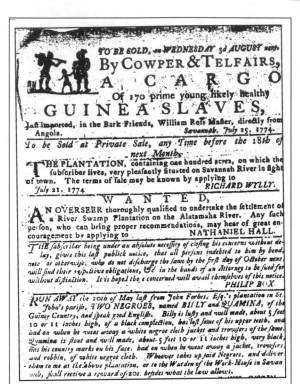

Advertising broadside, Savannah, 1774. Library of Congress USZ62-16876

Caribbean) to what became the United States. Nearly all were originally from West Africa, about half from present-day Angola and southern Nigeria. Different groups were concentrated in different colonies (e.g., 40 percent of Virginia's slaves were Ibos, compared to only 2 percent in South Carolina), but by emancipation (**354**) tribal identification and distinctions had largely been erased (**349**), and a distinctive African-American culture had emerged. In 1860 the black population of the United States was over 4.5 million; more than 90 percent were in the slave states, and all but 262,000 of those were enslaved. Today, roughly half of African-Americans live in the South, and about one Southerner in five is black.

93. Urban blacks aren't new in the South. In 1860 approximately 10 percent of Southern blacks lived in cities and towns. Some were free; others were enslaved house servants, craftsmen, or industrial workers. Not until this century, however, did the collapse of cotton agriculture and the relative comfort and freedom of urban life (even in the Jim Crow South) draw great numbers of rural blacks to Southern cities. Many others, of course, headed for Northeastern and Midwestern cities. Now most Southern blacks are city dwellers; in fact, more than half live in the twenty-nine Southern cities that have black populations over 100,000.

94. Rural blacks in the United States are nearly all found in the South. By 1860 most blacks worked as slaves in Southern fields, especially on Deep South cotton plantations, where many counties (and the states of Mississippi and South Carolina) had black majorities. As late as 1910, two-thirds of all blacks in the United States still lived in the rural South, and even today the rural black population is found mostly where cotton was grown (**173**). In 1980 Macon County, Alabama, had the highest proportion of black inhabitants in the United States (84 percent), followed by several other rural counties in the Deep South. But many counties in the Southern mountains and in west and south Texas—like most rural counties outside the South—have no black residents, or almost none.

95. Gullah (or Geechee) refers to the black people of the South Carolina and Georgia Sea Islands (**28**) as well as to their speech. Isolated on large plantations with minimal white supervision, Sea Island slaves were relatively cut off from both white and mainland African-American influence (though not from that of continuing new arrivals from Africa). The result was a culture—notably a creole language—that preserved many West African forms that blacks elsewhere lost, or never had. After emancipation many became small landowners, maintaining their independence. The bridges built since the 1920s and the recent Sea Island tourist boom have ended their isolation and now threaten independence as well. Television, off-island employment, and out-migration have eroded much of Gullah distinctiveness, but folk festivals, galleries, and the like may preserve some vestiges of it (**127, 519, 846**).

96. Creole, when applied to those of African or mixed-race ancestry, refers to Louisianans whose black or mulatto ancestors came to Louisiana in the late eighteenth century either as slaves of French planters or as *gens libre de couleur* fleeing the Haitian revolution. (Confusingly, "Creole" also refers to white Louisianans of French or Spanish colonial ancestry [**100**].) In the past, mixed-race Creoles distinguished themselves from those of more or less pure African descent and constituted one of the South's "little races" (**91**). They share both habitat and much of culture with Louisiana's Cajuns (**101**); many are French-speaking, most are Roman Catholic, and zydeco (**569**) is probably their best-known cultural export.

EUROPEAN-AMERICANS

ETHNIC IDENTITY AMONG SOUTHERN whites is relatively weak, perhaps because white Southerners' social standing has had little to do with national origins. Immigrants have been relatively rare since 1861, and the important distinction has been that between blacks and whites. Nevertheless, Southern whites do come from a variety of backgrounds.

97. **English** is the origin most white Southerners claim, giving credence to historian George Tindall's characterization of the region as "the biggest single WASP nest this side of the Atlantic." In fact, all of the U.S. counties where over half the inhabitants claim pure English ancestry are in Kentucky. Only in northern New England and the Mormon domain are the proportions even comparable. At the other extreme, however, two Texas counties on the Mexican border are among the handful of U.S. counties with virtually no English-origin population.

98. **Scotch-Irish** (Ulster Protestants of Scottish descent) came first to Pennsylvania; then, beginning in the 1770s, they fanned out down the Great Wagon Road (**40**) through Virginia, settling the Southern interior from the Carolina Piedmont to the Ozarks. Some historians have lately made a great deal of the "Celtic" ancestry of many Southerners, and certainly these hog drovers, subsistence farmers, long-rifle hunters, and whiskey distillers offered a striking cultural contrast to the English of both the Northeast and the lowland South. The census doesn't ask about religion, but of the five U.S. counties with the highest levels of "Irish" identification, two are in (Catholic) metropolitan Boston and three in (Protestant) Mississippi, Tennessee, and northern Florida.

99. **French Huguenots** came to all of the Southern colonies, but especially to South Carolina. In 1790 that state had the highest proportion (4 percent) of inhabitants of French origin. Although names like Lanier, Sevier, Huger, and Lenoir (pronounced *luh-NEER, suh-VEER, yew-GEE,* and *luh-NORE*) are both common and distinguished in the eastern South, these French Protestants quickly assimilated by intermarriage with the British. "French" in the South now means Louisiana, with extensions along the Gulf Coast to Texas and south Alabama. It comes in two flavors, both Catholic:

100. **Creoles,** when referring to whites, means the descendants of French (or, less commonly, Spanish) planters, merchants, government functionaries, etc., in colonial Louisiana. Many who stayed on after the United States got the colony in 1803 came from the French colony of Saint Domingue (later Haiti) or elsewhere in the Caribbean. Until World War I the French Quarter (Vieux Carré) of New Orleans was the center of this cultivated French-speaking society, depicted romantically in the stories of George Washington Cable, Grace King, Kate Chopin (**469**), and Frances Parkinson Keyes. By 1940 most Creoles had left the Quarter, but their architecture (**725, 890**) and cuisine (**690–96**) remain.

101. **Acadians (Cajuns)** are descended from French farmers exiled from Acadia (present-day Nova Scotia) by the British in 1755. Making their way to Louisiana, they settled in the swamps, along the bayous (**59**), and in the prairie country north and west of New Orleans and Baton Rouge, hunting and fishing, raising cattle, or (later) growing rice. Many now work in the oil refineries of southwestern Louisiana and east Texas. In a dozen parishes (counties) of Acadiana (**19**) a quarter or more of the population identify exclusively as French. English-only education (mandated in 1921) and the usual leveling influences mean that today only half as many Louisianans speak French at home as in 1970. Nevertheless, a quarter million still do, and Cajun music (**568**) and food (**690–93**) have lately and deservedly attracted admirers worldwide. While we're at it, "Castilians" have lived on an island in a bayou south of New Or-

leans since the 1700s, speaking a brand of Spanish still redolent of their original home in the Canary Islands. Over in Ascension Parish some folks speak Brule, a Spanish dialect strongly influenced by Cajun French.

102. Scottish immigrants (Scots from Scotland) were far less numerous than Scotch-Irish, but they were conspicuous in colonial North Carolina, where twelve thousand Highlanders were farming on the Cape Fear River in the 1770s. Many were Tories who left for Nova Scotia or returned to Scotland during the Revolution, but Gaelic was spoken in the area until the 1850s and North Carolina's Moore County has the fourth highest percentage of exclusively Scottish-identified residents in the United States. The annual Highland Games at Grandfather Mountain keep this heritage alive.

103. Germans in the Southeast are concentrated in Virginia's Shenandoah Valley and the North Carolina Piedmont, where "Pennsylvania Dutch" (German) farmers settled as early as the 1730s. Many belonged to such Pietist groups as the Moravians, Mennonites, and Brethren (or Dunkers) (**819**). Thousands of German Lutherans came through Charleston in the eighteenth century to settle in the South Carolina Piedmont. In the nineteenth and early twentieth centuries small groups of Germans established agricultural colonies in east Tennessee, eastern North Carolina, north Alabama, and elsewhere. But the really striking thing about Southerners of German descent is that there are so few of them east of the Mississippi. Most Deep South counties, in particular, have almost none.

104. Texas Germans, however, have been around since the 1830s in numbers large enough that German was once one of the official

North Carolina headstone, 1837. DixiePix

San Pedro Springs — "The Germans have established their beer gardens."

Texas Germans in the 1870s. *The Great South* (1875)

languages of the state (with Spanish and English). Thousands settled an area west of Houston during the nineteenth century, and other German colonies were planted near San Antonio, especially in the Hill Country around Fredericksburg (where close to half of the population reported only German ancestry in 1980). In the late 1800s Germans also began to farm the prairies of North Texas. Texas Germans are numerous enough, and from sufficiently varied backgrounds, to produce discernible differences between areas with Lutheran-Catholic, Methodist, and secularist traditions.

105. Other ethnic Texans include Mexican-Americans (**111**), of course, but also more exotic specimens. Beginning in the 1850s Czechs settled the plains south of Dallas and became efficient cotton farmers. Lavaca County is still nearly one-quarter Czech, but since 1930 most Czecho-Texans have moved to the city: Harris County (Houston) has the fourth largest Czech population in the United States. Polish Catholics from Silesia also began coming to Texas in the 1850s and established several farming communities southeast of San Antonio in counties still heavily Polish today.

106. Italians and Irish Catholics mostly avoided the South, as the plantation society had little to offer them, but enough Irish did settle in the South's major cities to give them well-established Irish-American communities. Especially notable are New Orleans, where residents of the Irish Channel neighborhood are known as yats (from their habitual greeting, "Where y'at?"), and Savannah, where St. Patrick's Day breakfasts include green grits. Sicilian peddlers and longshoremen were common in New Orleans as early as the 1850s, and some Italians came at the turn of the century to the Ap-

palachian coalfields and to truck-farming colonies in Louisiana, Arkansas, and Texas (where Italian names can still be found), but today most of the South's Italian-Americans are in south Florida.

107. Greeks first came to the South when they first came to America: some four hundred indentured servants were brought to New Smyrna, Florida, in 1768, but their descendants have been entirely assimilated. Few Greeks have come to the South since. Most who did came between 1880 and 1924, settled in cities, and took unskilled work; many subsequently opened small businesses, and most Southern cities today have Greek-owned restaurants and lunchrooms. But Greeks are a significant percentage of the population only west of Tampa, where they once dominated the sponge-diving industry: one-sixth of the residents of Tarpon Springs claim Greek ancestry.

108. Southern Jews have been, if not exactly few, at least far between. Although the South as a separate country would have the sixth largest Jewish population in the world, one observer has noted that "out of every 1,000 Americans, about 260 live in the South and about 30 are Jewish, but only two are Jews who live in the South—and one of those lives in Florida, which hardly counts." Sephardic merchants were found in seventeenth-century Charleston, and crypto-Jewish "conversos" survive in south Texas, left over from New Spain, but the South received little of the nineteenth- and early-twentieth-century Jewish immigration to the United States. Some Jewish peddlers settled in the region, and few Southern towns are without a Jewish-owned dry-goods store. Later generations' preferences and migration from the North mean that Southern Jews are increasingly found

Lexington, Mississippi, 1939. Marion Post Wolcott, Farm Security Administration/Library of Congress USF33-30590

in management and the professions rather than merchandising, and in the South's metropolitan areas rather than its smaller cities and towns. (See **821**.)

109. **The Jews of south Florida** are mostly migrants (many retired) from the urban Northeast. In fact, the Gold Coast from Miami to West Palm Beach is home to the third largest concentration of Jews in the United States, after New York and Los Angeles. This largely accounts for the significant numbers of Floridians with Austrian, Hungarian, Polish, Russian, Romanian, Israeli, and Baltic states origins. These nationality groups are rare in the rest of the South, although people of Polish descent are also found in Texas (where most are Catholic), and there's a significant Israeli presence in Myrtle Beach, South Carolina.

HISPANICS, ETC.

110. **South Florida's ethnic mix** accounts for most of the South's Cubans, Central and South Americans, Puerto Ricans, Jamaicans, Barbadi-

ans, and Haitians. A third of Miami households are now "Hispanic," most of them Cuban; in fact, a majority of the 800,000-plus Cuban-Americans live in metropolitan Miami, many having moved there after settling elsewhere in the United States. South Florida also has appreciable groups of other Latin Americans, especially Colombians and Puerto Ricans, the latter mostly migrants via the Northeast, as well as the largest Haitian and Jamaican communities outside New York City.

111. **Mexican-Americans** in Texas predate both Mexico and America, so not surprisingly some reject that label, preferring an old one, Tejanos, or a new one, Chicanos. Continuing immigration and high birthrates make this group the South's fastest-growing minority. In Texas nearly 4 million make up a quarter of the state's population. Starr County was 94 percent Mexican-American in 1980, and twenty-two of the twenty-four U.S. counties with Mexican-American majorities are in Texas, on or near the Mexican border. The populations of San Antonio and El Paso are 48 percent and 70 percent "Hispanic" respectively. Mexican-Americans are still rare outside Texas and southwest Florida, where they've recently come from Texas as agricultural workers. In other Southern states they're less than 3 per-

Mexican stone carvers in 1870s Texas. *The Great South* (1875)

cent—and usually less than 1 percent—of the permanent population, but Mexican and Mexican-American migrant workers are increasingly doing the field work of Southern agriculture (they now pick most of the bright-leaf tobacco crop, for instance), and they're also well represented in unpleasant industries like poultry processing.

ASIAN-AMERICANS

112. Chinese came to Texas and Louisiana as early as 1867 to pick cotton and build railroads, but nearly all were single men who returned to China, remained childless, or married white or black women and assimilated. (Houston now supports several competing Chinatowns, but its Chinese community, like other cities' smaller ones, is made up of more recent immigrants.) Mississippi is a different story. Chinese workers came to the Delta cotton fields about the same time, but many became owner-operators of small grocery stores serving the black community and were later joined by their wives. Under Jim Crow their status was intermediate between blacks and whites, and most became Southern Baptists. The community has been large enough to provide marriage partners for its members, and its numbers have increased, despite considerable out-migration.

113. Indians and Pakistanis are still rare in the South (outside Houston, which has the fourth largest Indian and Pakistani populations in the United States), but some are highly visible. Most are recent immigrants with high levels of education and tend to be found in Southern cities and university communities, but many small towns and rural areas shunned by native-born physicians are now served by Indian or Pakistani

Grundy, Virginia, 1994. DixiePix

practitioners. Also, as in other warm parts of the United States, many small motels are now run by Indian families, most of them Gujeratis from a Hindu commercial caste named Patel.

114. Koreans, Thais, Filipinos, Vietnamese, and Laotians, when found in the South at all, tend to be either in cities or near military bases. (The Siamese Twins [**118**] were an exception.) Many refugees from the Vietnam era were resettled in the South. Vietnamese fishermen have successfully relocated to several ports on the Gulf Coast from west Florida to east Texas, especially around Biloxi and Galveston Bay. Small enclaves of Hmong, for instance, can be found in unlikely places, and Houston has the third largest Vietnamese population in the United States, but many Vietnamese have left the South for California.

ETHNICALLY INTERESTING SOUTHERNERS

A FEW FOLKS OF exotic—or exotically mixed—backgrounds:

115. **Bilali Mohomet,** or Ben Ali, was a Muslim slave brought from what's now Sierra Leone to Sapelo Island, Georgia. Bilali practiced his faith as best he could, observing its holidays, praying to the east, and following Muslim dietary restrictions. Literate in Arabic, he compiled from memory a collection of extracts from an Islamic legal text (now in the Georgia State Law Library). Overseer of a plantation and its four-hundred-plus slaves for an absentee owner, he organized a force of eighty armed slaves to defend against the British in 1813, telling his master, "I will answer for every Negro of the true faith, but not for the *Christian dogs* you own." He raised his twelve children as Muslims, and his descendants (now called Bailey) still live on Sapelo Island. Frederick Douglass's (**389**) biographer has speculated that Douglass's Bailey ancestors may come from this line.

116. **Osceola** (1800?–38), a half-English Seminole chief, led a guerrilla war to prevent removal of the Seminoles from their homeland ("They cannot live in that cold country where only the oak tree grows"). Treacherously captured under a flag of truce, he was imprisoned in Florida and then near Charleston, where he inspired public sympathy by "his handsome person, his melodious voice, his large dark eyes, his bravery, and his fate." Sympathy was not enough to keep the "captive eagle" alive, and he died after four months in prison.

117. **Archibald Grimké** was the son of Sarah and Angelina's (**267**) brother Henry, a Charleston lawyer, and his slave Nancy Weston. After Henry's death, his legitimate son Montague ignored his will and turned Nancy out to support herself and her sons (not easy: she was crippled in one arm), but when he married, he took his half brothers back as his servants and had their mother jailed when she protested. After the Civil War, patrons sent the boys to Lincoln University. In 1868 Angelina saw her nephew mentioned in an antislavery paper and reunited the family. Archibald became a Boston lawyer, editor of a Negro journal, the *Hub,* and a prolific author. In 1894 he became U.S. consul general to Santo Domingo. He was vice-president of the NAACP and longtime president of the American Negro Academy.

Osceola. Library of Congress USZ62-356

Eng and Chang Bunker. Library of Congress USZ62-3928

118. Eng and Chang Bunker (1811–74), the Siamese Twins, left their native Siam (now Thailand) in 1829 to tour the world. Eng and Chang retired to Wilkes County, North Carolina, married (respectively) sisters Sarah and Adelaide Yates, became farmers, and produced twenty-two children (twelve and ten, if you're curious), to the consternation of their neighbors.

119. Ephraim E. Lisitzky (1885–1962), a major figure in the revival of modern Hebrew, was born in Minsk. He came to America as a teenager and eventually became principal of New Orleans's excellent Hebrew School. His poetry includes *Medurot Do'akhot* ("Dying Campfires"), an epic based on American Indian legends, in the style and meter of "Hiawatha," and

Be-Oholei Kush ("In the Tents of Cush"), based on Negro folktales, spirituals, and sermons. His Hebrew autobiography was translated as *In the Grip of Cross-Currents*.

120. Reuben Greenberg is a black Oklahoman who got his name and his religious affiliation from a Jewish grandfather. A former rodeo cowboy and political science professor, he's now the popular police chief of Charleston, South Carolina. (Innovative, too: he has been known to patrol on roller skates.) Once, when criticized for giving a policeman time off for a Confederate reenactment, he responded, "Well, you all have always told me that one boy in gray is worth ten in blue."

The Old Ways

SOUTHERNERS BROUGHT WITH THEM some distinctive ways of doing things. Up the hollers, out in the swamps, and even downtown, some still do them that way. Others are starting to do them that way again. (The *Foxfire* books are a good source, if you want to do them, too.)

121. Wrought iron is the medium of Philip Simmons (b. 1912), a black Charlestonian. Apprenticed to a blacksmith in 1925, he looked about him when horseshoeing jobs dried up and was inspired by local decorative ironwork. He made an old-style forge from a hundred-year-old pattern and began putting his mark on Charleston, adding his own motifs (fish, birds, "pecan leaves," and "wiggle tails") to traditional designs. Now he's famous: his work is in the Smithsonian and other museums, he's in the South Carolina Hall of Fame, he won a National Heritage Fellowship Award, a Charleston church

Detail from a gate by Philip Simmons. Courtesy of the South Carolina State Museum

Edgefield pot. Red Piano Too Art Gallery, St. Helena Island, S.C

has a Philip Simmons Garden, and a book has been written about him.

SOUTHERN POTTERS

122. **The Piedmont (15)**, thanks to its clay deposits, was where early potting started. The first notable potters, beginning about 1750, were North Carolina Moravians, but by 1825 there were Jugtowns in Georgia, Alabama, and North Carolina (the best known). Most of the pottery was simple, undecorated, and functional, including pottery grave markers. The most exotic was the face jug or, more aptly, "ugly jug," with a grotesque face on one side. Folks argue about whether blacks or whites invented it, but nobody says it ain't ugly. The glazes—one is called tobacco spit—may have spread from an Edgefield, South Carolina, pottery run by Dr. Abner Landrum, who may have read about similar Chinese glazes. (Landrum must have been a bit batty over pottery: his children had names like Wedgwood.) Folk pottery almost died out, although some of the old potting families (like the Coles and Cravens of North Carolina, who have been at it since the eighteenth century) hung on by adopting modern shapes and glazes and concentrating on tableware rather than storage jars. They're flourishing again—a favorite outing in North Carolina is an all-day trip to "the potteries."

123. **Dave, a slave,** was one of Edgefield's most famous potters. He often signed his pieces and sometimes inscribed them with his own poetry: for example, "Dave belongs to Mr. Miles / wher the oven bakes & the pot biles," or "Great & noble Jar / hold Sheep goat or bear," or "This noble jar will hold twenty [gallons] / fill it with silver then you will have plenty," or "The Fourth of July is surely come / to sound the fife and beat the drum," or (our favorite) the single word "Ponderosity."

THE SOUTH HAS HAD its share, and maybe more, of *art* potters.

124. **George Ohr** (1857–1918), a/k/a the Mad Potter of Biloxi, wasn't mad at all, just aggressively eccentric. His grotesque shapes with beautiful glazes won a medal at the 1904 St. Louis fair and were featured in *Harper's Weekly.* Writing to the U.S. Potters Association, he said, "I send you four pieces, but it is as easy to pass judgment on my productions from four pieces as it would be to take four lines from Shakespeare and guess the rest." Convinced that the government would one day buy the lot, he packed up his six thousand pieces in crates and opened a car repair shop. The government never came through, but someone did, and now his work is very pricey indeed.

125. **Newcomb pottery** (1895–1940) was an effort by Tulane's H. Sophie Newcomb Memorial College (for women) to provide respectable employment for its graduates (feminism meets the arts and crafts movement). Professional male potters threw shapes chosen by the women (feminism had its limits), who then decorated them. No two pieces were alike, and designs were based on Southern plants and animals. Newcomb was one of the most important art

potteries of the era: its pots were shown and sold widely, and it won eight medals in international exhibitions in its first twenty years.

AFRICAN SURVIVALS

WHEN YOU THINK OF Southern quilts and baskets, you may think of the work of white Southerners: handsome, utilitarian baskets and traditional patchwork or appliquéd quilts, often beautifully done. You may think of the distinctive American Indian baskets, which vary from tribe to tribe. But you may never have seen a quilt that reflects surviving African aesthetic values.

126. **Black quilts,** like jazz, value improvisation, and their aesthetic ideals are often clearly African: strong, contrasting colors and large designs (African clothing shows status, and the signals must be clear), multiple patterns (num-

Strip quilt with log-cabin-style center square, c. 1935, by Mrs. Floyd McIntosh, Pinola County, Mississippi. Collection of the Mississippi State Historical Museum

ber and complexity once showed royal or priestly position), use of strips (many African looms were four to nine inches wide), and asymmetry. Many quilts have all these characteristics, even when using patterns originated by whites: for example, a log-cabin block that would be one of many in a white quilt can be the whole of a black one, or the center section; if several blocks are used, they can be variations on the *idea* of the log-cabin block rather than dutifully repeated designs.

127. **The coiled baskets** of the Sea Islands (**28**) are almost identical to the baskets of Senegal and Angola and were used for the same purpose—winnowing rice and storing and carrying produce. Older baskets were made of rush to withstand hard use; later baskets are made of sweet grass, which is softer and easier to work but not as sturdy. Basket sewing flourishes in Charleston, along Route 17 at Mount Pleasant, South Carolina, and elsewhere along the coast—keep your eyes open. Makers pride themselves on their originality within the traditional techniques, and the best baskets now command art prices.

FOLKLORISTS DISTINGUISH BETWEEN "HOODOO" (conjuring) and "voodoo" (the folk religion), but common usage doesn't.

128. **Haiti** is where the *vodu* (gods) of Dahomey met the saints of Roman Catholicism, and hoodoo was born—an elaborate conjuring system in which doctors work through mojo hands (mojos, for short), pouches holding ingredients for hexing: fingernails or hair from the intended victim or beneficiary, lizard skins, goofer dust (graveyard dust), etc. It came to Louisiana with slaves and free blacks after the Haitian revolution.

129. **"New Orleans** is now and has ever been the hoodoo capital of America," Zora Neale Hurston (**507**) wrote in 1935. "Hoodoo, or Voodoo, as pronounced by the whites, is burning with a flame in America, with all the intensity of a suppressed religion," she added, and as far as we can tell, it still is. The *Wall Street Journal* has reported that Schwab's department store in Memphis sells twenty-one tons of hoodoo supplies a year, not all to tourists.

Sweet-grass baskets. DixiePix

Hoodoo supplies sold here. DixiePix

130. John the Conqueror root (St.-John's-wort) is a favorite hoodoo ingredient. Hurston gives a voodoo recipe for winning a court case: "Take one-half pint whiskey, nine pieces of John the Conqueror Root one inch long. Let it soak thirty-eight hours till all the strength is out. (Gather all roots before September 21.) Shake up good and drain off roots in another bottle. Get one ounce of white rose or Jockey Club perfume and pour into the mixture. Dress your client with this before going to Court."

131. Marie Laveau, queen of conjure, was (confusingly) a mother-daughter team in New Orleans. The tomb of Marie I (1794–1881) is in St. Louis Cemetery No. 1 and is still sought by pilgrims. Marie II was born in 1827 and was famous for her power among a huge circle of blacks and whites. She was also famous for her "hoodoo dances," which were great hype but just pleasure dances, not hoodoo, according to Luke Turner, who claimed to be her nephew and taught hoodoo to Zora Neale Hurston.

132. Influences of hoodoo are everywhere, when you start to look. Read the novels of Julia Peterkin (**519**). Notice how often the blues mention mojos or John the Conqueror or the seventh son of a seventh son. (W. E. B. Du Bois assumed everyone would understand when he said the Negro was "a sort of seventh son, born with a veil, and gifted with second sight.") Think about the modern magical realism of writers like Gloria Naylor, in *Mama Day,* and very young writers like Tina McElroy Ansa, whose heroine in *Baby of the Family* is born with a caul and thus can see spirits.

133. Many African burial practices survive in the rural South: a wake and a fine funeral and procession calm a restive spirit. William Faulkner, in *Go Down, Moses,* described a grave marked by "shards of pottery and broken bottles and old brick and other objects insignificant to sight but actually of a profound meaning and fatal to touch, which no white man could have read." Grave objects include things last used by the dead (usually broken), especially items as-

Tomb of the first Marie Laveau. Betty Swanson/Historic New Orleans Collection 1978. 144.438

Child's grave, Hale County, Alabama, 1936. Walker Evans, Farm Security Administration/Library of Congress USF342-8176A

sociated with water. An African belief that the dead become white *bakulu* who live underwater may account for this, and for the fact that grave goods in Africa and the United States are often white.

134. **The bottle tree,** once common throughout the South, originated in black folk culture but is now an equal-opportunity lawn ornament. A young black woman in Eudora Welty's (**510**) "Livvie" describes "bare crepe-myrtle trees with every branch of them ending in a colored bottle, green or blue. . . . bottle trees kept evil spirits from coming into the house—by luring them inside the colored bottles, where they cannot get out again." (They moan when the wind blows.) Cedars, stripped of their greenery, were most popular, for their shape and their resistance to rot. You'll be lucky to find one today—they're rare, and their purpose is largely forgotten.

The bottle tree survives as a logo. Bottletree Bakery, Oxford, Miss.

135. **The ring shout** is a compromise between the African tradition of religious dance and the Calvinist banning of dance: it's a dance that's not a dance, and a shout that's not a shout (the name seems to come from the Arabic *saut).* Moving counterclockwise, single file, the wor-shipers follow the directions of a lead singer, keeping feet on the floor and never allowing the legs to cross (which would be dancing)—the back foot never passes the front foot. "Shout" refers to the fast shuffling step, to the dance itself, or to the prayer meeting at which it is done.

FOLK MEDICINE

136. **Both blacks and whites** have elaborate systems of folk medicine. In the black community, herbalists need not practice hoodoo, but most hoodoo practitioners are also herb doctors who treat physical and mental ills (and are often patronized by blacks and whites). When you hear people complain of "high blood," they don't mean blood pressure: they're talking about the balance between "sweet" (high) blood and "bitter" (low) blood that is believed to control

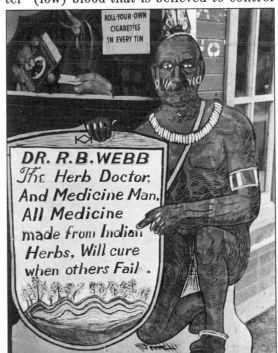

Arkansas herb doctor advertises his wares, 1938. Farm Security Administration/Library of Congress USF33-11697-M2

health. The mountain South has been particularly dependent on folk healers. J. C. Gunn's *Domestic Medicine, or Poor Man's Friend,* published in Knoxville, Tennessee, in 1830, went through one hundred editions by 1870.

137. **Healing talents**—cooling the heat of burns, curing "thrash," stopping bleeding—are something you're born with. When the young Harry Crews (**446**) fell into a cauldron of water boiling to scald hogs, a healer came: "I stopped burning before he ever started talking. He talked to the fire like an old and respected adversary, but one he had beaten consistently and had come to beat again. . . . he cursed the fire, calling it all kinds of sonofabitch, but the words neither surprised nor shocked me. The tone of his voice made me know that he was locked in a real and terrible conflict with the fire."

Southern Style

OTHER DISTINCTIVELY SOUTHERN WAYS have emerged in more recent times.

NAMING PRACTICES

THERE ARE IDENTIFIABLY SOUTHERN names, although most Southerners don't have one.

138. **Family names** are often used as given names for both male and female Southern children, especially among the upper class or aspirants to it—that is, those with access to family names of some distinction. "It's a way to keep the family names alive," says novelist Lee Smith. "We don't do hyphenated names." This can lead to gender-bending anomalies like guys named Shirley or Beverly and girls named Cameron, Fletcher, or Dabney.

139. **Double names** are often used for both men and women. Drew Jubera suggests that this is "a carry-over from a tradition in Scotland and Ireland, where so many people shared the same first name that they began adding their middle names to differentiate themselves." Sometimes a common given name is combined with a family name. "I was Lee Marshall growing up," says Lee Smith. "My cousins lived next door, and they all had two names. When we were called to dinner, it would take forever." Especially in the Deep South and Southwest, the combination is often just two given names, or even nicknames: Joe Bob, Tommy Lee, Peggy Sue, Bobbie Ann.

140. **Jr., II, III, etc.,** are more common in the South—another sign of filiopietism, or maybe just lack of imagination. Rex Taylor looked at the frequency of such names among men in nineteen U.S. cities. Five of the top six cities were Southern (the other was Baltimore); highest was Richmond. Fort Worth and Oklahoma City were more like Midwestern and Northeastern cities. Lowest were the Western cities—Olympia, Sacramento, and Cheyenne.

A well-known "Jr." with the title of one of his songs, on a suitable background. DixiePix

141. **"Big" and "Little"** are sometimes used informally among both black and white, especially in the Deep South, to distinguish between relatives with the same name. Thus "Little Willie" and "Big Edna" may refer not to stature, but to the existence of Big Willie and Little Edna.

142. **Diminutives** for men are more often retained into adulthood in the South. Thus, James Earl Carter, Jr., is known as Jimmy, and his brother was called Billy. Similarly, Martin Luther King, Jr., was called Marty at least as late as his graduate school years.

143. **Distinctive men's names.** Wilbur Zelinsky used telephone books to identify men's given names that are more common in the South. Many are nicknames elsewhere: Jim, Bob, Joe, Jack, Willie, Jerry, Ray, Fred. Others are just names that don't get used much (by white men) outside the South: Eugene, Clyde, Ernest, Marion, Earl(e), Lee, Floyd, Gerald, Harvey, Wilbur, Louis, Wayne. (If there are similar names for women—Dixie?—they haven't been as well documented.) Use one of these distinctive names in a double name and you get things like James Earl, as in James Earl Carter, James Earl Jones, James Earl Ray. Or Lee Harvey, as in— oh, never mind.

144. **The classic Southern male name.** Use a diminutive with one of these distinctive names and you get something *really* Southern, like Billy Ray Cyrus, Jerry Lee Lewis, or Billy Clyde Puckett (hero of Dan Jenkins's novel *Semi-Tough*). Some Southern guys have apparently found this part of their heritage a liability: Billy Don Moyers actually went to court to change his name, and Jimmy Earl Carter dropped his middle one somewhere along the way. On the other hand, Pennsylvanian Joe Namath (**869**) found it

useful to be "Joe Willie" while playing ball for 'Bama, and New Yorker Paul Crosby did better as a country singer when he moved to Texas and changed his name to Jerry Jeff Walker.

145. **Initials** as de facto given names are used more often by Southern men than by their Northern peers. Remember J. R. Ewing on *Dallas?* This isn't a matter (as it is with the British) of discouraging familiarity. You first-name one of these guys by calling him R.G. or whatever.

146. **Nicknames** seem to be more common among Southern men than Northern ones, although we don't have any hard data on it. Particularly in the rural and working-class South, one distinguishing characteristic or incident in childhood can stick you with a moniker for life. Some nicknames are based on physical characteristics (Red, Whitey, Shorty, Runt, Fats, Peanut, Satchel-mouth, Tree), others on personality or who knows what (Fireball, Hoss, Killer, Dog, Hotrod, Snake, Mojo, Bear). Junior is also common as a nickname, and not unknown as a given one. One of the best-known Deep South male nicknames, among both black and white, is

Some nicknames lack sensitivity: Zebulon, North Carolina, 1939. Southern Historical Collection, University of North Carolina Library, Chapel Hill

Bubba. It comes from the childish pronunciation of "brother," and the female equivalent ought to be Sissy but is probably more often Missy. Although the name has lately acquired political connotations (**417**), Bubbas actually come from all classes and all levels of sophistication. We know one who teaches classics. No lie.

THE KING'S ENGLISH

How ELVIS TALKED.

147. "Y'all" (usually one syllable) is undoubtedly the most widely recognized Southernism, and one of the most widespread, found in every Southern dialect from Cajun Louisiana to Appalachian West Virginia. It's a useful replacement for the second-person plural that modern English has lost, which is why Southerners use it, and why they get annoyed when it's misapplied to one person by ignorant Yankees poking fun. The referent can be a little vague (you and whomever you choose to associate yourself with), but it is a plural pronoun. (A recent development, perhaps to emphasize this, is the Southern hyper-plural "all y'all.") Eighty percent of Southerners own up to saying "you-all" occasionally; most non-Southerners only say it when mocking Southerners, but it may be creeping in among the young.

148. "Ma'am" and "sir" are respectful forms of address used in the South, especially for older persons. Hank Williams, Jr., sings that "we say grace and we say 'ma'am' "—and he's right on both scores. The Southern Focus Poll reports that 80 percent of Southern parents teach their children to use these forms with adults, compared to only 46 percent of non-Southern parents.

149. "Mess" is a good old usage (recall the biblical mess of pottage or the army mess hall) that means roughly a sufficiency of some kind of food. It has been preserved in the South, usually with reference to greens or fish. It's less than a slew.

150. "Piss-ant" is related to "pismire," an archaic word for ant, and it's a fine Southern epithet, combining implications of excrement and insignificance. After Pearl Harbor, Secretary of State Cordell Hull, a Tennessean, reportedly called two Japanese envoys "hickory-headed piss-ants" (but he presumably said "pith-anth," since he spoke with a lisp).

151. Other archaisms have also hung on longer in the South than elsewhere. "Ain't goin' to study war no more" yields three examples: "study" for contemplate, "ain't," and the double negative as an intensifier. Other examples include the useful word "yonder," "tote" for carry, "poke" for bag, "foot" instead of feet ("six foot tall"), "come" for came, and the antecedent *a-* with verbs ending in *-ing* ("he come a-running").

152. "Doublewide," on the other hand, is a new coinage, referring to a type of mobile home. Since trailer-houses now comprise more than half of the new housing in the South, it's almost axiomatic that someone who doesn't know what

Singlewide with satellite dish, South Carolina, 1994.
DixiePix

a doublewide is isn't a Southerner. You don't have to be a Southerner to know this, but the South does have over half of the nation's mobile homes.

153. **"Branch," "fork," and "run"** are subregional synonyms for creek, found only rarely outside the South. "Brook," on the other hand, isn't an indigenous Southern word at all—or wasn't until the real estate developers started using it.

154. **"Mamaw" and "Papaw"** are common, though by no means universal, Southern forms of address for grandmother and grandfather.

155. **Carbonated beverages** are pretty much a Southern invention (**212, 704–8**), but there's no consensus on what to call them. The Southern Focus Poll finds that 36 percent of Yankees call the stuff "pop," but only 9 percent of Southerners do. Southerners are also less likely to say "soda" or "soda pop," more likely to say "soft drink" or to use "Coke" generically. A few old-fashioned Southerners still say "dope," a reference to an early not-so-secret ingredient.

156. **African survivals** include words like banjo, goober, mojo, benne, okra, gumbo, hoodoo, boogie, and jazz (notice how many have to do with food and music), as well as "unh-uh" and "uh-huh" for no and yes. The extent of other survivals is a subject of hot debate, but as early as 1860 Daniel Hundley, a genteel Alabamian (**933–36**), was complaining about "Southern provin-cialisms and Africanisms" in the speech of white common folk.

157. **"Dinner,"** in the South, used to mean the midday meal—the principal meal of the day, as in many agricultural societies. The lighter evening meal was "supper." But as Southerners have moved to town, the major meal has moved to evening, and its name has moved with it (except, in many cases, on Sunday). According to the Southern Focus Poll, 57 percent of Southerners now eat dinner in the evening; only 40 percent still eat supper. (Among non-Southerners, the numbers are 65 percent and 32 percent.) Some feel it's a shame, recalling the great old gospel hymn "Suppertime," or even observing that Jesus ate a last supper, not a last dinner.

158. **The War Between the States** (WBTS) used to be the preferred Southern label for the late

A farmers' dinner, 1939: the women stand while the men eat. Marion Post Wolcott, Farm Security Administration/Library of Congress USF-52663-D

unpleasantness. Groups like the United Daughters of the Confederacy (**344**) say that "Civil War" accepts the implication that the conflict was between parts of a single nation. But this distinction seems to be a lost cause itself. Asked what the war between the North and South is called, 62 percent of Southerners now say Civil War, only 6 percent say WBTS, 13 percent say something else (like the War of Northern Aggression)—and 20 percent don't know. (It's Civil War to 71 percent of non-Southerners, WBTS to 3 percent.)

159. "Fixing to" and "might could" (i.e., might be able to), on the other hand, are Southernisms more common now than a generation ago, according to linguist Guy Bailey. The Southern Focus Poll shows that Southerners are three to four times as likely as other Americans both to hear and to say "fixing to" and "might could."

SOUTHERN ACCENT(S)

SOUTHERNERS NOT ONLY USE different words, they pronounce the same ones differently.

160. The post-vocalic *r*—that is, *r* after a vowel, as in *hard, cord,* or *her*—is omitted in many (though not all) Southern accents. Thus, garden becomes *gahden* (or, in Tidewater Virginia, *gyahden*). Mark Twain observed that "the educated Southerner has no use for an *r,* except at the beginning of a word," but linguists find that pesky consonant creeping into Southern speech these days, especially among the middle class and, there, especially among women.

161. "Pure Elizabethan English" has *not* been preserved in isolated parts of the South, despite

what you may have heard. Linguist Michael Montgomery dismisses such assertions as "pretty much complete exaggerations." It does appear, however, that "(1) the speech of the coastal areas like the South Carolina Low Country and the Virginia Tidewater resembles that of southeastern England in some ways; (2) the speech of the Lower South resembles in part that of London and southern counties of England; and (3) the speech of the Upper South is akin to that of northern England, and of Scotland and Northern Ireland."

162. Slow speech, similarly, is *not* a Southern characteristic, despite the general impression to the contrary. Montgomery reports that Southerners speak just about as many words per minute as other Americans. Some words get drawn out, though. Novelist Reynolds Price observes differences in "the tones of voice, the lit-

Reynolds Price. Photograph by Curt Richter

eral pitches and rhythms that ride the music of thought. Southerners employ more notes of the scale than other Americans; they need them for their broader reach of expression." Lewis Grizzard pointed out, for instance, that "Southerners can probably say 'shit' better than anybody else. We give it the ol' two-syllable 'shee-yet,' which strings it out a bit and gives it more ambience, if words can have ambience." Mark Twain said, "The Southerner talks music."

"STUDIES HAVE SHOWN . . ."

SOCIAL SCIENTISTS HAVE TURNED up some interesting regional differences in behavior.

163. **Smiling** appears to be a Southern custom. Ray L. Birdwhistell found smiling among middle-class folk on the street most common in Atlanta, Louisville, Memphis, and Nashville, followed by cities in the Midwest, then New England, and, last, western New York. Within the South, those from lowland areas were more

likely to be smiling than those from the Appalachian region. Such differences can be misunderstood: "In one part of the country, an unsmiling indi-

A famous smiler. National Archives

vidual might be queried as to whether he was 'angry about something,' while in another, the smiling individual might be asked, 'What's funny?' "

164. **Touchiness** seems to be characteristic of young Southern white men. Richard Nisbett brought white male students into the laboratory on a pretext and insulted them. Northerners addressed as "asshole" laughed it off or ignored it, but Southerners bristled. Subsequent tests showed that Southern subjects had heightened blood levels of stress-related hormones and testosterone, but Northern ones didn't.

165. **Taking it easy** is apparently a Southern custom, although shared with Californians. Robert V. Levine examined indicators of "the pace of life" in thirty-six American cities: walking speed in public, speed of a bank transaction, speed of postal clerks, and proportion wearing wristwatches in downtown areas. Only two of nine Southern cities were above average (Houston and Atlanta, barely); fourteen of eighteen Northeastern and Midwestern cities were. The fastest cities were Boston, Buffalo, and New York. But the West was slow, too: the slowest cities were Fresno, Memphis, San Jose, Shreveport, Sacramento, and (the slowest) Los Angeles.

166. **Helpfulness** is a Southern trait, according to Levine and his colleagues. They looked at behaviors like picking up an "accidentally" dropped pen, helping someone with a "hurt leg" pick up a bundle, making change for a quarter, helping a "blind" person cross the street, and mailing a "lost" letter. Five of the top six cities were Southern; only Atlanta and Shreveport were below average. Least helpful were Los Angeles, New York, and, dead last, Paterson, New

Jersey. Southerners did especially well in the situation (making change) where they were *asked* to help a stranger. But Southerners don't help just *anybody:*

167. **Chivalry** appears to be a Southern male characteristic. Bibb Latané and James Dabbs, Jr., had a woman drop pencils or coins on elevators in Atlanta, Seattle, and Columbus, Ohio. Over two-thirds of Georgia men helped the damsel in distress; only a third of Yankee men did. But almost as many non-Southern men also helped a hapless male, while only 12 percent of the Georgians did. Southern women also defer to male competence: they were as likely as non-Southern women to help another woman, but less than half as likely to help a male klutz. Of course things may have changed since 1976, when this study was published.

Chivalry, as portrayed by an Atlanta cartoonist, c. 1900.
Albert Volberg

Three

Boom and Bust

AGRICULTURE, COMMERCE, AND INDUSTRY

The old South rested everything on slavery and agriculture, unconscious that these could neither give nor maintain healthy growth. The new South presents a perfect democracy, the oligarchs leading in the popular movement—a social system compact and closely knitted, less splendid on the surface, but stronger at the core—a hundred farms for every plantation, fifty homes for every palace— and a diversified industry that meets the complex needs of this complex age.

—HENRY GRADY, 1886

Somebody said, well, then—said, you smart mouth—said, what color is a prejudice?...Say, it's green. That's the color it is. It's green. And, beloved hearts, if you ain't got that green you a second-class citizen anywhere in the world.

—BROTHER DAVE GARDNER

Before the War

WHETHER IT COULD "MAINTAIN healthy growth" or not, the economy of the Old South gave white Southerners the highest average standard of living in the world in 1860, even counting those (the majority) with no direct stake in the plantation system. Among the principal products:

168. **Corn** was grown by Southern Indians when Europeans first arrived, and it soon became a staple of the diet (**648–62**) for Southern hogs, horses, mules, and people. In the 1840s the upper South states were major corn producers (Tennessee led the nation). As late as the 1920s the South produced nearly a third of the nation's corn, mostly for Southern consumption. Crops like soybeans have partly replaced corn, but it's still important for silage and there's no substitute for homegrown sweet corn on the table.

169. **Tobacco** was smoked by Indians for religious and medicinal purposes, but Englishmen lit up for fun in colonial Virginia and Maryland.

(Tobacco, one said, "purgeth surperfluous fleame and other grosse humors.") Sot-weed became the South's first important export crop, and it remained important where cotton wouldn't grow. Today many varieties are cured in different ways for snuff, chewing tobacco, pipe tobacco, cigars, and cigarettes, but the big distinction is between the flue-cured bright leaf grown from Virginia to Florida, especially in North Carolina, and air-cured burley, grown mostly in Kentucky and Tennessee.

170. **Indigo** was of major importance only in colonial South Carolina (**234**), where it accounted for a third of the colony's exports by 1775. American indigo dyed Revolutionary War uniforms, but the loss of the British market and subsidies, East Indian competition, and the spread of cotton culture doomed it, which is just as well: "indigo Negroes" had notoriously short life expectancies.

171. **Rice** got started in seventeenth-century South Carolina, often tended by slaves from rice-growing parts of West Africa, and it soon became the dominant cash crop of coastal South Carolina and Georgia. In the 1880s, however, East Coast rice production began to fall as Southwestern production soared; by 1900

Billy Compton works tobacco, North Carolina, c. 1940.
Marion Post Wolcott, Farm Security Administration/Library of Congress USF33-30512

South Carolina rice field. *The Great South* (1875)

Louisiana, Texas, and Arkansas produced nearly all of the nation's rice crop, and they still do. Pumps, threshers, etc., now make rice production much less labor-intensive, but a museum in Georgetown, South Carolina, shows how and where it used to be grown. (See **671**.)

172. **Sugarcane** became economically important in Louisiana only after granulation methods from the Caribbean were introduced in 1795, but by 1850 Louisiana slaves were producing over 100,000 metric tons of sugar a year. Most American sugarcane is now cut by migrant labor, but most still comes from Louisiana, although since early in this century Floridians have grown it in the muck south of Lake Okeechobee (**55**). The United States has protected its sugar producers from foreign competition by a tariff since 1789.

Picking cotton. Marion Post Wolcott, Farm Security Administration/Library of Congress USF33-30628

173. **Cotton** was grown on the Sea Islands (**28**) in the eighteenth century, but it became King (**6**) only after the cotton gin (**235**) made cultivation of the more adaptable short-staple variety profitable. In the early nineteenth century cotton often made up more than half of all U.S. exports. Four million bales were produced in 1860, and production continued to increase after emancipation, peaking at 9 million bales in 1900. The boll weevil (**72**) and foreign competition ate into Southern domination of the world market, but cotton remained a mainstay of the region's economy until after World War II.

174. **Hemp** became a major crop in Kentucky and Missouri as cotton boomed in the Deep South: it provided rope and bagging for baling. After the Civil War, however, metal strapping and imported jute replaced hemp for these purposes, and the plant survives today only in the

Cutting cane near New Iberia, Louisiana, 1938.
Russell Lee, Farm Security Administration/
Library of Congress USF33-11861-M1

wild and on bootleg plantations where it is grown for smoking, a use that was known in antebellum times but wasn't considered a problem. Hemp is reportedly once again the principal cash crop of several Southern states, although statistics are rather unreliable.

175. **Horses** were highly valued by the Old South's gentry, who prided themselves on their horsemanship. Fox hunting and pseudo-medieval ring tournaments (**912**) displayed their skill; racing (**850**) showed their wealth and knowledge of horseflesh, and let them gamble. When a Yankee visitor observed that his host's stables were more comfortable than his slave quarters, the planter replied, "Two of my horses are worth more than any eight of my slaves." Tennessee walking horses and Kentucky thoroughbreds are now the best-known Southern breeds—but don't forget the wild ponies of Chincoteague Island, Virginia, celebrated in Marguerite Henry's children's books.

176. **Mules** have less class than horses, but they've been more important in the South. Our first president was also the first Southern mule-breeder. By 1860 the South had about half of the country's mules. "Forty acres and a mule" (**355**)

Mule harness for sale, Russellville, Tennessee, 1937. Edwin Locke, Farm Security Administration/Library of Congress USF33-04241

was the hope of newly freed slaves, and mules bred in the upper South were essential to the economy of the entire region. The South's mule population peaked at over 3 million about 1930. William Faulkner wrote of the "sheer and vindictive patience" of the mule, who will "work for you ten years for the chance to kick you once," but Harry Crews (**446**) has praised "the abiding genius of a good mule" in a marvelous testimonial too long to quote here.

177. **Hogs** came to Jamestown with the first English settlers (wild ones were already here, thanks to Spanish explorers), then moved across the upper South with the pioneers. Pig-

Lawn ornaments for sale near Fayetteville, North Carolina. Jack Delano, Farm Security Administration/Library of Congress USF34-43312-D

meat became central to high and low Southern cuisine (**637–45**); lard was used for lighting, salve, and soap. Some 20 million Southern hogs gave their lives in 1850. Raising "wood hogs" was an undemanding activity—just turn loose to forage for acorns and such, then slaughter for home use or drive to market—and the name of the University of Arkansas Razorbacks commemorates this easygoing lifestyle. Although production peaked around 1900, the South still accounts for a quarter of U.S. pork.

Richmond, 1865. Library of Congress

Economic Consequences of the War

ROBERT PENN WARREN CALLED the Civil War the South's Great Alibi, but there's no question that it destroyed, among other things, the Old South's economy.

178. Two-thirds of the South's wealth vanished between 1860 and 1865. Henry Grady said of the returning Confederate veteran, "He finds his house in ruins, his farm devastated, his slaves free, his stock killed, his barns empty, his trade destroyed, his money worthless; his social system, feudal in its magnificence, swept away; his people without law or legal status; his comrades slain and the burdens of others heavily on his shoulders." Over $2 billion invested in slaves was lost at emancipation—a rather cold-blooded way to look at it, but that's why economics is called the dismal science. Bonds and currency were worthless; the sharecropping system evolved in part because planters had no cash with which to pay their laborers. Other holdings lost or destroyed included livestock

(over 30 percent of the South's horses, cattle, and hogs), railroad track (most of the South's nine thousand miles destroyed, often twisted around trees to make "Sherman bow ties"), and real estate: cities like Atlanta, Columbia, and Richmond were in ruins, and Jackson, Mississippi, was called Chimneyville when Sherman finished with it.

179. Confederate government expenditures of $2.1 billion (when a dollar was still a dollar) went down the spout. And that doesn't count expenditures by individual states.

180. Dead or wounded were some 450,000 Southern men, more than half of all Confederates under arms and roughly a quarter of the able-bodied male population *including* non-combatant blacks. Nearly 100,000 were killed in action, twice that number wounded, 160,000 dead from disease or accident. Every third household lost a son or father. The ablest leadership of the South was literally decimated: 77 of the 425 Confederate generals died on the battlefield.

181. Support for veterans, widows, and orphans burdened Southern state governments well into the twentieth century. Southerners had a double burden: federal taxes for Union veterans' benefits, state taxes for Confederates. Shelby Foote unearthed the amazing fact that one-fifth of the Mississippi state budget in the first year of peace went for artificial limbs.

The 1930s

FOR WHATEVER REASONS, THE South was a long time recovering. "The nation's number-one economic problem" was President Roosevelt's characterization of the South in 1938—pretty impressive, considering that the Depression was going on at the time. But FDR was right. The government's *Report on Economic Conditions of the South* revealed some distressing facts:

182. **Per capita income** in 1937 was $314, about half the figure for the rest of the country. Adjusted for inflation, the South's income put it near the level the World Bank uses to define "less developed countries" today.

183. **Half of the South's labor force were farmers,** and more than half of America's farmers were Southerners. Southern farmers' incomes were only $186 per capita in 1929, a relatively *good* year for the rest of the country.

184. **Half of the South's farmers were tenants or sharecroppers** who didn't own the land they farmed. Tenants paid rent, sharecroppers split their crop with their landlords—either way, their situation was precarious. Per capita income for the average cotton tenant was $73.

185. **Southern farms were small and inefficient.** The average was seventy-one acres, and

one out of four was smaller than twenty acres. With more than half the nation's farms, the South had only one-fifth of its farm machinery.

186. **More than half the South's farmers raised only cotton,** and that was a risky business. Over 2 million Southern families depended on a staple whose price was subject to violent fluctuations, often 40 percent or more, from year to year.

187. **Erosion and soil depletion** were consequences of the poor farming practices that tenancy encouraged. The South had one-third of

Soil erosion, Georgia, 1941. Jack Delano, Farm Security Administration/Library of Congress USF34-43859-D

Tenant farmer houses, Georgia, 1938. Marion Post Wolcott, Farm Security Administration/Library of Congress USF34-51593D

U.S. farmland, but three-fifths of both the nation's fertilizer bill and its badly eroded land. Gullies covered as much area as South Carolina. And floods aggravated by runoff were a perennial danger for valley dwellers: they drove 750,000 people from their homes in 1927.

188. **Industrial wages** were better than farmers' incomes, but they still weren't good—an average $865 per year, compared to $1,219 outside the South. Most of that difference was because Southern industries like textiles and tobacco required fewer skilled workers.

Tending spindles in a Mississippi cotton mill, 1939. Russell Lee, Farm Security Administration/Library of Congress USF34-31963-D

189. **Child labor** was declining, but 108 of every 1,000 Southern children ten to fifteen years old were gainfully employed in agriculture or industry, more than five times the rate for the rest of the country.

190. **Lower tax revenues** were an inevitable result of poverty. State and local governments in the South actually taxed their citizens at a slightly higher rate than the national average, but still collected only about half the average per capita. This meant less money for everything from education to public health.

191. **A high birthrate** aggravated many of the region's problems. With roughly a quarter of the nation's population, the South had about a third of its children—and one-fifth of its tax revenues to educate them with. In 1936 Southern public school expenditures were $25 per child, about half the U.S. average. Support for segregated black schools was especially paltry.

A sharecropper's children. Southern Historical Collection, University of North Carolina Library, Chapel Hill

192. **Southern housing was substandard.** Even in urban areas, a quarter of households didn't have flush toilets, and in rural areas over 90 percent didn't have running water (one-fifth didn't even have privies). "By the most conservative estimates," the *Report on Economic Conditions* argued, "4,000,000 southern families should be rehoused. This is one-half of all families in the South."

193. Migration from the rural South had become a flood by the 1930s. One fourth of those born in the Southern countryside had left for Southern cities or for the North. Like many Third World economies, the South suffered a "brain drain": one-half of eminent Southern-born scientists in the 1930s no longer lived there. Boosters liked to point to a population that was 97.8 percent native-born in 1930, but one thing this meant was that hardly anyone was coming to the South.

194. Health costs money, and the government report observed that "the low-income belt of the South is a belt of sickness, misery, and unnecessary death." Low public-health budgets meant high rates of syphilis and malaria **(69)**. Overcrowded housing meant pneumonia and tuberculosis. Poor sanitation meant hookworm **(67)**. A diet of fatback and cornpone meant pellagra.

The report could also have mentioned black lung in the South's mines and brown lung in its textile mills.

195. Natural resources weren't a problem. The South had some of the nation's best farmland, 40 percent of its forests, a fifth of its soft coal, two-thirds of its oil, nearly all of its phosphates and sulfur, etc., etc. "The paradox of the South," the report concluded, "is that while it is blessed by Nature with immense wealth, its people as a whole are the poorest in the country. Lacking industries of its own, the South has been forced to trade the richness of its soil, its minerals and forests, and the labor of its people for goods manufactured elsewhere."

Kentucky coal miners. Caufield & Shook Collection, Photographic Archives, University of Louisville

NO. 4 MANTRIP & MINE SUPERINTENDENT.

The 1990s

IN SOME WAYS—AND in some parts of the South—things have sure changed since the 1930s. Even some black politicians, like Andrew Young (**397**), now talk like Brother Dave Gardner about green as the important color.

196. Industrialization was the answer, everyone agreed (except some planters concerned about their labor force and a few skeptics like the Agrarians [**922**]). And Lord knows the South has industrialized. As measured by percent of the labor force employed in industry, it's now the country's most industrialized section—and North Carolina is the most industrialized state. The agricultural labor force has dropped from half of the total to under 5 percent, and Southern agriculture has increasingly become "agribusiness." One telling statistic: the percent of cotton picked by machine went from 10 percent to 90 percent between 1950 and 1970.

Mechanical cotton picker. Marion Post Wolcott, Farm Security Administration/Library of Congress USF33-30550-M3

197. The South's birthrate declined as it moved from agriculture to industry. Since the mid-1950s it has been slightly *lower* than the U.S. average.

198. Interregional migration now flows the other way, as the South's booming economy slows out-migration and attracts migrants from other regions. Shortly after 1960 more whites began moving to the South than were leaving it; a decade later, the same was true for blacks. Now more than one of every eight residents of the Census South was born outside it. The South's population has increased rapidly in consequence. Texas has now replaced New York as the second most populous state, and Florida should overtake the Empire State early in the next century.

199. Personal income is still lower in the South—only Virginia and Florida are above the national average—but a cost of living about 10 percent lower than average largely offsets that difference.

200. Rural poverty is still a problem. Nine out of ten of the South's new jobs in the 1980s were in Texas, Florida, and a dozen metropolitan areas elsewhere. A poverty rate over twice the U.S. average still characterizes (1) the old cotton belt, where the problems are much the same as in the 1930s and the poor mostly black; (2) parts of Appalachia, where depressed energy prices have tanked the coal industry and the poor are nearly all white; and (3) a band of south Texas agricultural counties, where most of the poor are Mexican-American. This gives the South three of America's four major concentrations of rural poverty (the fourth is less a "concentration" than a Western archipelago of Indian reservations). The Commission on the Future of the South has called this combination of a flourishing metropolitan economy and stagnant rural areas "the two Souths." The title of the commission's report tells the story: *Halfway Home and a Long Way to Go.*

201. The process continues. In the 1990s eight of the top ten states in the growth of manufacturing plants were in the South. In 1992–94 over half the nation's new jobs and ten of the top thirteen states in jobs added per 100,000 population were Southern, the top three being North Carolina, Mississippi, and Kentucky. An analyst told the *Wall Street Journal* that "stark differences" in operating costs and "attitude toward business" explain the South's success.

202. Subsidies reflect the South's pro-industry attitudes and help to reduce operating costs as well. Mississippi pioneered relocation "incentives" in the 1930s; in the dozen years after 1956 the South was responsible for seven-eighths of the country's subsidized bond financing. Alabama holds the current record, with a $250-million-plus package for Mercedes.

203. Low wages have been attractive. The South's average manufacturing hourly wage is well below average, due primarily to an "industry mix" that requires less high-paid skilled labor and to the relative absence of labor unions, reinforced by right-to-work laws.

204. Foreign investment is increasingly important. Nearly 9 percent of South Carolinians now work for foreign-owned companies, almost twice the U.S. average. There are over fifty German-owned companies in Spartanburg County alone: the nearby section of Interstate 95 is known lo-

cally as the Autobahn. "We are the Germans' Mexicans," one cynic has remarked.

205. Automobiles are the classic heavy industry, and since the 1980s increasingly a Southern one. Tennessee has a $1.2-billion Nissan plant and a $3-billion Saturn one. Kentucky's Toyota factory ran $2 billion; South Carolina's BMW cost $450 million; Alabama's heavily subsidized Mercedes-Benz factory will cost $300 million. All told, these factories represent a $7-billion investment to create some twenty thousand well-paid jobs.

206. Branch plants and offices of Yankee and foreign firms are still the typical pattern. Moreover, absentee owners have acquired many indigenous Southern enterprises—from tobacco and furniture factories to *Southern Living* magazine and Lone Star beer. Only one in five of the Fortune 500, the largest U.S. industrial corporations, is headquartered in the South, and only one in seven of the top 100. The same is true for the Service 500, the nation's largest service corporations.

The Burroughs-Wellcome building in Research Triangle Park, North Carolina, designed by Paul Rudolph (see **738**). DixiePix

SOUTHERN ENTERPRISE

WHAT KINDS OF BIG corporations does the South have? Let's look at the Fortune 500.

207. Snowbirds. In recent years some large U.S. corporations have not just invested in the South but relocated there. Among them: American Airlines, Greyhound, and Penney's (to Dallas), and UPS (to Atlanta). Penney's claims its 1988 move saves it $60 million a year in operating expenses.

208. New Southern start-ups. Here Texas leads the South, with major competitors in new fields of endeavor ranging from computers (Texas Instruments, Compaq, Dell) to cosmetics (Mary Kay). All told, the Lone Star State is home to a third of the South's big industrial corporations, more than the next three states—Georgia, Virginia, and North Carolina—combined. It also leads in service corporations.

209. Oil is still the mainstay of the Texas economy, and in dollar terms it's the major industry in the South as a whole. The South's three largest industrial corporations are Exxon, Mobil, and Shell. Altogether, a couple of dozen of the South's hundred or so Fortune industries produce and distribute oil and gas or provide services to those who do. Most are in Texas or adjoining states, but don't forget Ashland Oil of Kentucky.

210. Textiles. Outside Texas, a good many Southern companies made the Fortune 500 the old-fashioned way: by spinning and weaving and knitting the product of those fields of cotton. Major examples of this traditional "New South" industry are Burlington Industries, James River,

Alamance Mill, North Carolina. North Carolina Museum of History, Raleigh

Springs Industries (**245**), and a half dozen others.

211. The South's fields, forests, and mines still fuel many of the region's other large industries. They process raw materials like timber (Georgia-Pacific) and ore (Reynolds Metals) or farm products like chickens (Tyson Foods) and corn (Brown-Forman distilleries). The International Home Furnishings Market brings some seventy thousand people twice a year to High Point, North Carolina, a major center of the furniture industry. But tobacco is no longer among these products. Cigarette factories are still found in Kentucky, Virginia, and especially North Carolina, but the headquarters and most of the expense-account jobs have decamped or been kidnaped to points north or, as in the case of Liggett and Myers, overseas. Even the maker of Skoal and Copenhagen snuff (**710**) has its headquarters in Greenwich, Connecticut. Red Man chewing tobacco, however, still comes from Pinkerton Tobacco Co. of Richmond.

212. Soft drinks (704–8), like tobacco, are a vice the South has profitably shared with the rest of the world. Here, too, some corporate headquarters have moved on: number two Pepsi, for instance, from North Carolina to New York State. But two of the biggest look to be

Atlanta's gift to the world. Caufield & Shook Collection, Photographic Archives, University of Louisville

staying in Dixie: number one Coca-Cola in Atlanta and number three Dr Pepper/7-Up of Dallas, although the latter was bought in 1995 by a British company.

213. **Transportation** has become something of a Southern specialty. Altogether, the South has seven of the top ten companies in this area, including snowbirds UPS and American Airlines (the two biggest) and Greyhound, plus other airlines, train lines, pipelines, shipbuilders, and trucking companies, and innovative Federal Express of Memphis. The South also has its share of large utilities.

214. **Retailing** is another area where the South holds its own. Southerners haven't become a nation of shopkeepers, but the region is home to Wal-Mart (the nation's largest retailer [**247**]);

J. C. Penney, and another dozen or so of the top fifty retail chains: supermarkets and convenience stores, drugstores, and dealers in building supplies, appliances, and electronics. The corporate headquarters are scattered across ten states.

215. **Commercial banking** has come on strong in recent years, thanks to an innovative interstate compact that allowed Southern banks to operate across state lines before other folks got the idea. A quarter of the nation's largest commercial banks are now headquartered in the South, six of them in North Carolina alone, including the South's three biggest: NationsBank (**227**), First Union, and Wachovia. For once, Texas isn't in the picture.

NOTABLE SOUTHERN COMPANIES

A FEW OF THE more interesting:

216. **Brown-Forman** of Louisville has been making Old Forester bourbon since 1870 (during Prohibition it was licensed to sell medicinal alcohol). Over the years it has diversified by ac-

Kentucky's gift to the world. Caufield & Shook Collection, Photographic Archives, University of Louisville

quisition and now markets wines, brandy, scotch, gin, California Cooler, and Lenox china as well as regional favorites Jack Daniel's (**661**), Early Times, and the world's best-selling liqueur, Southern Comfort. Until 1966 the company's president was always a member of the Brown family, and the company still hires by a publicly announced principle of nepotism, encouraging children and grandchildren of good employees to apply.

217. **Kress Stores** began in 1896 when Pennsylvanian S. H. Kress opened his first in Memphis. Kress's wasn't the first five-and-ten-cent store, but it was the first to eliminate the middleman, which was an improvement on Woolworth's scheme. By 1900 there were a half dozen stores in the South, and it was onward and upward from there. Kress himself moved to Fifth Avenue and amassed a considerable art collection, some of which he left to Southern museums.

Kress's prospered in its Memphis birthplace. DixiePix

Piggly Wiggly introduced many innovations. DixiePix

218. **Piggly Wiggly,** the world's first self-service grocery store, was also a Memphis enterprise, founded in 1916 by Clarence Sanders. The first grocery with checkout stands, the first with prices marked on all items, the first with refrigerated produce cases—Piggly Wiggly has long since been eclipsed by other supermarkets, but it's still in business as a regional chain.

219. **Morrison's Cafeterias,** begun in Mobile in 1920, has expanded to become the nation's largest cafeteria chain. Shopping-mall cafeterias are increasingly where you go to find traditional Southern fare. As Alex Haley observed, "Today if I were looking for greens—collard, mustard, or turnip—I'd go to Luby's in San Antonio, Morrison's in Mobile, S&S in Knoxville, or Piccadilly in Memphis. When people go to these cafeterias, they act as they do in churches. Their posture, gestures, and actions all say reverence."

220. **Delta Air Lines,** founded in 1924 by World War I flier Collet Everman Woolman, was the world's first crop-dusting service, to fight the boll weevil. It soon began carrying airmail and flew its first passengers (between Dallas and Jackson, Mississippi) in 1929. When Woolman

died in 1966, his company had become the most productive domestic airline in the country, thanks to excellent relations with its largely nonunion workforce, reinforced by policies of avoiding layoffs and filling all positions by promotion from within the company. The first airline to employ the "hub and spoke" system, Delta now maintains several hubs in the United States and one at Frankfurt. Delta flies over 80 percent of the flights at the nation's second busiest airport, giving rise to the Southern folk saying that even if you go to hell you'll have to change planes in Atlanta.

221. **Frito-Lay** started in Depression-era Texas, when Elmer Doolin bought the recipe for a tasty corn chip from a Mexican who wanted $100 to get back home. Doolin's mother, Daisy Dean Doolin, started cooking Fritos in her kitchen, and the rest is junk-food history. Frito acquired Lay's, an Atlanta potato chip company, in 1961. Headquartered in Plano, Texas, and now owned by PepsiCo, Frito-Lay has forty plants nationwide and produces one-eighth of all the snack food consumed in the United States, over $4 billion worth of Fritos, Chee-Tos, Tostitos, Doritos, and other treats every year.

222. **The Southland Corporation** took on too much debt in the 1980s and now belongs to the Japanese, but its headquarters are still in Dallas, where in 1927 an ice company got the idea of selling milk, eggs, and bread from its docks and the convenience store was born. Originally called Tote'm Stores (**151**) and decorated with (what else?) totem poles, in 1946 the outlets became 7-Elevens, to indicate their hours. When founder Joe Thompson died in 1961, there were six hundred of them; now, of course, they are ubiquitous, with over four thousand in Japan alone.

223. **Tyson Foods** has over $5 billion in annual sales of six thousand products in fifty-seven countries, but the Springdale, Arkansas, giant's bread and butter is chickens—over 17 million a week, a quarter of the U.S. market and more than its three biggest competitors combined. It has been in the chicken business since 1935, when John Tyson took a truckload to Chicago and made $235. The founder's son Don calls his employees "Tyson people" (not employees), encourages employee stock ownership, discourages labor unions, and requires his executives to wear khakis: "If we all wore suits," he says, "we'd sit here in the office, and we don't make money in here. We make it out in the field."

224. **Holiday Inns** were founded by Kemmons Wilson of Memphis in 1952, after an unpleasant family car trip to Washington. Wilson's first Holiday Inn (named after a Bing Crosby movie) offered private baths, air-conditioning, telephones, a swimming pool, free ice, free parking, and a kennel for the family dog. Holiday Inns soon became a chain of franchised motels offering standardized quality and guaranteed room rates. Holiday Inn University in Olive Branch, Mississippi, trained innkeepers, and by 1968 there were one thousand inns in the United States and abroad. The founder began meetings with prayer and insisted that each guest room's Bible be opened to a different page each day; many Holiday Inns had chaplains on call, and none had a bar until the 1960s. But after Wilson's retirement, modern management changed the corporate ethos: the company got into casinos, and new British owners moved its headquarters to Atlanta. There are now some sixteen hundred Holiday Inns worldwide, including one in Beijing.

225. **Food Lion** has grown since 1957 from a sin-

gle Salisbury, North Carolina, supermarket to a chain of hundreds of stores with billions of dollars in annual sales, dominating the market almost everywhere it does business—which is, for now, mostly in the Southeast. (A 1991 attempt to expand into Texas was a costly failure.) The company's philosophy is to do "1000 things 1% better," and its operating expenses are one-third below the industry average. Food Lion has been criticized for various shortcomings by the NAACP, the feds, the food workers' union, and *Primetime Live,* but the many small original investors in Salisbury will hear nothing against the company: a $1,000 investment was worth over $16 million thirty years later. Customers who appreciate Food Lion's guaranteed-lowest prices like it, too.

226. Cracker Barrel Old Country Stores started in 1969, when Dan Evins built a restaurant and gift shop at his Shell station near Lebanon, Tennessee. He stopped selling gas five years later; by then he had ten Cracker Barrels serving travelers on Southern interstates. Now there are nearly two hundred, most of them still in the South. The food is good cheap down-home grub, the decor is comfortable kitsch, the employees are efficient and friendly (turnover is half the industry average). Homosexual employees were once not welcome, but the company loosened up when protests threatened its expansion into northern states in 1991. (Protests or not, profits were up 50 percent that year.)

227. NationsBank is the largest of several Southern banks that saw their opportunities in the 1980s and took them. It traces its roots to a Charlotte bank founded in 1874, but more immediately to North Carolina National Bank, formed by a 1960 merger. The next year NCNB began operations in Florida. As soon as inter-

NationsBank's new headquarters building dominates the Charlotte skyline. DixiePix

state banking was allowed (**215**), it gobbled up banks in Georgia, South Carolina, Virginia, and Maryland, and in 1988 Texas's giant bankrupt First RepublicBank. It adopted its new, ambitious name when it merged with C&S/Sovran in 1991. By 1995, with NationsBank as America's third largest bank and crosstown competitor First Union at number six, Charlotte had become the country's third largest banking center, closing fast on number two San Francisco. The explosive growth of NationsBank has been driven by its CEO, Hugh McColl, Jr., an ex-marine given to remarks like "I expect the Herculean" and "Crush the sons of bitches and have a nice day." The company's grandiose new headquarters building is known locally as the Taj McColl.

228. **SAS Institute, Inc.,** was founded in 1976 by two North Carolina State University professors to market their statistical analysis software package. By 1994 SAS had a fancy new "campus" near North Carolina's Research Triangle Park, eleven U.S. regional offices, operations in 60 countries, and over 3 million users of its software in 120 countries. The company routinely leads the industry in percentage of revenue devoted to R&D, and its emphasis on problem-solving and user feedback was distinctive until competitors began to copy it. The company may also have been underestimated: "The competition saw us as a bunch of naive yokels who just fell off the turnip truck," says one vice-president. Remarkable employee benefits including fitness centers, on-site health care, day care for children, and help with elderly relatives keep turnover under one-seventh of the industry average.

Southern food, new-style. Courtesy of TCBY Enterprises, Inc.

229. **Columbia/HCA Healthcare,** now headquartered in Nashville, is by far the nation's largest hospital chain, three times larger than its nearest competitor. Its 175,000 employees made it the country's thirteenth largest private employer in 1995; 308 hospitals and 125 outpatient centers in the United States—more than half of them in five Southern states—generated revenues of roughly $15 billion. It has done for health care what Wal-Mart (**247**) and Southwest Airlines did in their fields: used purchasing muscle and high-tech methods to slash costs, lower prices, increase share, and expand. Chief strategist is Richard Scott, a former Kansas City doughnut-shop owner.

230. **"TCBY"** is arguably The Country's Best Yogurt (frozen) and certainly its biggest franchisor of that untraditional Southern treat. A single Little Rock store in 1981, "TCBY" had grown by 1995 to nearly three thousand outlets in the United States and from China to Qatar, with sales over $100 million a year. Its headquarters are still in Little Rock, and, with Wal-Mart, it seems to be one of the few big Arkansas businesses untouched by scandal. Most of the yogurt now comes from a plant in Dallas.

231. **Blockbuster Entertainment Corporation** began in 1982 as a homely Fort Worth video store started by David Cook, a software guy whose wife liked movies. Blockbuster differentiated itself from competitors by its large stock of old movies, high-tech inventory control, and the decision not to carry X-rated films. In 1987 Cook was bought out by some former Waste Management, Inc., executives, including founder Wayne Huizenga, who moved the headquarters to his hometown of Fort Lauderdale and pursued a policy of aggressive expansion. Blockbuster's

logo is now on nearly four thousand video rental outlets worldwide, and the company has moved into music retailing and video games.

232. Compaq Computers was founded in Houston in 1982 and made the Fortune 500 within four years, the first company ever to do that. Its founders, three executives from Texas Instruments, caught the PC wave just as it was cresting, and their buttoned-down management style saved them from the costly mistakes of more freewheeling computer entrepreneurs. Moreover, Compaq's machines were not just compatible with IBM's but better, and the company kept new products coming so fast that Big Blue had to scramble to keep up. There are no reserved parking spaces in the company lot, but this is not your laid-back Silicon Valley company: folks dress like IBMers. By 1990 more than half of Compaq's sales were overseas, and in 1994 it shipped 4.8 million PCs, which made it the industry's number one.

233. Ritz-Carlton Hotels. With all the successful Southern companies being bought up by Yankee and foreign investors, it's nice to find the opposite story. In 1983 Atlanta real estate developer William B. Johnson used some of his Holiday Inn and Waffle House money to buy the name of the venerable hotel chain. He also got the aging hotel in Boston, the only Ritz in North America, and spent $22 million to restore it. His Atlanta-based company now owns three Ritz-Carltons and manages twenty-five more, worldwide, offering the traditional grand style: twenty-four-hour room service, twice-a-day maid service, and splendid restaurants à la César Ritz. In 1992 Ritz-Carlton became the first hotel company to win the Malcolm Baldridge National Quality Award.

SOUTHERN INVENTORS AND ENTREPRENEURS

A FEW OF THESE folks went north to make their contributions, but a remarkable number stayed home to do it. A sampling of down-home talent:

234. Elizabeth Lucas Pinckney (1722–93) was probably born in Antigua. Educated in England, Eliza was left at age sixteen by her British officer father to manage three of his South Carolina plantations. Experimenting with indigo (**170**), she found a strain suitable to local conditions and learned how to produce dye from it. Her success set off the South Carolina indigo boom. She married into the remarkable Pinckney family of South Carolina: her sons Charles Cotesworth and Thomas carried on the family tradition as prominent soldiers and politicians.

235. Eli Whitney (1765–1825), a Yale graduate from Massachusetts, came south to be a tutor. At a dinner party in 1793 he learned that one worker took one day to separate one pound of short-staple cotton from its seed. Within ten days he designed a gin that eventually let one worker produce fifty pounds of cotton a day. In eight years cotton exports increased over a hundredfold. Litigation, business miscalculations, and bad luck kept him from making much money on the gin, but he opened a firearms factory in Connecticut that revolutionized manufacturing by using interchangeable parts.

236. Jean Lafitte (1780?–?1826), the Pirate King, was technically a privateer, but whatever he was, his navy and artillery made the governor of newly American Louisiana very nervous. His panache made him a hero to the Creole citizenry, however, and so did his prices: his plunder from the Spanish merchant fleet was for sale at a place called the Temple, in the swamps south of New Orleans, which John Maginnis has described as "Louisiana's first discount shopping center." Soon after Lafitte helped Andrew Jackson beat the British at the Battle of New Orleans in 1815, he found it prudent to move his operations to Galveston. Soon after that, he annoyed the U.S. Navy by sinking one of its ships and slipped away, presumably into retirement.

237. Cyrus McCormick (1809–84), born in Virginia, had little formal education, but in 1831 he patented a hillside plow, and the same year invented his famous reaper. He eventually concentrated his manufacturing operations in Chicago. He worked to prevent the Civil War, but when it came, his reaper let the North feed its people and sell grain abroad. After the war he gave money to revive the South's educational institutions, and he always remained a Virginian: he was president of Chicago's Virginia Society.

238. William Gregg (1800–67), raised in Georgia, ran a successful business in Columbia, South Carolina. Retiring early for health reasons, he bought a small cotton factory to amuse himself and made it successful. Healthy again, he moved to Charleston. Convinced that the South should spin and weave cotton, not just grow it, he published articles on the topic, then founded an incorporated cotton mill with nine thousand spindles, three hundred looms, and its own village, Graniteville (pop. 900), the first example of what became the typical Southern mill village. Gregg provided excellent housing, a library, and compulsory schooling for children. He sold direct from the plant, avoiding middlemen, and he made a bundle.

239. Richard Gatling (1818–1903) was the son of a North Carolina inventor. He patented a rice-sowing machine in 1839, then invented a hemp-breaking machine and a steam plow. He moved to St. Louis to manufacture farm equipment. During the Civil War he began to think about ordnance, invented a marine steam ram, and worked on the rapid-fire gun that (fortunately for his native state) was not adopted by the U.S. Army in time to do much damage. After the war he continued to tinker, inventing a motor-driven plow in 1900. Gatling's gun is the source of the gangland term "gat."

240. Miriam Florence Folline Leslie (1836?–1914) of New Orleans moved north when her first marriage was annulled, remarried, and became editor of *Frank Leslie's Lady's Journal.* Frank Leslie owned an empire of magazines, most with his name in the title. Pub-

Miriam Florence Folline Leslie. *Dictionary of American Portraits* (Dover, 1967)

lisher and editor soon fell in love, got divorces, and married each other. The Leslies entertained lavishly in New York and Saratoga. When Frank died, Mrs. Leslie had her name legally changed to Frank Leslie and took over the business, with huge success. She also wrote books, including the catchy title *Are Men Gay Deceivers?*

241. R. J. Reynolds (1859–1918) developed Camel cigarettes, which once claimed the loyalties of nearly half of America's smokers. Reynolds liked to pretend he was just a country boy, but he was a college graduate who used his family's money to start a chewing-tobacco factory in Winston (next door to Salem), North Carolina, in 1874. His company was gobbled up by the American Tobacco Trust (i.e., by James "Buck" Duke of Durham), but he got $3 million for it and got the company back when the trust was busted. He introduced Camels and developed a large and loyal customer base by giving them away to soldiers in World War I. He had thought about calling them Kaiser Wilhelm cigarettes, but luckily chose a name intended to evoke images of Turkey.

242. Asa Candler (1851–1929) didn't invent Coca-Cola (**212, 705**), but by 1891 he had bought the company, for $2,300. After he put the funny-tasting tonic on the path to being the world's most popular soft drink, his family sold out in 1919 for $25 million. Candler, realizing that the profits on flavored water could support advertising on an unprecedented scale, set out to make the Coke logo ubiquitous and damn near succeeded. His system of franchised bottlers generated some other great family fortunes. A devout Methodist, Candler was noted for his philanthropy: he gave millions to Emory University, prevented an Atlanta real estate panic by buying $1 million worth of homes, once

Asa Griggs Candler. Courtesy Emory University/*Dictionary of American Portraits* (Dover, 1967)

intervened in the cotton market to avert a crisis, and as Atlanta's mayor motorized the fire department and improved the water system largely at his own expense.

243. Duncan Hines (1880–1959), a Kentuckian, was a slow starter (he worked in the printing business until he was fifty-eight), but when he hit his stride, he built an empire. His 1935

Restaurant sign in Albany, Georgia, 1962. *U.S. News & World Report*/Library of Congress U9-8339-9

Christmas card was a list of 160 "superior eating places" he had found in his business travels. Word-of-mouth popularity encouraged him to publish it as *Adventures in Good Eating* in 1936. *Lodging for a Night* followed, and by 1948 he was selling 250,000 books a year and his name had come to stand for quality and integrity. Building on that, he formed a food company licensing the Duncan Hines label and an institute to publish his books. In 1957 Procter & Gamble bought it all. When he died, "Recommended by Duncan Hines" signs (leased from his company) adorned ten thousand businesses.

This advertisement read: "A buck well spent on a Springmaid Sheet."
Reproduced by permission of Springs Industries

244. David Marshall Williams (1900–75) of Cumberland County, North Carolina, was in solitary confinement for fighting with his warden, while in prison for shooting a sheriff's deputy poking around one of his whiskey stills, when naturally his thoughts turned to the question of how to make a rifle with a short-stroke gas piston. Later, at the start of World War II, the U.S. government asked the same question, and he was ready with the idea for what became the M1 carbine. No less an authority than Douglas MacArthur credited U.S. victory in the Pacific to Carbine Williams's invention.

245. Elliott White Springs (1896–1959) took over his family's Fort Mill, South Carolina, textile mills in 1931. The South's other cotton mill magnates tended to be solemn and private men, but "the Colonel" was a decorated World War I flier, a playboy, and generally a colorful character. He promoted his products in the 1940s and 1950s with ads that referred to bras as "lunglifters" and girdles as "ham hampers" (to "protect your assets"). The ads were too risqué for the *Saturday Evening Post,* but Springs Mills (now Springs Industries) became the nation's largest producer of bed linen and its third largest textile company. Springs also pioneered profit sharing, health insurance, recreation facilities, and subsidized hot meals for its employees, and it has contributed generously to the Carolina towns where it operates.

246. Colonel Harland Sanders (1890–1980), one of the best-known Kentuckians of our time, was actually an Indianan who left home at age twelve and worked at a variety of jobs before he opened a Corbin, Kentucky, filling station in 1929. Out of the back he served down-home food so good that he got named an honorary colonel by the governor and was endorsed by Duncan Hines. In 1952 he franchised his secret herbs and spices and his pressure-frying method for chicken; soon his white suit, string tie, and goatee graced hundreds of Kentucky Fried Chicken outlets. An indefatigable promoter, he traveled over 200,000 miles in one year. In 1964 he sold the company, but stayed on as a spokesman (not always reliable: he said the company's new Extra Crispy batter tasted like wallpaper paste). When he died, his body lay in state in the Kentucky state capitol. His old company, now part of the PepsiCo empire, has become the healthier-sounding KFC. Almost half of its thousands of outlets are abroad, and its U.S. customers consume a million chickens a day. (See **665.**)

247. **Sam Walton** (1918–92) had a boss who wouldn't listen to his ideas about running a store, so in 1962 Sam started his own. Wal-Mart, headquartered in Bentonville, Arkansas, became the nation's largest retailer. The formula was simple: attention to detail, locations in small towns within a day's drive of a distribution center, high-tech inventory control, bulk buying, a friendly greeting at the door, a no-questions return policy, and "Everyday Low Prices." Walton also built a unique corporate climate with annual employee ("associate") meetings like high school pep rallies, a stock-ownership plan, and bonuses based on sales growth. Despite policies like not stocking girlie magazines and discouraging employee adultery, the company has expanded successfully from its small-town Southern base. Local newspapers don't like Wal-Mart (it spends about one-third of the industry average on advertising), and local businesses often suffer from the competition, but one stock analyst wrote: "Wal-Mart deserves accolades for bringing low-cost merchandise to people struggling to make ends meet in small communities in the Farm Belt and Oil Patch." Sam Walton received the Presidential Medal of Freedom in 1992, the year of his death.

Mary Kay Ash, cosmetics queen. Mary Kay Cosmetics, Inc.

248. **Mary Kay Ash** (b. 1918?) says her priorities are God first, family second, career third. She began her Dallas-based direct-sales cosmetics company in 1963 to "give unlimited opportunity to women," and based it on the Golden Rule. That, and an incentive program that has put over 7,500 of the company's 375,000-plus salespeople in pink Cadillacs (or the equivalent), have made more women millionaires than any other company, given Mary Kay Cosmetics over $1.5 billion in annual sales, and put it among *Fortune*'s "Most Admired Corporations in America."

249. **Robert Edward "Ted" Turner, III** (b. 1938), grew up in Savannah, attended (unhappily) two Southern military academies, and was sent by his father to Brown, where he majored briefly in classics, preferred sailing, debating, and carousing, and was expelled for having a fe-

Ted Turner. Turner Broadcasting System, Inc.

male guest in his room. After his father's death, young Ted took over the family billboard business and built it into the Turner Communications empire, largely by seeing the possibilities of communications satellites. To feed his cable "superstation," Turner acquired the Atlanta Braves (**853, 879**) baseball team, the Atlanta Hawks basketball team, and the film library of MGM studios—just for starters. He founded the Cable News Network in 1980 and Turner Network Television in 1988. He remained an avid yachtsman, winning the 1977 America's Cup. *Business Monthly* said he "looks like Clark Gable and sounds like Huey Long," and he has described himself as "a Southern folk hero"; he owns three plantations and has sons named Beauregard and Rhett. But is it just our imagination, or has he really become less Southern since his marriage (his third) to Jane Fonda?

250. **Chris Whittle** was born in Etowah, Tennessee, in 1947. While still at the University of Tennessee he started a publishing company aimed at other collegians. Later, he was inspired to offer Nissan *all* of a new campus magazine's ad space, a simple idea that led to a variety of free-to-readers publications directed at captive audiences in, for example, doctors' waiting rooms. One of the most interesting was *Southern Style,* a remarkably well edited women's magazine sponsored by Procter & Gamble and distributed to beauty parlors. In 1989 Whittle's controversial Channel One began to put free news programs—and commercials—in schools; he then hired prominent authors to write books, salted with ads and distributed free to "opinion leaders." A classic big-idea man (weak on detail), Whittle finally overreached himself in the 1990s with his Edison Project, a planned chain of proprietary semipublic schools, but it was great fun while it lasted.

Consumer Behavior

AFFLUENCE AND URBANIZATION HAVEN'T effaced all regional differences. Indeed, they've given Southerners the resources to create some new ones.

Geographer Wilbur Zelinsky looked at several hundred special-interest publications and organizations. Among the differences:

251. **Women's magazines.** Southern women were relatively unlikely to read *Cosmo.* They preferred *Ingenue, Glamour,* and magazines with titles like (pick one) *True/Secret/Mod-*

ern/Real/Intimate (pick another) *Story/Romances/Screen/Confessions.*

252. Participatory sports. Southerners were likely to read gun and hunting magazines like *Field and Stream, Sports Afield, Outdoor Life, Shooting Times, Gun World,* and *American Cooner.* More were members of the National Wildlife Federation and the National Rifle Association. On the other hand, fewer read *Ski, Skiing, Dune Buggies, Cycle World, Water Skiier, Skin Diver, Yachting,* and *Salt Water Sports,* and fewer were members of the Izaak Walton League, the Amateur Trapshooting Association, the National Field Archery Association, the American Badminton Association, the National Horseshoe Pitchers Association, the Soaring Society of America, and the American Bowling Congress.

253. Gardening patterns are different in the South, with more members of the American Camellia Society and the American Rose Society and fewer of the iris, orchid, and rhododendron societies. States'-rights doctrine may explain why there are more members of the National Council of State Garden Clubs and fewer of the Garden Club of America.

IN GENERAL, ZELINSKY FOUND Southerners to be underrepresented in various activities—or at least less well read and well organized.

254. Animal lovers may be rarer in the South. Anyway, there are fewer readers of *Bloodhorse, Chronicle of the Horse, Thoroughbred Record, Western Horseman, Popular Dogs,* and *Pure-Bred Dogs* and fewer members of everything from the International Arabian Horse Federa-

tion to the International Federation of Homing Pigeon Fanciers.

255. Southern hobbyists are either rarer or less compulsive about it. Fewer belong to the American Philatelic Society, the American Numismatic Society, the National Model Railroad Association, Antique Motor Car Clubs, and the International Brotherhood of Magicians. Fewer read *Trains, Model Railroader, Railroad Model Craftsman, Flying Models, Sky & Telescope, Camera,* and *Gourmet.*

256. The arts—well, ditto. The South has fewer readers of *American Artist, Art in America,* and *Art News,* fewer members of the Amateur Chamber Music Players Association, the Metropolitan Opera Guild, and the Society for the Preservation & Encouragement of Barbershop Quartet Singing in America.

257. Self-help and do-good may proceed along more traditional lines in the South. Anyway, there are fewer readers of *Psychology Today;* also fewer members of Common Cause, the League of Women Voters, the War Resisters League, and the Humane Society.

OUTFITS LIKE SIMMONS AND Mediamark track consumer patterns, and Michael J. Weiss pulled a bunch of their data together in a book called *Latitudes and Attitudes* (1994). A summary:

258. Southerners buy fewer fresh croissants, Weight Watchers frozen desserts, bagels, apples, oranges, recliners, woks, stationary power tools, personal computers, home fax machines, boom boxes, plush dolls and animals, Nintendos, condoms, home pregnancy tests, sailboats, powerboats, BMWs, Cadillacs, Ford Escorts, sport/utility vehicles, and used cars. They buy less Ben & Jerry's ice cream, home gym equipment, Tupperware, Obsession for Men, dental floss, lemon-lime soda, ground coffee, herbal tea, white wine, red wine, Bud, Coors, and Miller. Southerners are less likely to be liberals, gay rights supporters (except in Atlanta, Houston, and Dallas), or willing to pay 10 percent more for "green" products. Southerners do less mall shopping, going to state fairs, joining fraternal orders, moviegoing, video renting, lottery playing, jogging, golfing, overnight camping, bowling, and racquetball playing. On television, they're less likely to watch baseball, pro football, pro basketball, *The Simpsons,* C-Span, *Saturday Night Live, America's Funniest Home Videos, Roseanne,* and MTV. They're less likely to listen to classical music, classic rock, folk music, modern rock, and heavy metal. They're less likely to read the *New Yorker, Gourmet, Family Circle, Vanity Fair, USA Today,* and (except in Atlanta, Dallas, Houston, and Miami)

Playboy. They own less stock (valued at over $10,000) and fewer cats.

WELL, WHAT *DO* THEY DO?

259. **Southerners buy more** white bread, bacon, Twinkies, fast food, mobile homes (**152**), Old Spice, cigarettes, mouthwash, hunting rifles, Mustangs, Camaros, Firebirds, domestic light trucks, and Busch Bavarian. Southerners are more likely to be conservatives, direct-mail respondents, concerned about endangered species, in favor of school prayer, and opposed to abortion (except in metropolitan areas). Racial differences in musical taste mean that Southerners are more likely to listen to country music (except in the Deep South), gospel music (especially in the Deep South), and hip-hop (only in the Deep South). They're more likely to watch *A Current Affair, Oprah, Donahue,* and daytime soap operas, more likely to read the *National Enquirer,* and they own more dogs.

Four

The Southern Nation

THE CONFEDERACY AND ITS LEGACY

For every Southern boy fourteen years old, not once but whenever he wants it, there is the instant when it's still not yet two o'clock on that July afternoon in 1863 . . . and it's all in the balance, it hasn't happened yet, it hasn't even begun yet, it not only hasn't begun yet but there is still time for it not to begin.

—WILLIAM FAULKNER

Fiddle-dee-dee. War, war, war. This war talk's spoiling all the fun at every party this spring. I get so bored I could scream.

—SCARLETT O'HARA

LOOK, SHELBY FOOTE took twenty years and three thousand pages to write his American *Iliad*. Lesser mortals have devoted their entire lives to it. People fight about why the War happened and can't even agree on what to call it (**158**). A few short paragraphs can't do it justice, but you can't talk about the South without saying something about its experiment with nationhood.

The Peculiar Institution, Pro and Con

WE'RE NOT TAKING SIDES in the quarrel over whether the fight was "about" slavery, but it wouldn't have happened without it.

PROSLAVERY THOUGHT

AFTER THE 1830s THE official line was increasingly that slavery was not just a necessary evil but a positive good, both for society as a whole and for the slaves themselves, ordained by God (**827**).

260. **John C. Calhoun** (1782–1850) was a practicing politician and the Old South's leading political theorist. (Fiercely intellectual, he tried once to write a poem, produced the single word "Whereas," and never tried again.) He argued that slavery was "the most safe and stable basis for free institutions in the world" and tried to find ways to protect it, short of secession. His idea of requiring a "concurrent majority" to protect minority rights (like those of Southern slaveholders) is still discussed, though seldom under that label.

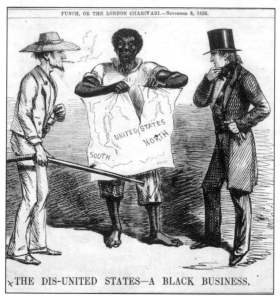

The Sectional Conflict, an English view. *Punch* (1856)

John C. Calhoun. Library of Congress USZ62-3786

261. **Thomas Roderick Dew** (1802–46) became president of his alma mater, William and Mary (**833**), in 1836. A prominent anti-tariff spokesman and author of a treatise on slavery entitled *A Review of the Debates in the Virginia Legislature of 1831 and 1832*, he defended the institution partly because it allowed the white woman to stop being a "mere 'beast of burthen'" and to become "the cheerful and animating center of the family circle."

262. **George Fitzhugh** (1806–81), author of *Sociology for the South* (1854) and *Cannibals All!* (1859), compared slavery favorably to Northern industry. Describing free laborers as "slaves without masters," he was one of the few to follow the proslavery argument to its logical conclusion that white workers would be better off enslaved. A genial adversary, he debated abolitionists and was a reluctant secessionist despite his strong pro-Southern views.

WHITE WOMEN WERE PROMINENT among the defenders of slavery. Some examples:

263. **Caroline Gilman** (1794–1888) also argued that slaves were better off than Northern workers. In 1838 she wrote: "Long before the manufacturer's task in other regions is closed, our labourers were lolling on sunny banks, or trimming their gardens, or fondling their little ones, or busy in their houses, scarcely more liable to intrusion than the royal retirement of a Guelph or a Capet." Caroline Lee Hentz (**464**) (like Gilman, a migrant from Massachusetts) offered similar testimonials in her novels.

264. **Susan Petigru King** (1824–75) defended slavery in *Lily: a Novel* (1855): "There are many cases of bad masters, just as there are many instances of bad fathers; but we should scarcely argue for the necessity of doing away with parental control. . . . Not one human being was placed in this world to enjoy happiness, but I know that [slaves] have as much contentment in a general way and in their way as we have."

265. **Louisa S. McCord** (1810–79), poet, dramatist, and essayist on social questions like the duties of women, wrote anonymously or under her initials in influential Southern journals. Her defense of slavery was aggressive: "We do *not* say it is a necessary evil. . . . We proclaim it, on the contrary, a Godlike dispensation, a providential caring for the weak, and a refuge for the portionless." She argued that "Christian slavery" was "the brightest sunbeam which Omniscience has destined for [the Negro's] existence." During the war she was unceasing in her charitable activities and put her money where her mouth was by clothing and arming her son's entire company.

WHITE SOUTHERN ANTISLAVERY THOUGHT

SOME WHITE SOUTHERNERS ACTIVELY opposed slavery, sometimes as a moral evil, but more often because they thought it was bad for whites. They often found it expedient to leave the South.

266. **Levi Coffin** (1798–1877) was a North Carolina Quaker (**819, 903**) who while still a child supposedly helped slaves to escape. He became a merchant in Indiana and the self-styled president of the Underground Railroad. The legend of the railroad contains much exaggeration, but there's no question that Coffin's house was an authentic station.

Forward (1967). Jacob Lawrence depicts a tale of the Underground Railroad. North Carolina Museum of Art, Raleigh

267. **Sarah and Angelina Grimké** (1792–1873 and 1805–79), aristocratic Charlestonians, became radical Yankee abolitionists. As a girl, Sarah wanted to be a lawyer, and she might have been less trouble if they'd let her. Visiting Philadelphia, she met some Quaker kindred spirits, so she and Angelina moved north and became Quakers, too. But they soon left the Quakers in the dust. The Charleston police threatened to jail Angelina for her abolitionist *Appeal to the Christian Women of the South* (1836) if she ever came home. The sisters were also feminists: Sarah argued that "women ought to feel a peculiar sympathy in the colored man's wrong, for, like him, she has been accused of mental inferiority, and denied the privileges of a liberal education." (See **117**.)

The Grimké sisters. *Dictionary of American Portraits* (Dover, 1967)

"The great compromiser," Henry Clay of Kentucky. Engraved by W. J. Edwards from a daguerreotype by Matthew Brady/*Dictionary of American Portraits* (Dover, 1967)

268. Henry Clay (1777–1852) is remembered as "the Great Pacificator," author of the Missouri Compromise and other attempts to resolve sectional differences, an economic nationalist, and a perennial also-ran for president. This Kentucky slaveholder also favored emancipation, though only if freedmen were returned to Africa. He and other prominent Southerners who felt the same helped found the American Colonization Society in 1817.

269. Cassius Marcellus Clay (1810–1903) sought a career in Kentucky politics, but his emancipationist views were, to say the least, unpopular (**835**). It wasn't a matter of conscience, he said, but a question of what was good for Kentucky's economy. He served the Union as minister to Russia from 1861 to 1869.

Cassius Marcellus Clay. Engraved by John C. Buttre from a photograph by Matthew Brady/ *Dictionary of American Portraits* (Dover, 1967)

270. Hinton Rowan Helper (1829–1909), a North Carolina yeoman, wrote *The Impending Crisis of the South,* using statistics to show that slavery would ruin the South, damning "the lords of the lash," and calling on nonslaveholders to seize power. Although banned in the South, his book was widely read elsewhere; after it was published he removed himself to New York, and in 1862 he was appointed U.S. consul in Buenos Aires. Although opposed to slavery, Helper was no friend to blacks: three of his later books were virulently racist.

SOME SOUTHERN WOMEN CONFIDED their doubts about slavery to their diaries.

271. Ella Gertrude Clanton Thomas (1848–89) wrote in her diary (**446**), "Southern women are I believe all at heart abolisionists [sic] but there I expect I have made a very broad assertion but I *will stand* to the opinion that the institution of slavery degrades the white man

more than the Negro and oh exerts a most dele-terious effect upon our children."

272. **Mary Boykin Chesnut (447)** wrote in *her* diary that slavery was "a curse to any land," a "hated institution," "a *monstrous* system & wrong & iniquity," etc. "Men and women are punished when their masters & mistresses are brutes and not when they do wrong." Her spe-cial complaint was that "like the patriarchs of old our men live all in one house with their wives & their concubines, & the Mulattoes one sees in every family exactly resemble the white children."

The Price of Blood, A Planter Selling His Son (1868), by Thomas Satterwhite Noble. Morris Museum of Art, Augusta, Ga.

Early Secessionists

WHEN THE INTERESTS OF the South's planta-tion economy and slave society seemed to be threatened by the North, some Southerners con-cluded that secession was the answer (**400**). Some of the more important, or at least colorful:

273. **William Lowndes Yancey** (1814–63) was Southern-born, but his stepfather, a New En-gland preacher-schoolmaster, sent him to North-ern academies and Williams College. He became a newspaper editor, an Alabama planter (after marrying wealth), and a politician. Eager to see slavery extended into the territories, he became an avid secessionist. He led the Southern walk-out from the Democratic convention in 1860 (**410**), then led Alabama's secession conven-tion. As a states'-rights Confederate senator he was an outspoken opponent of Jefferson Davis's centralizing tendencies.

William Lowndes Yancey. Library of Congress USZ62-36284

274. **Robert Barnwell Rhett** (1800–76) changed his name from Smith and pursued a ca-reer in South Carolina politics. With a manner as aristocratic as his new name, he became a prosecession congressman and briefly a senator. Like William Yancey, he ended up a bitter en-emy of Jefferson Davis, whom he blamed for the failure of the Southern revolution.

275. **Albert Gallatin Brown** (1813–80), the son of a poor farmer, eventually became a U.S. sena-

tor and Mississippi's leading fire-eater (**400**), then a Confederate senator. More of a Southern nationalist and less of a states' righter than many secessionists, Brown defended fellow Mississippian Jefferson Davis in the Confederate Senate. At the end, he sponsored a bill to induct slaves into the Confederate Army. (It passed, but not in time to be implemented.) After the war he supported sectional reconciliation.

276. **Louis Trezevant Wigfall** (1816–74) was active in South Carolina's dangerous politics, killing one man and wounding another in duels (**914**), before he went bankrupt and moved to Texas. Texans sent him back east to the U.S. Senate, where he worked to reopen the slave trade and to derail any compromises that might prevent secession. He became a Confederate hero by rowing to the besieged Fort Sumter and, without authorization, personally demanding its surrender. He served the Confederacy first as an undistinguished general, then as an obstreperous senator, toward the end declaring that he would prefer to see the Confederacy defeated rather than arm slaves for its service.

277. **Edmund Ruffin** (1794–1865), from a distinguished Virginia family, became a pioneering agricultural scientist with his work on fertilizer. But after 1856 he served the cause of Southern independence full-time as a writer and agitator. He fired the first shot at Fort Sumter (**306**) and one of the last shots of the war—into his own head, rather than submit to what his suicide note called "the perfidious, malignant and vile Yankee race."

Louis T. Wigfall. Library of Congress USZ62-11238

Edmund Ruffin. National Archives

Southern Unionists

MANY SOUTHERNERS WHO HAD no problems with slavery opposed secession, but after it happened most white Southerners supported the Confederacy whether they owned slaves or not (most didn't). Among those who didn't go along:

278. **James L. Petigru** (1789–1863) was attorney general of South Carolina in the 1820s and was considered the state's most distinguished lawyer. A leading Whig and consistent Unionist, he went against public opinion to join Andrew Jackson (**433**) in opposing nullification. Later, he favored the Compromise of 1850 and opposed secession, observing in 1860 that "South Carolina is too small for a republic and too large for a lunatic asylum."

279. **Sam Houston** (1793–1863) is best known for commanding the Texas republic's army against Mexico and becoming its first president. Virginia-born, he had lived with the Cherokees in his youth and been governor of Tennessee, a position he resigned to escape an unhappy marriage and to live with the Cherokees again. As governor of Texas in 1861 he was deposed for refusing to swear allegiance to the Confederacy. Earlier, as senator, he had been censured by the Texas legislature for his devotion to sectional compromise.

280. **John Marshall Harlan** (1833–1911) was a Kentucky Whig slaveholder who opposed secession. After it came, he served as a colonel in the Union Army and became an active Republican after the war. Appointed to the Supreme Court in 1877, he often differed with his conservative brethren, never more memorably than with his dissent in *Plessy v. Ferguson* (**365**), in which he declared that "our Constitution is color-blind."

281. **William Gannaway "Parson" Brownlow** (1805–77) grew up in east Tennessee and became a jackleg Methodist preacher and a newspaper editor. His wickedly anti-Confederate editorials in the *Knoxville Whig* got him deported to Union territory, where he continued to write anti-Rebel propaganda. Returning to Tennessee with the Union Army, he became that state's governor in 1865. But, like Hinton Helper, he disliked blacks as much as he disliked secessionists.

282. **Andrew Johnson** (1808–75) was another east Tennessee Unionist, a self-made tailor who entered politics as a champion of the common (white) man against "stuck up aristocrats." As U.S. senator he supported public education and a homestead act. He also supported slavery (and was a small slaveholder himself), but he stoutly opposed secession and refused to resign his Senate seat when Tennessee left the Union. Lincoln sent him back home as military governor of occupied Tennessee, then picked him as vice president in 1864, which put him in the White House when Lincoln was assassinated (**437**).

Confederate Politicians

THE CONFEDERACY'S POLITICAL LEADERS aren't as well known as its soldiers, probably for good reason. General Lee once complained that they did nothing but "eat peanuts and chew tobacco." Here are four you ought to know about anyway.

President Jefferson Davis and Varina Howell Davis. Library of Congress USZ62-5962

Vice President Alexander Stephens. Library of Congress USZ62-13709

283. Jefferson Davis (1808–89), the first and only president of the Confederacy, was born in Kentucky (like Lincoln) but grew up in Mississippi. After West Point, he alternated life as a planter with army service, notably in the Mexican War, and a career as congressman, senator, and secretary of war. After his first wife (Zachary Taylor's daughter) died, he married the scintillating Varina Howell. President Davis's devotion and sacrifice are unquestioned; historians disagree about his effectiveness, but it hardly matters now. Imprisoned for two years after the war, he was never tried. Davis's last years were spent at his home, Beauvoir (**726**), writing vindications of the Lost Cause. Ilis U.S. citizenship was restored posthumously, a century later.

284. Alexander Hamilton Stephens (1812–83) was a Georgia congressman who voted against Georgia's secession but accepted the majority's decision, then helped establish the Confederacy and became its vice president. A Constitutional Unionist before the war, he was a thoroughgoing states' righter during it and often quarreled with Jefferson Davis. After the war he wrote *A Constitutional View of the Late War Between the States* and served in the U.S. Congress and as governor of Georgia.

285. Judah P. Benjamin (1811–84) was America's first Jewish cabinet officer—in the Confederate cabinet. He was also the first Jew to be elected to the U.S. Senate (from Louisiana, in 1852). Famous for his proslavery speeches, he became Confederate attorney general, then secretary of war, then secretary of state, a post he held until the end of the war. Davis's most trusted adviser, Benjamin infuriated some Confederates by offering to trade emancipation for British or French recognition and, late in the war, by advocating that slaves be armed to fight for the Confederacy. After Appomattox he fled to England, where he continued his distinguished legal career and was soon appointed queen's counsel.

Judah Benjamin as an English lawyer, 1886. *Library of Southern Literature* (1907)

Clement C. Clay. DixiePix

286. Clement C. Clay (1816–82), son of the governor of Alabama and a strong states' righter, resigned from the U.S. Senate when Alabama seceded, and went on to serve in the Confederate Senate. In 1864 he went as a spy to Canada, where he helped to organize a Confederate raid on St. Albans, Vermont. Falsely accused of involvement in Lincoln's assassination, he turned himself in and returned to private life after his release in 1866. He was a good friend of Jefferson Davis's, which may be why he's portrayed on the Confederate one-dollar bill.

Military Men (and One Woman)

CONFEDERATE OFFICERS

THE CONFEDERACY'S SOLDIERS HAD some of the greatest-sounding names (considered just as words) of the nineteenth century, names like Jubal Early and Josiah Gorgas and Bushrod Johnson and Ambrose P. Hill. Sterling Price and Fitzhugh Lee. Earl Van Dorn, Edmund Kirby-Smith, Felix Zollicoffer, and Simon Bolivar Buckner. John Bankhead "Prince John" Magruder and John Sappington Marmaduke. Even the tiny Confederate Navy gave us Raphael Semmes and Matthew Fontaine Maury. We can't begin to list the military figures you'd need to know to be a true buff, but they'd certainly include these:

287. Robert E. Lee (1807–70) came from a distinguished Virginia family. Like many Confederate generals, he graduated from West Point and fought in the Mexican War. A career soldier who freed his slaves and belonged to a society supporting colonization of freedmen in Liberia, he opposed secession and was offered the command of the Union Army at the outbreak of war, but refused to draw his sword against his native state. His genius as commander of the Army of Northern Virginia is unquestioned. And he really was a remarkable human being. As Union general Montgomery Meigs put it: "He was one with whom nobody ever wished or ventured to take a liberty, though kind and generous to all subordinates, admired by all women, respected by all men. He was the model of a soldier and the very beau ideal of a Christian man." After Appomattox he accepted the presidency of

Patriotic flour: Robert E. Lee as a brand name, 1939.
Dorothea Lange, Farm Security Administration/Library of
Congress USF34-20227-E

Stonewall Jackson. *Library of Southern Literature* (1907)

Washington College (**840**) and worked for sectional reconciliation. He would not have approved, but he also became a central figure in the cult of the Lost Cause (**332–43**).

288. **Thomas "Stonewall" Jackson** (1824–63) is second only to Lee in the Confederate pantheon. Jackson taught at the Virginia Military Institute (**834**) and supposedly earned his nickname at First Manassas, when General Barnard Bee exclaimed, "See, there stands Jackson like a stone wall!" His character was described as "absolutely without blemish," if somewhat strange. A devout Presbyterian said to believe "in the vigorous use of the bayonet and the blessings of Providence," Jackson was known to his troops as Old Blue Light for the gleam in his eye during battle. He died at Chancellorsville, his last words being "Let us cross over the river and rest in the shade of the trees." Lee later said that Jackson would have given him a decisive victory at Gettysburg. Roanoke's oldest

black Presbyterian church honors him with a stained-glass window, for founding a Sunday school for slaves.

289. **James Longstreet** (1821–1904), lieutenant general, C.S.A., served primarily with the Army of Northern Virginia, at one point commanding half the forces. "Old Pete" fought with distinction in the early campaigns but was criticized for disappointing performances later. After Appomattox he joined the Republican Party and served as federal postmaster and marshal. Angry Southerners discounted his military accomplishments, suggesting that he deliberately lost at Gettysburg, but recent historians have redeemed his reputation as a judicious and dependable soldier.

290. **Pierre Gustave Toutant Beauregard** (1818–93) was a Creole (**100**) who resigned from the U.S. Army in 1861 to become a Confederate general. After commanding at Fort Sumter, he was the hero of First Manassas, but

P. G. T. Beauregard. Library of Congress

he was widely blamed for the lack of a victory at Shiloh, and was banished to coastal defense in South Carolina and Georgia. In 1864 he was recalled to Virginia, where he was largely responsible for the successful defense of Petersburg. Later he became a railroad company president in his native Louisiana.

291. **J. E. B. Stuart** (1833–64), a Virginian whose eyes "sparkle[d] with the merry glance which ladies love," was a lover of music and dancing, a devoted husband and father, and a conscientious Methodist. Described by one of his peers as "unconscious of the feeling of fear," he was a dashing cavalry commander with a trademark plumed hat, famous for his ride around McClellan's entire army in 1863. Lee said Stuart "never brought me a piece of false information," although at Gettysburg he didn't bring any information at all, for which some (not Lee) criticized him. Fatally wounded at

Yellow Tavern, he broke an early promise to his mother and drank whiskey for the first time when a doctor prescribed it to ease his pain. When Lee heard of Stuart's death, he said, "I can scarcely think of him without weeping."

292. **Braxton Bragg** (1817–76) fought ably in Mexico before becoming a Louisiana sugar planter, but as commander of the Army of Tennessee he left much to be desired. Despite hypochondria and genuine ill health, excessive caution and frequent failure of nerve, an authoritarian style, incessant quarrels with subordinates, and an anachronistic devotion to the bayonet charge, he was not relieved of command until after U. S. Grant made his shortcomings painfully obvious in the campaign for Atlanta.

293. **Nathan Bedford Forrest** (1821–77)—"the Wizard of the Saddle" to some, to others the villain of the massacre of surrendering black troops at Fort Pillow—was arguably the ablest Confederate general in the West. Raised poor in

Nathan Bedford Forrest rides in Memphis. DixiePix

Tennessee, he speculated in cattle and slaves before buying plantations in Alabama and Mississippi. Army advancement came slow because he wasn't a West Pointer, but he rose from private to lieutenant general. An intuitive military genius known for his audacity, he had twenty-nine horses shot from under him and killed thirty men in hand-to-hand combat. Apparently he didn't say, "Get there fustest with the mostest," but did say (when told the enemy was before and behind him), "Attack in both directions." After surrender he became the Ku Klux Klan's (**358**) first grand wizard. Many black Memphians are annoyed that Forrest Park in Memphis honors him.

294. **Leonidas Polk** (1806–64) combined the callings of sugar planter, Episcopal bishop of Louisiana, and major general in the Army of Tennessee. As a churchman he was instrumental in founding the University of the South

The Right Reverend Leonidas Polk. Library of Congress

(**836**). As a soldier he commanded troops at Shiloh, Perryville, and Chickamauga and was killed in action. For much of the war he had the misfortune to serve under Bragg, who had the habit of blaming his subordinates for his reverses.

295. **Patrick Cleburne** (1828–64), sometimes called the Stonewall Jackson of the West, was Anglo-Irish, a former British soldier, and an Arkansas druggist when the war began. He served at Shiloh, Chickamauga, and other big ones, rose from captain to major general, and was twice commended by the Confederate Congress, but he was another of Bragg's unfortunate subordinates. He urged in 1864 that slaves be freed and armed (a proposal suppressed by Davis) and was killed at the Battle of Franklin. Gay activists have lately claimed him as one of theirs, but the evidence is pretty flimsy.

296. **John Clifford Pemberton** (1814–81) was a Philadelphia Quaker who went to West Point and was cited for bravery during the Mexican War. Strong states'-rights views and a Virginia wife led him to support secession in 1861. As a Confederate general ordered to hold Vicksburg (**313**) at all costs, he mounted a valiant defense, but after a prolonged siege he surrendered on the Fourth of July 1863. "I am a Northern man," he said. "I know my people. . . . I know we can get better terms from them on the 4th of July than any other day of the year." Regarded as untrustworthy thereafter, after Appomattox he retired to a farm outside Philadelphia.

297. **Stand Watie** (1806–71), brigadier general, C.S.A., was a leader of the pro-Confederate faction of the Cherokee Nation. His brigade conducted numerous guerrilla actions in the Indian Territory and fought at the Battle of Elkhorn

Tavern, in Arkansas. He had the distinction of being the last Confederate general to surrender.

Stand Watie, Confederate Cherokee.

298. John Singleton Mosby (1833–1916) was involved in a shooting affray as a university student, but his jail sentence was annulled by the Virginia legislature. He practiced law before joining the Virginia Cavalry. In 1863 he organized the Partisan Rangers, a guerrilla band that disrupted Union operations in northern Virginia and Maryland so successfully that the area became known as Mosby's Confederacy. "The Gray Ghost" became famous for his daring, and he was made colonel in 1864. After the war he became a strong Republican and served as U.S. consul in Hong Kong and attorney in the Justice Department. Regarded as a scalawag (**403**), he died in Washington.

"The Gray Ghost." Library of Congress B8184-10613

299. Sally Louisa Tompkins (1833–1916) came from a fine Virginia family. At the outbreak of war she opened a hospital in Richmond so efficient that she was commissioned as a captain to retain her services when it was brought under military supervision. The only female officer in the Confederate Army, she never accepted a salary.

300. William Clarke Quantrill (1837–65) was a young Ohio schoolteacher before he moved to Kansas in 1857. He originally sided with the free-state forces but joined the Confederates when war began. As Captain Quantrill he captured Independence, Missouri, in 1862. A year later, notoriously, Quantrill's band of three hundred irregulars sacked Lawrence, long a nest of free-state guerrillas (who had their own atrocities to answer for); some 150 male citizens of Lawrence were killed in cold blood. Quantrill himself was later killed by Union forces in Kentucky. Former Quantrill's Raiders like Cole Younger, Bloody Bill Anderson, and Frank and Jesse James went on to postwar careers as bandits.

FINALLY (HE WASN'T A Confederate soldier, but he thought he was helping the Cause and there's nowhere else to put him):

301. John Wilkes Booth (1838–65) was born the son of a famous actor in Maryland and became a popular stage figure himself. An ardent Southerner, he served in a Virginia militia unit that helped put down John Brown's (**353**) uprising, but he continued his acting career in the North during the war. He joined a conspiracy to assassinate Lincoln, and the plan was realized on April 14, 1865, at Ford's Theater in Washington, when Booth shot Lincoln in the head, crying "Sic semper tyrannis." Fleeing to Virginia,

Satan tempts John Wilkes Booth. Library of Congress USZ62-8933

he was killed when the tobacco barn in which he was hiding was set on fire by Union troops to force him out. Three coconspirators and the mother of another were hanged; four others were imprisoned.

SOUTHERNERS WHO WORE THE BLUE

MOST SOUTHERN SOLDIERS WENT with their states, but some did not. Four of the most interesting:

302. **Winfield Scott** (1786–1866) was a Virginian and a professional soldier whose brilliance in the Mexican War won him the Whig nomination for president in 1852. In 1861 he remained with the Union and urged an "Anaconda" policy: blockade the Confederacy on the east and south, control the Mississippi to cut it off on the west, then wait for the new nation to collapse. After George McClellan's contrary views prevailed, ill health and McClellan's hostility led Scott to retire in November 1861, but his plan remains one of history's great what-ifs.

303. **George Henry Thomas** (1816–70), like Scott, stayed with the U.S. Army. Despite unjust suspicion about his loyalty, he became one of the Union's most effective commanders, lauded by Sherman as "splendid, victorious, invincible in battle." Known as the Rock of Chickamauga for his defensive triumph there, Thomas's greatest victory came at Nashville, where he destroyed the Army of Tennessee. Repudiated by his home state of Virginia, he was made a citizen of Tennessee by that state's legislature.

304. **David Glasgow Farragut** (1801–70) was born in east Tennessee, joined the navy at age nine, and rose through the ranks. Commanding the Union blockade in the western Gulf of Mexico, he captured New Orleans in a daring assault in 1862. In 1864 he said, "Damn the torpedoes, full speed ahead," and sailed under heavy fire through a minefield to attack a Confederate squadron in Mobile Bay. In 1866 he became the first admiral in the U.S. Navy.

305. **Philip St. George Cooke** was a Virginia-born general who commanded Union cavalry for a while, then finished the war in charge of recruitment, but his family was more remarkable than his war record. His son was a Confederate general and refused to speak to him for years. Three daughters married generals, one Union and two Confederate (one of the latter was J. E. B. Stuart). Many families, including Mrs. Abraham Lincoln's, had similar stories.

Civil War Battles and Sites

TEN THOUSAND MILITARY ACTIONS took place during the War, according to Shelby Foote, including "76 full-scale battles, 310 engagements, 6337 skirmishes, and numerous sieges, raids, expeditions, and the like." Here are some events and places we know you've heard of, and why you've heard of them. Also a few you may not recognize.

Inside Fort Sumter. Currier & Ives

306. Fort Sumter, in Charleston Harbor, received the first shot of the Civil War. When the Union garrison refused to leave Southern soil, Edmund Ruffin (**277**) pulled the first lanyard to open the bombardment, at 4:30 A.M. on April 12, 1861. After thirty-three hours Union commander Robert Anderson surrendered. (Ironically, Major Anderson was a Kentuckian, while the commander of Confederate artillery was an Ohio native.) The attack mobilized Northern public opinion in support of Lincoln, who soon issued a call for volunteers.

307. The First Battle of Manassas (known in the North as Bull Run) took place in July 1861. Many spectators (mostly congressmen and reporters) came from nearby Washington to watch an easy Union victory, but Confederate forces repulsed an attack; then a minor counterattack caused panic among the retreating Union forces, who fled back to Washington, along with the spectators. The disorganized Confederates didn't realize the extent of the rout and missed the opportunity to seize Washington. The Second Battle of Manassas took place in the same area a year later, with pretty much the same result.

308. The *Monitor* and the *Merrimack*. After the USS *Merrimack* was armored and commissioned as the CSS *Virginia* it had a high old time sinking Union vessels in Hampton Roads, off Norfolk, until the USS *Monitor* arrived. Their four-hour battle on March 9, 1862, was the first ever between ironclads and resulted in a standoff.

The CSS *Virginia* and the USS *Monitor*.

309. Glorieta (New Mexico) put a stop to an ambitious Confederate attempt to reach California's gold fields and unblockaded coast. In March 1862 Colorado Volunteers defeated a Confederate force who had previously seized Santa Fe, and forced them back through the desert to Texas.

310. The Valley Campaign of 1862 is still studied by aspiring soldiers. With fewer than 17,000 men in Virginia's Shenandoah Valley, Stonewall

Second Manassas. Currier & Ives

Jackson immobilized the 100,000 troops of four federal armies. Making masterful use of strategic diversion and interior lines of communication, he shuttled his "foot cavalry" from one engagement to another—then left his adversaries wondering where the hell he was when he slipped off to help Lee outside Richmond.

311. **Chancellorsville** (Virginia) is described as "Lee's masterpiece," a brilliant victory over Union general Joseph Hooker in May 1863, which opened the way to Pennsylvania. But it was a Pyrrhic victory: Stonewall Jackson was killed by friendly fire.

312. **Gettysburg** was the "high-water mark of the Confederacy," the end of Lee's invasion of the North in the summer of 1863. When Confederate troops stumbled on Union forces under

George Meade near this small Pennsylvania town, they drove them back but didn't pursue them. (They were hampered by a lack of the information that cavalry could have provided: Stuart was off on a raid that took him to the rear of the Union Army.) The next morning Union reinforcements arrived and held off an attack. The third day "Pickett's Charge" was temporarily successful, but General Pickett's weakened division couldn't maintain its advance. After Union reinforcements forced a retreat, Meade reported to Lincoln that the enemy had withdrawn "into his own country."

313. **Vicksburg** fell on the Fourth of July 1863, the day Lee began his retreat from Gettysburg. After several attempts to capture "the Gibraltar of the Confederacy," Grant had besieged the town and its 20,000 defenders with 71,000 men and a fleet of gunships. After seven weeks, with the civilian population living in caves and facing

starvation, General Pemberton (**296**) surrendered. This gave the Union control of the Mississippi, effectively cutting the Confederacy in two. The Fourth of July was not observed in Vicksburg until after World War II.

314. **Sabine Pass,** "the Thermopylae of the Confederacy," was a great morale-booster after Gettysburg and Vicksburg. In September 1863 Union general Nathaniel Banks attempted to invade Texas by landing at the mouth of the Sabine River on the Texas-Louisiana border. Lieutenant Richard Dowling and 46 soldiers with six cannons held off four gunboats and twenty-two transport ships carrying 5,000 soldiers, sinking two gunboats, crippling another, and capturing 350 sailors.

315. **Lookout Mountain** (Chattanooga, Tennessee), "the battle above the clouds" in November 1863, ended in defeat and disgrace for Braxton Bragg. When asked if Bragg had thought he held an impregnable position, Grant replied, "Well, it *was* impregnable." The loss at Chattanooga, soon after those at Gettysburg and Vicksburg, dashed Confederate hopes on three major fronts.

316. **Andersonville Prison,** in southwestern Georgia, was opened in February 1864 to house Union prisoners from Virginia. From the beginning, food, sanitation, and medical care were miserably inadequate, and there was no housing at all—prisoners built their own huts. At one point the prison's twenty-six and a half acres held 33,000 prisoners. Thirteen thousand died, many from dysentery, scurvy, and gangrene. Yankee prisons weren't much better, and with less excuse, but after the war they hanged Andersonville's Swiss-born commandant, Captain Henry Wirz, anyway.

317. **Spotsylvania,** in May 1864, saw what may have been the hardest fighting of the war. Like many Grant vs. Lee encounters in Virginia in the last year of the war, it's hard to say who won. Grant's losses of eighteen thousand or so were twice the Confederates', but Lee could less well afford it. Grant didn't break through to Richmond, but he kept coming.

318. **The Crater** appeared suddenly on July 30, 1864, when Pennsylvania coal miners serving in the Union Army exploded eight thousand pounds of powder in a tunnel they had dug under Confederate lines at Petersburg, Virginia. The explosion killed 278 Confederates and blew a hole 170 by 70 feet, 30 feet deep, but Union general Ambrose Burnside failed to follow up effectively, and his attack was repulsed with heavy losses.

319. **Sherman's March to the Sea** in the fall of 1864 took 65,000 Union soldiers from Atlanta to Savannah. Union general William T. Sherman ordered his troops to live off the countryside, and "bummers" quickly escalated to vandalism and plunder. Facing only token opposition, the army devastated an area sixty miles wide and two hundred miles long. The immediate result was to menace the Carolinas and Lee's rear; more lasting legacies include the jaunty air "Marching through Georgia" and several generations of bitterness.

320. **The fall of Richmond.** President Davis and the Confederate government left beleaguered Richmond on April 2, 1865, and that night they drove old Dixie down. When Union troops entered the next day, they found severe damage from fire and looting. A week later, on April 9, Lee surrendered to Grant at nearby Appomattox (**30**). Other Confederate armies surrendered soon after.

Confederatalia

THE CONFEDERACY HAD SOME trouble getting its act together, flag-wise.

The Stainless Banner on Confederate sheet music. Library of Congress USZ62-33407

321. The Bonnie Blue Flag was the unofficial first flag of the Confederacy, designed by some Mississippi ladies early in 1861. Their version featured a magnolia tree on a white background, with a white star on a blue field in the upper left, but it was soon simplified to just the star and blue field. It inspired the song (**326**) but was soon replaced by—

322. The Stars and Bars (**770**). Often used erroneously to refer to the battle flag (**323**), this label properly denotes the flag flown over the Confederate capitol in Montgomery on the day of Lincoln's inauguration in March 1861. It origi-

The Stars and Bars. DixiePix

nally had seven stars, but soon acquired six more (**3**). It served as the new nation's flag for two years, but it was never officially adopted by the Confederate Congress. After its similarity to the Stars and Stripes led to confusion on the battlefield, it was replaced in combat by—

323. The battle flag. Adopted by the Army of Northern Virginia after First Manassas, this was originally square (the rectangular form had official standing only as a naval jack). Popular with Confederate veterans' organizations—ironically because it was a "soldiers' flag" that lacked

A multicultural T-shirt at the North Carolina state fair. DixiePix

other flags' political connotations—it remains an icon for many white Southerners, especially members of Confederate descendants' groups. Since the 1970s country-music and Southern-rock groups have used the flag to symbolize Southern pride of a less historical sort, and it's also a symbol for many athletic teams, notably those of the University of Mississippi (**844**). Unfortunately, to others it has come to stand for white supremacy, and the NAACP has vowed to oppose its state-sponsored display (e.g., in the Georgia and Mississippi state flags). Conflict over the flag now seems a perennial feature of Southern life.

324. The Stainless Banner was the Confederacy's first official flag, adopted only in 1863. It featured the popular battle flag in the upper left corner of a white field. Alas, this flag proved as unsuitable as the Stars and Bars for battlefield

The Stainless Banner on postwar sheet music. Library of Congress USZ62-91833

use: except in a high wind, it was easily mistaken for a flag of truce, or even surrender. So one of the last acts of the Confederate Congress in March 1865 was to add a red band to the Stainless Banner's right edge.

THE NEW NATION NEVER got around to picking an official anthem at all, but it had some great songs. Four of the best:

325. "Dixie." Dan Emmett's tombstone in Mount Vernon, Ohio, says his " 'Dixie Land' inspired the courage and devotion of the Southern people and now thrills the hearts of a united nation." Three miles away, a gravestone for black musicians Ben and Lew Snowden claims "They taught 'Dixie' to Dan Emmett." Whatever, by 1861 "Dixie" was a popular minstrel-show walkabout that, as a Confederate propagandist put it, "expressed the negro's preference for this more genial and sunny clime, the land which is the negro's true home, and the only land where he is happy and contented, despite the morbid imaginings of ill-informed or misguided philanthropists." It seized the Confederacy by storm, became its unofficial anthem, and soon gave its name to the Southland (**5**). Repeated attempts have been made to give it more dignified lyrics (e.g., "Southrons! hear your country call you!"), but the Southern public has always preferred the ones about "buckwheat cakes and Injun batter" that "makes you fat and a little fatter."

326. "The Bonnie Blue Flag" was composed shortly after secession by an Irish variety artist named Harry McCarthy and was set to the tune of a popular air called "The Irish Jaunting Car." McCarthy styled himself "the National Poet of the South," and his song vied with "Dixie" as a Confederate anthem, even though the flag it referred to was soon replaced and McCarthy himself defected to the North. The last line goes: "So cheer again for the Bonnie Blue Flag that bears a Single Star!" (See **340**.)

327. **"Maryland, My Maryland"** was written in 1861 by James Ryder Randall, a young Marylander teaching in Louisiana, as a passionate appeal to Maryland to join the Confederacy. Lurid references to "the despot's heel," "the tyrant's chain," and "patriotic gore" (which provided a title for Edmund Wilson's study of Civil War literature) make it an unlikely official song for a fence-sitting state, but (set to the innocuous tune of "O Christmas Tree") that's what it is. The last verse is nonpareil: "Huzza! she spurns the Northern scum! / She breathes! she burns, she'll come! she'll come!"

"Patriotic gore" in Baltimore, 1861, led to the writing of "Maryland, My Maryland." Currier & Ives

328. **"The Yellow Rose of Texas,"** first published in New York in 1858, refers not to a flower, but to a mulatto girl. Popular with Confederate troops, it is still a Texas favorite, played recently at the official opening of one of Houston's several Chinatowns.

SOME OTHER ODDS AND ends about the Southern nation:

329. **The Great Seal** of the Confederacy was almost an afterthought, adopted only in 1863. The seal was made in England and brought through the blockade. It shows George Washington (a Virginian, after all) surrounded by a wreath of Southern crops, with the date of Jefferson Davis's inauguration and the motto *Deo vindice* ("With God as our defender"). The original is now in Richmond's Museum of the Confederacy.

Rebel R&R.

330. **Johnny Reb,** originally a derogatory label by Union troops for the Confederate soldier, was taken up by the Confederates themselves. Sometimes reduced to simply "Johnny," it gave rise by analogy to "Billy Yank." Another word for rebs was "butternuts," which originally referred to some poor Tennessee troops whose uniforms were dyed tan with sap from the butternut tree.

331. **The rebel yell** probably originated as a hunting cry. First heard in battle at First Manassas (**307**), it was a high-pitched yelp, quite different from the cheers and huzzahs of Union troops. It was later used as the brand name for a bourbon "made and sold only below the Mason-Dixon line" (but owned by a British company) and in the 1960s as an ironic newsletter title by the Southern Students Organizing Committee, a civil rights group.

Southern Students Organizing Committee button from the 1960s. Collection of the Mississippi State Historical Museum

The Cult of the Lost Cause

THE GREAT COLUMBIA CLASSICIST Moses Hadas (born in Atlanta) once observed, "A conquered people has no glories but departed ones." He probably didn't have the South in mind, but he could have. The Confederacy died in 1865, but its memory lingered on—and still does, for some. It was never more potent than at the turn of the century.

The Lost Cause portrayed in *The Birth of a Nation*.
Museum of Modern Art Film Stills Archive

332. **The Lost Cause** began simply as the title of an 1866 Civil War history, but the concept soon acquired religious potency. Presbyterian divine James Henley Thornwell (**827**) spoke of the South's purifying "baptism of blood." The Southern Methodist Church adopted a hymn based on Stonewall Jackson's last words (**288**), and in 1912 Cornelia Branch Stone of the United Daughters of the Confederacy published a "UDC Catechism for Children." Asked what her faith was, the young Juliette Gordon Low, founder of the Girl Scouts (**945**), replied, "My faith is my papa's faith, the Confederate faith." Katharine

Du Pre Lumpkin's father said of his children, "Their mother teaches them their prayers. I teach them to love the Lost Cause." And when Father Abram Joseph Ryan's niece was asked who killed Christ, she replied, "O yes I know, the Yankees."

ICONS OF THE RELIGION

333. **Popular prints of Confederate leaders** and other patriotic subjects soon adorned Southern walls. By 1900 about 150 had been published, mostly by Northern presses. A visitor in 1871 wrote, "Upon the walls were portraits of Gen. R. E. Lee, and Stonewall Jackson, and Jefferson Davis—indeed, the two first-mentioned I see everywhere in the South, in private as well as in public houses—and other Rebels of distinction."

The Last Meeting of Lee and Jackson (1869), by E. B. D. Julio. Museum of the Confederacy, Richmond, Va.

334. THE BURIAL OF LATANÉ (1864), by William D. Washington, was a favorite painting. It shows white women, children, and slaves mourning. No adult white males were present because godless Yankee troops refused to let the dead hero's captured brother stay for the funeral and wouldn't let a clergyman through the lines to read the service. The painting was displayed in Richmond to raise contributions for wounded soldiers, and in the 1870s the *Southern Magazine* gave away copies with subscriptions.

335. OTHER PRINTS FROM FAVORITE PAINTINGS included *The Lost Cause,* which shows an infantryman coming home to his ruined cabin; *The Last Meeting of Lee and Jackson,* which shows an imaginary encounter on the eve of Chancellorsville; and *The Surrender of General Lee to General Grant at Appomattox, April 9, 1865,* by Louis Guillaume (**30**).

SACRED TEXTS

EVERY RELIGION HAS ITS holy writ, and this one was no exception.

336. **Lee's Farewell to the Army of Northern Virginia,** sending them home with "the satisfaction that proceeds from the consciousness of duty faithfully performed," was often committed to memory and recited.

EX-CONFEDERATES AND THEIR CHILDREN also took comfort from an assortment of poems, some set to music. Three examples, of many:

337. **"The Burial of Latané,"** by John R. Thompson: "Gently they laid him underneath the sod / And left him with his fame, his country,

Suitable for framing. Library of Congress

and his God." The poem appeared in the *Southern Literary Messenger* within a month of Latané's death, had wide circulation as a broadside, and inspired Washington's painting.

338. **"Magnolia Cemetery,"** by Henry Timrod, one contender for the unofficial title of poet laureate of the Confederacy, foresaw monuments (**341**) yet to come:

Sleep sweetly in your humble graves,
Sleep, martyrs of a fallen cause!
Though yet no marble column craves
The pilgrim here to pause.

In seeds of laurel in the earth
The blossom of your fame is blown,

And somewhere, waiting for its birth,
The shaft is in the stone.

339. "The Conquered Banner," by Father Abram Joseph Ryan, a Confederate chaplain and, like Timrod, a contender for poet laureate, gave some widely ignored advice:

Furl that Banner, for 'tis weary;
Round its staff 'tis drooping dreary;
Furl it, fold it, it is best;
For there's not a man to wave it,
And there's not a sword to save it,
And there's not one left to lave it
In the blood which heroes gave it;
And its foes now scorn and brave it;
Furl it, hide it—let it rest.

Father Abram J. Ryan. *Library of Southern Literature* (1907)

HYMNS, HOLIDAYS, AND SERVICES

340. "Dixie," "Maryland, My Maryland," and "The Bonnie Blue Flag" (325–27) were as much anthems of the Lost Cause as of the Confederacy itself. "The Yellow Rose of Texas" (**328**), on the other hand, was quietly returned to her home state.

341. Holidays of the Lost Cause were Lee's birthday (January 19) and Confederate Memorial Day. Different states celebrated different memorial days, in the good states'-rights tradition, but ten finally agreed on Jefferson Davis's birthday, June 3. Dedications of the South's many war monuments were solemn and elaborate occasions: 200,000 people attended the dedication of the Davis statue in Richmond in 1907.

342. Confederate veterans' gatherings were also occasions for Lost Cause oratory and devotions, especially the annual reunions of the United Confederate Veterans, founded in 1889. At one point a full quarter of all Confederate soldiers who survived the war belonged to the UCV. Its magazine ceased publication only in 1932, and its last reunion wasn't until 1951 (three veterans attended). The last surviving veteran died in 1959.

OUR FAVORITE SPOKESMAN FOR THE LOST CAUSE

343. Basil Lanneau Gildersleeve (1831–1924), a Charlestonian, read the entire Bible by his fifth birthday, graduated from Princeton at seventeen, and got a Ph.D. from Göttingen after five semesters. Except for time spent in the

Confederate cavalry, where he received a crippling leg wound, he taught at the University of Virginia and later at the new Johns Hopkins University. His *Latin Grammar* (1867) was the first of many books and articles. In 1880 he founded the *American Journal of Philology*, which he edited for forty years. In *The Creed of the Old South* (1915) he summed up his feeling about the war: "It is something to have belonged in deed and in truth to an heroic generation." "That the cause we fought for and our brothers died for was the cause of civil liberty and not the cause of human slavery, is a thesis which we feel ourselves bound to maintain whenever our motives are challenged or misunderstood, if only for our children's sake."

North Carolina billboard, 1995. DixiePix

Stars and Bars. (One could ask why the UDC wanted a *federal* patent in the first place.) Membership has declined since 1980 from 35,000 to about 22,000.

Contemporary Groups with a Confederate Heritage

THEY'RE NOT WHAT THEY were in the Lost Cause era, but they're still around.

344. The United Daughters of the Confederacy was founded in 1894 to consolidate the activities of a number of women's memorial groups. Open to female descendants of the Confederate military or civil service, it no longer assists veterans' widows and orphans, but it's active in a variety of philanthropic and educational activities. Recently Illinois's black junior senator was instrumental in denying the organization a federal patent for its seal, which incorporates the

345. The Sons of Confederate Veterans, on the other hand, is growing rapidly, largely in response to attacks on the Confederate flag. With "camps" throughout the United States and abroad (including one among the descendants of Confederate expatriates in Brazil), the UDC's male counterpart had approximately 25,000 members in 1995—a handful of them black. This was still a long way from the 160,000 peak membership of the United Confederate Veterans, but it was up 50 percent in three years. Two related groups are the Order of the Confederate Rose, an auxiliary for wives of Sons, and the Military Order of the Stars and Bars, restricted to the male descendants of Confederate officers.

346. The Kappa Alpha Order was founded in 1865 at what's now Washington and Lee University (**840**). The fraternity venerates Robert E. Lee as its "spiritual founder" and upholds the ideal of the Southern gentleman (**933**): "the chivalrous warrior of Christ, the knight who loves God and country, honors and protects pure womanhood, practices courtesy and magnanimity of spirit and prefers self-respect to ill-gotten wealth," as one of the founders put it. Most of the hundred-plus chapters, mostly in the South, hold an annual Old South Ball. Some chapters' deployment of Confederate symbolism has recently occasioned unpleasantness, but the order's ideals have at least some multicultural appeal: in 1994 the president of the University of Florida's chapter was of Asian-Indian descent, its vice-president was Cuban-American, and its members included Jews, Asian-Americans, and one black.

347. **The Confederate Air Force** came along about ninety years too late, when some Air Corps veterans in Texas started collecting World War II airplanes. Now they have an airfield and museum in Midland, squadrons and detachments in thirty states and four countries, and 137 vintage warplanes, which they display at an annual air show. All officers are colonels, and patches on their uniforms say: "This is a CAF aviator. If found lost or unconscious, please hide him from Yankees, revive with mint julep and assist him in returning to Southern territory."

Five

The Central Theme

RACE AND POLITICS

Race permeates Southern politics like the twilight mist hanging in the marshlands that slither with the sounds of night creatures. It is always just below the surface of every public utterance, a chorus of whispers in the clatter of elective politics.

—ELI EVANS

The core of the Old South . . . consists of a single thing. . . . an ancient and ongoing dialogue between masses of white and black people. Desperately evil though long stretches of that relation

*have been, and are, the South is the single region
that has continued to avoid an emotional impasse
of the sort that blights so much of the nation. And
during those centuries of ceaseless interaction,
millions of individuals moved together to form the
heart of a life unlike any other on earth.*

—REYNOLDS PRICE

HISTORIAN ULRICH PHILLIPS wrote that the "central theme of Southern history" has been the struggle to maintain white supremacy. Maybe. Anyway, from the first the South has been pretty much a two-race society in which white Southerners called the shots.

Race from the Start

EPISODES IN THE HISTORY of Southern race relations:

SLAVERY, 1619–1865

348. The first blacks in the Virginia colony were twenty indentured servants brought to Jamestown on a Dutch frigate in 1619 (blacks had accompanied Spanish expeditions to what is now the United States a century before that). As early as 1640 some blacks were being illegally held in bondage after their term of indenture, and slavery was legally recognized in Virginia in 1661. The institution soon spread to other colonies, especially to Southern plantations. By 1690 the wholesale importation of enslaved Africans (**92**) was under way, either from the West Indies or directly from West Africa via the notorious Middle Passage.

349. Legal importation of slaves ended in 1807, as required by the Constitution, some decades before it ended in the Caribbean and Latin America. At emancipation most black Americans were at least three generations removed from Africa, and the age and sex distributions of the black population were more balanced than elsewhere in the hemisphere. Also unlike slaves elsewhere, Southern slaves were dispersed and usually outnumbered by whites, which helps explain the blurring of tribal distinctions among African-Americans and the relative absence of slave insurrections in the United States. (The United States was also the only New World society to free more slaves than it imported—more than eight times as many.)

Shackles. North Carolina Museum of History, Raleigh

A slave ship. Library of Congress USZ62-10607

350. Slave rebellions and conspiracies were not uncommon in the antebellum South (there were at least 250), but most were small and all were suicidal. Two of the most ambitious conspiracies were suppressed before coming to fruition: Gabriel Prosser's, in Richmond in 1800, and Denmark Vesey's, in Charleston in 1822. In only three cases did insurrections reach the point of battle between substantial bodies of slaves and whites. In 1739 on Stono Creek near Charleston "Cato's rebellion" took the lives of twenty whites and a larger number of slaves, and 1811 witnessed a revolt on several Louisiana plantations, but the bloodiest and best-known U.S. slave insurrection was that led by Nat Turner.

351. DENMARK VESEY (1767?–1822), bought at age fourteen by a slaver named Vesey, was called Télémaque (i.e., Telemachus—later corrupted to Denmark) because of his intelligence and beauty. He lived in Charleston, where he won $1,500 in a lottery, bought his freedom, and became a carpenter. His planned slave revolt, involving blacksmiths to make weapons and a white barber to make wigs and whiskers of European hair, was betrayed (so we'll never know what the wigs were for). He and thirty-four other blacks were hanged, thirty-four were sent out of state, and sixty-one were acquitted. Four whites were fined and imprisoned. In response, the state legislature started an arsenal, which became The Citadel (**834**) in 1841.

352. NAT TURNER (1800–31), a field hand and slave preacher in Southampton County, Virginia, was called the Prophet by fellow slaves. In-

Nat Turner's rebellion as depicted in an antiabolitionist tract, 1831. Library of Congress USZ62-38902

spired by visions, Turner recruited sixty to seventy followers and in 1831 led them in the slaughter of some sixty whites. At least 120 unimplicated blacks were murdered in retaliation; Turner and his twenty surviving followers were tried and hanged. The rebellion led the slave states to tighten their regulation of slavery (e.g., by enacting laws against teaching slaves to read), and Southern whites closed ranks against Northern abolitionists, whom they blamed for the revolt. (See **527**.)

353. JOHN BROWN (1800–59), a white abolitionist, led twenty-one men, five of them black, in a doomed attack on the U.S. arsenal at Harpers Ferry, Virginia (now West Virginia), in October 1859. Financed by Northern abolitionists and believing himself "an instrument of God," he intended to establish a black republic in the mountains as a base for overthrowing slavery al-

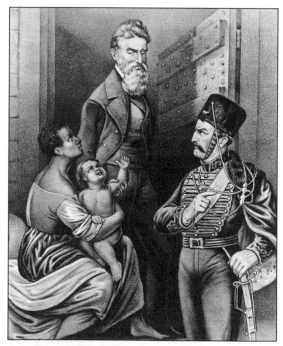

John Brown goes to his hanging (an antislavery view). Library of Congress USZ62-1284

together. Ironically, the first to die at the raiders' hands was a free black railroad employee. No slaves rose to join Brown, but a dozen were liberated involuntarily before U.S. marines led by Colonel Robert E. Lee (**287**) quelled the insurrection, killing ten of Brown's men. Seven more, including Brown himself, were hanged. Many people, including Abraham Lincoln, condemned the raid as useless, if not worse, but Ralph Waldo Emerson said Brown would make "the gallows glorious like the cross," and the song "John Brown's Body" became an anthem for antislavery forces.

EMANCIPATION AND RECONSTRUCTION, 1865–77

354. **Emancipation** came about piecemeal in the South, as it had earlier in the North. Con-

Emancipation, 1863. Currier & Ives

gress provided in 1862 for compensated emancipation in the District of Columbia, but Delaware, Maryland, and Missouri rejected similar plans, and no other jurisdiction even contemplated the prospect. Lincoln's proclamation of 1863 "freed" only slaves in areas under Confederate control (i.e., where the proclamation was unenforceable); effective emancipation in those areas had to await their surrender. In some parts of the South even news of the proclamation was slow to arrive. The black holiday "Juneteenth" supposedly commemorates the day in 1865 when Texas slaves heard the news. Not until the Thirteenth Amendment was ratified in December 1865 was the abolition of "involuntary servitude, except as punishment for crime" complete.

355. **"Forty acres and a mule"** was what many freedmen thought was coming to them after emancipation when, it was rumored, expropriated and abandoned Confederate land would be distributed to former slaves. Christmas 1865 was widely thought to be the date, but it came and went without any action. Something of the sort might have been a good idea—without land or resources, most Southern blacks were soon reduced to something like serfdom—but aside from a few wartime experiments in the Sea Islands (**28**), no land was ever given to ex-slaves. Today the phrase serves as the name of filmmaker Spike Lee's production company.

356. **Black Codes** were swiftly enacted by the white governments of almost every Southern state soon after the surrender. They excluded blacks from juries, voting, and public office, forbade them to testify against whites in court, and in some states virtually required them to work for whites. Extensive violence was also directed against blacks and white Republicans, culminat-

ing in massive race riots in Memphis and New Orleans in 1866.

357. **Congressional Reconstruction** saw Republicans in Congress respond with a variety of laws and three constitutional amendments to protect the rights of the freedmen and, not incidentally, to sustain Republican majorities in the conquered states. The first enactments, over solid Democratic opposition and President Andrew Johnson's (**437**) veto, imposed military government on the South, disfranchised prominent Confederates, set conditions for the readmission of states to the Union, and guaranteed Negro suffrage (in the South, that is: blacks couldn't vote in most Northern states at the time).

Ku Klux Klan mask. North Carolina Museum of History, Raleigh

An unreconstructed view of Reconstruction. Library of Congress USZ62-8788

358. **The Ku Klux Klan** was apparently founded as an innocent fraternal order by six Confederate veterans in Pulaski, Tennessee, in 1866. It soon turned to terrorizing blacks and white Republicans, however, and the idea caught on: scores of such organizations—some with the same name, some not—sprang up in every Southern state, usually acting as a secret para-

military arm of the Democratic Party to intimidate Republican voters and politicians, and to kill hundreds of them. In the 1870s federal anti-Klan measures, conservative Democratic leaders' growing uneasiness, and, finally, the election of Redeemer (**405**) governments put the Klan out of business. But a night-riding tradition had been established: it continued in less organized forms, directed against wife-beaters, revenue agents, real estate speculators, and other undesirables, as well as in defense of white supremacy. (See **367**.)

359. **The Compromise of 1877** occurred when congressional Republicans set out to steal the presidency for Rutherford Hayes from the Democrat Samuel Tilden (**411**). White Southern Democrats in Congress went along in exchange for federal recognition of Democratic administrations in South Carolina and Louisiana, a Southerner in Hayes's cabinet, several pork-barrel projects, the removal of federal troops from the South, and restoration of "home rule." This left the Southern states in the hands of white Democratic Redeemers (**405**).

THE JIM CROW ERA, 1878–c. 1960

Key to the consolidation of white control was the disfranchisement of black voters. A number of ingenious ways were found to do this, as well as some breathtakingly crude ones.

360. LITERACY TESTS became popular after 1880, when Mississippi required that prospective voters demonstrate that they could read and "understand" the state constitution. Registrars obviously had room for discretion, which they did not hesitate to employ. Other states soon added refinements. Virginia, for instance, required voters to write from memory the answers to a complicated series of questions, and South Carolina required that ballots be correctly deposited in each of eight separate boxes (with voting officials free to help, or not). The Voting Rights Act of 1965 struck down the use of such "tests and devices" when they appeared to reduce voter registration—which was, after all, the point.

361. POLL TAXES appeared in most Southern states between 1889 and 1908, when someone noticed that an annual tax of one or two dollars (cumulative in some states) had the dual effect of decreasing black voting and blunting the Populist challenge from poor whites. Politicians seeking poor-white votes later led several states to repeal these taxes, but five still levied them in 1964, when the Twenty-fourth Amendment prohibited such taxes in federal elections. In 1966 the Supreme Court outlawed them altogether.

362. GRANDFATHER CLAUSES allowed five Southern states to exempt voters from the new literacy and property qualifications. In three states they exempted those who could vote before 1867 or were descended from someone who could; in two other states they exempted veterans, including Confederate veterans, and their descendants. In either case, they exempted hardly any black folks.

363. THE WHITE PRIMARY rested on the argument that a political party is a private association free to select its own members—that is, to say who can vote in its primaries. In Southern states where the Democratic nomination guaranteed election, a Democratic primary for whites only was obviously even more efficient than poll taxes and literacy tests. In a series of decisions between 1941 and 1953, the federal courts rejected this view of what a party is, and thus its implications.

364. **The Atlanta Compromise** was W. E. B. Du Bois's (**391**) disapproving label for a speech by Booker T. Washington (**390**) at the Atlanta Exposition of 1895, which appeared to accept seg-

Booker T. Washington. Library of Congress USZ62-25624

regation as the price for black progress in the South. "In all things that are purely social," Washington said, "we can be as separate as the fingers, yet one as the hand in all things essential to mutual progress." He urged whites to recognize the economic value of black labor, urged blacks to pursue education and self-help, and pleaded for interracial cooperation. All this earned him a reputation for statesmanship among progressive whites, but the distrust of more militant blacks like Du Bois.

365. *Plessy v. Ferguson* arose when Plessy, a Louisiana "octoroon" (one-eighth black), was arrested for entering a railroad coach reserved for whites, under a state law requiring "equal but separate" accommodations for black and white passengers. In 1896 the Supreme Court upheld the constitutionality of Louisiana's law, rejecting the "assumption that the enforced separation of the two races stamps the colored race with the badge of inferiority" (**280**). The *Plessy* decision opened the door to enforcing segregation in all public accommodations, and Southern states swiftly enacted laws to do that.

366. **"The nadir"** is historian Rayford Logan's label for the early years of the twentieth century. Stripped of the vote, segregated by custom and increasingly by law, without effective legal protection or even the protection slaves had as property, Southern blacks were reduced to dependence on the goodwill of whites. As sharecroppers (**184**), most were in a condition of near peonage. Lynching had peaked in the 1890s but continued at a rate of fifty to a hundred a year. This period was also one of large-scale urban race riots (one of the worst was in Atlanta in 1906). These riots, amounting in some cases to pogroms, were not just Southern: over twenty cities across the United States witnessed them in the "Red Summer" of 1919.

367. **The second Ku Klux Klan** was formed in 1915 by William J. Simmons, a self-styled "colonel" from Alabama, who was inspired by the success of *The Birth of a Nation* (**496, 955**) and the idea of selling robes and memberships. In the 1920s it spread throughout the South and beyond, claiming 2 million members at its peak. It appealed to native white Protestants in all re-

Jim Crow water fountains. Standard Oil (New Jersey) Collection, Photographic Archives, University of Louisville

Cross-burning, Deland, Florida, 1975.
U.S. News & World Report/Library of Congress U9-31229-17

gions with its support for Prohibition and opposition to immigrant Roman Catholics. It was almost incidentally antiblack, anti-Asian, and anti-Semitic. Corruption, internal conflict, violence, the opposition of several powerful Southern newspapers, and, ultimately, tax troubles and World War II brought it down. Several small, independent Klan groups were active in opposition to the civil rights movement of the 1960s, and a few are still in business, but their numbers are negligible and the white-supremacist fringe has moved on to less picturesque organizations.

368. **The Great Migration** of blacks from the South began during World War I, when factory jobs opened up in the cities of the Northeast and Midwest. Although over the next decades more whites than blacks left the South, the effect on the South's black population was striking. In 1900, 90 percent of U.S. blacks lived in the South; by 1965, only 40 percent did, and one out of four Southern-born blacks—over 3 million of them—lived outside the South.

THE CIVIL RIGHTS ERA, 1954–68

369. *Brown v. Board of Education of Topeka, Kansas, et al.,* decided by unanimous vote of the Supreme Court on May 17, 1954, ruled that segregation of the public schools is unconstitutional, overturning *Plessy v. Ferguson.* (Two years later, the Court would rule against segregation on interstate transportation.) A later ruling ordered that school desegregation proceed "with all deliberate speed": although some school districts in border states were desegregated the following autumn, elsewhere in the South compliance was slower.

370. **Emmett Till,** a black fourteen-year-old from Chicago, was lynched in Leflore County, Mississippi, in August 1955, for whistling at a white woman. William Faulkner remarked, "If we in America have reached that point in our desperate culture when we must murder children, no matter for what reason or what color, we don't deserve to survive, and probably won't." But Till's murderers were never convicted.

371. **The Montgomery bus boycott** began in December 1955 after Rosa Parks was arrested for refusing to give a white man her seat on a Montgomery city bus. The boycott by black bus riders lasted over a year before the city agreed to a favorable settlement, and it brought prominence to the twenty-six-year-old minister of the Dexter Avenue Baptist Church, Martin Luther King, Jr. (**393**). In 1957 King would become the first president of the Southern Christian Leadership Conference (SCLC, or "Slick").

372. **The Southern Manifesto** was issued in March 1956, asserting states' rights and pledging to resist federally imposed desegregation. It was signed by Senator Harry F. Byrd (**431**) of Virginia and one hundred other congressmen, including every Southern senator except Estes Kefauver and Albert Gore of Tennessee and majority leader Lyndon Johnson (**439**) of Texas. In 1959, as part of Byrd's strategy of "massive resistance," Prince Edward County, Virginia, closed its public schools rather than desegregate.

373. **Little Rock** was the scene of the first civil rights confrontation widely covered by national television. In September 1957, under court order to desegregate Central High School, Governor Orval Faubus (**426**) mobilized the state militia to prevent a handful of black students from enrolling. President Eisenhower reluc-

tantly sent federal troops to enforce the court order.

374. **The sit-ins** began on February 1, 1960, when four black students from North Carolina A&T sat at Woolworth's lunch counter in Greensboro and refused to leave until served. The tactic quickly spread to other black campuses in the South, and in April the Student Nonviolent Coordinating Committee (SNCC, or "Snick") was formed. (SNCC's first president was Marion Barry, later a flamboyant mayor of Washington.)

375. **The Freedom Riders** left Washington by bus in May 1961, headed for New Orleans, to confront and expose segregation in bus terminals. The integrated group of thirteen met vio-lent mobs and indifferent (when not complicit) police in Anniston, Birmingham, and Montgomery. After the riders were beaten and their bus burned, Attorney General Robert Kennedy sent six hundred federal marshals to Montgomery to protect them. Their numbers growing, the riders continued to Jackson, Mississippi, where they were arrested and jailed under state segregation statutes.

376. **The Albany Movement** began in November 1961 to oppose segregation in Albany, Georgia. In the following months hundreds of demonstrators, including Martin Luther King, were jailed, but local authorities' insistence on "law and order" on *both* sides meant that the Albany protests ended inconclusively.

The Greensboro sit-ins. Jack Moebes for the *Greensboro News & Record*

James Meredith at the University of Mississippi, 1962. *U.S. News & World Report*/Library of Congress U9-8556-24

377. **The University of Mississippi (844)** saw mob violence in October 1962, when James Meredith, the school's first black student, enrolled. Encouraged in their opposition by Governor Ross Barnett (**427**), rioters took over the campus. Two people were killed, and twenty thousand troops were sent to restore order.

378. **Birmingham,** described by Martin Luther King as the most segregated city in America, was targeted by the Movement (now with a capital M) beginning in April 1963. Sit-ins, marches, boycotts, and other demonstrations met police dogs and fire hoses, coordinated by police commissioner Eugene "Bull" Conner. News photographs and television coverage shocked the world. Soon afterward, Governor George Wallace vowed, "Segregation now, segregation tomorrow, segregation forever," but two black students were enrolled in the University of Alabama without violence. In September four young black

Birmingham Civil Rights Memorial. Brian Ward, *Square Talk*

girls died when Birmingham's 16th Street Baptist Church was bombed. The Klan was presumed to be behind the bombing, but no convictions were ever obtained.

379. **Medgar Evers,** NAACP field secretary, was shot to death at his home in Jackson, Mississippi, June 12, 1963. His white assassin, Byron

De La Beckwith, was finally convicted in 1994; two earlier trials had ended in hung juries.

380. The March on Washington brought 200,000 people to the Lincoln Memorial on August 28, 1963, to demand an end to racial discrimination. This peaceful gathering was marked by Martin Luther King's "I Have a Dream" speech.

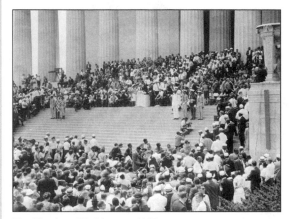

The March on Washington, 1963. *U.S. News & World Report*/Library of Congress U9-10360-23

381. The Mississippi Summer Project brought hundreds of (mostly Northern white) college students to the state in 1964, where they taught over two thousand black children in forty-one "freedom schools" and organized a "freedom vote" in which over eighty thousand disfranchised black Mississippians participated. The violence the project encountered—eighty beatings, thirty-five shootings, thirty-five church bombings, thirty house bombings, and six murders—focused media attention on the Magnolia State, especially after the abduction and murder of James Chaney, Michael Schwerner, and Andrew Goodman, one black and two Northern white volunteers.

382. The Civil Rights Act of 1964 was passed by a Congress exasperated with white Southern resistance to desegregation, and it was signed into law by President Johnson on July 2. It forbade racial discrimination in employment, public housing, and places of public accommodation.

383. Selma, Alabama, was the focus of national attention in March 1965, when a march on its way to the state capital of Montgomery to protest voting-rights abuses was broken up at the Pettus Bridge in Selma and marchers were beaten by the police. Two days later, three white ministers were beaten, and one of them died. All this drew thousands more marchers, including many politicians and celebrities, and even more television coverage to this small Dallas County town, formerly best known as the site of a Confederate supply depot.

384. The Voting Rights Act of 1965 provided federal registrars for jurisdictions where discrimination had been most flagrant (**361**). Its provisions originally applied to the five Deep South states, Virginia, and some counties of

Registering to vote in Mississippi, 1965. *U.S. News & World Report*/Library of Congress U9-14513-10

North Carolina. (Alaska was included, almost incidentally.) The immediate consequence was a striking increase in the number of blacks registered to vote (in Mississippi, from 6 percent of those eligible in 1965 to nearly 60 percent in 1968), a striking increase in the number of black officeholders, and striking changes in the behavior of white officeholders.

INTERESTING RECENT DEVELOPMENTS

SOME THINGS HAVE REALLY changed.

385. **White support for school segregation** is now no higher in the South than anywhere else—around 5 percent. In 1959, 72 percent of Southern white parents objected to sending their children to school where even "a few" of the children were black, compared to 7 percent of non-Southern white parents.

386. **The poverty rate for black families** in the South is now comparable to that for the rest of the country. In 1970 it was twice as high, but during the 1970s the percentage of black families in poverty fell in the South, while increasing in all other American regions. In fact, in the 1980s the Southern rate fell *below* that for the North Central states.

387. **More blacks have been moving to the South** than leaving it since the early 1970s, echoing a migration turnaround that occurred a decade earlier for whites (**198**) and reversing a population flow that once seemed a given in American demography (**368**). The percentage of American blacks who live in the Census South had dropped to around 40 percent, but it is once again a majority.

388. **Blacks are more likely to hold elected office** in the South than in any other region. Though blacks are still underrepresented among elected officials everywhere, a higher percentage of blacks hold office—and a higher percentage of officeholders are black—in the South than anywhere else. In 1994 two-thirds of America's 8,015 black elected officials were in the South, 1,450 in Mississippi alone.

NOTABLE BLACK LEADERS OF THE SOUTH

JUST A SAMPLE.

389. **Frederick Douglass** (1817–95), child of a slave woman and (presumably) her white master, worked at various occupations in Maryland, teaching himself to read and write, before he escaped in 1838. An eloquent platform speaker, he published three important autobiographies (**448**) and founded an abolitionist and women's-rights newspaper, the *North Star*. A loyal Republican, he held a variety of federal positions after the Civil War, including minister to Haiti. In 1884 his second marriage, to his white secretary, scandalized even Northern whites, but he had recognized as early as the 1840s that the race problem was not merely Southern.

390. **Booker T. Washington** (1856–1915) came "up from slavery" (**449**) via a West Virginia coal mine and the Hampton Institute, working his way through as a janitor. After teaching at Hampton, he founded Alabama's Tuskegee Normal Industrial Institute (**839**) in 1881 and soon became the most powerful black in the United States (**364**). An advocate of self-help, he created the National Negro Business League in 1900. John Spencer Bassett of Trinity College

wrote in 1903, "Washington is a great and good man, a Christian statesman, and take him all in all, the greatest man, save General Lee, born in the South in a hundred years." (Bassett almost lost his job for that.) Washington's dying words were: "Take me home. I was born in the South; I have lived and labored in the South; and I wish to die and be buried in the South."

391. **W. E. B. Du Bois** (1868–1963), Booker T. Washington's great rival, was a man of many talents, but diplomacy wasn't one of them; he was forever leaving jobs where he had annoyed people and going to other jobs where he annoyed people. He mourned Stalin as "calm, simple, and courageous." What's more, he was a Yankee. So why's he in here? He taught sociology at Atlanta University; he edited the NAACP's *Crisis* and published many Southern black writers; *The Souls of Black Folk* is still important (everyone cites his idea of black "twoness—an American, a Negro; two souls, two thoughts, two unreconciled strivings; two warring ideals in one dark

body, whose dogged strength alone keeps it from being torn asunder"); and he came around enough to say that "the future of American Negroes is in the South."

392. **A. Philip Randolph** (1889–1979) was born in Crescent City, Florida. In 1925 he organized the Brotherhood of Sleeping Car Porters. As its president, he was one of the best-known labor and civil rights leaders of his day. He organized *three* marches on Washington: one in 1941 that led to establishment of the Fair Employment Practices Commission; one in 1958, in support of the *Brown* decision; and the last, in 1963 (**380**), perhaps the culminating moment of the civil rights movement.

393. **Martin Luther King, Jr.** (1929–68), was a son of Atlanta's black bourgeoisie, his mother a teacher, his father a greatly respected Baptist minister. His academic career at Morehouse (**837**) and Boston University was at best undistinguished (his doctoral dissertation was largely

W. E. B. Du Bois. Library of Congress USZ62-16767

Martin Luther King, Jr. Robert J. Doherty Collection, Photographic Archives, University of Louisville

plagiarized), but it introduced him to the ideas of Thoreau and Gandhi on civil disobedience. Those ideas bore fruit in 1955, when as a young minister in Montgomery he organized that city's bus boycott (**371**). As president of the Southern Christian Leadership Conference, King went on to lead nonviolent demonstrations (nonviolent on the Movement's side, anyway) throughout the Deep South, culminating in the March on Washington (**380**). King was named *Time* magazine's Man of the Year, and in 1964 he won the Nobel Peace Prize. But attempts to take the Movement outside the South and to broaden its agenda to include economic issues were not particularly successful. King was in Memphis to support a sanitation workers' strike when he was assassinated, on April 4, 1968. Atlanta's King Center carries on his work, and his widow, Coretta Scott King, guards his legacy.

394. **Barbara Jordan** (1936–96) was a young Houston lawyer when she became the first woman ever elected to the Texas State Senate and a power in Texas politics. In 1972 she was elected to the U.S. Congress (she and Andrew Young were the first black Southerners in that body since 1898). She earned national fame as a powerful speaker during the impeachment hearings against President Nixon. Her keynote address to the 1976 Democratic convention confirmed that judgment, and she was named Best Living Orator by the International Platform Association. She retired in 1978 to teach at the University of Texas. Though suffering from muscular dystrophy, she continued to speak, notably at the 1992 Democratic convention.

395. **Jesse Jackson** (b. 1941) grew up in Greenville, South Carolina. He left the University of Illinois for North Carolina A&T, a black college where they'd let him be quarterback. He got there too late for the sit-ins (**374**) but became active in the Congress of Racial Equality (CORE). After seminary in Chicago, he joined the staff of SCLC, working with Martin Luther King on marches and demonstrations. When

Barbara Jordan at the 1976 Democratic Convention. *U.S. News & World Report*/Library of Congress U9-32934-12

The young Jesse Jackson. *U.S. News & World Report*/Library of Congress U9-35896-29

King died, Jackson moved to seize the leadership of the fragmented civil rights movement, using his Chicago-based Operation PUSH to negotiate concessions from businesses and banks, running for mayor of Chicago, lending his good offices to negotiations with Third World dictators, and generally staying in the limelight. A powerful speaker in the traditional Southern black-preacher mode, he ran for president in 1984 and 1988 and won enough delegates to be a factor in the Democratic conventions. His Rainbow Coalition has never really come together, but he remains a force in Democratic Party politics.

396. **John Lewis** (b. 1940) was born in Troy, Alabama, and got caught up in the civil rights movement while a Baptist seminary student in Nashville. In 1963 he became chairman of the Student Nonviolent Coordinating Committee (SNCC) but resigned to protest that organization's increasing militancy and secularization. While working as director of the Southern Re-

Civil-rights leaders at the 1964 Democratic Convention (left to right: John Lewis, SNCC; Aaron Henry, Mississippi Freedom Democratic Party; Roy Wilkins, NAACP; James Farmer, CORE). *U.S. News & World Report*/Library of Congress U9-12470-26

gional Council's Voter Education Project, he was severely beaten, but he maintained his commitment to nonviolence and racial reconciliation. He has since pursued a career in Georgia politics, and he's now an influential Democratic congressman, representing an Atlanta district.

Ralph Abernathy and Andrew Young. *U.S. News & World Report*/Library of Congress U9-19031-6

397. **Andrew Young** (b. 1932) was born in New Orleans and educated at Dillard, Howard, and Hartford Theological Seminary. An ordained United Church of Christ minister, he became active in the Southern Christian Leadership Conference and then in politics. Diplomacy has been his job no matter where he was: in negotiations between blacks and whites or within SCLC itself; in Congress, where he served three terms; in the United Nations, where he was ambassador 1977–79; in Atlanta, where he was mayor 1982–90; and in his recent job as cochair of the Atlanta Olympic Committee.

Southern Politics

INSOFAR AS SOUTHERN POLITICS have been *Southern*—that is, different from anybody else's—it has usually been a matter of race. Notice how often that subject comes up in what follows.

POLITICAL LABELS

THE SOUTH'S COLORFUL POLITICS have given rise to some colorful expressions to describe the actors.

398. "Tertium quids" was a phrase popularized in 1806 by John Randolph of Roanoke, who thought his fellow Virginians Jefferson and Madison had betrayed their principles of decentralized government and free trade—that is, states' rights and the interests of agriculture. Randolph sought a "third thing," opposed to both the Federalists and the Jeffersonians. Most "quids" were Southerners like Randolph, Nathaniel Macon, and John Taylor of Caroline.

399. "Wool hats" was a contemptuous term applied in the 1820s to Andrew Jackson's working-class and rural supporters. Fashions in inexpensive headgear changed, but the term stuck. It was revived in the 1890s by the Populists, who applied it to themselves and wore it proudly.

400. Fire-eaters were antebellum Southern radicals who vigorously advocated slavery, states' rights, and eventually secession (**260–65, 273–77**). John Brown's raid and Lincoln's election strengthened their hand, and in 1861 their views prevailed.

401. Copperheads weren't Southerners, and it's not a Southern term, but without the South there wouldn't have been any. Northern Republicans used it during the Civil War, referring to the poisonous reptile, to condemn antiwar Democrats. Although Republicans saw them as pro-Confederate, most were just anti-Negro and/or opposed to Eastern industrial interests. Mostly Midwestern farmers, they favored a peace settlement within a restored Union, and their movement died after the Northern military victories in 1864.

402. Carpetbaggers were Northern white Radical Republicans who came South during Reconstruction and advocated equal rights for freedmen, the establishment of public schools, and disfranchisement of many former Confederates. Hundreds held office at all levels during Reconstruction, usually put there by the votes of freedmen. The label implied that these were shiftless opportunists who brought only what assets would fit in a carpetbag, and the term has survived in the South as a label for Yankee migrants the speaker disapproves of.

403. "Scalawags" was a derogatory term for native Southern white Republicans during Reconstruction. (Before the war, it meant simply "rascal.") Most belonged to the moderate wing of the Republican Party that offered the freedmen political and civil equality but nothing more, and hoped to attract white voters with a program of economic development. Many scalawags had been antiwar and anti-Confederate Whigs and were viewed by other Southern whites as traitors; by siding with the freedmen, they also earned the wrath of white supremacists. The term is still in use: for example, *Southern Parti*

san magazine gives its Scalawag Award to white Southerners it deems disloyal to the South.

404. The lily-whites and the black and tans were opposing factions of the Southern Republican Party during and after Reconstruction. The lily-whites were a motley collection of former Whigs, businessmen, and simple racists who sought to exclude blacks from their party. The black and tans were the interracial faction. Black disfranchisement removed their core voting bloc, but they kept some influence and patronage by successfully contesting the seating of lily-whites at Republican national conventions. This ended in 1928, when the convention seated mainly lily-whites and set the stage for black voters' switch to the Democratic Party.

405. The Redeemers or Bourbons (what you call them depends on whether you see them as liberating the South or as the Southern analogue to the reactionary European monarchs) were the conservative white Democratic successors to the Republican state governments of Reconstruction. Historians disagree about whether they were a "new class" of businessmen or simply the old planter class returned, but whoever they were, they promoted the textile industry, imposed conservative economic policies, and disfranchised blacks.

406. Yellow-dog Democrats were white Southerners who would rather vote for a yellow dog on the Democratic ticket than for a Republican. Once the backbone of the Solid South (**11**), these reflexive Democrats are now an endangered species.

407. "Big Mules" originally meant anti–New Deal urban business interests in 1940s Alabama. Since then the term's meaning has broadened to include any wealthy and powerful political faction.

408. "Dixiecrats" was a nickname for the States' Rights Democratic Party in the 1948 presidential election. The label was subsequently applied to other conservative Southern Democrats.

409. Boll weevils were conservative-to-moderate Southern Democrats in Congress during the early years of the Reagan presidency (1980–88). Although Republicans were a minority in the House, the support of this faction occasionally gave them a working majority.

PIVOTAL PRESIDENTIAL ELECTIONS

CERTAIN ELECTIONS HAVE MARKED turning points in the South's relation to the rest of the country.

410. 1860 was a four-way race, set up by divisions over slavery. Stephen Douglas of Illinois supported slavery too weakly for Southern Democrats, who backed Kentuckian John C. Breckinridge. Southern Unionists, disliking Republican Abraham Lincoln, formed the Constitutional Union Party and nominated John Bell. In the election, Douglas carried Missouri; Bell carried Kentucky, Virginia, and Tennessee; Breckinridge carried all the other slave states. Lincoln finished last even in the border states, but won every Northern state except New Jersey. Even before his inauguration seven Deep South states seceded.

411. 1876 showed that both North and South had learned to compromise. Democrat Samuel

The four-way election of 1860. Library of Congress USZ62-14827

South Carolina were challenged, the race was sent to Congress, where the Compromise of 1877 (**359**) gave Southern Democrats the end of Reconstruction and Republicans the presidency.

412. **1928** saw the first serious fissure in the Solid South, when only the Deep South stayed with the historic party of white supremacy to vote for Democrat Al Smith against Republican Herbert Hoover. Most white Southerners had reservations about Smith, a New York City Catholic opposed to Prohibition, and many Protestant clergymen led the way in deserting the ever-more-liberal Democrats.

Tilden beat Republican Rutherford Hayes in both the popular and electoral votes, but when the electoral votes of Florida, Louisiana, and

The Deep South stays solid for Al Smith, 1928.

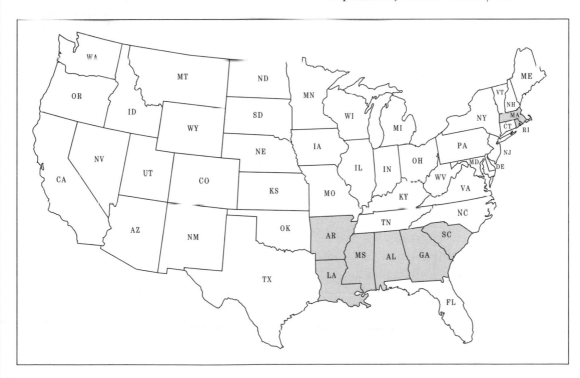

413. **1948** reversed the pattern: this time the Deep South deserted the Democrats. Southern Democrats dissatisfied with President Harry Truman's civil rights positions formed the Dixiecrat (**408**) Party. Its nominee, Governor Strom Thurmond of South Carolina, carried only Alabama, Louisiana, Mississippi, and South Carolina and did not prevent Truman from winning an electoral majority, but the Dixiecrat revolt marked another milestone in the breakup of the Solid South.

414. **1964** again saw the Deep South desert the Democrats, this time to support an actual Republican. Many white Southerners displeased with Lyndon Johnson's liberal social programs and civil rights initiatives voted for Senator Barry Goldwater of Arizona, a thoroughgoing conservative who had opposed the Civil Rights Act of 1964 (**382**) on principle. Goldwater carried only six states: Alabama, Georgia, Louisiana, Mississippi, South Carolina, and his home state.

415. **1968** was something of a rerun of 1948, as Alabama governor George Wallace asserted that there wasn't "a dime's worth of difference" between Republican Richard Nixon and Democrat Hubert Humphrey, and mounted a third-party candidacy. Wallace ran strong among white rural and working-class voters, Nixon carried traditional Republicans and the white middle class, and Humphrey got the votes of newly enfranchised blacks and the South's few white liberals. Wallace carried five Deep South states; Nixon and Humphrey split the rest of the South. But Wallace took votes from the Republican, not (like Thurmond in 1948) the Democrat. Otherwise Nixon's victory in 1968 would have been the first Southern Republican landslide. As it was, he had to wait for that until 1972.

416. **1976** showed that the Democrats could temporarily solidify the South by nominating a native son. Jimmy Carter was liberal enough to overcome non-Southern Democrats' reservations about a governor of Georgia, but he wasn't seen as a "typical Democrat," so he could still appeal to some conservative white Southerners. Those votes plus solid majorities among blacks gave Carter every Southern state but Virginia, and he beat incumbent Gerald Ford. The victory was short-lived, however. In 1980 the only Southern state Carter carried was Georgia, as he lost to Republican Ronald Reagan, the first of three landslide Republican presidential victories in the South.

George Wallace congratulates Jimmy Carter at the 1976 Democratic Convention. *U.S. News & World Report*/Library of Congress U9-32974-29

417. **1992** started out like 1976. The Democrats nominated a native son. Bill Clinton was liberal enough to overcome non-Southern Democrats' reservations about a governor of Arkansas, but he wasn't seen as a "typical Democrat," so he could still appeal to some conservative white Southerners. (Clinton's choice of a running mate, Senator Al Gore of Tennessee, produced the so-called double Bubba (**146**) ticket, the

first time since before the Civil War that a major party had nominated two Southerners.) But this time it didn't work: Clinton won, but with only 47 of the South's 157 electoral votes. And even that victory was short-lived. In the 1994 midterm elections the nation followed the South's lead and elected Republican majorities in both houses of Congress. For the first time in 120 years most of the South's congressional delegation were Republicans, including the leadership of both the House and the Senate.

MEN OF THE PEOPLE

SURE, THE SOUTH HAS politicians like everybody else's, but the interesting ones are like *nobody* else's. "Southern demagogues" flourished in the century after Appomattox. Some were racists, some weren't, some faked it. A few were liberal, some conservative, most a bewildering mixture. Outside Louisiana, you don't see their like much these days. Here's a sampling.

418. **Benjamin R. "Pitchfork Ben" Tillman** (1847–1918) was a Confederate veteran whose bad luck at cotton farming made him skeptical about Redeemer (**405**) government and receptive to the reforming ideas of the Farmers Alliance. As governor of South Carolina in the 1890s he pursued populist goals like higher corporate taxes and railroad regulation within the Democratic Party, while working for the disfranchisement of blacks (achieved in 1895). As U.S. senator (1894–1918) he supported free silver and greenbacks, low tariffs, and the Spanish-American War, while opposing Theodore Roosevelt's regulatory measures. Poor white farmers liked his fiery rhetoric in support of their economic interests and against the Charleston

"That South Carolina cyclone, or the terrible tantrums of the untamable Tillman," *Washington Post*, 1896. Library of Congress USZ62-9901

newspaper, the state university ("seedbed of the aristocracy"), and "the black beast."

419. **Thomas Edward Watson** (1856–1922) was a Jeffersonian agrarian (**918–21**) from a rich Georgia slaveholding family. Elected to Congress in 1890, he served farmers' interests with legislation like that establishing rural free mail delivery. Unlike Tillman, Tom Watson encouraged blacks and poor whites to cooperate on economic issues, which led the Democratic Party to rig the elections of 1892 and 1894 against him. He joined the Populist Party, running as its candidate for vice president in 1896 and for president in 1904 and 1908. Embittered by his lack of success, he became an anti-Catholic and anti-Semitic editor and supported the revival of the Ku Klux Klan. (The 1915 lynching of Leo Frank owed something to his in-

fluence.) He served as a U.S. senator for the last two years of his life.

420. **James K. Vardaman** (1861–1930) was known to campaign in a white suit on a wagon drawn by twelve white oxen. He appealed to Mississippi poor whites with a combination of agrarian reform and vicious anti-Negro rhetoric. As governor (1904–8) he regulated the railroads and abolished the convict-lease system—and called for closing all black schools. As U.S. senator (1913–19) he supported Wilson's progressive reforms—and defended lynching. His opposition to American entry into World War I cost him his seat and ended his career in 1918.

James Vardaman. Library of Congress USZ62-38765

421. **Coleman Blease** (1868–1942) was a perennial candidate for office in South Carolina from the 1890s to the 1930s, a controversial but ineffectual governor from 1910 to 1914, and an undistinguished U.S. senator in the 1920s. He turned the universal opposition of the state's newspapers into an asset, appealing to millworkers' resentment of corporations and aristocrats. He also appealed to their racism, defending lynching by observing that "whenever the Constitution comes between me and the virtue of the white women of the South, I say to hell with the Constitution."

422. **Eugene "Farmer Gene" Talmadge** (1884–1946) served several terms as governor of Georgia in the 1930s and 1940s. "The wild man from Sugar Creek" was a gifted orator whose populist rhetoric, folksy ways, and red galluses endeared him to rural voters, while his adamant opposition to New Deal spending won him the quiet support of corporate interests. Quaintly corrupt ("Sure I stole, but I stole it for you"), he began by defending Georgia's traditional agrarian lifestyle but in the 1940s became a more and more outspoken racist. His son Herman succeeded him as governor and later served as U.S. senator.

423. **Theodore Bilbo** (1877–1947) came from a well-off family, studied law at Vanderbilt, became a progressive governor of Mississippi in 1916, later a loyal New Deal senator, and America's most notorious bigot in the 1940s. Plagued throughout his career by sexual and financial scandals, he was a champion of the common man against a catalog of enemies that included "farmer murderers, poor-folks haters, shooters of widows and orphans, international well-poisoners, charity hospital destroyers, spitters on our heroic veterans, rich enemies of our public schools, private bankers, international debt cancellers, unemployment makers, Pacifists, Communists, munitions manufacturers, and skunks who steal Gideon Bibles"—also the corporations until the 1940s, when, supposedly, the corporations bought him off. About that time he be-

gan to race-bait in a serious way, publishing *Take Your Choice: Separation or Mongrelization.* Charges of corruption and his advocacy of violence to keep blacks from voting led the Senate to refuse him his seat in 1947, but he drew his salary until his death later that year.

424. **Huey Pierce Long** (1893–1935) built a political machine on the foundation of poor, rural Louisianans who loved him. As governor after 1928 and U.S. senator after 1932 "the Kingfish" ruthlessly consolidated nearly all governmental power in Louisiana for himself, using high cor-

porate taxes to pay for all manner of welfare and public works projects. His Share Our Wealth Society attracted a strong national following, and he was preparing to run for president when he was assassinated in 1935 (**775, 974**). His younger brother, Earl, continued in Huey's populist footsteps as three-time governor between 1939 and 1960, and was a pioneer in protecting the voting rights of Louisiana's blacks (they voted for him). But Earl was memorable less for all that than for his bigger-than-life flamboyance and his involuntary commitment to a mental institution in 1959.

425. **James Elisha "Big Jim" Folsom** (1908–87) was elected governor of Alabama in 1946 by a farmer-labor coalition against the Big Mules (**407**), but a conservative legislature thwarted his plans for expanded social services, educational improvement, and repeal of the poll tax; his opposition to the Dixiecrats (**408**) in 1948 was unpopular; and a paternity suit didn't help. He won a second term in 1954, though, and got much of his program through before he offended voters with his racial liberalism—for example, by saying that the state legislature's

Big Jim Folsom (the little man's big friend) and friends. *U.S. News & World Report*/Library of Congress U9-1042-29

Huey P. Long in the U.S. Capitol. Library of Congress USA7-35057

"nullification" of the *Brown* decision (**369**) was "like a hound dog baying at the moon." Running for a third term in 1962, he was race-baited into third place by a former protégé, George Wallace.

426. Orval Faubus (1910–94) ran for governor of Arkansas in 1954 as a moderate populist. As governor he brought blacks into the leadership of the state Democratic Party and oversaw the desegregation of public transportation. He will be remembered, however, for sending the National Guard to block desegregation of Little Rock's Central High School in 1957. President Eisenhower responded with what Faubus described as "the military occupation of Arkansas," and the school was desegregated. Faubus became a segregationist hero and won an unprecedented four more terms as governor.

427. Ross Barnett (1898–1987) was the youngest of a poor Confederate veteran's ten children. He worked his way up to president of the Mississippi Bar Association. With support from the segregationist Citizens Council, he was elected governor in 1959. His moment of glory came in 1962 when his public defiance of a court order to integrate the University of Mississippi (**377, 844**) set off a riot that led to the deployment of federal troops. A vehement racist with a folksy style, Barnett was also famous for putting his foot in his mouth. He once asked a Brazilian military officer whether his country had problems with integration; told that it didn't, he said, "Wait 'til it hits you, boy."

428. George Corley Wallace (b. 1919), once an amateur boxer, became a pugnacious opponent of desegregation. Beginning in Alabama politics as a racial moderate and economic liberal, he reputedly decided not to be "outniggered" again after losing a 1958 gubernatorial election, and

Governor George Wallace stands in the schoolhouse door at the University of Alabama. *U.S. News & World Report*/Library of Congress U9-9930-20

won in 1962. He "stood in the schoolhouse door" in a largely symbolic attempt to prevent the desegregation of the University of Alabama, and civil rights violence in Birmingham (**378**) and Selma (**383**) took place on his watch. He was a force in national politics in 1968 (**415**) and 1972 (when he was shot and crippled on the campaign trail), but his appeal had faded by 1976. In 1982, having renounced his segregationist past, he was again elected governor of Alabama, this time with substantial black support. Increased highway and educational spending were among his less well known legacies.

429. Lester Maddox (b. 1915) grew up poor in Atlanta and became a local character with newspaper ads for his fried-chicken restaurant that also offered his thoughts on integrationists and other liberals. In 1964 he gave out ax handles for supporters to use on any blacks who wanted to eat at his establishment, then sold the place rather than desegregate it. In 1966, with no previous political experience, he ran a grassroots campaign for governor and won. His

Governor Lester Maddox of Georgia. *U.S. News & World Report*/Library of Congress U9-19668-A-10

term was marked by fiery states'-rights and segregationist rhetoric, but little in the way of action to prevent integration. Barred from succeeding himself, he ran again in 1974 but lost to a moderate. For a while he ran a tourist shop in Underground Atlanta, selling, among other things, autographed souvenir ax handles.

Two POLITICIANS OF DIFFERENT stripes:

430. Edward Hull "Boss" Crump (1874–1954) wasn't an agrarian demagogue: he was an urban boss. A successful businessman, he was elected mayor of Memphis in 1909, 1911, and 1915 and congressman in 1930, but more important than his offices was his political machine, which controlled Memphis for decades and dominated Tennessee elections during the 1930s and 1940s. The Crump machine was noteworthy because it involved and depended on Memphis's black voters—an unusual pattern for Deep South politics. It lost much of its statewide power after it backed a loser in the 1948 U.S. Senate election.

431. Harry Flood Byrd (1887–1966), like Boss Crump, wasn't a demagogue—he was a Virginia aristocrat—but he, too, built an effective machine. In his case, a statewide network and effective disfranchisement of both black and poor white voters kept him in the Senate for thirty-two years and his conservative candidates in office from the 1920s to the 1960s, working for states' rights, pay-as-you-go government, and segregation. The machine distanced itself from the New Deal liberalism of the national Democratic Party and tacitly supported Republican presidential candidates in the 1950s and 1960s. Changing demographics, the 1965 Voting Rights Act (**384**), and Byrd's death did it in.

SOUTHERN PRESIDENTS

THE SOUTH PRETTY MUCH kept its demagogues for itself. Here are some of the politicians it exported, the good, the bad, and the ugly.

432. The Virginia Dynasty. Four of the first five presidents were Virginians, from the Father of Our Country to the author of the Monroe Doc-

Thomas Jefferson of Monticello, painting by Rembrandt Peale (**750**). Courtesy Princeton University/*Dictionary of American Portraits* (Dover, 1967)

trine, with a Renaissance man (**729**) and an author of *The Federalist Papers* in between. Not bad. Washington, Jefferson, Madison, and Monroe each served two full terms, thirty-two of the nation's first thirty-six years, 1789–1825. Some think it's been downhill ever since.

433. Andrew Jackson wasn't a Virginia Gentleman. Born in North or South Carolina (the two states fight about it), "Old Hickory" was really a Tennessean, and so was his down-home wife, Rachel. Hero of the Battle of New Orleans in 1814, Democrat with both big and small *d*, champion of the common man, scourge of the

Old Hickory, on the grounds of the Tennessee state capitol. DixiePix

Indian, president 1829–37, strong Unionist (in opposition to John C. Calhoun [**260**]).

434. William Henry Harrison and John Tyler—"Tippicanoe and Tyler, too"—were Virginia Whigs, although Harrison lived in Ohio when they were elected president and vice president in 1840. The old Indian fighter died of pneumonia a month after giving a record-length inaugural address on a very cold day. Tyler served out the term, alienating congressional Whigs by vetoing most of Henry Clay's nationalistic legislation. Back home in Virginia, Tyler became a secessionist and eventually a Confederate congressman. (Harrison's Midwestern grandson Benjamin was president 1889–93.)

435. James Knox Polk, a Tennessee Democrat born in North Carolina, beat Henry Clay in 1844. Parallels to Lyndon Johnson are unavoidable: an activist president, master of Congress, impresario of the Mexican War, but not the popular leader needed by a nation increasingly divided (over slavery). He also retired after one term, although unlike Johnson, he'd intended to from the beginning. He was succeeded by the Whig—

436. Zachary Taylor, Mexican War hero, Louisiana slaveholder, and yet another Virginia-born president. Elected in 1848 with the votes of most Southern states, Taylor surprisingly turned out to be a fervent nationalist and opponent of slavery in the territories. He got sick at a Fourth of July celebration in 1850 and died; otherwise, Daniel Webster observed, there would have been a civil war that year.

437. Andrew Johnson, the last undeniably Southern president for nearly a century, succeeded to the office when Lincoln was assassi-

Andrew Johnson of Tennessee, with his 1864 running mate. Library of Congress USZ62-14616

nated in 1865. A Unionist who was still at heart a states'-rights Tennessee Democrat (**282**), Johnson tried to achieve sectional reconciliation, pardoning ex-Confederates and acquiescing in their retention of political and social control (**356–57**). That might have been Lincoln's plan (who knows?), but Johnson lacked Abe's popularity and political skill. In 1866 outraged Northern voters returned a hostile Congress that impeached him and came within one vote of removing him from office. In 1874 he came back to Washington as Tennessee's senator and continued to oppose Republican Reconstruction policies.

438. **Woodrow Wilson** was born in (yes!) Virginia, son of an ardent Confederate, and except for his college days at Princeton, spent his first thirty years in the South. He married a Georgia girl. He admired *The Birth of a Nation* (**955**) and Robert E. Lee. He was a Democrat, a Calvinist, a moralist, and a paternalistic segregationist. He called the South "the only place in the world where nothing has to be explained to me" and called himself a Southerner. So why is there any question about whether America's president from 1913 to 1921 was Southern? Maybe because he was governor of New Jersey before that.

ASIDE FROM WILSON (if you count him), there were no Southern presidents between the 1860s and the 1960s, and the two on either end were accidents. During these Wilderness Years several Southerners were nominated for *vice* president on Democratic tickets and a few were even elected. But, as one of them (John Nance Garner, vice president 1933–41) memorably observed, that office isn't worth "a pitcher of warm spit." Unless you get lucky. . . .

439. **Lyndon B. Johnson,** like Andrew, was a Southern states'-rights Democrat who suc-

Ol' Lyndon.
*U.S. News &
World
Report*/Library
of Congress U9-
17563-25

ceeded from the vice presidency on the assassination of a Northern president and was eventually driven from office. As a Texas senator Johnson had been a nominal member of the conservative Southern bloc, but he made up for it as president by pushing through liberal Great Society legislation, including important civil rights bills (**382, 384**). Biographer Robert Dallek argues that the outlines of the Great Society were a direct response to the Southern experience. Could be, but LBJ's unpopularity with white Southern voters in 1964 (**414**) spelled the end of the Solid South. His unpopularity with

liberals in his own party in 1968, primarily over the Vietnam War, spelled the end of his presidency: he did not seek reelection.

440. **James Earl "Jimmy" Carter** was a born-again Baptist peanut merchant, Annapolis graduate, and governor of Georgia, who capitalized on widespread images of a really *new* South to win the Democratic nomination in 1976 as an unabashed Southerner. He largely governed that way, too, with many black and white Southerners as advisers and key appointees (and his foreign policy moralism reminded some of Woodrow Wilson's). A combination of bad economic conditions, perceived impotence overseas, and what he diagnosed as national "malaise" brought him down after one term.

441. **William Jefferson "Bill" Clinton,** Georgetown and Yale, governor of Arkansas, and Southern yuppie, didn't inhale marijuana smoke or fight in Vietnam, but he beat Texans George Bush (soi-disant) and Ross Perot (undeniable) in 1992. (Bush, a New Englander by birth and education, moved to Texas and went into the oil business in 1950. We don't claim him.) Clinton's Southernness, like Carter's, didn't seem to hurt him, and may even have helped to persuade voters that his liberal social and economic policies didn't mean he was soft on crime, excess spending, or foreign enemies of the United States. (But see **417.**)

Six

Grit Lit

WRITERS AND LITERATURE

Southerners did not publish, did not write, did not read.

—ELLEN GLASGOW

The South has produced writers as the Dark Ages produced saints.

—ALFRED KAZIN

Nonfiction since the Beginning

FOLKS IN THE SOUTH have been telling their stories for a long time. They used to pretend they were true.

MYTHMAKERS

THREE EARLY ONES:

442. Captain John Smith (1580–1631), Renaissance paladin, believed *vincere est vivere* ("To conquer is to live") and boasted in print of killing three Turkish champions in tournaments and of surviving Indian wars, Turkish slavery, and worse. His "rescue" by Pocahontas is part of American mythology. Whether historian or fabulist, Smith is our first important author: he wrote eight books about his Virginia experiences and gave us the first description of the Southern good life. His definition of history could be a motto for the South: "History is the memory of time, the life of the dead, and the happiness of the living."

443. William Byrd, II (1674–1744), the most important Southern writer before Jefferson, wrote many works in assorted genres while running a 180,000-acre empire and living the agrarian ideal (**918**) "like one of the patriarchs [with] my flocks and herds, my bondmen and bondwomen, and every sort of trade amongst my own servants, so that I live in a kind of independence on every one but Providence." He saw bad effects from "this unchristian traffick of making merchandize of our fellow creatures": slaves "blow up the pride, & ruin the industry of our white people." His coded diaries document his sex life and provide our best single source about colonial Virginia.

Captain John Smith. Library of Congress USZ62-55182

William Byrd, II. Library of Congress USZ62-42108

444. Mason Locke "Parson" Weems (1759–1825), whose books like *God's Revenge against Adultery, The Effects of Drunkenness,* and *The Bad Wife's Looking Glass* sought to "dulcify and exalt human nature," was headed for oblivion until he got into the mythmaking business with his *Life of Washington.* It went into countless editions. (He invented the fable of the cherry tree in the fifth.)

THE MYTHMAKING BUSINESS HAS continued (see chapter 12). In a class by himself:

445. W. J. Cash (1900–41) wrote one book, *The Mind of the South,* and then hanged himself. Cash was an admirer and protégé of H. L. Mencken (his writing shows it), and his history should be taken with a grain of salt, but the book is still in print, still shaping how people think about the South, for better or for worse. Cash debunked the plantation myth while asserting the historical continuity of white Southern racism, individualism, and romanticism. The "savage ideal" of intolerance, the Southern "rape complex," the "proto-Dorian bond" among white men—he had a gift for memorable labels.

DIARIES, COLLECTED NARRATIVES, MEMOIRS, ETC.

446. Hundreds, perhaps thousands, of Southern diaries, letters, and memoirs have been published, with more appearing every day. A good oldie is *The Secret Eye,* Georgian Ella Gertrude Clanton Thomas's diaries from 1848 to 1889 (**271**). A fine book of family letters is *The Children of Pride: A True Story of Georgia and the Civil War* (1972). Malcolm Bell, Jr., uses family letters to dissect the Butlers of Georgia in *Major Butler's Legacy: Five Generations of a Slaveholding Family* (1987). Five good modern memoirs: Ben Robertson's *Red Hills and Cotton* (1942), a poetic meditation on family, the South, and agrarianism (**918–21**); Willie Morris's *North toward Home* (1967), about a Mississippi boy who goes to New York; Albert Murray's *South to a Very Old Place* (1971), about a black Alabamian who returns to the South; Harry Crews's *A Childhood: The Biography of a Place* (1978), about growing up in rural south Georgia during the Depression; Ruthie Bolton's *Gal: a True Life* (1994), a searing account of growing up poor, black, and abused that could be subtitled "Love Lifted Me."

447. Mary Boykin Miller Chesnut (1823–86), the Old South's most famous diarist (**272, 914**), grew up in South Carolina society, was daughter and wife to U.S. senators, and knew everyone who was anyone in the Confederacy. Begun in 1861, her diary became a self-conscious—and very fine, but not necessarily honest—literary production as years went by. Its 400,000 words have been excerpted in various forms, the best being an edition by C. Vann Woodward.

Mary Chesnut

Over six thousand slave narratives were published between 1703 and 1944.

Frederick Douglass

448. MORE THAN ONE HUNDRED ANTEBELLUM NARRATIVES by escaped or freed slaves (including some in Arabic) were important abolitionist propaganda.

Although they were rarely challenged by slavery's defenders, later historians either didn't know about them (in 1939 one said that "the slaves themselves never told" what slavery was like) or didn't take them seriously (Ulrich Phillips thought that "abolitionist editing" meant "their authenticity is doubtful"). Historians have only recently begun to put these accounts to use, but they have been a pervasive influence on modern black writers. Two important narratives are *The Autobiography of Frederick Douglass* (**389**) and *Incidents in the Life of a Slave Girl,* by Harriet Jacobs (thought until recently to have been written by her editor). *Incidents* is written like a Victorian domestic novel but shows a woman making hard choices in a world of sexual complexity (e.g., "It seems less degrading to give one's self, than to submit to compulsion").

449. POST-EMANCIPATION ACCOUNTS include ex-slaves' autobiographies, of which probably the best—certainly the best known—is Booker T. Washington's *Up from Slavery.* During the Depression the Federal Writers' Project interviewed over 2,200 ex-slaves in seventeen states, yielding about 3.5 million words of narrative. Scholars almost completely ignored this extraordinary resource for years, perhaps intimidated by the problems of working with an unrepresentative sample, interviewed years after slavery mostly by white interviewers at a time when candor between the races was unlikely— and by the added complication that the project's staff altered some interviews. But, as C. Vann Woodward has said, "The norm for historical sources is a mess, a confusing mess, and the task of the historian is to make sense of it."

Fanny Kemble. Library of Congress USZ62-79733

TRAVELERS' AND VISITORS' ACCOUNTS

450. **Visits to the South** spawned 2,703 books before 1955, according to one study. Early travel writing was meant to lure colonists or to document flora and fauna and Indian life. Antebellum visitors included foreigners like Charles Dickens, Alexis de Tocqueville, Harriet Martineau, and Frances Trollope, and equally fascinated Yankees like James Kirke Paulding, Joseph Holt Ingraham, and Frederick Law Olmsted (who left us detailed descriptions, with measurements, of all sorts of buildings). After the war, Edward King's *The Great South* reflected—and encouraged—a new reconciliation with the Old South.

451. **Fanny Kemble** (1809–93), a successful British actress, married Southern planter Pierce Butler (**446**) in 1834 and moved south. She was divorced (not amicably) in 1849. In 1863 she published her *Journal of a Residence on a Georgian Plantation in 1838–1839.* She

was a shrewd and articulate observer, forthright in her hatred of slavery, less straightforward in her scorn for Southern planters (no surprise there). (See **950.**)

452. David Hunter Strother (1816–88), who wrote under the name of Porte Crayon, was a native of what is now West Virginia and cousin to several writers, including John Pendleton Kennedy (**463**). He wrote and illustrated (**53**) travel pieces for *Harper's* beginning in the 1850s, reaching an estimated quarter million people each month. Like the Southwestern humorists (**458**), he depended heavily on wit and irony. Unlike them, he worked hard to present an accurate view of blacks and mountaineers. His service with the Union Army (yes, Union) is chronicled in his diary *Personal Recollections of the War by a Virginian.*

PORTE CRAYON SKETCHING

Virginia Illustrated (1857)

453. James Agee (1909–55), a Knoxville boy, went to Exeter and Harvard but came south to Alabama to write *Let Us Now Praise Famous Men* (1941), with masterly photographs by Walker Evans. This remarkable book is really a piece of literary performance art: we watch a writer write about the lives of tenant farmers. Critics hated it, and it sold fewer than six hundred copies; reissued in 1960, it became a classic. (See also **523.**)

454. Writers of all persuasions still roam the South. John Howard Griffin darkened his skin, traveled through the South, and wrote about it in *Black Like Me* (1961). *An Asian Anthropologist in the South* (1977), by Choong Soon Kim, needs no comment. *A Turn in the South* (1989) isn't V. S. Naipaul's best, but it's not bad. Black Northerner Eddy L. Harris toured the South by motorcycle and discovered some Confederate virtues *(The South of Haunted Dreams,* 1993). There have been a dozen more in recent years.

Nineteenth-Century Belles Lettres

AS THE SOUTH ACQUIRED a distinct identity, it became evident even in the titles of journals: *Southern Literary Messenger* (1834), *Southern Review* (1828), *Southern Literary Gazette* (1828), *Southern Quarterly Review* (1842).

455. Edgar Allan Poe (1809–49) edited the *Southern Literary Messenger* for three years, supported Southern writers and institutions, but rarely wrote about anything obviously Southern (although some critics see allegories of guilt about slavery). His life, on the other hand, was Southern Gothic at its finest: he suf-

Edgar Allan Poe. Library of Congress USZ62-10610

457. William Wells Brown (1816?–84), born a slave in Kentucky, escaped to the North, where he wrote a well-known narrative and became an abolition and temperance lecturer. His many other books include *The Anti-Slavery Harp: A Collection of Songs for Anti-Slavery Meetings* (1848); a play (probably the first by a black American); *Three Years in Europe; or, Places I Have Seen and People I Have Met* (1852); and four histories. He's best known for *Clotel* (1853), a novel (definitely the first by a black American) based on the rumor that Thomas Jefferson had a daughter with one of his slaves. Melodramatic and didactic, it condemns American race relations and advocates integration. He ended his life as a Boston physician.

HUMOR OF THE OLD SOUTHWEST

458. "Southwestern humor," mostly from Georgia, Alabama, and Tennessee between the 1830s and the Civil War, was the Old South's unique

fered from alcoholism and depression, had difficulty making a living, and (like Jerry Lee Lewis) married his thirteen-year-old cousin. He invented the short story and the detective story, and his poetry influenced the French Symbolists, who in turn influenced modern poets like T. S. Eliot.

456. William Gilmore Simms (1806–70), like many antebellum Southerners, began as a patriotic American but became increasingly Southern and defensive: in 1852 he contributed to *The Proslavery Argument.* He actually made his living writing (more than eighty books: novels, stories, essays, poetry, criticism, biography, history, and plays) and editing (ten journals). He is best known for three series of historical romances. Most readers like *The Yemassee* (1835) best.

William Gilmore Simms. Library of Congress USZ62-12702

contribution to American literature. A. B. Longstreet said it aimed to capture "the manners, customs, amusements, wit, dialect, as they appear in all grades of society"; typically, an urbane narrator depicted native shrewdness outwitting pretentious sophistication, sometimes his own. (Simon Suggs says, "Mother-wit can beat booklarnin' at *any* game.") Bawdy, earthy, and often violent, it must have been a relief after the stilted pretension of contemporary novelists and poets.

459. **Augustus Baldwin Longstreet** (1790–1870) was the first and most influential of the Southwestern humorists. A Yale-trained lawyer, judge, newspaper editor, Methodist minister, and president of four colleges (Emory, Centenary, Mississippi, and South Carolina), he used his wide experience to write social history in which poor whites got equal time, for a change. *Georgia Scenes* (1835) is his most important book.

Davy Crockett. Engraving by Thomas B. Welch from a painting by S. S. Osgood/ *Dictionary of American Portraits* (Dover, 1967)

460. **Davy Crockett** (1786–1836) is in the long line of Southern writers from John Smith to James Dickey who haven't felt limited by the facts in retelling their lives. His *Narrative of the Life of David Crockett, of the State of Tennessee* (1834), written with Thomas Chilton, is more tall tale than autobiography, a splendid example of the unlettered but wily backwoodsman who can "run faster, jump higher, squat lower, dive deeper, stay under longer, and come out drier, than any man in the whole country"—still a stock character. Crockett served in Congress, died a hero at the Alamo, and was resurrected by Walt Disney in the 1950s.

Augustus Baldwin Longstreet. Library of Congress USZ62-9845

BEYOND SOUTHWESTERN HUMOR

461. Mark Twain (Samuel Langhorne Clemens, 1835–1910) was raised in Hannibal, Missouri, by Southern parents. A former printer, riverboat pilot, and Confederate soldier (he deserted), he began writing Southwestern humor but soon transcended the genre. He is remembered for novels like *The Adventures of Tom Sawyer* (1876), a wild combination of Gothic horror and childhood innocence; *Huckleberry Finn* (1884), from which, Hemingway said, "all modern American literature comes"; and *A Connecticut Yankee in King Arthur's Court* (1889), a pessimistic spoof denying the possibility of progress. Fame and honor didn't offset financial reverses and the deaths of two daughters and his wife, which left him a bitter old man.

Mark Twain. Library of Congress USZ62-28784

462. The plantation novel began before the Civil War but reached full flower in reaction to defeat. Stories of aristocratic romance narrated by devoted old slaves, idyllic depictions of a society too pure and good to survive in a crass, commercial world, had an odd appeal to Northern publishers and book buyers as well as an obvious one to white Southerners. One of James Branch Cabell's characters explains how it works: "I love to prattle of 'ole Marster' and 'ole Miss,' and throw in a sprinkling of 'mockin'-buds' and 'hants' and 'horg-killing time,' and of sweeping animadversions as to all 'free niggers'; and to narrate how 'de quality use ter cum'— you spell it c-u-m because that looks so convincingly like dialect—'ter de gret hous.' Those are the main ingredients."

463. JOHN PENDLETON KENNEDY (1795–1870), lawyer and politician, invented the plantation novel with *Swallow Barn* (1832), in which the plantation myth (**912–17**) is already fully realized. Here's a description of a visit to the quarters: "I came here . . . expecting to have my sympathies excited towards them as objects of commiseration. . . . I will not say that, in a high state of cultivation and of such self-dependence as they might possibly attain in a separate national existence, they might not become a more respectable people; but I am quite sure they never could become a happier people than I find them here."

464. CAROLINE LEE HENTZ (1800–56), prolific plantation novelist, is best known for *The Planter's Northern Bride* (1851), an answer to *Uncle Tom's Cabin,* in which she stoutly defends slavery, railing against Northern "wage-slavery," offering endless illustrations of black inferiority, and portraying an evil abolitionist who incites a slave uprising (and also, lest she appear biased,

an honorable abolitionist). All this must have distressed her parents and friends in Massachusetts, where she was born and raised.

465. THOMAS NELSON PAGE (1853–1922), the most important writer of plantation novels, gave his readers exactly the South they wanted. He was not first to use the faithful retainer as narrator (467), but he perfected the character. His success allowed him to give up law and become a literary lion, moving in high society and traveling in Europe. He was elected to the American Academy of Arts and Letters and was made ambassador to Rome by Woodrow Wilson. "Marse Chan" is his most frequently anthologized story.

466. **Augusta Jane Evans Wilson** (1835–1909) wrote didactic domestic novels that were na-

Augusta Evans Wilson. *Library of Southern Literature* (1907)

tionwide best-sellers, despite her show-off prose style and abstruse allusions, or perhaps because of them (nineteenth-century readers yearned for uplift). A staunch Confederate, she broke her engagement to a staunch Yankee in 1860 and wrote *Macaria; or, Altars of Sacrifice* (1864), which was smuggled through the blockade, reprinted in New York, and banned by a Yankee general. *St. Elmo* (1866) rivaled *Uncle Tom's Cabin* in total sales, and countless girls were named after the heroine, Edna Earle (there's one in Eudora Welty's *The Ponder Heart* [510]). Wilson's theme was that women should follow God's desires, not their own. (But could she have given up her fame with the grace she demanded of her heroines?)

"**Local colorists**" was the category for dozens of late-nineteenth-century authors who wrote about their parts of the South. That dismissive label has been abandoned, which probably improves their reputations. Many were important purveyors of the plantation myth; others wrote about sturdy yeomen or quaint rustics up the hollers. Two to be aware of:

467. JOEL CHANDLER HARRIS (1848–1908) was an able publicist for old Uncle Remus and his tales of Br'er Rabbit, told "in the simple but picturesque language of the Negroes, just as the Negroes tell them." Harris said Uncle Remus had "nothing but pleasant memories of the discipline of slavery," but the tales show clever critters winning by cunning what they can't win by strength. Uncle Remus was Harris's creation, but the stories were authentic black folktales, many with African origins. Harris was a popular and prolific writer, a longtime colleague of Henry Grady (**7, 997**) at the *Atlanta Constitution,* and an influential critic and editorialist on issues like race and economic development.

Joel Chandler Harris. Albert Volberg

Some of his thirty-plus books offer sympathetic portraits of Georgia "crackers."

468. CHARLES WADDELL CHESNUTT (1858–1932), son of free North Carolina blacks, served as principal of the black normal school in Fayetteville before he moved to Ohio, passed the bar, and opened a court-reporting firm, which prospered and gave him time to write. His first published story, in 1887, was the *Atlantic Monthly*'s first story by a black writer. The narrator of the stories in *The Conjure Woman,* Uncle Julius, is modeled on Uncle Remus but turns the faithful servant into a subversive whose tales show the injustices of plantation life, so Chesnutt can "lead people out, imperceptibly, unconsciously, step by step" to an awareness of the rights of blacks.

469. **Kate Chopin** (1851–1904) lived most of her life in St. Louis's French Catholic community. In a youthful diary, she complained about "men whose only talent is in their feet," observed that a flirt just had to ask "What do *you* think?" to succeed, and said she hoped to avoid "the useless degrading life of most married ladies." Despite her bad attitude, she made a good (and happy) marriage. She then moved to Louisiana (**732**), where she discovered the Creoles and Cajuns of her fiction. Back in St. Louis after her husband died, she wrote to make money, with immediate success, but her second novel, *The Awakening* (1899), was condemned as immoral: "Its disagreeable glimpses of sensuality are repellent," one critic wrote, and another said that "the purport of the story can hardly be described in language fit for publication." Even her own library withdrew her book, and the St. Louis Fine Arts Club kicked her out. Her work languished in the ghetto of "local color" until the 1970s, when feminist critics rediscovered its subtle characterization and the modernity of its moral ambiguity.

470. **Walter Hines Page** (1855–1918) left North Carolina for New York, where he edited the *Atlantic Monthly* and founded and edited *World's Work.* He supported the New South (**7**) movement but was strongly critical of almost everything about his birthplace. He founded Doubleday, Page & Company (for which we're grateful) and published Southerners like Ellen Glasgow (**498**), Sidney Lanier, Thomas Dixon, Jr. (**496**), Charles Chesnutt (**468**), and Booker T. Washington (**390, 449**). He continued to work for change in the South and became less public in his criticism—training in diplomacy that later stood him in good stead as ambassador to the Court of St. James's.

Twentieth-Century Fiction and Poetry

ANTEBELLUM LITERATURE DEVELOPED A repertoire of distinctive themes that marked Southern literature into the twentieth century: the plantation tradition, vernacular humor, local color, and the black story of ascent to freedom. But it wasn't great literature—until suddenly, in the 1920s, it was. What happened?

Willie Morris. W. R. Ferris Collection, University of Mississippi Special Collections

WHY SO MUCH SOUTHERN LITERATURE?

471. **"Great writers are exiles,** either spiritually or geographically," says critic Louis Rubin, and it rings true. Earlier Southern writers were embedded in their communities, but when modernity intruded in this century, many young people's experience differed from the community's received wisdom. Rubin says that "the impulse to write is the impulse to give order and definition to one's world, and such a desire can arise only out of need." All this applies to black writers as well as white, of course.

472. **Living outside the South** often triggers writing: Katherine Anne Porter said living abroad "gave me back my past and my own house and my own people—the native land of the heart." Robert Penn Warren "became a Southerner by going to California and to Connecticut and New England." Willie Morris realized that in New York "the sensitive outlander might soon find himself in a subtle interior struggle with himself, over the most fundamental sense and meaning of his own origins." Most Southern writers seem to have said something similar, and many have been hit by double or triple whammies—having a Yankee parent, or being Roman Catholic or Jewish or gay or even just very bookish or very poor.

473. **Mississippi,** the least modern state when modernity began to intrude, produced a mess of writers, black and white. Willie Morris thought it "the only state in the Union (or certainly one of a half dozen in the South) which had produced a genuine set of exiles, almost in the European sense: alienated from home yet forever drawn back to it, seeking some form of personal liberty elsewhere yet obsessed with the texture and the complexity of the place from which they had departed as few Americans from other states could ever be."

ALTERNATIVELY:

474. **The experience of defeat.** Walker Percy: "Why has the South produced so many good writers? Because we got beat." Hunter S. Thompson: "I've always felt like a Southerner. And I always felt I was born in defeat. And I may

have written everything I've written just to win back a victory. My life may be pure revenge."

CHARACTERISTICS OF SOUTHERN LITERATURE

NONE OF THESE IS unique to Southern letters, but, taken together, they do seem to describe the phenomenon. We'll let Southern writers speak for themselves.

475. **A sense of history.** Allan Gurganus: "I'm an imaginative historian. It's my obligation to dream out of history." William Faulkner, in *Intruder in the Dust:* "Yesterday today and tomorrow are Is: Indivisible: One." Robert Penn Warren's character Jack Burden: "If you could not accept the past and its burden there was no future, for without one there cannot be the other, and . . . if you could accept the past you might hope for the future, for only out of the past can you make the future." Black writers, too, are drawn to the past in search of their identity. Ernest J. Gaines: "I was trying to go back, back

Ernest Gaines. W. R. Ferris Collection, University of Mississippi Special Collections

into our experiences in this country to find some kind of meaning to our present lives."

476. **A sense of place.** Eudora Welty: "I am myself touched off by place. The place where I am and the place I know . . . are what set me to writing my stories. [Southerners feel] passionately about Place. Not simply in the historical or philosophical connotation of the word, but in the sensory thing, the experienced world of sight and sound and smell, in its earth and water and sky and in its seasons." Ernest Gaines: "I wanted to smell that Louisiana earth, feel that Louisiana sun. . . . hear that Louisiana dialect. . . . there's no more beautiful sound anywhere."

477. **A sense of community,** rooted in place. Louis Rubin: "What makes the oft-remarked Sense of Place in Southern fiction so important is the vividness, the ferocity even, with which it implies social and community attitudes." Josephine Humphreys: "The natural setting of Southern fiction is not wilderness nor farm nor city. It is town. For the most part, . . . that is the place that has seemed most fitting for the kind of stories we have wanted to tell—narratives of the human community."

478. **Family** can be the most important community. The Southern writer who does *not* write about family is an oddity. "The South is the South's cousins, honey" (Allan Gurganus, *Oldest Living Confederate Widow Tells All*). Ben Robertson, quoting a family letter: "Life is but a day at most, then why not spend it among one's own?"

479. **Love of storytelling.** Robert Penn Warren: "Storytelling and copulation are the two chief forms of amusement in the South. They're inexpensive and easy to procure." The emphasis is

Robert Penn Warren. W. R. Ferris Collection, University of Mississippi Special Collections

"the complex Southern tactic of assaying a sort of running start, a joke before the joke, ten assumptions shared and a common stance of rhetoric and a whole shared set of special ironies and opposites." Roy Reed: "No discussion, sermon, or quarrel should be telescoped when it can be drawn out all afternoon with endless opportunity for dodging, feinting, and keeping one's position obscured. . . . Indirection is not dishonesty. It is simply a matter of style." Allen Tate: "The typical southern conversation is not going anywhere; it is not about anything. It is about the people who are talking." Its goal is "to make everybody happy."

481. **Love of language** may be directly related to early and frequent encounters with the Bible. Eudora Welty: "How many of us, the South's writers-to-be of my generation, were blessed in one way or another, if not blessed alike, in not having gone deprived of the King James Version of the Bible. Its cadence entered into our ears and our memories for good. The evidence, or the ghost of it, lingers in all our books."

Eudora Welty. W. R. Ferris Collection, University of Mississippi Special Collections

on what W. J. Cash called "that innocent love of personal detail native to Southerners," on the concrete and particular rather than abstractions. A character in Nancy Lemann's *Lives of the Saints* understands this: "Then Mr. LaSalle started philosophizing to me about women 'You see, dawlin, women like to be led. Women are the weaker sex. It's human nature, precious,' he said. 'Cut it out, you two,' said Henry. As a rule, Southerners do not like philosophical conversations."

480. **A leisurely, conversational approach** that's deeper than it appears. Will Barrett, in Walker Percy's *The Last Gentleman*, describes

482. **A culture steeped in religion.** Mary Ward Brown: "People talk about God the way they talk about the weather, about His will and His blessings, about why He lets things happen." White and black experience may differ a bit here—black religion has been heavier on support and salvation, white heavier on guilt—but both stress "the grave who counts us all" (Allen Tate).

483. **Race** has been what Allan Gurganus calls a subject of "unending terror and fascination and unending richness" for many white writers, and certainly it was the great subject for a generation of black ones (**509, 512**). But some very Southern white writers hardly talk about it at all. Lee Smith couldn't identify with Faulkner: "It might have been set in New York or Greece or somewhere. . . . In the county that I grew up in, there were no black people." Doris Betts agrees: "I come out of yeoman farmers and Piedmont red clay country. There weren't many

Alex Haley. W. R. Ferris Collection, University of Mississippi Special Collections

slaves there, and there wasn't an aristocratic tradition at all." Even many Southern black writers don't see race relations as their main theme. Like Zora Neale Hurston, Jean Toomer, and others in the Harlem Renaissance, they're looking to their pasts, to their roots—loss of community is their subject. Robert Deane Pharr was one of the first, in *The Book of Numbers* (1969), followed by Randall Kenan, Clifton Taulbert, Tina Ansa, Chalmers Archer, James Alan McPherson, and others. Many black writers now call themselves Southerners and speak of the sense of community, shared experience, manners, food. Alex Haley said Southerners, black and white, were "raised better than people in the North." Alice Walker: "I think there's hope in the South, not in the North."

484. **The Southern grotesque.** Flannery O'Connor, who wrote it best, also talked about it best: "I have found that any fiction that comes out of the South is going to be considered grotesque by the Northern critic, unless it is grotesque, in which case it is going to be considered realistic." Some Southerners get all defensive and flustered when the topic comes up, but most of us have just learned to quote the inimitable O'Connor: "Whenever I'm asked why Southern writers particularly have a penchant for writing about freaks, I say it is because we are still able to recognize one. To be able to recognize a freak, you have to have some conception of the whole man." Seriously, "The novelist with Christian concerns will find in modern life distortions which are repugnant to him, and his problem will be to make these appear as distortions to an audience which is used to seeing them as natural . . . to the hard of hearing you shout, and for the almost-blind you draw large and startling figures."

485. The influence of Faulkner has been hard to ignore. He has been a blessing and a burden for other Southern writers, most of whom until recently either tried to write like him or tried *not* to write like him. Flannery O'Connor: "No one wants his mule and wagon stalled on the same track the *Dixie Limited* is roaring down. [Faulkner's presence] makes a great difference in what the writer can and cannot permit himself to do." Allan Gurganus: "I've tried to blow in the wind that is always sort of swooping off of William Faulkner's work." But Eudora Welty demurred: "It was like living near a big mountain, something majestic—it made me happy to know it was there, all that work of his life. But it wasn't a helping or hindering presence. Its magnitude, all by itself, made it something remote in my own working life. When I thought of Faulkner it was when I *read.*"

486. Being called a Southern writer can get tiresome. Flannery O'Connor said, "The woods are full of regional writers, and it is the great horror of every serious Southern writer that he

Doris Betts. Photo by Jerry Bauer

will become one of them." Doris Betts complains about "that cramped quality of being a southern writer." Florence King's greatest regret is being "tagged as a Southern Writer . . . I still get letters from Emory and Vanderbilt grad students writing theses on 'Studies in Neo-Agrarian Torment.' I don't like Southern writing; all the novels seem to be about three generations of women who sit on the porch and talk for 400 pages."

FOUR LITERARY MOVEMENTS WITH SOUTHERN ROOTS

487. The Fugitives (fleeing the "high-caste Brahmins of the Old South") began in 1914 in Nashville as a philosophical discussion group under guru Sidney Mttron (yes) Hirsch (**500**). After World War I, with John Crowe Ransom as mentor, they concentrated on poetry, publishing a "little magazine," the *Fugitive*. The leading Fugitives—Ransom, Allen Tate, Donald Davidson, and Robert Penn Warren (**508**)—all became, at the very least, major poets. Studying poetic modernism and reading H. L. Mencken forced them to confront the effects of modernity on the South and led them to take their stand as Agrarians (**922**).

488. "The Southern Renaissance" (or Renascence) was a phrase coined by writer Frances Newman (**502**) in the *New York Herald Tribune* in 1925, referring to the flowering of Southern literature. It had hardly begun—almost no one we think of as a Renaissance writer had published by then—but the Fugitives were in full bloom, and other promising writers were budding: T. S. Stribling, DuBose Heyward, Evelyn Scott (**503**). Actually, Newman was egotistical enough to see herself as a one-woman renaissance.

489. **The Harlem Renaissance** of the 1920s was largely the product of expatriate black Southerners like Langston Hughes (Joplin, Missouri), James Weldon Johnson (**497**) (Florida), Zora Neale Hurston (**507**) (Florida), and Arna Bontemps (Louisiana). They didn't just write about black life in the urban North; they tried to come to terms with the rural Southern culture of their childhoods. Three magazines were especially important: the NAACP's *Crisis,* edited by W. E. B. Du Bois (**391**); the Urban League's *Opportunity* (subtitled *A Journal of Negro Life),* edited by Virginian Charles S. Johnson (**838**); and the *Messenger,* published by the Brotherhood of Sleeping Car Porters (founded by A. Philip Randolph [**392**]).

490. **The New Criticism** sprang from the intellectually fecund atmosphere at Vanderbilt in the 1930s. Inspired by John Crowe Ransom's critical theories, his students Cleanth Brooks and Robert Penn Warren (**508**) began a critical revolution in *Understanding Poetry* (1938) by rejecting emphasis on biography and literary history: "(1) Emphasis should be focused on the poem; (2) Discussion of all poems should be specific, concrete and inductive; (3) A poem, if it is to be fully understood, must always be treated as an organic system of relationships and never thought to be included in one or more isolated parts." That book was followed by *Understanding Fiction* (Brooks and Warren, 1943) and *Understanding Drama* (Brooks and Robert B. Heilman, 1945). They radically changed the teaching of literature.

Langston Hughes, a major figure in the Harlem Renaissance. Library of Congress USZ62-43605

Cleanth Brooks. W. R. Ferris Collection, University of Mississippi Special Collections

THE REPUBLIC OF LETTERS

George Garrett, man of letters. Photo © University of Virginia

491. Southern "men of letters"—the old phrase for it—have always interpreted the job description broadly. Edgar Allan Poe (**455**) and William Gilmore Simms (**456**) are classic examples, combining the callings of poet, fiction writer, critic, and editor. Their twentieth-century heirs have often worn an additional hat, that of teacher. Many of the Fugitives–Agrarians–New Critics filled the bill, and there are dozens working today. Many studied with two remarkable teachers:

492. WILLIAM BLACKBURN (1899–1972) was a professor (at Duke), not a writer. His Elizabethan poetry course was incandescent—learned, theatrical, fearless. His "composition" class emphasized the craft of fiction, using Brooks and Warren's text (**490**) ("Show, don't tell" should be his epitaph). He was gruff, devastating, and in-spiring—in exactly the right balance, as a partial list of his students shows: William Styron (**527**), Guy Davenport, Mac Hyman, George Zabriskie, Reynolds Price, Wallace Kaufman, Anne Tyler (**532**), Fred Chappell, James Applewhite, Angela Davis-Gardner, Charlie Smith, and Josephine Humphreys.

493. LOUIS D. RUBIN, JR. (b. 1923), is a writer (nearly fifty books and counting) and editor of distinction, founder of one of the most influential small presses in America, Algonquin Books (**494**), and arguably the most important living critic of Southern literature. His students include notable scholars (Anne Goodwyn Jones, Lucinda MacKethan, Anne Bradford Warner), editors (Shannon Ravenel), and writers (John Barth, Lee Smith, Annie Dillard, Sylvia Wilkinson, Kaye Gibbons).

Louis Rubin. *The Chapel Hill News*

Commercial publishing is more than ever a New York/New England enterprise. However,

494. SMALL SOUTHERN PUBLISHERS are flourishing. Algonquin Books of Chapel Hill publishes dozens of Southern writers and an important annual, *New Stories from the South*. Nashville's John Sanders reprints Southern classics. Oxmoor House, the publishing arm of *Southern Living*, covers cooking, gardening, quilting, and expensive coffee-table books *(Land of the South* is an excellent atlas). Yoknapatawpha Press does Mississippi writers, with a strong line in Faulkneriana. August House covers folktales, folk humor, and fiction. Atlanta's Peachtree has an eclectic list including classic Southern fiction, Doug Marlette's cartoons, and Lewis Grizzard's third wife's memoirs, and Longstreet Press is similar. John Blair has an interesting miscellaneous line, and Jonathan Williams's Jargon Society has published poetry, photography, and *White Trash Cooking*.

495. SOUTHERN UNIVERSITY PRESSES have published much of the South's history, poetry, autobiography, and serious fiction since the first Southern university press was founded at North Carolina in 1922. University presses are especially valuable for keeping worthy books in print, a job most commercial houses have abandoned. In 1994 Georgia listed 126 Southern books, Tennessee 109, and North Carolina Press 105. LSU's *Encyclopedia of Southern History* (1979) and North Carolina's *Encyclopedia of Southern Culture* (1989) made our work much easier.

A PASSEL OF TWENTIETH-CENTURY LITERARY FIGURES

SOME NAMES TO KNOW, and why:

496. **Thomas W. Dixon, Jr.** (1864–1946), is best known for *The Clansman: An Historical Romance of the Ku Klux Klan* (1905)—bad history and worse literature, but a million-seller and the basis for *The Birth of a Nation* (**955**). Dixon wasn't an ignorant bigot, he was a well-educated bigot: graduate of Wake Forest and Johns Hopkins, state legislator, lawyer, actor, playwright, movie producer, and Baptist minister (with huge churches in Boston and New York). He wrote nearly thirty books and made and lost several fortunes.

Thomas Dixon. Library of Congress USZ62-110941

497. James Weldon Johnson (1871–1938) led a remarkable life as a school principal, publisher, lawyer, songwriter and lyricist on Broadway, consul to Venezuela and Nicaragua, editor, poet, writer of autobiography *(Along This Way)* and fiction *(The Autobiography of an Ex-Coloured Man)*, Fisk professor, and longtime field secretary of the NAACP. He's best known for *God's Trombones: Seven Negro Sermons in Verse* and his poem "Lift Every Voice and Sing" ("the Negro national anthem"). His use of black folk material and language was innovative and influential.

498. Ellen Glasgow (1873–1945) set out to write a social history of Virginia in fiction. She pondered the "evasive idealism" of Southern society, the tradition of the Southern lady (she

Ellen Glasgow. Library of Congress USZ62-103578

helped found the Equal Suffrage League of Virginia), and the reconciliation of past and present. She said the South needed a good dose of blood (she didn't mean blue, though she wrote about the declining aristocracy) and irony. Her own irony was heavy-handed at first, but by 1904 she'd found the balance, and *The Romantic Comedians* (1926), *They Stooped to Folly* (1929), and *The Sheltered Life* (1932) are witty comedies of manners. Her 1942 Pulitzer Prize was for a lesser effort, clearly belated recognition of her life's work. Louis Rubin has called her "simply, the first really modern Southern novelist."

499. James Branch Cabell (519) (1879–1958) was born in Richmond to a father with old family and a mother with new money. His time at William and Mary was difficult: he was known for his yellow gloves and cane, and was called Sister. He left college under a cloud of rumor, deeply hurt by the gossip. He came home to find his parents separated (unthinkable in Richmond society) and his mother smoking and drinking cocktails (ditto). Cabell worked successfully as a journalist, despite rumors that he had murdered his mother's lover (his cousin). His autobiographical mytho-comical fiction satirized Richmond society, and his success was assured when a New York court suppressed his novel *Jurgen* for lewdness. He's nearly forgotten today—his work is a little too fey for late-twentieth-century audiences.

500. Sidney Mttron Hirsch could be called the father of the Fugitives **(487)**. The son of a merchant, he grew up (like Frances Rose "Dinah" Shore) Jewish in Nashville. He ran away to sea, became heavyweight champion of the Pacific Fleet, and came home via the Far East, Europe, and New York. On the way he soaked up Buddhism and Taoism, Rosicrucianism, the occult, etymology and other ologies, and bits of odd languages. He was a sculptors' model for Rodin and Gertrude Vanderbilt Whitney, and a friend of Gertrude Stein and Edwin Arlington Robinson. He wasn't a writer, exactly, but in 1913, for Nashville's May Festival, he wrote a pageant involving chariot races, six hundred actors, three hundred sheep, and one thousand pigeons. No wonder the young Fugitives-to-be, mostly ministers' sons and suchlike, were enthralled.

501. Elizabeth Madox Roberts (1886–1941) won critical and popular acclaim for her novels *The Time of Man* (1926) and *The Great Meadow* (1930). Captivated by the pioneer experience, she lyrically explored the vast distance (physical and metaphorical) between the settled coast and the frontier. Historian Clyde Wilson has called her "the grandmother of modern Southern writers," who "rendered the American pioneer experience into art as well as it has ever been rendered." In Southern academic circles she's having something of a vogue as the South's Virginia Woolf.

502. Frances Newman (1883–1928) wrote acerbic reviews, an erudite study of the short story, and two elegant, tightly controlled stream-of-

H. L. Mencken called Frances Newman "a violet of the Sahara." Courtesy Enoch Pratt Free Library, Baltimore

consciousness novels about the elegant, tightly controlled, suffocating lives of aristocratic Southern women: *The Hard-Boiled Virgin* (banned in Boston) and *Dead Lovers Are Faithful Lovers*. She's known today chiefly for coining the phrase "Southern Renascence" (**488**) but ought to be known for her novels.

503. Evelyn Scott (1893–1963), born Elsie Dunn, changed her name at age twenty when she ran off to Brazil with the married head of Tulane's tropical medicine school. She seems to have been *born* a radical feminist, and her autobiographical *Background in Tennessee* and *Escapade* should be the next trend in women's studies. *The Wave*, a big avant-garde Civil War novel (really), was praised for its "intellectual lucidity" and "powerful and bitter moral vision," but it does go on and on: each chapter is a separate short story with new characters. Faulkner's publisher suggested that *The Sound and the Fury* would "place Faulkner in company with Evelyn Scott."

504. Caroline Gordon (1895–1981), novelist and short story writer, was a generous adviser and friend to Flannery O'Connor, Walker Percy, and decades of students. Her response to the manuscript of Percy's first novel was thirty-two typed pages, beginning, "You've made every mistake it is possible for a beginner to make." Percy (not just in gratitude) has called her "one of the modern masters of the short story." As literateur Allen Tate's (**487**) wife she was also hostess to the entire Southern literary world.

505. William Faulkner (1897–1962) spent most of his life in Oxford, Mississippi. During World War I he joined the Canadian Air Force but saw no action. After a spell of posturing and bad poetry (locals called him Count No 'Count), he

The wall of McDonald's, Oxford, Mississippi. DixiePix

The young Thomas Wolfe. North Carolina Collection, University of North Carolina Library, Chapel Hill

found himself by founding mythical Yoknapatawpha County (15,611 people, 2,400 square miles, "William Faulkner, sole owner and proprietor"), the setting of most of his fiction. As the champion modern American (not just Southern) writer, he's known for difficult points of view and convoluted sentences and he reveled in modernist techniques, but he wrote about a traditional world (Ralph Ellison admired his handling of black life), and he was the greatest storyteller of them all. Critical success doesn't sell books, however: when Malcolm Cowley published *The Portable Faulkner* in 1948, all the novels were out of print. After that nadir Faulkner's fame, sales, and influence increased: he won the Nobel Prize in 1950, a Pulitzer in 1955 (finally) and another in 1963, and today country-music lyricists can casually drop his name into lyrics. Pretty good for a high school dropout.

506. **Thomas Wolfe** (1900–38) wrote of his youth in Asheville, Chapel Hill, and New York. He controlled the form of his first novel, *Look Homeward, Angel,* but nothing thereafter. His editor, Maxwell Perkins, radically changed *Of Time and the River,* and another editor created Wolfe's later "novels" from the million words of

manuscript left when he died. His relations with editors continue to provide fodder for scholars, who rarely talk about what he actually *wrote.* Wolfe spoke directly to generations of young adults. Doris Lessing has said that "he did not write *about* adolescence: to read him is to re-experience adolescence"—dreadful idea. Critics harp on his flaws, perhaps a bit embarrassed that he once moved them in ways better writers did not.

507. **Zora Neale Hurston** (1903–60), from all-black Eatonville, Florida, studied at Howard and at Barnard, where anthropologist Franz Boas encouraged her interest in Southern black folklore. A Harlem Renaissance (**489**) star, she wrote fiction (*Their Eyes Were Watching God,* 1937), autobiography (*Dust Tracks on a Road,* 1942), essays, drama, and folk studies (*Mules and Men,* 1935 [**128–30**]). But she died alone and poor, and her books were gradually forgotten. Maybe they weren't angry enough: they were about strong black communities, and

Zora Neale Hurston. Photo by Alan Lomax/Library of Congress USZ61-1859

black women with gumption and intelligence, and a South that leavened its segregation and discrimination with "human touches." Alice Walker (**530**) rediscovered Hurston in the 1960s and bought her a tombstone that read, "A genius of the South." She has now influenced a generation of readers, particularly black women, but you don't have to be black or female to appreciate her use of language and her deft portrayal of a culture.

508. **Robert Penn Warren** (1905–89) astounds. The sheer volume of his work would be overwhelming even if it weren't masterful—in every genre. He's the only writer to have won Pulitzers for poetry *and* fiction. He also won about every other prize (except the Nobel) and was the nation's first poet laureate. As a New Critic (**490**) he transformed the study of literature. As an editor *(Southern Review)* he nourished other writers. As an essayist he formed our thinking

about the South and American race relations. He thought of himself, however, as a poet and of poetry as "a way of getting your reality shaped a little better." James Dickey (**515**), a fair wordsmith himself, says, "When he is good, and often when he is bad, you had as soon read Warren as live."

509. **Richard Wright** (1908–60) is known for *Black Boy,* a didactic fictionalized autobiography, and especially for *Native Son,* which won him a Guggenheim before it was finished, was a Book-of-the-Month Club selection, and sold 200,000 copies in three weeks. Extremely influential and extremely controversial, *Native Son* offers in Bigger Thomas, its protagonist, one of the memorable characters of modern American fiction. Wright's friend Ralph Ellison observed, however, that "Bigger Thomas had none of the finer qualities of Richard Wright, none of the imagination, none of the sense of poetry, none of the gaiety." Ellison found *Native Son* simplistic, too narrow, too "sociological."

Richard Wright. Library of Congress USW3-39285D

510. Eudora Welty (b. 1909) has a "shining fidelity to place" (her phrase about Faulkner) that made her a great documentary photographer before she became a great writer. Add perfect pitch for Southern speech, clear-eyed compassion for overlooked lives, and a wry sense of humor, and you get stories that are simply wonderful. They're in *Collected Stories*. Maybe the best of the novels are *Losing Battles* and *The Optimist's Daughter* (which won a Pulitzer in 1973), though it's not an easy choice. See also *One Writer's Beginnings* (a memoir) and *The Eye of the Story* (criticism).

511. Tennessee Williams (1911–83), Mississippi-born dramatist, won Pulitzers for *A Streetcar Named Desire* (1948) and *Cat on a Hot Tin Roof* (1955) (**960**) and most of the other applicable awards. In good Southern fashion, he invented much of his biography, which is *not* the same as his plays, despite strong resemblances ("I write from my own tensions"). *The Glass Menagerie* (1944) was his first hit. His plays often made highly successful movies ("I want to reach a mass audience"). He was always a mess, and it caught up with him in the 1960s: his work and his reputation declined. Like many other Southern writers, he wrote about outsiders: "the faded and frightened and difficult and odd and lonely," the disturbed, the oversensitive—some of the most memorable characters in modern theater.

A streetcar named Desire. Historic New Orleans Collection, acc. no. 1974.25.37.103

512. Ralph Ellison (1914–94) is known chiefly for *Invisible Man* (1952), his only novel, but a great one. (Henry Louis Gates, Jr., calls it "an encyclopedia of black culture.") Unlike Richard Wright, Ellison refused to limit himself to "the uneasy sanctuary of race" and chose, in his words, "to affirm those qualities which are of value beyond any question of segregation, economics, or previous condition of servitude." He wrote twenty-one stories, a number of essays, and a legendary incomplete second novel—350 pages were lost in a house fire, and he left 1,000–2,000 pages of manuscript, soon to be published. He called himself a Southern writer; like many others, he wanted to understand history to be free of it.

513. Walker Percy (1916–90) was an M.D. who never practiced, from a distinguished and literary Mississippi family, and one of the South's surprisingly numerous Roman Catholic writers. He was profoundly serious but not preachy: "A good deal of my energy as a novelist comes from *malice*—the desire to attack things in our culture." Novels like *The Moviegoer* and *The Last Gentleman* offer insight, but rarely resolution. "Life is fits and starts, mostly fits. Life doesn't have to stop with failure." Writing out of a long family history of depression and suicide, Percy said he "would like to think of starting where Faulkner left off, of starting with the Quentin

College student/moviegoer Walker Percy (in light-colored trousers), in Chapel Hill. North Carolina Collection, University of North Carolina Library, Chapel Hill

Compson who *didn't* commit suicide. Suicide is easy. Keeping Quentin Compson alive is something else."

514. Flannery O'Connor (1925–64) found success early (easy publication and prestigious fellowships), but at age twenty-five she contracted disseminated lupus and went home to Milledgeville, Georgia, where she became increasingly crippled and died at thirty-nine. An unlikely amalgam of Catholicism and Southwestern humor (**458**), her work reveals a mordant wit and a faultless ear for Southern speech, but it makes many readers uncomfortable. Her stories—in which, as one critic wrote, "the repulsive good defeats the urbane evil"—can be as garish as the roadside attractions that once dotted the South. In her world, the desperate need for Christian salvation requires a violent response like John Donne's: "Batter my heart, three-personed God . . . / That I may rise and stand, o'er throw me, and bend / Your force to break, blow, burn and make me new."

515. James Dickey (b. 1923) is a poet (*Buckdancer's Choice*, 1965), a novelist (*Deliverance*,

1970 [**962**]), teacher, major prizewinner, sometime actor, former adman, eternal ladies' man, and liar. George Garrett says the Southern talent for storytelling leads some writers like Harry Crews and James Dickey "to invent new and colorful lives and selves as a part of their art." Dickey himself admits "the creative possibilities of the lie." (Another writer has said, "Dickey sounds like he's lyin' even when he's tellin' the truth.") Good thing he's a good writer.

516. A. R. Ammons (b. 1926) has won all the poetry prizes and fellowships, including a MacArthur, and Harold Bloom calls him "the central poet" of our generation. He's also prolific, with twenty-eight books at last count. Critics have praised his "exquisitely unencumbered technique" and his "entrancing Southern storytelling voice." Even his titles can be marvelous: *Garbage; The Really Short Poems of A. R. Ammons; Shit List, or, Omnium-gatherum of Diversity into Unity.*

A. R. Ammons. Photograph by Curt Richter

517. Ernest J. Gaines (b. 1933) is best known for *The Autobiography of Miss Jane Pittman* (1971), a million-seller that became a TV movie (**959**) that won nine Emmys. All his work is set in fictional Bayonne, Louisiana, and it's richly historical, realistic without being polemical. "Black writers have to do more than work out their anger on paper," he has said. His books not only sell, they've won him innumerable grants and prizes.

518. Charles Wright (b. 1935) won the prestigious 1993 Ruth Lilly Poetry Prize, to add to his National Book Award, PEN Translation Award, and a clutch of others. His family was classically Southern. His mother dated Faulkner's brother Dean and was called "the fairest flower of the Delta" by writer William Alexander Percy. His great-grandfather caught a minié ball in his palate while yelling "Charge" at the Battle of Shiloh. His poetry is Southern, too. Kathleen Agena says he has a "mad sense of language."

Charles Wright. Nancy Crampton

He says he writes about "landscape, and the idea of God," and adds, "I wanted to be thought of as a Southern writer." Happy to oblige.

The Pulitzer Prize is given for many reasons, not all of them literary. William Faulkner and Ellen Glasgow both got it late, and for the wrong books; in 1933 T. S. Stribling's politics were clearly more laudable than his prose; etc. Here are some winners that we haven't already mentioned. Most are worth reading, and all are worth thinking about.

519. JULIA M. PETERKIN, *Scarlet Sister Mary* (1929). Wife of a plantation manager, Peterkin wrote sympathetic novels, praised by blacks and whites, about the self-sufficient Gullah community (**95**). W. E. B. Du Bois (**391**) said, "She is a Southern white woman, but she has the eye and the ear to see beauty and know truth." The heroine of this one is strong, sensual, and smart.

James Branch Cabell and Julia Peterkin. South Caroliniana Library, University of South Carolina

520. CAROLINE MILLER, *Lamb in His Bosom* (1934). A fine novel about the hard life of a pioneer wife and mother in the Georgia backwoods. It won the French Prix Femina, was a bestseller, and went through nearly forty editions before going out of print.

Gone With the Wind merchandise, Underground Atlanta. DixiePix

521. MARGARET MITCHELL, *Gone with the Wind* (1936). Sold a million copies the first year and, at last count, was the most popular novel of this century. A novel critics love to hate: "the fantasies of a fatally genteel and superficial imagination," a "camp classic," "narrowly patriotic, prudish, melodramatic, and sentimental." Readers love it, which must explain why it beat out Faulkner's *Absalom, Absalom* for the Pulitzer. Them that's got shall get. (See **956**.)

522. MARJORIE KINNAN RAWLINGS, *The Yearling* (1939). A serious, unsentimental writer (see also *Cross Creek* and *South Moon Under),* Rawlings "suffered from having her beautiful pas-

toral story . . . made into a lachrymose Disney movie, so that ever after she has been thought of, when remembered at all, as a sentimental juvenile writer," says critic Clyde Wilson.

523. JAMES AGEE'S *A Death in the Family* (1958) may not be a great novel, but it's a great book. The prologue has inspired music (**626, 720**) and dance (by Alvin Ailey [**628**], 1961). It's set in Knoxville when, as Agee put it, "I lived there so successfully disguised to myself as a child." Alfred Kazin said Agee's "power with English words can make you gasp"—and his evocation of childhood will make you weep. (See **453** and **780**.)

524. HARPER LEE, *To Kill a Mockingbird* (1961). Lee's only novel, written from the point of view of a child, tackles perennial Southern themes of race and community. It was a selection of the Literary Guild and the Book-of-the-Month Club and made a fine movie (**964**).

525. SHIRLEY ANN GRAU, *The Keeper of the House* (1965). A good read and a good book. Family, miscegenation, strong women, and revenge. What more can you ask?

526. KATHERINE ANNE PORTER, *Collected Stories of Katherine Anne Porter* (1966). Another Southern writer who "improved" her childhood (on a Texas dirt farm) for the press, Porter led a glamorous, difficult life and seemed to write best when it was most difficult. She was a great short story writer (Eudora Welty admired the "invisible surface" of her style). We wish whoever borrowed our copy would return it.

527. WILLIAM STYRON, *The Confessions of Nat Turner* (1968). A "meditation on history," condemned by many black scholars for bad faith

William Styron. Photograph by Curt Richter

and bad history but defended as history by Eugene Genovese and C. Vann Woodward. A more telling charge has been that it's bad psychology. Woodward called it "the most profound fictional treatment of slavery in our literature," but think about the competition.

528. JAMES ALAN MCPHERSON, *Elbow Room* (short stories, 1978). A Savannahian with a Harvard Law degree, McPherson teaches writing at the Iowa Writers Workshop, where he earned his M.F.A. He has won all the big fellowships. He has said of his characters: "Certain of these people happen to be black, and certain of them happen to be white; but I have tried to keep the color part of most of them far in the background, where these things should rightly be."

529. JOHN KENNEDY TOOLE, *A Confederacy of Dunces* (1981). Toole, a brilliant misfit who entered Tulane at age sixteen, killed himself in 1969 at age thirty-two. His mother unsuccessfully shopped the novel around to publishers before persuading Walker Percy to sponsor it. LSU Press published it in 1979 and sold over forty thousand copies in a year. Percy describes the protagonist as "intellectual, ideologue, deadbeat, goof-off, glutton," "slob extraordinary, a mad Oliver Hardy, a fat Don Quixote, a perverse Thomas Aquinas rolled into one."

530. ALICE WALKER, *The Color Purple* (1983). Walker is one of many Southern writers whose work has offended other Southerners, especially after it reached mass audiences through the movies. (Thomas W. Dixon [**496**], James Dickey [**515, 962**], Pat Conroy, and Tennessee Williams [**511, 960**] also come to mind). Some black men detested the male characters in *The Color Purple*—novelist Ishmael Reed called the film a "Nazi conspiracy." But Walker would be important if she had done nothing else but rediscover Zora Neale Hurston (**507**), and she has also won tons of fellowships and prizes. Not bad for a sharecropper's daughter.

531. PETER TAYLOR, *A Summons to Memphis* (1987). Taylor wrote about the subtle social codes of the urban upper-middle class and the "dislocation and slow destruction of the family as an institution" (Andrew Lytle)—"manners privately practiced, standards privately held" (Walter Sullivan). Allen Tate was briefly his teacher: "I asked him to leave the class after about two weeks. The simple truth is that he did not need to know anything I could teach him. He had a perfection of style at the age of 18 that

Peter Taylor. Photograph by Curt Richter

I envied. If the South has produced a Chekhov, he is Peter Taylor."

532. ANNE TYLER, *Breathing Lessons* (1989). Raised on communes and in Raleigh, educated at Duke, Tyler writes about "a Baltimore with only Southern exits" (Robert McPhillips). Miss Welty's literary daughter, Tyler considers family and privacy, lives where not much happens. We prefer *Dinner at the Homesick Restaurant* and *The Accidental Tourist.*

533. We're stumped. So many wonderful writers, so little space. We can't begin to do right by Ellen Douglas, Elizabeth Spencer, Mary Lee Settle, or George Garrett. Then there's Madison Smartt Bell, Wendell Berry, Doris Betts, Larry Brown, Fred Chappell, Pat Conroy, Harry Crews, Clyde Edgerton, Kaye Gibbons, Ellen Gilchrist, Gail Godwin, Allan Gurganus, Barry Hannah, Donald Harington, William McCranor Henderson, Josephine Humphreys, Randall Kenan, Bobbie Ann Mason, Cormac McCarthy, Jill McCorkle, Michael McFee, Lewis Nordan, Charles Portis, Reynolds Price, Lee Smith, etc. . . . We won't even try to list the young ones with only a book or two to their credit.

THE SOUTHERN MYSTERY

WITH ALL THE *SERIOUS* writers we haven't discussed, it seems frivolous to talk about hammock reading. But mysteries with Southern settings, by Southern writers, are coming on strong these days. Three authors of more than commercial interest:

534. James Lee Burke, best known for his books featuring Cajun detective and boat-dock owner Dave Robicheaux, is unsurpassed at portraying the seamy side of his native Gulf Coast—"that quasi-rural slum culture that has always characterized the peckerwood South: ramshackle nightclubs with oyster-shell parking lots; roach-infested motels that feature water beds and pornographic movies and rent rooms by the day or week; truck stops with banks of rubber machines in the restrooms; all-night glaringly lit cafes where the smell of fried food permeates the counters and stools as tangibly as a film of grease" (from *In the Electric Mist with Confederate Dead*).

535. **Carl Hiaasen,** reporter and columnist for the *Miami Herald,* has developed a strong sideline in fast-paced and funny stories of crime and chicanery among the drug dealers, Yankee tourists, real estate developers, theme park operators, and assorted other lowlifes that populate modern south Florida. In books like *Skin Tight, Double Whammy,* and *Native Tongue,* it's hard to miss the strong undercurrent of nostalgia for the old Florida of crackers, Seminoles, and swamps.

536. **Patricia D. Cornwell** is a former police reporter who worked for the Virginia chief medical examiner's office and did a biography of Mrs. Billy Graham before writing *Postmortem,* the first of her award-winning mysteries starring Richmond forensic pathologist Kay Scarpetta. Cornwell's books are set in a modern, urban South with modern, urban creeps and psychopaths to provide the corpses for her heroine to autopsy.

IT'S NOT TOO FAR off the mark to say that insofar as there has been *American* music, it has been *Southern* music. See if you don't agree.

Southern Religious Music

ELEVEN O'CLOCK ON SUNDAY morning is said to be the most segregated hour of the week, and certainly religious music has been a racially divided affair. But that doesn't mean that black music and white music haven't profoundly influenced each other.

TRADITIONAL WHITE SACRED MUSIC

537. **White spirituals** came out of the great revival periods of the eighteenth and nineteenth centuries (**823–24**), when worshipers needed more personal, intense music. Folk hymns and religious ballads like "Amazing Grace" and "Wayfaring Stranger" put religious texts to secular tunes. Camp-meeting spirituals like "Won-

"The family sang line by line." *The Great South* (1875)

drous Love" have simpler texts, frequent repetition, refrains, and inserted tag lines: they're easily taught by "lining out." Often using old-fashioned modal or gapped scales, they were published in shape-note books and were sung mostly in rural areas.

538. **Shape-note hymnody** uses shaped note heads to represent the notes of a scale. The old system, sometimes called fasola, uses four syllables; tunes are harmonized in three or four parts with the melody in the tenor and are sung unaccompanied. Reynolds Price has called the result "that eerie set of hymns, harsh as scraped glass but hot as mystic transport." *The Sacred Harp,* the best known hymnbook, was first published in 1844 by two Georgians; the latest revision came out in 1992 and sold fifteen thousand copies in three years. Singers sit in a hollow square, grouped by part, with a leader in the middle. This isn't concert music; it's energetic, unsubtle, and best when you're in the square.

"Amazing Grace" (New Britain). *Southern Harmony,* 1854

539. **A newfangled seven-shape system** caught on after the Civil War and is still in use, although it's more popular with worshipers than with folklorists. Among seven-noters there's another schism, between those who sing unaccom-

WELCOME
SACRED HARP SINGING

Embroidery by Ethel Mohamed. W. R. Ferris Collection,
University of Mississippi Special Collections

isfying occasion combining four Southern obsessions—religion, music, food, and conversation.

540. **White gospel music** comes in several forms. Country gospel is just country music with religious content, often recorded by performers like Roy Acuff (or Elvis, for that matter) along with their secular repertoire; the close-harmony duo, like the Louvin Brothers, is popular. Gospel quartets, usually all male, do both soulful and up-tempo numbers, with or without instrumental accompaniment. The Statesmen, the Blackwood Brothers, and the Jordanaires (who later sang backup for Elvis) are good examples, as are the Statler Brothers, who became stars when they switched to secular music. Composer Albert Brumley contributed more than six hundred songs to the repertoire, including such standards as "If We Never Meet Again," "Turn Your Radio On," and "I'll Fly Away." In recent years, pop-flavored numbers have captured a market that extends well beyond the South, but many of the performers, like Amy Grant, are Southerners.

panied and those who use instruments (which these days can include drums and electric guitars). For all shape-note singers, however, an all-day singing and dinner on the grounds (those words always go together) is a deeply sat-

BLACK SPIRITUALS AND GOSPEL MUSIC

541. **Black spirituals,** like white ones, grew out of nineteenth-century camp meetings (**825**), where the races mingled freely. The balance of white and African ancestry in black spirituals is a matter of hot debate: the ring shout (**135**), which is definitely African, uses call and response, but call and response was also common in white evangelical churches, and part-singing came from whites. Black spirituals are about trial, sorrow, and the hope for freedom. Frederick Douglass wrote, "A keen observer might have detected in our repeated singing of 'O Canaan, sweet Canaan, I am bound for the land of Canaan' something more than a hope of reaching heaven." Concert performances of spirituals by groups like the Fisk Jubilee Singers (**838**) introduced them to a wider public in the late nineteenth century. Soloists like Roland Hayes, Marian Anderson, and Paul Robeson broadened the audience. In the 1930s and 1940s spirituals surviving in parts of the South, especially the Sea Islands (**28**), were recorded and archived in the Library of Congress.

542. **Black gospel music** emerged early in this century from the potent mix of blues, spirituals, ragtime, and shape-note. It has dominated black religious music and has had a symbiotic relationship with black secular music (**566**). Like the blues, it produced an abundance of legends, like Sister Rosetta Tharpe of Cotton Plant, Arkansas, whose raw, bluesy style made her the hit of the Newport Jazz Festival in 1978; Clara Ward ("queen of the moaners") and the Ward Singers, who toured with Aretha Franklin's father; the Five Blind Boys of Mississippi, whose ecstatic screaming style produced similar hysteria in the congregation; and the Dixie Hum-

mingbirds, an influential, long-lived quartet who recorded with Paul Simon. North Carolina's Shirley Caesar is one of today's leading gospel artists.

Traditional Secular Music

543. **Folk music** was first collected for publication in William Francis Allen's *Slave Songs of the United States* (1867). Black spirituals got most of the attention until an Englishman named Cecil Sharp traveled southern Appalachia between 1916 and 1918 collecting folk songs and ballads. Sharp hinted at an exciting (if imaginary) fossilized English folk culture preserved in the mountains (which explains why the public was so dubious about "hillbilly" music when it appeared: it didn't sound at all like "Barbara Allen"). Platoons of collectors have been "catching songs" and folktales ever since.

544. **Protest songs** in the South are at least as old as slave spirituals, but in the twentieth century they became important tools of the labor and civil rights movements, which adapted

Striking textile workers. Jack Delano, Farm Security Administration/Library of Congress USF33-20926

songs new and old to the struggle. Some great ones are "Which Side Are You On?," "Dark as a Dungeon," "We Shall Not Be Moved," "Oh, Freedom," and, of course, "We Shall Overcome" (the Revised Standard Version of C. A. Tindley's "I'll Overcome Some Day"). The folk fad circa 1960 (**598**) had young Americans of all political persuasions (well, almost all) humming along.

The Birth of the Blues—and Ragtime and Jazz

IN THE YEARS JUST before 1900, otherwise probably the low point in their history (**366**), black Southerners brought forth three remarkable musical forms: ragtime, the blues, and jazz. Each was the product of obscure and often anonymous genius.

RAGTIME

545. **Ragtime** piano music, created almost entirely by black Southerners, has roots in minstrel-show cakewalks, most of them composed, ironically, by Northern white men burlesquing the Southern black tradition. Classic ragtime had a strict form (an opening flourish and contrasting sections), a strong bass line, syncopation ("ragged time") possibly derived from banjo music, and melodies echoing plantation songs and dances. (Later, Tin Pan Alley used "rag" to mean almost any swingy song, as in "Alexander's Ragtime Band," but we're not talking about that.) Early ragtime was a product of the outer South. Several pioneers lived in St. Louis, where Tom Turpin's Rosebud Cafe nourished their activity. Turpin, a former Nevada gold miner, wrote

Street musicians, Montgomery, Alabama, 1939. Marion Post Wolcott, Farm Security Administration/Library of Congress USF33-30321

"Harlem Rag" (1897), the first published rag by a black composer.

THE BLUES

BLUES originally came in three varieties, geographically defined.

546. **Delta blues,** the ur-blues, originated with anonymous black musicians in the Mississippi Delta (**22**), south of Memphis. These blues ain't nothing but a good man singing about feeling bad, usually accompanied by guitar (often fretted with a bottleneck) and sometimes by harmonica. The classic three-line, twelve-bar pattern, where the second line repeats the first and the third rhymes, is found in Celtic ballads, but Delta bluesmen like Charley Patton (**586**), Son House, Robert Johnson (**587**), and Big Joe Williams made it their own, and the blues became for the Jim Crow period what spirituals had been in slavery times.

547. **The Piedmont blues** of the Carolinas and Georgia were more influenced by ragtime, white

Mississippi John Hurt, by Lamar Sorrento. Red Piano Too Art Gallery, St. Helena Island, S.C

country music, and popular song than their Delta counterpart. Smaller black populations and less rigid segregation than in the Deep South probably account for that. Piedmont bluesmen like Blind Blake (**588**), Blind Boy Fuller, Reverend Blind Gary Davis, and Blind Willie McTell also usually displayed greater instrumental virtuosity, if less passion, than their Mississippi cousins. From the eastern South musicians like Josh White, Sonny Terry, and Brownie McGhee went to New York, where they figured in the folk-music revival.

548. **Texas blues** were also eclectic, incorporating flamenco licks from Mexico and (after 1930) influences from white Western swing (**559**). The lyrics of singers like Blind Lemon Jefferson, Clarence "Gatemouth" Brown, and Lightnin' Hopkins tended to have a stronger narrative line than the Delta blues. Migrants like T-Bone Walker and Albert Collins kept the Texas blues

tradition alive in California to influence young West Coast bluesmen. It has survived in Texas largely in the music of white musicians (most of them Austin-based) like Stevie Ray Vaughan, Marcia Ball, Delbert McClinton, Lou Ann Barton, and the Fabulous Thunderbirds.

FROM THESE ROOTS CAME many other kinds of music, some called blues, some not.

549. **Boogie-woogie** is a piano style developed around 1900, probably in New Orleans. Just uptempo twelve-bar blues over a driving, repetitive bass figure, boogie-woogie moved with Southern blacks to the North, where it was often called barrelhouse music after its natural habitat. Developed and popularized by musicians like Cow Cow Davenport and Pine Top Smith, both from Alabama, boogie-woogie became a popular-music craze in the 1930s, often in big-band arrangements. Later it returned to the South and the original blues instrument as guitar boogie, a species of country music.

550. **Chicago blues** are basically the Delta blues, taken north by migrants from the Deep South, electrified, and backed with a band. The process  began before World War II with artists like Big Bill Broonzy (b. Scott, Mississippi), the first of the two harmonica-playing Sonny Boy Williamsons (b. Jackson, Tennessee), and pianist-composer Memphis Slim (b. Memphis). Important postwar figures include Mississippians Muddy Waters, Howlin' Wolf, Jimmy Reed, songwriter Willie Dixon, and slide guitarist Elmore James as well as singer Koko Taylor and mouth harpist Junior Wells, both from Memphis.

This Delta diaspora was concentrated in Chicago, but the incomparable John Lee Hooker went to Detroit instead.

551. **Vaudeville blues** were women's business: orchestrated, theatrical, jazz-flavored stuff by powerful female singers like Georgia's Ma Rainey, Houston-born Victoria Spivey, Bessie Smith of Chattanooga (**589**), and Ethel Waters from Chester, Pennsylvania (of all places). Performed in touring revues (**574**) and eventually recorded, this music was so well known that it came to be thought of as "classic" blues, but coming from sophisticated composers like W. C. Handy (**590**), it was hardly that, and it's probably better regarded as an early form of pop music.

John Lee Hooker. Connie Ives—Hot Shot Photos

552. **Blues shouting** came later, during the swing era of the 1940s, and it was for guys. Identified largely with Kansas City, it numbered among its exponents local boy Big Joe Turner, Oklahoman Jimmy Rushing, and Arkansan Jimmy Witherspoon. This form of declamatory band-backed blues singing contributed to—

553. **Rhythm and blues** (R&B), the 1950s name for the "race music" of the 1940s: a jumped-up, often orchestrated, dance-worthy kind of blues, with a heavy backbeat later picked up by rock and roll. Notable Southern-bred R&B artists included bluesmen like John Lee Hooker and Muddy Waters, blues shouters like Big Joe Turner and Wynonie Harris, and band singers like Ruth Brown and Big Mama Thornton as well as vocal groups like the Drifters (with Clyde McPhatter and, later, Ben E. King). Originally segregated in the "chitlin circuit" of black night-clubs and juke joints, R&B mesmerized white teenagers across the South who tuned it in on black-oriented radio stations like Nashville's WLAC. Early black rock and rollers like Little Richard, Fats Domino, Chuck Willis, and Bo Diddley came directly out of this tradition.

554. **Swamp blues,** a minor but interesting genre, originated in the Baton Rouge area, where musicians like Slim Harpo, Lightnin' Slim, Lonesome Sundown, and Lazy Lester developed a unique, rocking, Cajun-influenced blues style, captured after 1948 on Excello records. It appealed particularly to British rockers of the 1960s (the Rolling Stones covered Harpo's "I'm a King Bee," for instance, and the Kinks recorded Lazy Lester's "I'm a Lover Not a Fighter") and eventually contributed to the development of zydeco (**569**). Among the few surviving exemplars is "swamp boogie queen" Katie Webster.

NEW ORLEANS JAZZ

555. **Dixieland jazz** started when black musicians in the Crescent City got hold of cast-off

Preservation Hall preserves New Orleans jazz. DixiePix

probably of African origin, was—like "jitterbug" and "rock and roll"—originally a coarse reference to copulation. By a natural process "jazz music" came to refer to the stimulating sounds coming out of New Orleans's red-light district.

556. **White Dixieland** came along early. Nick La Rocca learned jazz cornet as a New Orleans teenager, and by 1916 he was in Chicago leading a group called Stein's Dixie Jass Band (the first recorded use of the word "jazz" in this context). The next year the all-white group moved to New York as "the Original Dixieland Jazz Band"— which, of course, it wasn't—made the first jazz recordings, and triumphantly toured England. La Rocca was not the last New Orleans jazzman whose whiteness was an asset (Al Hirt and Pete Fountain come to mind), but he was not merely a rip-off artist: he composed "Tiger Rag," "Clarinet Marmalade," and other classics.

Country Music

Civil War military band instruments. To European instruments and popular American tunes, African-Americans added what came to be called the swing. Originally played by marching bands for wedding and especially funeral processions, jazz moved indoors, acquired piano and often banjo accompaniment, but kept its basic shape: melody usually in the trumpet, with clarinet and trombone supplying filigree, and bass (or tuba) and drums for rhythm. Jazz funerals can still be found (**609, 760**): a band plays the body to the graveyard with the mournful strains of "Just a Closer Walk with Thee"; then the funeral party, including "second line" cakewalkers, parades back home to raucous songs like "Didn't He Ramble?" The word "jazz,"

MEANWHILE, WHITE FOLKS WERE doing their own thing, especially in the Southwest and the Southern uplands, where they didn't have many black folks to make music for them.

557. **Country (or country and western) music** really got under way when phonographs and radio programs (especially, after the 1930s, broadcasts from Nashville's Grand Ole Opry) turned isolated rural folks into a mass audience. The first country-music hit was Fiddlin' John Carson's "Little Old Log Cabin in the Lane," recorded by Ralph Peer in Atlanta in 1923. Even Peer thought it was "pluperfect awful," but it set off a boom in "hill-billy" music, which *Variety* called the "sing-song nasal-twanging vocalizing"

Mountain musicians, 1937. Ben Shahn, Farm Security Administration/Library of Congress USF3301-06258-M2

of Southern mountaineers with "the intelligence of morons." But there was gold in them thar hills, and Peer struck it again in 1927 in Bristol, Tennessee, when a call for singers of "prewar melodies and old mountaineer songs" brought the Carter Family (**594**) and Jimmie Rodgers (**593**) to his studio.

COUNTRY MUSIC HAS ALWAYS been eclectic, and there has always been a tension between commercialization and "authenticity." Three important early variants emerged in the 1940s.

558. **Bluegrass** music, originated by Bill Monroe (**599**), builds on traditional string-band music, usually featuring guitar, banjo, mandolin, bass, fiddle and/or dobro (a form of slide guitar), but adds a driving bluesy rhythm, jazzlike displays of virtuosity, and gospel-inspired high vocal harmonies. A remarkable number of early bluegrass musicians passed through Monroe's Blue Grass Boys, among them Lester Flatt, Earl Scruggs, Jimmy Martin, Carter Stanley (of the Stanley Brothers), and Sonny Osborne (of the Osborne Brothers). College audiences picked up on bluegrass during the 1960s folk revival (Monroe

played at the 1963 Newport Folk Festival), and it's often heard today in strangely suburban settings. Bluegrass also lends itself to festivals: one of the biggest is Monroe's own, in Bean Blossom, Indiana.

559. **Western swing** is basically a Texas-accented big-band sound, featuring twin fiddles, horns, pedal steel guitar, accordion, and most anything else, playing an eclectic mix of country ballads, blues, and jazz. Especially popular in Texas and Oklahoma and among migrant white Southerners in California, it reflects Texas's ethnic mix (**17, 87, 104–5, 111–12**), combining old-time string-band music, Jimmie Rodgers (**593**), ragtime, Dixieland jazz, German band music, Mexican polkas, and the blues. Texan bandleader Spade Cooley once claimed the title "King of Western Swing," but Bob Wills (**600**) and His Texas Playboys are generally recognized as the music's major innovators and popularizers.

560. **Honky-tonk music,** as its name suggests, came out of the taverns of the Southwest, but its

George "Possum" Jones gets an award. Connie Ives—Hot Shot Photos

combination of keening steel guitar and weepy lyrics, often dealing with drinking, cheating, divorce, and other problems of middle age, is now found on country jukeboxes worldwide. It's pretty much a male genre, defined in the 1940s and 1950s by Ernest Tubb ("Walking the Floor over You") and Lefty Frizzell ("If You've Got the Money, Honey, I've Got the Time"), and almost personified by their fellow Texan George Jones ("He Stopped Loving Her Today"). "New Traditionalists" (**563**) often mine the same vein.

LATER DEVELOPMENTS HAVE INCLUDED:

561. **The Nashville Sound.** In the late 1950s, Nashville recording studios replaced pedal steel and fiddle with guitar and piano, added violins and backup vocal groups, and generally tried to imitate singer Eddy Arnold's success in decountrifying country music for a larger national audience. Chet Atkins—guitarist, producer, and RCA executive—is generally credited with (or blamed for) this development, in recordings like the Browns' "The Three Bells," Don Gibson's "Oh, Lonesome Me," Jim Reeves's "He'll Have to Go," and Skeeter Davis's "The End of the World."

562. **The Outlaws.** In the early 1970s some country musicians, mostly in Austin, rebelled against the smooth sonorities of the Nashville Sound and began to do it their way—simultaneously hip and stone country. In 1976 two of the leading outlaws, Texans Willie Nelson and Waylon Jennings, had a number one hit with "Good Hearted Woman," and the anthology *Wanted: The Outlaws* became country music's first platinum album. Their success ended their outlaw status: both Nelson and Jennings quickly won top music-industry awards, and Nashville absorbed this revolt without changing a great deal.

563. **The New Traditionalists.** In the early Reagan years a determinedly reactionary movement appeared, harking back to the pure older tradition. (In fact, *Pure Country* was the title of a film starring movement elder George Strait.) Kentucky's Ricky Skaggs, an accomplished bluegrass musician before becoming a solo artist, was influential early on, and North Carolina's Randy Travis was a very successful recruit, but it

Randy Travis. Connie Ives—Hot Shot Photos

Willie Nelson. Connie Ives—Hot Shot Photos

was primarily Strait's homage to the Texas honky-tonk sound that inspired a generation of singers traditional in both their music and their cowboy attire (thus, their label in the trade, "hat acts"). Ironically, the traditionalists have attracted larger audiences than the Nashville Sound ever did: Garth Brooks even made it to the cover of *Time* magazine.

Rock and Roll and Just Plain Rock

ROCK AND ROLL CAME to pass when country music met rhythm and blues. The influence went both ways.

564. **Rockabilly's** marriage of black and white styles was not unprecedented, but full stylistic miscegenation dates from Elvis Presley's (**606**) first release on Sam Phillips's Sun Records. Soon rockabillies were coming out of the woodwork: white boys from Norfolk (Gene Vincent), Lubbock (Buddy Holly), and everywhere in between, but most from within a couple of hundred miles of Memphis, where the influence of black music was strongest—for example, Conway Twitty (Friars Point, Mississippi), Carl Perkins (Tiptonville, Tennessee), Johnny Cash (Kingsland, Arkansas), Jerry Lee Lewis (Ferriday, Louisiana), Johnny and Dorsey Burnette (Memphis), Ronnie Hawkins (Huntsville, Arkansas), and Charlie Rich (Colt, Arkansas). Those from elsewhere, like Roy Orbison (Vernon, Texas) and the Everly Brothers (Brownie, Kentucky), tended to have noticeably "whiter" styles. As the fifties ended, so did rockabilly: Buddy Holly died, Elvis was drafted, Jerry Lee was ostracized for marrying his cousin. Most old rockabillies turned to pop, country, or generic rock and roll, but English revival groups and a few touring performers like Sleepy LaBeef keep the faith even today.

565. **Rockin' rhythm and blues.** In the wake of the rockabillies' success some rhythm and blues artists began to record for the new, larger (and whiter) audience. Some had already been listening to country music: it's no accident that Missourian Chuck Berry, whose songs shared many of its features (notably a strong narrative line), was one of the most successful with white audiences. Berry acknowledged the country influence, as did Tennessean Bobby "Blue" Bland, who said, "We used to listen to the radio every morning to people like Roy Acuff, Lefty Frizzell, Hank Williams, and Hank Snow."

ROCK AND ROLL SOON went national and lost its regional flavor, but in later years, occasional developments reminded rock fans where it all started. Two of the most significant:

566. **Soul music** was the 1960s transmutation of R&B. Unlike Detroit's slicker Motown Sound, which was aimed at a mass (i.e., national and mostly white) market, sweet soul music was down-home, secularized black gospel music. Pioneered by Ray Charles (**607**) and then by Sam Cooke (formerly of the Soul Stirrers), full-blown soul was exemplified by Southern-rooted black performers like Otis Redding, Aretha Franklin, James Brown, Wilson Pickett, Gladys Knight, Percy Sledge, Sam and Dave, and Joe Tex. Their audience included white Southern college students, who have since embalmed it as "beach music." Many of the session musicians were white boys from recording studios in Memphis and Muscle Shoals, and a guitar obbligato on Aretha Franklin's "Think" sounds an awful lot like "Dixie." But the collaboration worked: New

York producer Jerry Wexler said it was because "they were all Southerners."

567. **Southern rock** was white, an odd 1970s amalgam of classic Delta blues, hard-edged country music, early Southern rock and roll, and 1960s psychedelia. Longhaired country boys (Charlie Daniels's phrase) displayed attitudes and musical licks of the counterculture with a distinctively down-home spin, celebrating Southern rural life, Southern women, and Southern places. Duane Allman, session guitarist for many famous soul singers in the 1960s, brought his blues-style "slide" guitar to the Allman Brothers Band, and the Charlie Daniels Band celebrated the movement in its song "The South's Gonna Do It Again." Other important groups were the Marshall Tucker Band, Wet Willie, and Lynyrd Skynyrd, whose "Free Bird" has been called the redneck national anthem. The movement peaked about the time Georgian Jimmy Carter, who claimed to be a fan, won the presidency.

Cajuns at a fais-do-do, 1938. Russell Lee, Farm Security Administration/Library of Congress USF34-31634-D

Louisiana Music

AS USUAL, SOUTH LOUISIANA has its own way of doing things.

568. **Cajun music** was pretty much ignored outside Louisiana—and sometimes in it, too—until recently. It's played by a fiddle or two and a Cajun accordion, with triangle *(petit fer)* and guitar for rhythm. The local accordion is limited to four chords, so it's better for dancing than for plain listening. Lyrics are in Cajun French, of course. One classic is "Sweet Jole Blon" (i.e., *jolie blonde).* One relatively well known group is

the Balfa Brothers, and Doug Kershaw has introduced Cajun sounds to country music.

569. **Zydeco,** the music of *black* French Louisiana, was even more obscure than its Cajun cousin until it experienced a vogue in the 1980s. The word is a corruption of *les haricots* (beans—from the lyrics of one popular song), and the music is a sort of cross between R&B and Cajun. The accordion is front and center (usually no fiddles), with rhythm from triangle, washboard or "rub-board" (worn on the chest), and guitar. Some groups have recently added saxophone. Clifton Chenier (d. 1987) was the King of Zydeco in his generation; Rockin' Dopsie

and Buckwheat Zydeco are notable current performers.

Some Southern Aspects of Modern Jazz

AFTER JAZZ LEFT ITS Louisiana home, it settled in the cities of the North and West and underwent some startling changes. But Southern-bred musicians were still on the job. Two of the most baffling developments:

570. **Bebop** got its name from scat singers' "hey bop a rebop," which may have echoed the "*arriba!*" of Latin bands. Although forged in New York, "bop" was the creation of expatriate black Southerners, notably guitarist Charlie Christian (b. Bonham, Texas), pianist Thelonious Monk (Rocky Mount, North Carolina), saxophonist Charlie Parker (Kansas City), and trumpeter Dizzy Gillespie (**609**) (Cheraw, South Carolina). Beginning about 1940, they moved jazz in new, complex, and often obscure directions, away from simple harmonies and basic rhythms. In part, they were just bored, but they also meant to play music too difficult for the white musicians who got most of the well-paid gigs.

571. **Free jazz,** like bebop, was a Northern creation by black Southern musicians. An improvisational form that abandoned harmony and chordal structure altogether, free jazz nevertheless showed a strong blues influence, with instruments imitating the human voice. Most jazz historians date the genre from 1959, when Or-nette Coleman (b. Fort Worth) introduced it to New York's Five Spot Club. Later, saxophonist John Coltrane (Hamlet, North Carolina) took it to the limit with a forty-minute improvisation called "Ascension." Opinions differ violently about whether free jazz was a good thing, but its admirers included Leonard Bernstein and John Lewis (the musician, not the congressman [**396**]).

Pop Music

COMMERCIAL POP MUSIC HASN'T been a Southern speciality, especially after its consolidation in New York. Although many Southerners have been successful performers and songwriters, they've generally had to leave the South to do it. What *is* often "Southern," however, is the subject matter of American popular music. Three phenomena in particular are worth noting.

572. **Minstrel shows** became wildly popular throughout the United States in the 1840s, with blacked-up white men performing "plantation songs" that were usually either borrowed from Irish originals or written by Yankee composers like Thomas Rice, Dan Emmett, and Stephen Foster. Groups like the Virginia Minstrels and the Ethiopian Serenaders featured stock characters like the dim-witted Jim Crow and the dandy, Zip Coon. Only the banjo and bones these guys played (along with tambourine, fiddle, and accordion) had much to do with African-American culture, but after the Civil War, in a sad sort of feedback phenomenon, blacks formed their own troupes and wrote songs for the minstrel stage (**611**). By 1900 black-face minstrelsy was in decline, although it remained a fund-raising

Midcentury minstrel show. Caufield & Shook Collection, Photographic Archives, University of Louisville

option for small-town white civic clubs past mid-century.

573. **Tin Pan Alley** began a long love affair with Dixie around 1890, turning out literally hundreds of formulaic songs about the region. Many were simply "coon songs" in the minstrel-show tradition, but others expressed affection or nostalgia for the South in terms suitable for white singers, incorporating the moonlight and magnolias myth also evident in fiction (**462**). A process of national reconciliation was made explicit by songs like "It Doesn't Make Much Difference Now, Who Wore the Blue or Grey" (1914). This tradition died of exhaustion sometime after World War II, but many of its themes made the transition to country, rock, and soul music.

574. **Revues,** extensions of the minstrel and vaudeville traditions and precursors of the mod-

Tin Pan Alley's view of the South.

ern musical, proliferated in the 1920s and 1930s. In the era of Harlem's Cotton Club, revues often featured black singers, dancers, and themes—many inevitably Southern. Bessie Smith (**589**), for instance, played both black and white theaters with her shows like *Yellow Girl Revue, Steamboat Days,* and *Happy Times.* James P. Johnson, the composer of "Charleston," also wrote shows like *Black Sensations, Plantation Days,* and *Keep Shufflin'.* Pianist Eubie Blake had a hand in *Shuffle Along, Chocolate Dandies,* and *Blackbirds of 1930.* These shows were essentially Jim Crow versions of the *Ziegfeld Follies,* but they popularized Southern black "shimmy" dances, some of which became national crazes.

Low-Down Dancing

BLACK SOUTHERNERS IN PARTICULAR have put some moves on the world.

575. The Shimmy became after 1900 the generic name for a family of dances that called for women to shake their, ah, booties and, um, upper torsos. Clearly of West African origin, dances of this sort (also known as the Shake) were al-

Juke joint, Frogmore, South Carolina. DixiePix

ways popular in the South and came to fruition in turn-of-the-century juke joints (low-rent nightspots where black folks gathered to get down). New Orleans pianist Tony Jackson supposedly first applied the word "shimmy" to them; another black New Orleanian, Spencer Williams, wrote "Shim-me-sha-wabble" in 1917; soon white girls throughout America were wishing they could shimmy like their sister Kate. Dance crazes with these roots include everything from Balling the Jack (1913) to the Twist (1960); among the most popular were:

576. The Charleston. The dance that came to stand for the Roaring Twenties was being done by Southern blacks before 1900. Touring black revues took it to a wider audience, but its international vogue dates from 1923, when it was performed in the *Ziegfeld Follies* and James P. Johnson composed the song of the same name. The dance made stars of Ginger Rogers and Joan Crawford.

577. The Black Bottom. The name was said to refer to a neighborhood in Nashville, but one of the characteristics of the dance was slapping one's behind. Its history was similar to the Charleston's: a juke-joint dance spread by black touring companies, it became a rage after it was incorporated in a white Broadway show *(Scandals of 1926)* and accompanied by an eponymous song.

578. The Big Apple. Named for the Big Apple Club in Columbia, South Carolina, this dance captured a national following after 1935. Derived from an earlier dance called the Shout (**135**), the Big Apple involved several couples in a circle, with a caller (rather like a square dance). Couples took turns strutting their stuff in the center of the circle.

Clarksdale, Mississippi, 1939. Marion Post Wolcott, Farm Security Administration/Library of Congress USF34-52594-D

579. The Lindy Hop. This dance from the black South combined vigorous shaking movements with a frantic athleticism—spins, flips, even splits. It was part of black revues by the 1920s, and promoters seized on the coincidence of its name to tie it to the 1927 Lindbergh flight, but its real popularity with white dancers had to wait until the era of big-band swing in the 1930s. It evolved into the Jitterbug, then subsided into "jive" or "swing dancing."

OVER AGAINST THIS WEALTH of black invention, white Southerners can only offer:

580. The Southern square dance, rediscovered by Cecil Sharp (**543**) at the Pine Mountain Settlement School in the Kentucky mountains about 1915. He loved it because it was just what he was looking for: a clear survival of European dance forms like the cotillion and the quadrille. Unlike those, however, its successive steps are "lined out" by a caller.

581. Clogging, a freestyle dance, often of great individuality—people all dance together, but do whatever they want (a metaphor for the South's own brand of individualism within the tight-knit Southern community). The late 1950s produced precision clogging, another thing altogether, with costumes, tap shoes, and tight choreogra-

Precision clogging. Courtesy Apple Chill Cloggers, Chapel Hill, N.C.

phy. Clogging isn't an Elizabethan survival or a variant on the Irish jig; it's not even very old—perhaps from the 1920s.

582. **The Shag,** the state dance of South Carolina, a Lindy Hop cooled down by white teenagers vacationing on the Carolina coast. Now a constantly evolving popular art form, it has its own contests, festivals, and music ("beach music"). (See **566** and **969.**)

583. **Country dancing,** a recent label for both traditional Southwestern couple-dances like the Texas two-step and alarming, choreographed, semi-aerobic "line dances." Once confined to honky-tonks, these dances experienced a brief national vogue in the early 1980s, inspired by the John Travolta movie *Urban Cowboy,* but it was a decade later, helped along by instructional videotapes and television programs like the Nashville Network's *Club Dance,* that they really acquired a mass following. Now dances with names like the Electric Slide and the Tush Push, done to songs like "Boot-Scootin' Boogie" and "Achey-Breaky Heart," can be observed in dance clubs throughout the South and beyond.

A Southern Music Hall of Fame

BELIEVE IT: WE *KNOW* who's left out.

584. **Charles "Buddy" Bolden** (1877–1931) is a mysterious figure. We know only that he was a powerful trumpet player, led an early New Orleans jazz band, had an alcohol problem, and spent the last half of his life in the state insane asylum. He was never recorded, but he profoundly influenced other musicians and was

Buddy Bolden and his band. Historic New Orleans Collection

clearly a founding father of jazz. Among the legends that have grown up about him is that his trumpet could be heard fourteen miles away.

585. **Scott Joplin** (1868–1917) grew up in a musical family in Texarkana, went to Missouri, hung out at the Rosebud Cafe (**545**), studied at a music school in Sedalia, and published "Original Rags" in 1899. "Maple Leaf Rag" was an immediate best-seller, and Joplin turned out many worthy successors. Moving to New York, he invested much time and money in *Treemonisha,* a ragtime opera; when he couldn't get it produced, he cracked up and died in an asylum. Nearly sixty years later his music was rediscovered, *Treemonisha* made it to the Met, and Joplin was recognized as an American genius.

586. **Charley Patton** (1891?–1934), who grew up on a Delta plantation, largely defined the Delta style: down and dirty, with percussive accompaniment on guitar, often played with a bottleneck slide. He also largely defined the role of Delta bluesman: itinerant, illiterate, dissolute, womanizing (eight wives, by some accounts), in and out of jail. A popular local performer throughout the 1920s, he began to record in 1929, and songs like "Pony Blues" and "High Water Everywhere" have become classics.

587. **Robert Johnson** (1911–38) was the complete bluesman: an extraordinary guitarist (the first to use a bass line adapted from boogie-woogie),

a singer of great emotional intensity, and an unusually gifted songwriter. ("Who says Mississippi hasn't produced great poets?" novelist Ellen Douglas once asked. "Haven't you ever heard of Robert Johnson?") The rumor that he had bartered his soul for greatness was fueled by songs like "Me and the Devil Blues" and "Hell Hound on My Trail." (The movie *Crossroads* [1986] was loosely based on this story.) Other Johnson classics include "Sweet Home Chicago," "Dust My Broom," "Walking Blues," and "Come on in My Kitchen." Johnson died at age twenty-seven, killed by one of the many jealous husbands he left in his wake. In 1990 a set of his complete recordings sold a half million copies and won a Grammy.

588. **Blind Blake** was born in Jacksonville, Florida, or maybe in the Georgia Sea Islands, in the early 1890s, or maybe in the 1880s. He went by several names, and died in 1933, or maybe as late as 1940, in Chicago, or maybe in Florida. He lived in Atlanta for a while, although nobody knows what he was doing there (probably playing on street corners—maybe the young Josh White was his "lead boy" for a time). He definitely moved to Chicago, began making records in 1926, and became one of the most popular male blues artists of the 1920s with songs like "Diddie Wa Diddie" and "Hard Pushing Papa." Blake is known for a complex fingerpicking technique that adapted ragtime to the guitar and laid the basis for the Piedmont blues style. His innovations greatly influenced later blues-

men as well as white guitarist Merle Travis, who popularized fingerpicking in country music.

589. **Bessie Smith** (1894–1937) and her brother, orphaned, sang and danced for change on Chattanooga street cor-

ners until she joined a touring vaudeville company featuring Ma Rainey, the Mother of the Blues. In the 1920s Smith moved to Philadelphia and began to record. Her first record sold nearly a million copies; she made scores more in the next decade, while touring both black and white theaters with her own shows (**574**) featuring pop songs and blues classics like "Young Woman's Blues," "Mama's Got the Blues," "Back Water Blues" (about the 1927 floods), and " 'Tain't Nobody's Business If I Do." Smith recorded with many jazz greats, notably with Louis Armstrong on W. C. Handy's "St. Louis Blues," and influenced singers from Mahalia Jackson to Janis Joplin. Her unfettered and disorderly personal life fit the great blues tradition. She died in a Mississippi car wreck (apparently *not* the victim of racist neglect, as was widely rumored).

590. **W. C. Handy** (1873–1958), a Florence, Alabama, preacher's son, studied and taught composition at Huntsville College and played cornet with brass bands and a touring minstrel show. In the 1890s he heard the blues in rural Mississippi and began to compose paler works based on them. ("I hasten to confess that I took up with low folk forms hesitantly. . . . wondering if they were quite the thing.") In 1914 he wrote "St. Louis Blues," the most widely recorded popular song ever; other hits followed, including "Beale Street Blues" and "Yellow Dog Blues."

W. C. Handy is still on Beale Street. DixiePix

Satchmo. Historic New Orleans Collection

Moving to New York, he set up a music-publishing business and the country's first black-owned recording company. Blindness after the 1920s did not slow his entrepreneurial activities. His book *Blues: An Anthology* (1926) greatly influenced the Harlem Renaissance (**489**), and the title of his autobiography, *Father of the Blues* (1941), isn't far off the mark. Nat "King" Cole played Handy in the movie *St. Louis Blues* (1958).

591. **Jelly Roll Morton** (1890–1941), born Ferdinand Lemott, was raised by his grandmother in New Orleans. Supporting himself by a variety of jobs, some illegal (time as a pimp probably accounts for his nickname), after 1906 he played piano in touring shows while composing entirely original music—songs like "Jolly Roll Blues" and "King Porter Stomp"—that linked the ragtime of the 1890s with the jazz of the

1920s. By 1923 he had settled in Chicago, where he began to record and started his great band, the Red Hot Peppers. By 1930, however, he had fallen behind the times, and he was largely forgotten until Alan Lomax recorded him for the Library of Congress in 1938.

592. **Louis Armstrong** (1901–71) learned to play cornet in a New Orleans orphanage, where he'd been sent for shooting a gun in the street to celebrate New Year's. As a teenager he replaced King Oliver in Kid Ory's band and as cornet king of New Orleans. After the closing of Storyville (**31**) he joined Oliver's Creole Jazz Band in Chicago. An inimitable jazz singer and arguably the world's greatest jazz trumpet player, Armstrong influenced hundreds of musicians, wrote a score of jazz classics, appeared in a dozen movies, and became an all-round great showman. He toured triumphantly in Europe

and Africa and returned to New Orleans as King of the Zulu Mardi Gras crewe. His autobiography, *Satchmo,* was published in 1953 (the nickname is short for "Satchel mouth").

593. **Jimmie Rodgers** (1897–1933), known variously as the Father of Country Music, the Blue Yodeler, and the Singing Brakeman, was the son of a railroad worker from Meridian, Mississippi. Rodgers worked on the railroad himself until ill health forced him to seek a living in music. Greatly influenced by the Delta blues, Rodgers's songs recorded at Ralph Peer's Bristol session (**557**) were an instant success, and he went on to record "T for Texas," "Brakeman's Blues," and other million-sellers, some with jazz or Hawaiian backing groups (and some with black sidemen, including, once, Louis Armstrong). Although suffering from tuberculosis (which he sang about in "TB Blues"), he joined Will Rogers in 1931 in a series of benefit performances for dust bowl victims. He collapsed and died after a marathon New York recording session. In 1961 he was one of the first inductees (with Hank Williams and Fred Rose) to the Country Music Hall of Fame.

594. **The Carter Family**—A. P. Carter, his wife, Sara, and his sister-in-law Maybelle—came from Maces Springs, Virginia, to nearby Bristol to record with Ralph Peer (**557**); soon after, Peer took them to New Jersey to record a dozen more songs, including "Wildwood Flower" and their theme song, "Keep on the Sunny Side." On some 270 recordings—original compositions, traditional mountain songs, and reworked

popular tunes—Sara usually sang lead and played autoharp, Maybelle sang harmony and played guitar, and A. P. sang bass. Maybelle's "Carter Family scratch" picking influenced guitar players like Leadbelly and Woody Guthrie. Songs like "I'm Thinking Tonight of My Blue Eyes," "Lonesome Valley," "Will the Circle Be Unbroken?" and "Wabash Cannonball" reappeared during the folk revival of the 1960s and have also become staples of the bluegrass repertoire. After the group disbanded in 1943, the original members and their children continued to perform. June, daughter of "Mother Maybelle," became a successful solo artist and married Johnny Cash; June's daughter Carlene Carter is now also a country-music star.

595. **Thomas A. Dorsey** (1899–1993), the Father of Gospel Music, began in the 1920s as bluesman "Georgia Tom" but abandoned the blues for gospel music (a name he probably invented) in 1932. He wrote about five hundred gospel songs, including "A Little Talk with Jesus," "There Will Be Peace in the Valley," and "Precious Lord, Take My Hand," which was translated into thirty-two languages, recorded by Aretha Franklin, and sung by Mahalia Jackson at Martin Luther King's funeral (**605**).

596. **John Lomax** (1867–1948) traveled the South and West collecting folk songs, aided in later years by his son Alan and daughter Bess Lomax Hawes. He deposited more than ten thousand songs in the Library of Congress Archive of Folk Song, including blues from Muddy Waters and prison and work songs from Leadbelly (who accompanied him on a prison tour). Without Lomax, there would probably have been no folk revival in the sixties and Scouts around campfires would be silent.

Greene County, Georgia, prison camp, 1941. Jack Delano, Farm Security Administration/Library of Congress USF34-44770-E

597. Leadbelly (1888–1949), born Huddie Ledbetter to poor sharecropping parents, wandered as a youth, worked in Shreveport's red-light district, learned to play the twelve-string guitar and other instruments, and went to prison twice, for murder and assault. Although this sounds like the life of a classic bluesman, Leadbelly wasn't that. He's best known for other kinds of music: work songs, cowboy songs, dance tunes, ballads, and spirituals. After his second release from prison, he moved to New York, fell in with left-wing folksingers like Pete Seeger and Woody Guthrie, and began to write songs like "Bourgeois Blues" and "Scottsboro Boys." Always poor, he died the year before the Weavers had a number one pop hit with his song "Good Night Irene."

598. Woody Guthrie (1912–67), Oklahoma boy, union organizer, and street singer, wrote songs about the Depression. Alan Lomax recorded him for the Library of Congress in 1940. He wrote, or adapted, at least a thousand songs, and if you remember the sixties, you know some: "This Train Is Bound for Glory," "So Long, It's Been Good to Know You," etc. Folkies like Bob Dylan and Phil Ochs readily acknowledge his influence. "This Land Is Your Land," originally intended as a radical alternative to "God Bless America," wound up being used for television commercials.

599. Bill Monroe (1911–96), the Father of Bluegrass Music, was born in Rosine, Kentucky, youngest of eight children in a musical family. Raised in the shape-note tradition (**538–40**), he learned to play from relatives and a local black musician named Arnold Schultz. A singer and mandolin player, he developed the distinctive "high lonesome" vocal sound of bluegrass with his brother Charlie. In the late 1930s he formed the first version of the Blue Grass Boys and became a fixture on the Grand Ole Opry. By 1946, with the addition of Earl Scruggs's innovative three-finger banjo playing, the bluegrass sound was complete. Monroe wrote a dozen bluegrass classics, both secular ("Blue Moon of Kentucky," "I Hear a Sweet Voice Calling," "I'm Going Back to Old Kentucky") and sacred ("I'm Working on a Building," "Walking in Jerusalem"). He received all the obvious awards and was honored by the U.S. Senate on his seventy-fifth birthday.

600. Bob Wills (1905–75), the major early proponent of Western swing music, grew up as Jim Rob Wills in west Texas, oldest of a fiddle-playing father's ten children. He moved to Fort Worth in 1929, changed his name when he joined a medicine show with too many Jims, and played with the Light Crust Doughboys (sponsored by a flour company on a local radio station). Fired from the Doughboys for drinking, he formed what became the Texas Playboys, settling eventually at a radio station in Tulsa. The Playboys had a million-seller with Wills's "New San Antonio Rose" in 1940. Wills took the band to California, where Okie war-workers loved it; he continued to tour and to record and made several forgettable movies. His health failed in the early 1960s, but he lived to see his profound influence recognized. The best of many tributes was Waylon Jennings's song "Bob Wills Is Still the King."

601. **Roy Acuff** (1903–92), the King of Country Music, was born a Baptist preacher's son in a three-room shack in Maynardville, Tennessee. After sunstroke ended his minor-league baseball career, he played fiddle with a medicine-show band and in 1936 cut two classic records, "The Wabash Cannonball" and "The Great Speckled Bird" (a gospel song). Acuff was a regular with the Grand Ole Opry, and his wartime records like "Wreck on the Highway" were so popular that Japanese troops on Okinawa reportedly charged with the cry "To hell with Roosevelt! To hell with Babe Ruth! To hell with Roy Acuff!" Acuff sold over 30 million records in his lifetime, organized the powerful music-publishing company Acuff-Rose, and in 1962 became the first living performer to be inducted into the

Country Music Hall of Fame. A loyal Republican, he ran unsuccessfully for governor of Tennessee in 1948, and at the opening of the new Opryhouse in 1974 gave yo-yo lessons to President Richard Nixon.

602. **Hank Williams** (1923–53) was born and raised in small-town Alabama (that's right), sang in a church choir, learned guitar from a black street musician, and played on a Montgomery radio station before joining the Grand

Hank Williams on tour. DixiePix

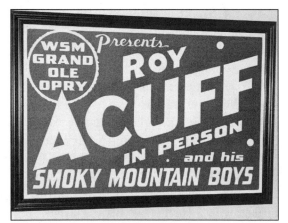

Roy Acuff at the Grand Ole Opry. DixiePix

Ole Opry in 1949. Fired by the Opry for drunkenness and divorced by his wife Miss Audrey, he died in the backseat of a car en route to a performance in 1953. By then he'd written and recorded two dozen classics, among them "Mind Your Own Business," "Moaning the Blues," "Cold, Cold Heart," "Half as Much," and "Your Cheatin' Heart." Over twenty thousand attended his funeral in Montgomery, and he has attained country-music immortality with almost as many songs *about* him as *by* him. His son Hank Jr. is also a star, with his own macho, country-rock sound and a string of Southern anthems like "The New South," "If Heaven Ain't a Lot like Dixie," and "If the South Woulda Won."

603. **Kitty Wells** (b. 1919), the Queen of Country Music, was born Muriel Deason in Nashville, took her stage name from a folk song, and began performing in the 1930s. In 1952 she became the first woman not part of a family group to be a genuine country star, with her number one hit, "It Wasn't God Who Made Honky Tonk Angels." Since then she has won all the big awards, sticking faithfully to her original country sound. Asked in 1995 which songs were her favorites, she replied, "I'm partial to those that made the most money." Her success paved the way for the next generation of female stars, notably Patsy Cline, Dolly Parton, Tammy Wynette, and Loretta Lynn.

604. **Johnny Mercer** (1909–76) grew up in Savannah. Before he was twenty-five he was recognized as an accomplished lyricist and was soon singing with Benny Goodman, Paul Whiteman, and Bob Crosby. (Music historian Peter Gammond observed that his "dry Southern drawl . . . gave his singing a distinctively good-natured character.") He collaborated with dozens of composers over four decades to produce such

gems as "Come Rain or Come Shine," "In the Cool, Cool, Cool of the Evening," "Too Marvelous for Words," "Hooray for Hollywood," "Blues in the Night," "That Old Black Magic," "One for My Baby," "Lazybones," and literally over a thousand more. He was cofounder of Capitol Records and won four Academy Awards.

605. **Mahalia Jackson** (1911–72) could only have come out of New Orleans's mix of blues, jazz, and gospel. In her teens she moved to Chicago and got a Decca contract in 1937. When "Move on up a Little Higher" sold a million copies and "I Can Put My Trust in Jesus" won the French *disque d'or* in 1951, an international career was launched. She entertained a Kennedy inaugural party and was the obvious choice to sing at the funeral of Martin Luther King, Jr.

606. **Elvis** (1935–77) eventually transcended the world of Southern music to become one of those mythic figures known to the world by their first names. (Of course it helped that his name wasn't, say, Robert.) But the Presley boy from Tupelo and Memphis, raised in the Assemblies of God (**815**), made his major contribution

The King with Duke University's best-known alumnus.
National Archives

to music history with his very first record in 1954: a country-flavored version of the R&B hit "That's All Right" backed with a bluesy rendition of the bluegrass classic "Blue Moon of Kentucky." This synthesis laid the foundation for rock and roll, and Elvis was well aware of where it came from: "The colored folk been singin' it and playin' it just the way I'm doin' now, man, for more years than I know. Nobody paid it no mind 'til I goosed it up." Eventually, like all too many other Southern musicians, he became the classic hero-victim, doomed by his own excesses. But the King remained to a remarkable extent what he was raised to be: a polite and humble gospel-singing Southern boy, who loved his mama, greasy food, and hanging out with the boys—and, never forget, a remarkable musical influence. As Bruce Springsteen said, "It was like he came along and whispered some dream in everybody's ear, and somehow we all dreamed it." (See **908, 968.**)

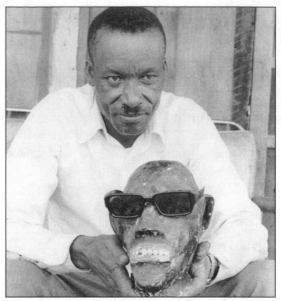

Sculpture of Ray Charles by Delta bluesman James "Son" Thomas. W. R. Ferris Collection, University of Mississippi Special Collections

607. **Ray Charles** (b. 1930), born Ray Charles Robinson in Albany, Georgia, learned to play piano after he went blind at the age of six. He had a couple of R&B hits in the 1950s, melding gospel and blues in songs like "I Got a Woman," anticipating later soul music, but his first monster hit was "What'd I Say," in 1959. Since then he has successfully recorded jazz, soul, and even country, as well as straight pop (**613**). His protean versatility exceeds even Elvis's, and his fame is sufficient to make him in demand for Pepsi commercials.

608. **B. B. King** (B. B. for "Blues Boy") (b. 1925) was born Riley Ben King in Indianola, Mississippi. Given his first guitar by a cousin, bluesman Bukka White, King grew up singing gospel music and worked as a farmhand, then as a disk jockey, while honing his complex, refined, jazz-

B. B. King, by Lamar Sorrento. Red Piano Too Art Gallery, St. Helena Island, S.C.

flavored guitar style. Extremely popular in the 1950s as a big-band blues performer, King caught on with rock audiences in the 1960s; he and his guitar "Lucille" influenced a generation of white guitarists. His pop-chart success with "The Thrill Is Gone" (1970) sent him from Las Vegas to Moscow as "Ambassador of the Blues." Recipient of innumerable awards and honorary degrees, King has been a generous supporter of institutions like the Delta Blues Museum, the University of Mississippi's Blues Archives, and the Center for the Study of Southern Culture. His new blues club on Beale Street (**45**) in Memphis is a major tourist attraction.

609. **Dizzy Gillespie** (1917–93), one of the fathers of bebop, was a showman as well as a supremely innovative musician. With his horn-rims, goatee, beret, puffed-out cheeks, and distinctive up-turned horn, Gillespie came to define the ideal of the cool jazz cat for many who had little understanding of or sympathy for what he was up to musically. In 1964 he announced his candidacy for president on a platform that included deporting George Wallace and making Ray Charles Librarian of Congress. His conversion to the benign Baha'i faith only added to his sweet nature and serenity, and his New Orleans–style jazz funeral (**555**) in New York, attended by thousands, featured Wynton Marsalis.

Ten Interesting Songs about the South

To CONCLUDE ON A musical note. Most of these songs were written by Yankees. For some Confederate songs (a couple of them written by Yankees, too) see **325–28**.

Stephen Foster. Caufield & Shook Collection, Photographic Archives, University of Louisville

610. **"My Old Kentucky Home"** (1853) is one of the best-known and was once one of the best-loved minstrel songs of the antebellum Pennsylvania songwriter Stephen Foster. The state song of Kentucky (with the verse about how "the darkies are gay" now bowdlerized), it is still sung at the start of the Kentucky Derby.

611. **"Carry Me Back to Old Virginny"** was written for the minstrel stage in 1878 by James Bland, "the Negro Stephen Foster." A Washingtonian who also composed "Oh, Dem Golden Slippers" and "In the Evening by the Moonlight," Bland later had a successful music-hall career in England before returning to the United States, where he died in obscurity and poverty. "Carry Me Back" is now the state song

"Carry Me Back to Ole Virginny" tobacco label, 1859. Library of Congress USZC4-2356

of Virginia, although there is a move afoot to replace it.

612. "Are You from Dixie?" is a better-than-average specimen of the genre of "Southern" songs that came from Tin Pan Alley (**573**) in the decades after 1890. Composed about 1915 by the same songwriting team that gave us "It's All a Dream" and "Just for Tonight," it was redone in the 1950s by the rockabilly group Joe Bennett and the Sparkletones.

613. "Georgia on My Mind" (1930) was one of many fine Southern-tinged songs written for a national pop audience by Indiana's Hoagy Carmichael. Ray Charles's (**607**) soulful 1960 version became a number one crossover hit, and a generation later it was a hit for country's Willie Nelson.

614. "Strange Fruit" was a grim dissent from the nation's musical love feast with the South. It's a chilling indictment of lynching, recorded by Billie Holiday in 1939. Five years later, white Georgia writer Lillian Smith used the title for a novel, and the song was later recorded by folksinger Josh White.

615. "That's What I Like about the South" was the signature song of singer-bandleader Phil

Harris (who also had the dubious distinction of recording some of the last "coon songs" with hits like "The Preacher and the Bear" and "The Darktown Poker Club"). This 1947 paean to Southern food came in the twilight of popular music's infatuation with the South. A few years later, Harvard mathematician-pianist-songwriter Tom Lehrer's "I Wanna Go Back to Dixie" delivered a coup de grâce to the dying Tin Pan Alley tradition by setting mock-nostalgic lyrics about pellagra, poll taxes, and boll weevils to a perky tune that could easily have been authentic.

616. "American Trilogy" was a crowd-pleasing closer for the Late Elvis. A Vegas-style medley of "Dixie," "The Battle Hymn of the Republic," and the black folk song "All My Trials," it had something for everybody.

617. "Detroit City" was written by Mel Tillis and became a hit for Bobby Bare in the early 1960s. With its repetitive "I want to go home" chorus, it's one of the best of the many country-music adaptations of the pop-music trope of longing for an idealized South. Otis Redding's "Sitting on the Dock of the Bay" is the soul equivalent, and the Indigo Girls' "Southland in the Springtime" brings the theme back to *fin de siècle* pop music.

618. "Sweet Home Alabama" by the Southern-rock group Lynyrd Skynyrd was a bellicose response to Canadian Neil Young's criticism of redneck ways in a song called "Southern Man." Released in 1975, it was immensely popular (in the South) and was part of the wave of regional pride and self-assertion that peaked with the election of Jimmy Carter.

619. "Tennessee" set off a process that won Atlanta rap group Arrested Development two

Grammy Awards. Described by member Baba Oje as a "dynamic, revolutionary musical vagabond family of the South," Arrested Development combines dreadlocks and traditional African garb with down-home themes to celebrate both the African and Southern rural roots of black Americans. Their music was described by a *New York Times* critic as a "blend of blues, reggae, funk, and straight-up hip hop."

Classical Music and Dance

THESE AREN'T USUALLY THOUGHT of as Southern specialities, but the South got there first and is finishing strong.

620. **Opera** arrived in the colonies as "ballad operas," comic plays with songs set mostly to traditional or currently popular melodies. (The first, and still best known thanks to Kurt Weill, is John Gay's *Beggar's Opera.*) In 1735 and 1736 Charleston was the scene of America's first ballad operas—John Hippisley's comical story *Flora, or Hob in the Well* and Charles Coffey's *The Devil to Pay.*

621. **The Moravians** who came to North Carolina (Salem, Bethania, and Bethabara) valued music, sacred and secular. All church services had music both "congregational and concerted," and music was nearly constant in the love feast and song hour. Most communities had a *collegium musicum,* an orchestra, and a chorus as well as several church choirs. Well-trained and musically sophisticated Moravian composers were the first Americans to write religious music with orchestral accompaniment.

North Carolina School of the Arts Symphony Orchestra. Charlie Buchanan

AGAINST ALL ODDS, THIS mostly rural and (for much of its history) poor region produced a number of performers and a couple of composers worth mentioning.

622. **Louis Moreau Gottschalk** (1829–69) was America's first piano virtuoso. Born in New Orleans, as a teenager he overcame considerable prejudice (one critic wrote, "An American com-

Louis Moreau Gottschalk. Library of Congress USZ62-56031

poser, good God!") to conquer Europe, including Berlioz and Chopin, with his playing, romantic looks, and novel compositions based on Afro-American and Creole music. Perhaps overconfident, he neglected his technique and other composers' music, and he lost his audience. People loved his sentimental pieces: the Library of Congress has "Last Hope" in twenty-eight editions, including the 1907 Presbyterian hymnal. His more sophisticated compositions based on ethnic styles are delightful evocations of another era.

623. **Olga Hickenlooper** (1882–1948), Texan and pianist, was the first woman to get a scholarship to the Paris Conservatoire—and she never looked back. Somewhere along the way she became Olga Samaroff, married Leopold Stokowski (1911 to 1923), had a great career (but retired early after an arm injury), and taught a roster of distinguished students at the Philadelphia Conservatory and Juilliard.

624. **William Grant Still**'s life (1895–1978) is largely a list of "firsts"—first American black to

compose a symphony played by a major orchestra, to compose an opera staged by a major company, to conduct a major U.S. orchestra, to conduct a major Southern orchestra, and one of the first to write for radio, movies, and television. Born on a Mississippi plantation, Still's route to eminence included a stint in the navy, a music degree from Oberlin, playing with W. C. Handy (**590**) and Eubie Blake, orchestrating for Artie Shaw and Paul Whiteman, studying with composer Edgard Varèse, and finally returning to the folk idioms of his roots. Leopold Stokowski called him "one of our greatest American composers."

625. **Maria Tallchief** (b. 1925) was an inspiration to little girls who loved ballet: if an Osage from Oklahoma could become the first American to dance at the Paris Opèra, a member of Ballets Russes, Balanchine's wife/muse, and the first, electrifying Firebird, maybe the world was ready for kids from Kingsport. Her fans didn't realize that her wealthy parents had taken her out of Oklahoma at age eight (to Beverly Hills, where she studied with the best, including Mme Nijinska).

626. **Leontyne Price** (b. 1927) is custodian of one of this century's great voices (she calls it "the instrument"); young singers routinely break the Tenth Commandment because of it. Miss Price began singing in church in Laurel, Mississippi, and has sung on the world's great stages. A close associate of composer Samuel Barber, she sang the premiere of his *Hermit Songs* and is permanently identified with his "Knoxville: Summer of 1915" (**523, 720**).

William Grant Still. Courtesy William Grant Still Music, Flagstaff, Ariz.

627. **Van Cliburn** (b. 1934) was the right man in the right place at the right time—a brilliant Texas pianist who won the first International Tchaikovsky Piano Competition in Moscow in 1958, at the chilliest point of the cold war. It made him a cultural hero like the astronauts: a *New York Times* headline read "Russians Cheer U.S. Pianist." He got a *Time* cover, a Broadway ticker-tape parade, and a presidential welcome home. His recording of Tchaikovsky's Piano Concerto No. 1 was the first classical album to sell a million copies. He played a heavy concert schedule for twenty years, then returned to private life. His fans had to settle for recordings until 1987, when he began appearing again.

628. **Alvin Ailey** (1931–89), great modern dancer and choreographer, left Texas at age twelve, but by then he was permanently Southern ("I have deep memories . . . sharecropping, picking cotton, people being lynched . . . the baptisms and the gospel shouts. . . . that early black experience colored everything that I did"). His choreography for the Alvin Ailey American Dance Theater used it all in a supercharged mix of dance styles and music (field hollers, gospel, blues, and jazz)—theater at its best.

THE SOUTH has all manner of fiddlers' conventions, blues and bluegrass festivals, and other down-home cultural gatherings, but it's starting to get some high-culture events worth attending, too. Here are four of the best.

629. **The Van Cliburn International Piano Competition,** begun in 1962, was conceived by the head of the Texas-based National Guild of Piano Teachers (which offered a $10,000 grand prize) and organized by an influential group of citizens and piano teachers in Fort Worth. The competition is unusual in giving *all* prizewin-

ners (usually six) two years of performances and free management. It has become a big deal, with TV and radio specials documenting its rigors, and major labels recording winning performances.

630. **The Spoleto Festival U.S.A.** was founded in 1977 by composer Gian Carlo Menotti in Charleston, South Carolina (a nice place to visit). It offers an annual orgy of drama, jazz, dance, classical music, and readings by some of the biggest names around, including many world premieres. It also provides training for young musicians in the Festival Orchestra and apprenticeships in arts management. It has intensive programs involving two thousand younger students a year, and reaches even more through videotapes and curriculum development projects. It generates 2,400 jobs and brings $73 million a year to South Carolina, doing well by doing good.

631. **The American Dance Festival** moved to the Sunbelt, like many other Yankee enterprises. Begun in Bennington, Vermont, by four giants of modern dance (Martha Graham, Hanya Holm, Doris Humphrey, and Charles Weidman), it came to Duke University in 1977, after thirty years in Connecticut. Every summer a faculty of fifty teaches 350 students, and the festival offers a feast of performances by the best professional companies. It has presented over four hundred premieres, including many works it has commissioned. It has also been important in reconstructing and preserving the works of master choreographers and establishing a modern dance archive. Critic Clive Barnes called it "the world's greatest dance festival."

632. **The International Ballet Competition,** sanctioned by UNESCO's International Dance

Committee, rotates between Varna, Helsinki, Moscow—and Jackson, Mississippi. In 1994, in Jackson, 131 dancers representing thirty-seven countries sought twenty-two medals and $55,000 in prizes, hoping to follow in the footsteps (so to speak) of 1969 winner Mikhail Baryshnikov.

Eight

Eating and Drinking

SOUTHERN CUISINE

My grandmother said cabbage boiled less than four hours would kill you. . . . Either we boil vegetables or we eat them raw—we have never put much stock in the scalding school of vegetable-cooking.

—BEN ROBERTSON

Hell, yes, we eat dirt! And if you haven't ever tried blackened red dirt you don't know what's good!

—ROY BLOUNT, JR.

The South excelled in two things which the French deem essential to civilization: a code of manners and a native cuisine.

—JOHN PEALE BISHOP

As novelist Reynolds Price observes, Southern cooking at its best offers America's "subtlest native food. Hardly a dish is less than a product of the joint skills, over three hundred years, of red, black, and white cooks and eaters." But it comes in many forms.

Four Kinds of Southern Cooking

633. Down-home Southern cuisine uses what Southern farms have historically produced: thus, corn (**168**) and pork (**177**) figure heavily. Everything from okra to pies is fried; Cajuns even deep-fry whole turkeys. (Walter Hines Page once observed that Southerners have suffered even more from fried food than from oratory.) Boiled vegetables are boiled a long time, and bacon grease is a sort of Dixie ghee. This food's bad for the heart but good for the soul: Immanuel Kant refused to eat food fried in pork fat because it interfered with his thinking, and look what *that* led to. Reynolds Price extols the standard summer lunch: "chicken and cured ham, corn pudding, green beans, spring onions, tomatoes, small limas, hot rolls, corn sticks, iced tea,

Dinner on the grounds, North Carolina, 1940. Southern Historical Collection, University of North Carolina Library, Chapel Hill

and lemon pie (with all the ingredients but the tea and lemons grown no more than twenty miles off)." Rarer now in Southern homes, this food is still available at innumerable plate-lunch restaurants, shopping-mall cafeterias (**219**), and interstate-highway chains like Cracker Barrel (**226**).

634. Soul food was simply the chic 1960s label for the funkier dishes of down-home Southern cooking. When black became beautiful, so did fried chicken, greens, and crackling cornbread. Leonard Bernstein served this food to the Black Panthers. Of course he could also have served it to the Knights of the Ku Klux Klan, if he'd wanted to make *them* feel at home. It's just the food of poor rural Southerners making the most of what's at hand, and there's been a lot of inter-racial recipe trading, too.

635. Big House Southern cuisine has provided many of the glories of American cooking. (In the South "Big House" means Ole Massa's place, not prison.) Like its country cousins, it reveals European, African, and American Indian influ-

Antoine's restaurant. Historic New Orleans Collection, acc. no. 1974.25.29.1

ences, but it's more labor-intensive and the ingredients are pricier. Smithfield ham and spoonbread replace pork chops and biscuits, or fatback and cornpone. There are subregional variations, but good cookbooks and *Southern Living* magazine have put the South's great food on the menus of country-club brunches everywhere.

636. **"New Southern cuisine,"** at its best, refers to traditional, fresh, local ingredients used in innovative ways. Chef Bill Neal's *Southern Cooking* (1985) is a good compendium. Neal's recipe for shrimp and grits is now a cliché in yuppie restaurants throughout the South (though no less tasty for that), but one trendy D.C. eatery advertises new Southern cuisine like monkfish with braised cabbage, roasted sweetbreads with mustard greens, and seared rare salmon with asparagus, fennel, and shiitakes over arugula. Greens aside, it's hard to say what's Southern about that: most Southerners probably can't pronounce "arugula" and wouldn't knowingly eat something called shiitakes. But this, too, shall pass.

Hog Heaven

637. **Pork** has been the meat of the South since before 1728, when William Byrd (**443**) sneered of his Carolina neighbors that "the only business here is raising of hogs, which is managed with the least trouble, and affords the diet they are most fond of." The Virginia aristocrat shouldn't have been so scornful: Richmond's E. M. Todd Co., the nation's oldest meatpacker (founded 1779), processes nothing but pork. As late as the 1960s nonfarm Southern households consumed 20 percent more bacon and 110 percent more lard than the national average. Most parts

of the pig are eaten one way or another, by somebody or other.

Three hogmeat dishes, one high-toned, one low-down, and one just down-home:

638. **Country ham**—the hindquarter of a year-old hog fattened on corn or peanuts, cured with salt (and sometimes sugar), given flavor and distinctive red color by smoke (usually hickory, but in some places oak, sassafras, corncobs, or peanut husks), aged for a year or more, and served baked, boiled, or sliced and fried—is one of the most splendid achievements of Southern cuisine. Smithfield, Virginia, is the best-known source, but the process was widespread in colonial Maryland, Virginia, and North Carolina and moved west unaltered to Kentucky and Tennessee; today those five states are the ham heartland. (Red-eye gravy is made by adding a little water or coffee to the residue left in the skillet when ham is fried. The resulting liquid—thin, dark, and salty—goes well with grits.)

Country ham. DixiePix

639. Chitterlings (pronounced and sometimes spelled "chitlins") are the small intestine of hog, sometimes boiled, but more often parboiled, battered, and fried. Tons are consumed by thousands of festival-goers at Salley, South Carolina's annual Chitlin Strut. Like brains and eggs for breakfast, hog jowl at New Year's, pork rind, head cheese, and souse (pickled ears, feet, etc.), chitterlings reflect the ability of rural Southerners, black and white, to use "everything but the squeal" at hog-killing time. The Park Sausage Company now sells them frozen and suggests serving them with champagne, but even as chic soul food the dish has an image problem: eating just doesn't get much lower on the hog than this.

640. Barbecue is the most Southern meat of all, long associated with political rallies and fire-department fund-raisers, and ideally served from a cinder-block building with a sign that says "BBQ." The word (which probably comes from an Indian root) can refer to a process, a dish, or an event; all three were well established by the eighteenth century (Washington barbecued at Mount Vernon). But Southerners disagree vehemently about how best to prepare 'cue. Texans and some Kentuckians even dissent from the regional consensus that barbecue means *pork*. In fact, Southern barbecue is like Europe's wines and cheeses—drive a hundred miles and the barbecue changes.

Andrew Jackson gets a grilling. Library of Congress USZ62-9647

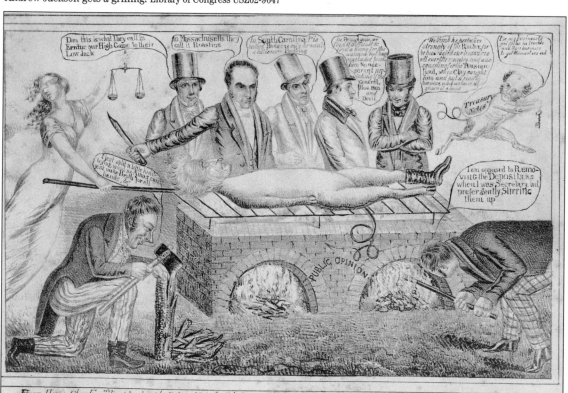

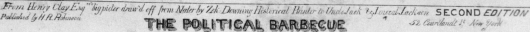

THE POLITICAL BARBECUE

THE MAGNIFICENT SEVEN

BARBECUE TRADITIONS WORTH KNOWING:

641. **Eastern North Carolina.** Simple and classic: smoked shoulder or whole hog, chopped or "pulled," dressed with vinegar and red pepper, and served with coleslaw, hushpuppies, and Brunswick stew. The mother church is Wilber's, in Goldsboro, but it's hard to get bad barbecue anywhere east of Raleigh.

642. **Western North Carolina** barbecue has equally devoted fans. Above the fall line, tomato sneaks into the sauce, sauce sneaks into the coleslaw (resulting in spicy red slaw), and the meat is offered sliced as well as chopped. Ground zero is Lexington, with sixteen barbecue joints for fewer than sixteen thousand people. Wayne "Honey" Monk of Lexington cooked for the 1983 Economic Summit in Williamsburg.

643. **Central South Carolina** serves pork with a distinctive sweet, mustard-based sauce, sometimes with rice (this *is* South Carolina). Traditional within an hour and a half of Columbia, it's now more widely available thanks to Maurice Bessinger of Columbia's Piggy Park, whose product is available in supermarket freezer cases around the South or shipped air-freight (1-800-MAURICE). On July 4, 1994, Bessinger served a record 9,725 pounds of barbecue.

644. **Generic Southern pork barbecue.** Moving west from the Carolinas, sauces get thicker, redder, and usually sweeter, and side dishes get less predictable. Baked beans, french fries, and onion rings appear. Hushpuppies yield to white bread, soda crackers, even (at McClard's in Hot Springs, Arkansas) tamales. Other meats join pork on the menu. But all the way to Kansas

Generic Southern pork BBQ. DixiePix

City (except in Texas and western Kentucky) barbecue means pork slow-cooked over aromatic hardwood fires, with sauce applied or on the side. Every Southern state has dozens of good joints and three or four great ones. Ask a native. (But don't ask two; they'll disagree.)

Home of Memphis "dry ribs." DixiePix

645. **Memphis** modestly claims to be the world's barbecue capital: its Yellow Pages list over eighty joints, and it's the scene of the annual World Championship Barbecue Cooking Contest. Memphis-style barbecue emphasizes ribs,

served either wet (with sauce) or dry (with a crusty, spicy "dry rub"). You can get good wet ribs elsewhere—South Side Chicago, for example—but dry ribs are unique to Memphis, and the Rendezvous is the place to get them, at least on your first visit. Alternatively, Lee Atwater's Red Hot & Blue chain now offers a facsimile to city dwellers throughout the Southern and Middle Atlantic states.

646. **Owensboro, Kentucky,** also claims to be the World Barbecue Capital, and it has its own barbecue festival. But it also has a unique brand of barbecue: mutton's the meat of choice. Why this should be, no one knows, but one pit boss estimates that Owensboro's dozen or so joints cook fifty tons a week in the summertime. The biggest and best known is the Moonlight Bar-B-Que Inn.

647. **Texas barbecue** is also, ah, something else. In the rest of the South beef brisket's an alternative to pork, if it's on the menu at all. But by the time you get to Dallas, barbecue means brisket—and Texans insist that that's what it *is*. Other Southerners may object, but Texans don't care, and there's no denying that Sonny Bryan's Smokehouse serves a meal worth a long detour. (If you keep going west, you run into folks who barbecue link sausages, bologna, and eventually goat.)

The Corn-fed-racy

648. **Corn,** like pork, turns up throughout Southern cuisine. Preferring the South's native grain to imported wheat and rye is like preferring pork to beef and lamb—a strong tendency, if not a general rule. This was noted in the 1860s by visiting Union soldiers, who called the South the "corn-fed-racy." A century later, nonfarm Southern households bought over two and a half times the national average of cornmeal. Corn appears in the forms noted below, as well as in corn pudding, turkey stuffing, batters for fried foods, and dumplings to go with greens.

HOMINY, GRITS, HOMINY GRITS, ETC.

THERE'S SOME CONFUSION HERE.

649. **Hominy** refers to dried whole corn kernels, boiled with lye to loosen the husk, then rinsed and dried again. The word and the process come from the Indians, who either stewed hominy whole or cracked it to make what English settlers came to call hominy grits. Canned, cooked hominy is available throughout the South and in black and Hispanic neighborhoods elsewhere.

650. **Grits** are the national dish of the South, so identified with it that "grit" has become a derogatory epithet for a white Southerner. A poor man's polenta, grits are now made from dried corn rather than hominy. Dressed with butter and salt or with red-eye gravy (**638**), grits are served with eggs at breakfast; gussied up with cheese, garlic, etc., they also make a side dish for dinner.

Grits, quick and quicker. DixiePix

651. **Hominy grits** is (confusingly) still just the full name for grits (even though they're not made from hominy anymore). That is, except in Charleston and environs, where the uncooked product is often called grist (hence, gristmill) and the dish itself hominy. Moreover, in coastal South Carolina "grits" is singular; elsewhere the word's usually plural.

MORE GRITSLORE:

652. **South Carolinians** may not know what to call grits, but they lead the nation in per capita consumption of them. The leading grits-eating cities are Charleston and New Orleans. (More grits are sold in New York City, with its large population of expatriate black Southerners, than in Atlanta, with *its* large population of expatriate white Northerners.) The World Grits Festival, held each April in St. George, South Carolina, features a grits-eating competition (of course) and also something called the Grits Roll, in which people dive into a tank of grits.

653. **Quaker Products** of Chicago has about 80 percent of the U.S. grits market; most of the rest belongs to Pillsbury subsidiary Martha White of Nashville. Both sell both regular (twenty-minute) and quick (five-minute) grits; "instant grits" are also available, plain or flavored, but no real Southern cook would admit to using them.

654. **Famous non-Southern grits-eaters** have included Ulysses S. Grant, who ate them in the White House, and Franklin D. Roosevelt, who had a special bowl for them at his place in Warm Springs, Georgia. Captain John Smith (**112**) also ate grits; he observed in 1629 that his Indian neighbors served grits with milk, but that's now a Yankee solecism.

CORNBREADS

ONE LINGUIST UNCOVERED OVER a hundred words for different kinds of cornbread in South Carolina alone. Among them:

655. **Cornpone** is the original cornbread, low-rent but still good eating: a batter of meal, water, and grease, baked. Southerners got this recipe from the Indians, who called the result something that sounded like *pone*. There are many ways to cook cornpone. You can put the batter on a hoe blade and stick it near the coals, for instance: what you get is hoecake.

656. **Hushpuppies** may or may not have begun as deep-fried cornmeal nuggets thrown to the hounds to shut them up. If they did, somebody soon figured out that these morsels were too good to waste, even on Old Blue. Additives vary—onion, sugar, self-rising flour—but your basic hushpuppy reflects the old Southern understanding that almost anything's better coated with cornmeal batter and fried: it gets straight to the point and just fries the batter. Hushpuppies are the classic accompaniment for fried fish and North Carolina barbecue.

Hushpuppies to go. DixiePix

657. Standard Southern cornbread is eaten plain or crumbled in buttermilk or pot likker (**669**). Southerners usually go light on the sugar and flour found in Yankee cornbread, and most prefer white cornmeal (and white grits); Yankees tend to prefer yellow meal (and not to like grits at all).

658. Crackling cornbread is studded with crispy-chewy "cracklings," which are what's left over when hog fat is cooked down for lard. They add taste, texture, and cholesterol to the basic recipe.

659. Spoonbread is the top of the cornbread line: a fluffy, steaming cornmeal soufflé made with butter, milk, and eggs. This elegant side dish seems to have originated in late-nineteenth-century Virginia. It's best served with a fine ham, but it's delicious with anything—or by itself, for that matter.

LIQUID CORN

660. Corn whiskey was first distilled in early Jamestown, but it became an industry when the Scotch-Irish (**98**) brought their ancient whiskey-making traditions to Pennsylvania, adapted them to the native grain, then fled federal excise agents to the Southern interior, especially Kentucky. There the first commercial distillery was established in 1783 by Evan Williams. Unless it's mellowed and aged into bourbon, corn whiskey is clear, raw (to most tastes), and potent "white lightning." It's still produced illegally throughout the upper South, where the age-old conflict between moonshiner and revenue agent is said to have given birth to stock car racing (**851**). But pride in workmanship is seldom what it used to be, and modern moonshine can be greatly hazardous to your health.

No more corn whiskey from this still. R. G. Potter Collection, Photographic Archives, University of Louisville

661. **Bourbon** is the South's gift to the world of whiskey, far removed from the corn whiskey of the eighteenth century. James Beam Distilling Co. was operating in Bourbon, Kentucky, by 1789, but bourbon as we know it dates from the 1820s, when Dr. James Crow introduced the sour-mash distilling process, and distillers began to filter their whiskey, mix it with water from limestone springs, and age it in charred white-oak barrels. This produces the smooth amber liquor of which a Kentuckian wrote, "One Small drink would Stimulate the whole Sistom. . . . It Brot out kind feelings of the Heart." Kentucky produces most of it and Jim Beam is the world's best-seller, but (thanks to a popular series of advertisements) Jack Daniel's (**216**) whiskey, rustic setting, and quaint employees now attract thousands of tourists to Lynchburg, Tennessee (pop. 361).

662. **The mint julep** is the classic Southern bourbon drink. Although "julep" is French (from Persian *gulab,* rose water) and recipes tend to be lyrical ("Take from the cold spring, some water, pure as the angels are," or "Mix into chilled limestone water to make a silvery mixture as smooth as some rare Egyptian oil"), it's just good American whiskey, sugar, a touch of pure water, and mint, served over crushed ice, ideally in a frosted silver julep cup. Sweet, cold, and treacherous. (Virginians and Kentuckians argue over whether the mint should be crushed, but no one else cares.) The julep has been the official drink of the Kentucky Derby since 1875, and more than eighty thousand are drunk at each running. Trying to snare the Olympics, Atlanta served juleps to the international committee and gave each an engraved cup. (It worked.) Given all this, it's dismaying to learn from the Southern Focus Poll that only one-fourth of

Southerners have drunk a julep, and only 10 percent know what's in one.

Other Southern Foods

SOUTHERN CUISINE ISN'T ALL pork and corn, hogmeat and hoecakes.

MEAT AND FISH

663. **Game** was common in the early Southern diet, and assorted wild birds, wild mammals, and the occasional reptile (**63**) are still found on Southern tables, fallout from the fact that Southerners are more likely to hunt than other Americans. Some dishes have attained stereotypical status, notably possum (**64**). Despite the query in the song "Is It True What They Say about Dixie?" few Southerners actually eat that marsupial, but it's true that most possum-eaters are Southern, and Alabama's tongue-in-cheek Possum Growers and Breeders Association of America once distributed thousands of "Eat More Possum" bumper stickers. Possum is said to go well with sweet potatoes.

664. **Catfish** used to be pulled out of river bottoms with chicken innards for bait—and who knew *what* they'd been eating? Consequently, these ugly scavengers used to be for poor folks. Now that they're raised commercially and sold without the whiskers, however, their succulent flesh has begun to get the market it deserves. Southerners usually eat them battered and fried, with hushpuppies, coleslaw, and ice tea, often at the catfish houses that have begun to be as common as barbecue joints, especially in

the lower South. But cats (sometimes under other names) have begun to turn up at fancy restaurants, too—and not just in the South.

665. **Southern fried chicken** is a cliché, and something of a fiction. Southerners don't all fry chicken the same way, or in any way that other folks don't. They don't even fry much more these days: only a third of Southerners prefer their chicken fried, compared to a quarter of non-Southerners. But historically, the dish has been the bedrock of Sunday dinner, what you have when the preacher's coming. And thanks to Colonel Sanders (**246**), the "finger-lickin' good" dish is now identified with the South from Denver to Dar es Salaam.

666. **Brunswick stew** is a sort of East Coast gumbo (**690**): chicken and other meat (squirrel is traditional but now rare) cooked with vegetables, usually including lima beans and corn. Essentially the same recipe makes Kentucky "burgoo." It's often served with rice or (in North Carolina) as a side dish with barbecue. Brunswick, Georgia, and Brunswick County, Virginia, both claim to have invented the dish.

FRUITS AND VEGETABLES

667. **Black-eyed peas,** or cowpeas, are probably one of the many African contributions to Southern cuisine. Like many other Southern vegetables (crowder peas, field peas, greens, and every kind of bean, for instance), they are cooked long and slow, with salt pork, ham hock, or just plain bacon grease. Combined with rice, black-eyed peas make hoppin' john, originally a coastal Carolina dish, but now popular throughout most of the South. Associated with good luck, black-eyed peas are eaten on New Year's Day in over

60 percent of Southern households, traditionally accompanied by greens (for wealth).

668. **Greens** (the boiled leaves of various plants, cultivated or wild) are a traditional Southern side dish. Turnip greens are more popular in the upper South, collards in the lower, but both are ubiquitous, as are mustard greens, kale, and many others. Wild varieties include dandelion greens, cress ("creasy greens"), and poke sallet, each the subject of at least one country song. Although some "new Southern cuisine" restaurants serve greens al dente, most eaters prefer them at least well cooked enough to yield pot likker, and many like them with vinegar. Ayden, North Carolina, and Gaston, South Carolina, both sponsor annual collard festivals to honor the most aromatic of Southern greens.

669. **Pot likker** is the liquid that remains after greens have been cooked for a long time with bacon or salt pork for flavoring. Served with cornbread, it's usually sipped, but one Atlanta restaurant treats it as a soup. Huey Long (**424**) described pot likker as "the noblest dish the mind of man has yet conceived," and defended the dunking of cornbread against the editor of the *Atlanta Constitution,* who believed it should be crumbled. Pot likker is thought by some to be an aphrodisiac.

670. **Okra** is, like cotton, a member of the mallow family. The plant has a lovely blossom, but its edible pod tends to be prickly—thus, the improved Clemson Spineless variety. When stewed, often with tomatoes, okra has a texture charitably described as mucilaginous, but breaded and fried it can be sublime. Okra makes a good pickle, too, but as home-front Confederates discovered, it's a poor coffee substitute. In Louisiana it's often used as the base for gumbo.

The pod of the gods. DixiePix

Okra probably came from Africa: the word has Ashanti roots; "gumbo," originally a synonym, is from the Bantu.

671. Rice is of culinary importance only in parts of the South, but its image as a Southern food

Lousiana store window, 1938. The sign says "Rice: Queen of the dinner table." Russell Lee, Farm Security Administration/Library of Congress USF34-31466-D

survives (e.g., in the logo of Uncle Ben), and where it's important it's very important indeed. Although no longer a South Carolina crop (**171**), it is still basic to low-country cuisine. (Charlestonians have been called America's Japanese because they eat rice and worship their ancestors.) It's also a Louisiana staple, served with red beans or gumbo, or in jambalaya.

672. Fried tomatoes, green or ripe, have long been a common Southern side dish (often served at breakfast), but only after the movie based on Fannie Flagg's novel *Fried Green Tomatoes at the Whistle-Stop Cafe* did they become a regional icon. Now green tomatoes—sliced, coated with cornmeal batter, and fried—are on the menus of innumerable "new Southern cuisine" restaurants.

673. Vidalia onions have now been grown for several decades in the neighborhood of Vidalia, Georgia, where the soil mysteriously makes them "sweet as Coca-Cola." They make fine relish or onion rings and are also delicious baked (sometimes with brown sugar to make them even sweeter). Some folks claim to eat them like apples.

674. Watermelon is a member of the gourd family, originally brought from Africa on slave ships. It's not unique to the South, but it came to be identified with the region, especially and stereotypically with black Southerners. Hope, Arkansas, was once best known for the quality and size of its melons, a dozen towns have watermelon festivals, popular varieties have names like Dixie Queen and Stone Mountain, and most Southerners learn the techniques of melon-thumping and seed-spitting early in life. Many recipes call for watermelon, including ones for

Ice-cold watermelon. Standard Oil (New Jersey) Collection, Photographic Archives, University of Louisville

wine and pickles, but in the Southern summer it's hard to beat simply cooled (ideally in a spring) and sliced. Salt is optional.

WHEAT BREAD

YES, IT MAKES A change from cornbread once in a while.

675. **Beaten biscuits** are something like the original eighteenth-century biscuit. They are unleavened and the dough is beaten with a mallet (or at least kneaded for a *long* time): the result's a hard little wafer perfect for eating with country ham. Although the work can now be done by machine, and the finished product can even be bought mail-order, beaten biscuits have become something of a luxury item, for special occasions only. For some reason they have held on longer in the upper South than in the lower.

676. **Today's ordinary Southern biscuit** is a fairly recent innovation: it requires baking soda, baking powder, and cheap white flour not widely

available until the late nineteenth century. But it's now universal: part of fast-food breakfasts, elegant brunches, and Mamaw's Sunday dinners—from scratch, from Bisquick, or from refrigerated cans of dough. Often made with buttermilk, it's big, soft, and fluffy and makes a great down-home breakfast served with sawmill gravy (sausage drippings, flour, and milk). White Lily or another low-gluten soft-winter-wheat flour makes the best biscuits.

CONDIMENTS

SOUTHERNERS HAVE CREATED A mess of them, and they're damn near all wonderful or at least interesting. Southern food (except, as usual, in New Orleans) has relied on fresh ingredients rather than lots of spices. Condiments add a kick without compromising the basic flavors. We have:

677. **Pickles, relishes, etc.:** pickles of all kinds (peaches, Jerusalem artichokes, watermelon rind, green beans, okra, green tomatoes, palmetto); relishes from the common chowchow to treats like Vidalia onion; catsups of walnut, mushroom, and green tomato; plus a beloved Johnny-Reb-come-lately, pepper jelly (tasty with cream cheese on a cracker).

678. **Hot sauces:** dozens of them, homemade (the most basic is fresh cayenne peppers steeped whole in vinegar, served in the Mason jar) and commercial (e.g., Texas Pete of Winston-Salem). The gold standard is Tabasco sauce, invented after the Civil War when Edmund McIlhenny came home to Avery Island, Louisiana, to find the family cane fields and salt-quarrying operation destroyed by Union troops. Some Mexican peppers he'd planted

Southern heat. McIlhenny Company

were still growing, though, and the sauce he devised—crushed capsicum peppers mixed with salt and aged, then blended with vinegar, strained, and bottled—spiced up the dreary food of Reconstruction. These days the sauce is aged for three years in white-oak barrels, but otherwise the recipe's pretty much the same. Tabasco sauce is labeled in fifteen languages and sold in over a hundred countries.

DESSERTS

MOST SOUTHERNERS HAVE A sweet tooth, and there are many great Southern desserts, especially pies: buttermilk, black bottom, coconut cream, banana, lemon meringue. . . . Some favorites:

679. **Sweet potato pie** is simple soul food: a favorite Southern vegetable mashed, sweetened, flavored, and baked in a crust. It was eaten by Henry VIII, who'd heard from the Spanish that this new vegetable called *batata* was an aphrodisiac. If that were so, Methodist church suppers would be more exciting.

680. **Pecan pie** starts with the tender, meaty fruit of a native tree with an Indian name, cultivated at Mount Vernon and Monticello; adds

butter and eggs and brown sugar, syrup, or molasses, maybe some bourbon or vanilla; and bakes it in a crust. Served with vanilla ice cream or whipped cream, there's nothing better or more Southern. Which makes it odd that (as food writer John Egerton notes) it wasn't found in cookbooks until after World War I.

681. **Chess pie** is another "old Southern recipe" that isn't exactly that. In the past, something like this sugar, butter, and egg delight went by a variety of names, including Jefferson Davis pie, but chess pie, so designated, appears to be a twentieth-century addition to Southern cookbooks. Despite that, the origins of the name are lost: it might be a corruption of *cheese* (no longer an ingredient, if it ever was), could have to do with storage in a pie *chest*, or might mean "just"—as in "It's ches' pie." Lemon and chocolate versions are fairly recent innovations.

682. **Key lime pie** is a Florida specialty, now adopted by the rest of the South. Tart Key limes—probably brought to the West Indies by Columbus and widely grown on the Florida keys before the hurricane of 1926—were the, uh, key ingredient, but ordinary Persian limes are often substituted. This is the aristocrat of the many sweetened-condensed-milk and graham-cracker-crust pies found in the South.

683. **Fried pies** are a natural: pie's good, fried food's good, so why not *fry a pie?* The little one-serving pocket is usually stuffed with fruit, but chocolate, coconut cream, sweet potato, and many other fillings have been observed. Like barbecue and corn dogs, fried pies are seldom prepared at home these days; they're bought cellophane-wrapped from convenience stores or fresh from the fryer at places like Atlanta's Varsity Drive-In.

684. Fruitcake is an inescapable part of a Southern Christmas. Although there's no real evidence that Southerners *like* fruitcake, they produce a lot of it. Trappist monks in Kentucky advertise theirs in the *New Yorker;* Corsicana, Texas, has not one but two mail-order operations; a Chattanooga bakery advertises "No Little Green Things"; and Georgia's giant Claxton Fruitcake Co. sells over two hundred tons a year. Bourbon in the recipe helps a lot.

SNACK FOODS AND CANDY

YOU WANT TO EAT between meals? Try these.

685. The corn dog started as a carnival treat, became a convenience-store snack, and is now in freezer cases for microwaving at home. It's just an all-American hot dog (market research shows that Southerners prefer 'em bright red), coated in a cornmeal batter, and—guess what?—*deep-fried.* Yum.

686. Boiled peanuts are a uniquely Southern treatment of the goober or pinder (both Gullah [95] words). Other folks eat them roasted, in the shell or out of cans, but only in the South (and not everywhere there) do households and roadside stands offer the unshelled groundnut

South Carolina roadside stand. DixiePix

boiled in very salty water for hours. How many hours is, as with many aspects of Southern cuisine, a matter for earnest discussion if not argument. The taste is an acquired one, and so's the technique: remove the shell with teeth and tongue, spit it out, and swallow the salty and sometimes mushy morsel.

687. Pralines have long since escaped their New Orleans birthplace to become a staple at Stuckey's throughout the South. Originally made with almonds, they now incorporate the native pecan in a creamy disk of caramelized sugar and butter (or cream).

688. The Goo Goo Cluster, invented in Nashville in 1912, was the first combination candy bar in America, melding chocolate, marshmallow, caramel, and peanuts (pecans in the Goo Goo Supreme) in a wonderfully sweet and gooey confection. Marketed as "the South's favorite candy" and "A Good Ole Southern Treat," Goo Goo has advertised for years on the Grand Ole Opry with the slogan "Go get a Goo Goo—it's good." The name is widely believed to refer to the Opry's initials, but the product is older than the broadcast; wherever it came from, the manufacturer observes that Southern babies demand it.

689. The Moon Pie is a wad of marshmallow sandwiched between two round, four-inch-diameter cookies. The classic, invented in Chattanooga around 1919, is covered with chocolate, but vanilla, banana, and coconut frostings have also been used, and a double-decker version was introduced in 1969. The Chattanooga Bakery, the pie's maker, has never advertised, but now sells over 50 million pies a year. Sales soared in the 1950s after Lonzo and Oscar recorded "Give Me an RC Cola and a Moon Pie." The Moon Pie's

DixiePix

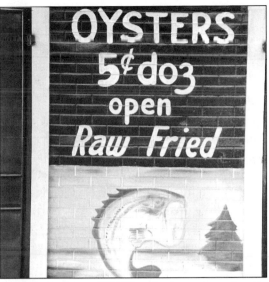

Abbeville, Louisiana, 1938. The price has gone up. Russell Lee, Farm Security Administration/Library of Congress USF33-11763-M2

appeal is a mystery to those who've never tasted one, but the pie has been celebrated by the Moon Pie Cultural Club (headquartered in Charlotte, North Carolina) and a book called *The Great American Moon Pie Handbook.*

Local Specialties

MANY PARTS OF THE SOUTH have their own tasty traditions. We've already looked at barbecue. Here are some more.

FOOD FROM THE LAND OF DREAMY DREAMS

NEW ORLEANS ISN'T A great barbecue town, but that doesn't matter at all. Here's what it has instead.

690. **Gumbo,** Bantu for okra, now refers to any of a number of flavorful stews unique to French Louisiana, some thickened with okra, others with the filé (powdered sassafras leaves) adapted from the Choctaw Indians. Gumbos

usually include vegetables (peppers, onions, celery, often tomatoes); spices and seasonings; sausage, ham, or other smoked pork for flavoring; and seafood and/or chicken. But they can also be made with beef or game, or in a vegetarian version for Lent. All are served with rice. In New Orleans, gumbo has a mystique similar to that of barbecue elsewhere in the South.

691. **Jambalaya** begins with smoked pork (its name comes from the French and Spanish words for ham) and it ends with rice, but almost anything in the way of vegetables, seafood, and meat can come between. Jambalaya, like the crawfish pie and filé gumbo that accompany it in a Hank Williams (**602**) song, makes a peppery, nourishing down-home meal all by itself. Gonzales, Louisiana, claims to be the Jambalaya Capital of the World, and it may well be.

692. **Crawfish** can be "mudbugs" if you're slumming, *"écrevisses"* if you're French or pretentious, possibly "crawdads," but never, never

"crayfish." They're freshwater crustaceans something like shrimp, gathered (or, increasingly, farmed) for such dishes as crawfish pie, crawfish bisque, and crawfish étouffée, or just to be boiled and served on heaping platters. Picking the meat is an acquired skill, but Louisianans now pinch the tails and suck the heads of over 50 million pounds a year, and the little fellers have become even more closely identified with Cajun cuisine than tasso (ham) or the tasty sausages called andouille and boudin. Elvis sang about them in *King Creole* (**968**).

693. **Blackened redfish** (spiced and seared to a char) was devised in living memory by chef Paul Prudhomme of K-Paul's Restaurant, whose smiling face is now almost as familiar as Aunt Jemima's once was. We include it here just to show that the spirit of innovation isn't dead in Louisiana cooking. Prudhomme was almost single-handedly responsible for the Cajun food craze of a while back, and every time you eat blackened anything, you should thank him.

Paul Prudhomme's restaurant. DixiePix

694. **Sandwiches** elsewhere tend to be second-rate meals at best, but in New Orleans even the sandwiches are good. The po' boy (poor boy) is the local hero sandwich, made with ingredients like roast beef or fried oysters on crusty French bread. The muffuleta is an indigenous Italian treat: cheeses and cold cuts with a garlicky olive dressing, served on a round sesame-seed bun.

695. **Cocktails** could be said to be a New Orleans invention (like brunch, at which they're often served). The word comes from *coquetiers,* egg cups in which an apothecary named Peychaud served his new digestive "bitters" (mixed with brandy) in the late eighteenth century. One famous New Orleans potation is the Sazerac, originally brandy flavored with bitters and absinthe, now whiskey, bitters, and anisette. Another is the Ramos gin fizz, a silky blend of gin, egg white, and cream, with a shot of soda, a squeeze of lemon, and a hint of orange flower water, shaken vigorously.

696. **Chickory café au lait and beignets** at the Café du Monde—oh, my. You can get them in Underground Atlanta or make them yourself, but somehow they just don't taste the same.

OTHER TREATS WORTH A TRIP

SOME OTHER PLACES HAVE a distinctive dish or two:

697. **Charleston** and the surrounding South Carolina Low Country offer a distinctive cuisine based on the abundant local seafood, invariably served with rice. She-crab soup originally got its flavor from crab roe, but crumbled hard-boiled egg yolks are now frequently substituted. Cookies, candies, and bread often include benne

(sesame) seeds, the word attesting to their seventeenth-century African origin.

698. Louisville, a river town with a large German population, may have more in common with Cincinnati and St. Louis than with cities further south, at least when it comes to food. A local specialty is the "hot brown," invented at the Brown Hotel in the 1930s: toast topped with turkey slices, and bacon or ham, smothered with white sauce and Parmesan cheese, and baked. Another is a chocolate-bourbon-pecan confection called derby pie. The name and original recipe are the property of a local restaurant, but passable imitations can be found everywhere. Louisville would like to claim the mint julep as its own, too, but that's overreaching.

699. The whole damn state of Texas has its own native cuisine, offering (besides beef brisket) such delights as chicken-fried steak. In general, as one moves west across the state the indigenous food becomes less Southern and more Mexican-influenced. But you can tell Texans are Southern by the way they argue about chili (with or without beans, with or without tomatoes, etc.): it's the same way other Southerners argue about barbecue. "Tex-Mex" food can now be found throughout the United States, even in the rest of the South, where it tends to be marketed and regarded as simply Mexican.

Potables

WHAT SOUTHERNERS DRINK THAT *isn't* made from corn:

700. Ice tea has been called "the ceremonial drink of the South," and Southerners do drink it year-round, in all settings. Eighty-seven percent of Southerners say they drink ice tea, and two thirds like it sweet: ice tea in the South is sometimes served with mint, sometimes with lemon, but usually with *lots* of sugar. Grady Nutt used to talk about the "40-weight" tea that he drank in the line of duty as a Baptist preacher.

701. Buttermilk is what's left over from the butter-making process. Whole milk, soured, yields a gelatinous goop called "clabber"; clabber, churned, yields sweet butter and a creamy, lumpy, sour residue—buttermilk. Aficionados (like Elvis) often crumble cornbread into it and spoon it up. Buttermilk as a drink is a country taste, and may be going out of fashion, but it's still widely used in biscuits, pies, pancakes, and other dishes. It can be bought powdered for those purposes.

702. Beer is viewed with suspicion by evangelical Protestants, but some pagans have always liked a cold one in the summer heat. Think of the short-lived "Billy" brand, endorsed by Jimmy Carter's hard-drinking kid brother, and country songs like "Red Necks, White Socks, and Blue Ribbon Beer." The best-known Southern brews are Jax and Dixie, from Catholic New Orleans, and Lone Star, "the National Beer of Texas" (**206**). Also, as elsewhere, boutique breweries have begun to produce designer beers for yuppies.

703. Scuppernong wine comes from a grape native only to the South, one of several North American varieties known as muscadines or fox grapes. Long a homemade product in the rural South—taken for medicinal purposes only, of course—it is now available from several Southern wineries. Its distinctive "foxy" taste offends connoisseurs but has its nostalgic partisans.

SOFT DRINKS AND THE SOUTH

704. Soft drinks are usually called that in the South (**155, 212**), which pretty much invented them and still leads the nation in consuming them ("Southerners need carbonation," writes novelist Nancy Lemann). The word "soft" is significant: these are nonalcoholic coolers suitable for Christians. The top ten soft-drink states are all in the South: North Carolina was recently number one, with over fifty gallons per year for every man, woman, and child in the state. It isn't just for breakfast anymore.

A North Carolina soft drink. DixiePix

705. Coca-Cola was introduced by Atlanta pharmacist John S. Pemberton in 1886—not incidentally the year Atlanta went dry. Made from extracts of cola nut and coca leaf, the *real* "classic Coke" did get its kick from cocaine, despite what the company says today. That stimulant was removed only at the turn of the century, by which time the brand had transcended its regional origins and was on the way to becoming a symbol of American civilization. Pepsi, the most successful of Coke's many imitators, is now headquartered in New York, but it was concocted in 1896 by a pharmacist in New Bern, North Carolina.

706. Dr Pepper is actually older than Coke, first sold in 1885 in Waco, Texas. Charles Alderton supposedly named his drink for Dr. Charles Pepper of Rural Retreat, Virginia, and Virginians claim it was invented in Dr. Pepper's pharmacy there. In 1988 the company merged with the most popular non-Southern soft drink, 7-Up (a St. Louis product, introduced in 1929), and the joint company is now headquartered in Dallas.

707. Mountain Dew is another disputed brew. The drink with the name that used to mean moonshine whiskey is claimed by Marion, Virginia, as a "tart and refreshing soft drink reminiscent of the culture and heritage of Southwestern Virginia," created by William H. Jones in 1961. Knoxville, Tennessee, contends that it was invented there by Barney and Ally Hartman. Dick Bridgeforth claims his father invented the final formula, with help from Marion's Mr. Jones. Wherever it came from, it is now the nation's sixth most popular soft drink, owned by PepsiCo.

708. Other soft drinks abound in the South, many of them with strictly regional or even local markets. Colas (all good with a handful of peanuts in the bottle) have

Blenheim Bottlers, Inc.

included Double Cola from Chattanooga and Royal Crown from Columbus, Georgia, which is also home to the Nehi line of approximately fruit-flavored drinks. Barq's of Biloxi has now diversified from root beer, its staple since 1898. Cheerwine, of Salisbury, North Carolina, advertises "The Taste That's . . . Um . . . Hard to Describe" (it leans toward cherry). When it comes to ginger ale, South Carolina has fiery Blenheim, Alabama has Buffalo Rock, and at the Foodmart in Boonesboro, Kentucky, the local Ale-8-One outsells all colas better than ten to one. Other local favorites are Jumbo Orange (Chattanooga), Big Red (Texas), Hoko Chocolate (the Shenandoah Valley), Dr. Enuf (Tennessee), and Pop Rouge (Louisiana—where else?). And don't forget Gatorade, invented for the Florida Gators football team by a Gainesville kidney specialist.

Oddments

SOUTHERNERS HAVE BEEN KNOWN to put many strange things in their mouths.

709. **Dry snuff** began as finely powdered tobacco sniffed by Indians through a tube called a *taboca*. Trendy seventeenth-century Europeans picked up the habit (and produced some lovely snuffboxes). But since colonial times Southerners haven't snorted the stuff, they've "dipped" it—put it in their mouths, where it releases nicotine through the gums. The names of popular dry ("scotch") snuffs—Bruton, Dental, Garrett, Honey Bee, Railroad Mills, Rooster, Society, Tops, Tube Rose—evoke the rural South of the 1930s. Which may be why dry snuff is now seen as something for old ladies and is outsold better than six to one by the "moist" snuffs popular with young men.

710. **Smokeless tobacco** properly refers to eating tobacco of all sorts, but it has come to be a popular euphemism for the moist snuff that baseball star Bobby Murcer sang about in his country-music hit of the 1980s, "I'm a Skoal Dippin' Man." Nearly a billion dollars' worth is now sold each year, 90 percent of it by U.S. Tobacco of Nashville and Greenwich, Connecticut, makers of Skoal and Copenhagen. In 1983 Skoal introduced Bandits, little tea-bag-like pouches that keep the snuff from getting between the user's teeth and obviate the need to spit, and Skoal is now available in cherry, mint, and wintergreen flavors.

711. **Chewing tobacco** is for real men. None of this "just a pinch" stuff. It was once used by American males in general, but it's now largely confined to those who can spit while working, like rural Southerners and major-league baseball players (it was recently forbidden for players below the major leagues). Still, at $500 million a year, chewing-tobacco sales are nothing to spit at. Forty-three percent of Southern men and 7 percent of Southern women say they've chewed. One popular chaw is Red Man.

712. **Headache powders** have been produced and consumed largely in the South. In fact, the Big Three—Goody's, BC, and Stanback—originated within a hundred-mile radius, in Winston-

Take a powder. DixiePix

Salem, Durham, and Salisbury, North Carolina, respectively. These fast-acting, foul-tasting, aspirin-based products are sold in little envelopes and are usually washed down with a soft drink. Goody's has been a sponsor of the Grand Ole Opry and the "official pain reliever" of NASCAR, endorsed by Roy Acuff (**601**) and Richard Petty (**874**), but it was acquired in 1995 by a New Jersey firm (which earlier bought out BC and moved its manufacturing operations to Memphis). To take a wholly Southern powder these days, you'll have to "snap back with Stanback."

713. **Dirt**—well, most Southerners never touch the stuff, but, yes, it's true that a few do take a little clay now and then, just to settle the stomach. (That's where South Carolinians' nickname "sandlappers" comes from.) A common practice in Africa, by the nineteenth century "geophagy" was widespread in the South among poor women and children of both races. Southerners have taken a lot of grief on this score, and it does no good at all to point out that the an-

Digging eating clay, near Siloam, Georgia, 1941. Jack Delano, Farm Security Administration/Library of Congress USF34-44526-D

cients treated illness by ingesting clay, or that kaolin is a key ingredient in one popular over-the-counter medicine.

Nine

Paintings and Porticoes

ARCHITECTURE AND ART

The South don't care a d——n for literature or art.
—WILLIAM GILMORE SIMMS, 1847

When you come to . . . painters, sculptors, architects, and the like, you will have to give it up, for there is not even a bad one between the Potomac mud-flats and the Gulf.

—H. L. MENCKEN, 1917

The region was as dependent aesthetically as it was economically. It imported its art—what little it got—as it did other consumer goods, from the North or from abroad.

—C. VANN WOODWARD

Architecture and the Decorative Arts

HISTORIC SOUTHERN BUILDINGS AND objects have suffered from acts of God and man. Three major fires and a killer hurricane hit eighteenth-century Charleston, and an earthquake struck in the nineteenth. Looting the South is almost a tradition: the British supposedly took some five hundred barrels of silverware when they left Charleston, and Union general B. F. "Spoons" Butler got his nickname for a reason. The climate (warm, moist, and hospitable to life—like termites and mildew) has destroyed much of what survived all that.

Yet it's easy to see that the rich lived elegantly. Early Southern decorative arts aped English styles, except in New Orleans, where they aped French. Many builders, painters, furniture makers, silversmiths, etc., came directly from Europe. But styles varied from region to region, and time to time, and some were unique to the South.

Southern Corinthian, 1850—corn, wheat, and tobacco—on a combination library and ballroom at the University of North Carolina. DixiePix

RURAL BUILDINGS

YOU CAN STILL FIND these here and there today, among the mobile homes (**152**).

714. **The log cabin** (or the log tobacco barn, or for that matter Lincoln Logs) might not have existed without the Swedes and Finns. These folks aren't usually considered major contributors to Southern culture, but they brought log construction to Delaware, whence the Pennsylvania Germans brought it down the Shenandoah Valley (**40**), and it became a symbol of the rural South.

Log dogtrot cabin (see **722**). Russell Lee, Farm Security Administration/Library of Congress USF34-31954-D

715. **Plantation houses** could be grand, and many of the surviving examples are (**732, 886, 926**). But far more common were establishments like the Louisiana one Frederick Law Olmsted visited in 1853: the house was a "small square log cabin, with a broad open shed or piazza in front, and a chimney, made of sticks and mud, leaning against one end," and a detached kitchen. "About the house was a large yard, in which were two or three China trees, and two fine Cherokee roses; half a dozen hounds; several negro babies; turkeys and chickens, and a pet sow, teaching a fine litter of pigs how to root and wallow. Three hundred yards from the house was a gin-house and stable, and in the interval between were two rows of comfortable negro cabins."

716. **Outbuildings.** The bigger the farm, the more buildings there were. Benjamin Latrobe wrote that they nestled around the house "as a litter of pigs their mother." Most everyone had a privy, a smokehouse (**637–38**), and usually a dairy or springhouse. Other things were often separate, too (one writer said that "there were nearly as many roofs as rooms"): kitchens (**721**), laundries, schools, offices, stables, carriage houses, storehouses, icehouses, barns, craft shops (for weaving, spinning, smithery), mule barns, duck houses, pig houses, chicken coops, dovecotes, corncribs, gristmills, rice threshing mills or sugar mills or cotton presses and gins, toolsheds, and water towers. Hampton plantation had an herb shed, greenhouses, and an orangery.

717. **Slave quarters** ranged from a single cabin to veritable subdivisions. Most slaves lived one family to a room—houses could have one, two, or four rooms, and varied greatly in comfort. Oddly, the houses that look least comfortable,

Street of slave cabins, the Hermitage plantation, Georgia. Library of Congress/Historic American Buildings Survey

the low windowless sheds of the South Carolina Low Country, strongly resemble eighteenth-century houses in the Congo. Large estates often had an overseer's house and a slave dining hall, kitchen, and hospital. Field hands could be scattered in villages around the plantation.

718. **Icehouses** were surprisingly frequent in the nineteenth century, even in the Deep South. They were pits as deep as thirty feet, sometimes just dirt-covered, sometimes elaborately roofed. Ice came from New England by sea and from Wisconsin and Illinois down the Mississippi.

719. **Tobacco barns** were (and are) everywhere in tobacco country. Tobacco (**169**) was cured in small structures near the fields. These days the

North Carolina tobacco barn, 1939. Southern Historical Collection, University of North Carolina Library, Chapel Hill

old log barns are falling to ruin as sheet metal and other unlovely materials replace them.

ADAPTING TO THE CLIMATE

SOUTHERN ARCHITECTURE HAS ALWAYS tried to be cool.

720. **Porches** are not uniquely Southern, but Southerners credit them with encouraging their sense of community, their literary heritage, and even the continuity of the race (there's not much to do sittin' on a porch waitin' for the house to cool off but tell stories or make out). Zora Neale Hurston (**507**): "It was the time for sitting on porches beside the road. It was the time to hear things and talk." The fatally cute country hit "Swingin' " is about a porch, and the porch's apotheosis is in "Knoxville: Summer of 1915," by Yankee composer Samuel Barber (**626**), with words from James Agee's (**523**) *A Death in the Family.*

721. **Detached kitchens** often went with larger farmhouses and even many city houses. This not only kept the heat out of the Big House, it kept the frequent kitchen fires from destroying the whole shebang.

722. **Raised houses with large windows** (often floor-to-ceiling) and porches to shade the windows caught cool breezes. They were often only one room deep, to encourage cross-ventilation, and sometimes had a cupola (belvedere) to create an updraft. The simplest two-room house was cooler and had more useful space when an open "dogtrot" (**714**) connected the rooms. Larger houses got the same effect with a grand entrance hall open from the front door to the back door.

A very large cupola, Waverly (1852), West Point, Mississippi. DixiePix

723. **The shotgun house** (you can fire a shotgun through it without hitting anything) is the low-rent version. One room wide and three rooms deep, with the gable end on the street, it's also open front to back. Could be poor man's Greek Revival, but John Michael Vlach argues that it came from Haiti and was perhaps originally African. It became the ubiquitous house of the poor; the most famous is Elvis's birthplace.

Shotgun houses, Memphis. DixiePix

THREE LOCAL VARIATIONS, ALL shaped by the heat:

724. **The South Carolina Low Country** came up with the "single house." A traveler wrote in 1799, "In Charleston persons vie with one an-

A Charleston single house. *The Great South* (1875)

Beauvoir (1853), home of Jefferson Davis, a typical raised cottage. Library of Congress D4-10564

other, not who shall have the finest, but who the coolest house," and the single house is an elegant solution. It's rectangular, short side abutting the street, and only one room deep (thus the name). Entertaining is often on the second floor. Each floor has a porch (piazza), usually oriented to catch the prevailing breezes. The lowest piazza has a solid door to the street for privacy and an entry to the house halfway down its length. A row of houses creates an elegant streetscape and affords seclusion: each house's piazzas face a drive or walled garden and the back of the neighbor's house.

725. New Orleans displayed less concern for cool breezes, but just as much for privacy and for providing an island of calm within the bustle of urban life. An old New Orleans house looks like an ordinary town house, but it is L-shaped, creating a quiet courtyard with two-story porches and semitropical plants. The wing in back, called a *garçonnière*, provided housing for young men of the family or for servants.

726. Lower Mississippi valley plantation houses were usually raised cottages with the public rooms on the second floor—as Benjamin La-

trobe said, "the best kind of house for the climate, namely, a mansion surrounded entirely by a portico or gallery of two stories. The roof is enormous."

ANTEBELLUM ARCHITECTURAL FASHIONS

ONCE SOUTHERNERS COULD AFFORD something not strictly utilitarian, they began to adapt architectural styles popular elsewhere. They did it with enthusiasm.

727. The Greek Revival in the United States started with the portico George Washington added to Mount Vernon; then Thomas Jefferson (**729**) and his friends Benjamin Latrobe and Robert Mills (**731**) turned to classicism for simpler, stronger, bigger, and more "American" forms than fragile Federal architecture offered. Greek Revival spread slowly through the South but was widely popular by the 1840s for public buildings and colleges as well as plantations. The North had Greek Revival houses, too, but they've become a symbol of plantation life,

Classical revival: *The Enigma* (1941), by Clarence John Laughlin (**782**). Copyright by the Historic New Orleans Collection (1981.247.1.1659)

Longwood (1860–61), Natchez, designed by Samuel Sloan. *Sloan's Homestead Architecture* (1861)

maybe because they make such spectacular ruins.

728. Gothic and other picturesque styles inevitably came to the South. Victorian romanticism (**912**) meant Southerners could be up to date by turning to medieval patterns. Gothic became popular for churches and some public buildings. For houses, Southerners altered Gothic, Italianate, and Moorish designs by keeping their beloved columns and all of their adaptations to heat. Architect Samuel Sloan wrote: "The detachment of the kitchen from the main building, the size of the ground floor, the necessity for large windows, wide doors and ample verandahs, the difference in the number of stories, and many other considerations all tend to render a design prepared for a northern man-

sion totally unfit for the wants and conveniences of a Southern family."

SOUTHERN ARCHITECTS AND BUILDERS

A FEW ARE FAMOUS, many forgotten.

729. Thomas Jefferson (1743–1826), a fine architect, was an enthusiast for classical design: "How is a taste in this beautiful art to be formed in our countrymen, unless we avail ourselves of every occasion when public buildings are to be erected, of presenting to them models for their study and imitation?" He worked closely with the architects of Washington, lending Pierre L'Enfant plans of twelve major European cities and letting Robert Mills spend two years using his architectural library. Of his own work, Mon-

Jefferson's Monticello (1769–1782), near Charlottesville, Virginia. Library of Congress USW3–35275–D

The Fireproof Building (1822–27), Charleston, designed by Robert Mills. DixiePix

ticello (his home), the University of Virginia (**843**), and the Virginia state capitol have been especially influential.

730. **William Jay** (1792–1837), an Englishman, introduced the Regency style to Savannah in 1817. His buildings are beautiful, and very English: a travel book published in London in 1836 describes "several very ambitious-looking dwellings, built by a European architect for wealthy merchants during the palmy days of trade; these are of stone or some composition, showily designed, and very large, but ill-adapted . . . for summer residences in this climate."

731. **Robert Mills** (1781–1855) of Charleston called himself "the first native American who directed his studies to architecture as a profession." With William Jay he introduced the Greek Revival style to the South, where it became as rampant as kudzu. In Washington he designed the Washington Monument, the Treasury Building, the Patent Office, and the Post Office. His work is self-consciously American: "I say to our artists: Study your country's tastes and requirements, and make classic ground *here* for your art. . . . We have entered a new era in the history

of the world; it is our destiny to lead, not to be led. Our vast country is before us and our motto Excelsior."

732. **Black builders and craftsmen,** slave and free, built much more than has usually been recognized. "Charles, free Mulatto," for example, signed a contract to build Destrehan, a large Louisiana plantation house. Other slave-built Louisiana houses include Cherokee, Oakland, and Kate Chopin's (**469**) house (now the Bayou Folk Museum). Isaiah Wimbush built Winsor Hall, in Greenville, Georgia, in 1836. A slave named Sandy did ornate plasterwork at Gaineswood, an ostentatious plantation at Demopolis, Alabama. James Bell was brought from Virginia to build three spiral staircases in a house in Alabama. Horace King, freed by the Alabama legislature, built the longest covered bridge (614 feet) then in existence. The elaborate plasterwork of the old Kentucky state capitol (1827–33) was done by Henry Mordecai.

733. LOUIS METOYER, son of ex-slave Marie Therese Coincoin, studied architecture in Paris in the early nineteenth century. He came home to build a house, church, and several other

buildings at his family's Melrose plantation, a thirteen-thousand-acre estate that became the center of the Isle Brevelle, a settlement of free blacks in Louisiana. Many of the buildings appear in the paintings of Clementine Hunter (**789**).

734. THOMAS DAY (1801?–61), a free black, owned North Carolina's largest antebellum cabinet shop, in the town of Milton. In 1850 he employed twelve people, including some slaves, to build interiors and furniture for private houses, for the governor, and for public buildings (e.g., Milton's Presbyterian church and the chambers of the Dialectic and Philanthropic Societies at the University of North Carolina). He must have been a talented diplomat: he was a Presbyterian deacon and a trustee of the town bank, and the North Carolina General Assembly passed a special bill to let him bring his wife from Virginia (blacks were not allowed to move across state lines).

BEFORE THE WAR, NORTHERN architects like William Strickland (buried in the Tennessee capitol he designed) worked in the South. After the War, Southern architects had to work in the North.

735. **Henry Hobson Richardson** (1838–86), from Louisiana, was educated at the University of Louisiana, Harvard, and the Ecole des Beaux-Arts in Paris. In 1862, back in Boston, he refused to swear allegiance to the Union and returned to Paris, writing to his Boston fiancée, "New Orleans is taken—governed by strangers. . . . I burned with shame when I read of the capture of my city and I in Paris." After the war, he worked in Boston, building in a highly romantic

A Northern building by a Southern architect: Trinity Church (1872–77), Boston, by H. H. Richardson. *American Architect and Building News* (1877)

and eclectic style. Trinity Church (1877) made "Richardsonian Romanesque" the dominant style of the day. Even Europeans admitted his genius.

THREE MODERN SOUTHERN ARCHITECTS (only one is a Southern architectural *modernist*):

736. **Edward Durell Stone** (1902–78) was born in Fayetteville, Arkansas (he called it a "hotbed of tranquility"), and studied architecture at Harvard and MIT. Despite his training, he felt that "the inspiration for a building should be in the accumulation of history." His most identifiable work used rectangular pavilions with columns. Washington's Kennedy Center, for instance, refers to the capital's classical architec-

Edward Durell Stone's North Carolina State Legislative Building (1959–63), Raleigh. DixiePix

ture: Stone thought it "should represent twenty-five hundred years of Western culture rather than twenty-five years of modern architecture." Remarks like that caused him to be scorned as a populist panderer to lowbrow taste.

737. John Portman (b. 1924) found fame with his glitzy Hyatt Regency Hotel in Atlanta (1967), which has a lobby-atrium twenty-two stories high. "I wanted to explode the hotel; to open it up; to create a grandeur of space, almost a resort, in the center of the city. . . . to take the elevators and literally pull them out of the walls and let them become an experience within themselves, let them become a giant kinetic sculpture." Later buildings vary that theme: Atlanta's Peachtree Center Plaza Hotel (1976) has its elevators on the *outside*. Portman has his

critics—for instance, Georgia historian Phinizy Spalding despised "the mass Portmania of a new society rich in material goods but dead culturally"—but he has certainly changed the face of Atlanta. When John Gunther characterized Atlanta's architecture as "rococola" in 1947, he couldn't have imagined what was coming.

738. Paul Rudolph (b. 1918), a Kentuckian who studied at Auburn, went on to study with Walter Gropius at Harvard and chaired Yale's architecture department, 1958–65. His chapel at Tuskegee (**839**) (1969) was toned down by the builders in an attempt to fit it into its surroundings, but it's still like the rest of his work: sculptural, personal, and at the least, interesting. His controversial Art and Architecture Building for Yale (1963) apparently inspired arson, but the Burroughs-Wellcome building (1972) (**206**) is a highlight of North Carolina's Research Triangle Park, and some colonnaded Southern houses led Kenneth Severens to call him "one of the first modernist champions of regionalism."

Paul Rudolph's chapel (1960–69) at Tuskegee University. DixiePix

John Portman's Peachtree Center Plaza (1976), Atlanta. DixiePix

FURNITURE, SILVER, AND OBJETS D'ART

THE ARTS OF THE SOUTH have been influenced by its rich assortment of cultures (see chapter 2). Much everyday furniture was made "on the place" by slave craftsmen or by yeoman farmers themselves. At the same time, the major seaboard cities had craftsmen as skillful as any in the country, and even inland towns like Lexington, Kentucky, managed to stay au courant.

THE THREE MAJOR centers of antebellum decorative art:

739. **Charleston,** the richest Southern city in the mid-eighteenth century. "Here the rich people have handsome equipages; the merchants are opulent and well-bred; the people are thriv-

ing and extensive, in dress and life; so that everything conspires to make this town the politest, as it is one of the richest in America" (*London Magazine,* 1762). Charleston even exported furniture and silver to the North and to England. In 1810 it had 81 cabinetmakers; between 1800 and 1825, 101 painters worked there. After the Panic of 1819, however, it lost some of its economic clout. (See **85, 889.**)

740. **Baltimore.** Still a Southern city, it became a busy and important port just before the Revolution, and it was an influential center of style well into the nineteenth century. Baltimore was known especially for its cabinetmakers (over 360 in 1820) and for silversmiths like Samuel Kirk and Son.

741. **New Orleans (86, 890).** A sleepy town of 8,000 in 1800, it was jump-started by the rise of

Silver coffeepot (c. 1750–60), by Alexander Petrie of Charleston. Collection of the Museum of Early Southern Decorative Arts

Bedroom furniture by Prudent Mallard, Waverly, Mississippi. DixiePix

King Cotton and the steamboat. By 1840 it had 100,000 people, plus at least 40,000 winter residents. All that cotton money attracted artists like Vaudechamp (**743**), architects like the Latrobes, Gallier, and the Dakins, and craftsmen like Frenchmen François Seignouret and Prudent Mallard. Someone had to build those expensive plantation houses, fill them with fashionable furnishings, and paint their owners' portraits. A page from Andrew Jackson's account book for 1821 shows a payment of $970.25 (a pretty penny) to Seignouret for furniture and fabrics.

Fine Arts

Still Life—Basket of Peaches (c. 1865), by Thomas Addison Richards. Morris Museum of Art, Augusta, Ga.

EVERYBODY KNOWS THERE'S NO Southern art, right? H. L. Mencken and W. J. Cash and Yankee art historians and even C. Vann Woodward said so. But pioneering shows at the Corcoran Gallery (1960) and the Virginia Museum (1983) proved them wrong, and the South is now a hot topic in art-history circles (**900**). This chapter would have been a lot shorter fifteen years ago.

742. **In colonial times** painters mostly did portraits, which were status symbols as well as decorative objects. The middle class usually had to settle for "folk" painters, local or traveling. Highly trained itinerant artists painted the rich (if the rich didn't go abroad). The only city big and wealthy enough to support a local portrait painter was Charleston (**763**).

743. **Cotton wealth** brought artists, many of them foreigners, and some stayed. Many, intelligently, were snowbirds, coming only for the winter. Big rich New Orleans was especially attrac-

Mrs. Algernon Wilson (1756), by Jeremiah Theus. Collection of the Museum of Early Southern Decorative Arts

tive: Jean Joseph Vaudechamp left in 1834 with $30,000, "a good painter and a gentleman, having made his fortune in three years" by painting portraits (seventy-eight are known). The long list of well-known painters who worked awhile in the South includes the Peale family (**750**), Samuel F. B. Morse, Gilbert Stuart, George Catlin, Eastman Johnson, and Edgar Degas (yes, that Degas). Several major Kentucky painters regularly traveled downriver to Natchez and New Orleans (see, for example, **753**).

744. Landscape painting came late and grew slowly because travel was difficult, but plantation and town views were published in the United States and Europe. In the 1830s George Cooke wrote about the South's "varied beauties" in the *Southern Literary Messenger* and painted *Tallulah Falls*. T. Addison Richards's (**754**) *Georgia Illustrated* (1843) offered steel engravings based on his sketches. Richards complained in 1853 that "little has yet been said, either in picture or story, of the natural scenery of the Southern States," and compared the South's "mystical lagunes, in whose stately arcades of cypress, fancy floats at will through all the wilds of past and future" to "the magnificence of the Hudson, and the Delaware and the Susquehanna."

745. Still-life painting was a sideline for many Southern painters. T. Addison Richards's book on flower painting, *The American Artist* (1838), reflected its growing popularity (**742**). Pictures of dead fish and game are common (Southerners have always been hunters). Oddly enough, there are only two known paintings of cotton: Rosetta Raulston Rivers did one of bolls in 1899, and Nell Choate Jones painted blossoms in 1936.

Meadowlark (1914), by George Lewis Viavant. Morris Museum of Art, Augusta, Ga.

746. Sculpture in the nineteenth century was mostly monumental or funeral, much of it (even Civil War monuments) commissioned from outsiders. Edward Virginius Valentine was probably the best nineteenth-century Southern sculptor; he even managed to make a living in Reconstruction Richmond and was sculptor of Robert E. Lee's tomb (**840**). In New Orleans, Achille Perelli did lots of portrait busts and funeral sculpture, but he's better known for his watercolors of dead game.

747. Scenes of black life, like plantation novels (**462**), captivated Northerners. They ranged from sensitive to stereotyped, and even the best of them can make modern viewers uncomfortable, but they're an important historical record. In 1860 Eastman Johnson exhibited his popular

In the Cottonfields (c. 1885), by William Aiken Walker.
Morris Museum of Art, Augusta, Ga.

The Old Plantation Home, by Currier & Ives.

Negro Life in the South in New York. Thomas Moran showed his *Slaves Escaping through the Swamp* in 1863. Winslow Homer painted blacks in Virginia in the 1870s (e.g., *The Visit from the Old Mistress),* and Southerners like William Aiken Walker (**771**) did very well indeed painting views of black life for tourists. (Walker offered one to a relative, who replied, "I cannot have one in my kitchen anymore. Why should I want one on the wall?")

748. **Currier and Ives** (active 1835–1907), publishers of popular prints, were major contributors to the myth of the Old South, offering Spanish moss, steamboats, happy darkies, elegant aristocrats, and stately homes—often all in the same picture. Many of their Southern scenes were drawn by Fanny Palmer, who was born in England, lived in New York, and never visited the South.

749. **After the War,** the South was shown inhabited entirely by blacks or by no one at all. Landscapes became the bread and butter of locals like the Brenner family and Paul Sawyier in Kentucky and visitors like William Morris Hunt, Winslow Homer, and Martin Johnson Heade (Henry Flagler's pet artist [**883**]). Joseph Rusling Meeker, who served on a Union gunboat on the Mississippi, was so enchanted that he came back to spend thirteen summers painting in the Delta heat. In 1873, when Edward King wrote in *Scribner's Monthly,* "Louisiana today is Paradise Lost," New Orleans was rife with landscape painters (**769**). W. J. Cash's description of the

A Louisiana Swamp (c. 1870), by Joseph Rusling Meeker. Morris Museum of Art, Augusta, Ga.

South fits their work: "The country is one of extravagant colors, of proliferating foliage and bloom, of floating yellow sunlight, and, above all, perhaps, of haze . . . a sort of cosmic conspiracy against reality in favor of romance."

SOUTHERN PAINTERS WHO LEFT THE SOUTH

MOST CAME BACK REGULARLY to paint.

750. **The Peale dynasty** includes the Maryland-born brothers Charles Willson Peale (1741–1827) and James Peale (1749–1831); Charles's sons Raphaelle, Rembrandt, and Titian; James's daughters Sarah, Anna, and Margaretta; Charles's nephew Charles Peale Polk; and Charles Willson's great-great-granddaughter Ella Sophonisba Hergesheimer (1873–1943). All were painters; some left the South and some stayed. Charles painted fourteen portraits of George Washington and founded several museums and the Pennsylvania Academy of Fine

Arts. Anna was a well-known miniaturist. Rembrandt ran the Peale Museum in Annapolis. Ella, a fine portraitist and still-life painter, worked in Nashville.

751. **Washington Allston** (1779–1843), of the South Carolina Allstons, showed his talent early, so his family sent him off to Newport, Rhode Island, that "his nervous and high-strung organization might be recruited by a more bracing air." Later, Harvard gossip said he had painted "a woman, stark naked." He used his inheritance to travel and to study under Benjamin West at the Royal Academy. He was a hit in England but returned to the United States when a dishonest agent wasted all his money, and his painting was never the same. The South claims

Washington Allston. Library of Congress USZ62-51928

him gladly, because he was, said Jessie Poesch, "the brightest star on the American artistic horizon in the early nineteenth century."

752. Thomas Sully (1783–1872) was born in England and raised in Charleston, Richmond, and Norfolk. He moved north when marriage radically raised his expenses. Settling in Philadelphia, he continued to paint often in the South. He did over two thousand portraits (art historian Henry Tuckerman said, "One always feels . . . in good society among his portraits") and about five hundred other pictures. The North Carolina legislature commissioned *The Passage of the Delaware by the American Troops under the Command of General Washington,* but it was too big for the space and ended up in Boston.

753. William Edward West (1788–1857) painted in Natchez and New Orleans, then went to Italy, where he painted the last life portrait of Byron. Trading on that connection, he hung out with literati and financiers in Paris and London and became a welcome bon vivant. Bankrupt from financial speculation, he came home—fortunately for us, because in 1838 he painted the first known portrait of Lee.

754. T. Addison Richards (1820–1900) was born in London but considered himself a Southerner. In 1845 he moved from Georgia to New York for study at the Art Students League and a distinguished career with the American Academy of Design, Cooper Union, and NYU. The

South remained a favorite subject, though he was as eloquent on the difficulty of travel as on its beauties (**744**): "the by-ways are miserable, the people ignorant, the fare scant and wretched, the expense of travel disproportionately great."

755. Louis Remy Mignot (1831–70), a Charlestonian, studied in the Netherlands and worked in New York. He traveled to Equador with his friend Frederic Edwin Church and became a sort of honorary member of the Hudson River School. After the outbreak of war, his Southern loyalty made him leave the United States forever (though it did not make him go home and enlist). He was a success in London, exhibiting at the Royal Academy and at the Paris Exposition of 1867. Henry Tuckerman, in

Robert E. Lee in the Uniform of a Lieutenant of Engineers, United States Army (1838), by William Edward West. Washington/Custis/Lee Collection, Washington and Lee University, Lexington, Va.

Detail from *Landscape in Ecuador* (1859), by Louis Remy Mignot. North Carolina Museum of Art, Raleigh

his *Book of the Artists* (1867), said of him, "He is a master of color, and some of his atmospheric experiments are wonderful."

756. Conrad Wise Chapman (1842–1910), the son of a painter, was living in Rome with his parents when the War broke out. He sold paintings to raise money for a ticket home and joined the Confederate Army, for which he painted military installations around Charleston. Thirty-one small, elegant oils survive. After the war he refused to set foot in the United States and shuttled between Europe and Mexico until old age drove him to seek refuge with relatives in Virginia.

757. Elliot Daingerfield (1859–1932) studied at the Art Students League and established a studio in New York. After 1885 he summered in Blowing Rock, North Carolina. He went through a symbolist period of bad poetry and religious painting. That was his best-known work, but now his still lifes and timeless Southern landscapes are widely appreciated, at least by Southerners.

Submarine Torpedo Boat H. L. Hundley, Dec. 6, 1863 (1864), by Conrad Wise Chapman. Museum of the Confederacy, Richmond, Va.

758. Anne Goldthwaite (1869–1944), painter and outspoken feminist, studied at the National Academy of Design, then went to Paris, where she helped organize the Académie Moderne and knew Gertrude Stein, Isadora Duncan, and Henri Matisse. She opened a studio in New York, had a piece in the Armory Show of 1913, and taught at the Art Students League after 1922.

New Orleans Ragging Home (1974), by Romare Bearden. North Carolina Museum of Art, Raleigh

Every summer (before air-conditioning) she returned to her native Alabama to paint with "the lightness of touch of the well-bred Old South, with the disenchanted wisdom of Paris added."

759. William H. Johnson (1901–70), from Florence, South Carolina, was the first black student at the National Academy of Design, won a scholarship to study abroad, worked in Europe, married a Dane, and returned to Harlem in 1938. He was perhaps too talented; he could adapt to any style (postimpressionism, expressionism) and make it look good. He's best known for his late work, painting the South of his roots in a "primitive" style, which he picked up from modernist Europeans. He's one of many black artists who left the South but returned (like black writers) in their work, as is—

760. Romare Bearden (1914–88), who moved north as a child but spent summers in the South. "I never left Charlotte, except physically." He got a math degree from NYU, then studied at the Art Students League under George Grosz. After the army he studied on the GI Bill at the Sorbonne, where he met Braque and Brancusi. He used collage and montage to create a kind of cubist narrative painting. "I thought about who I was and what I liked. I paint out of the tradition of the Blues, of call and recall." It works.

761. So many others. James McNeill Whistler, whose mother was a Southern girl and brother a Confederate Army surgeon; Jimmy always claimed he was a Southerner, even though he grew up in his native New England and in Russia, made his career in England, never set foot south of Washington, and didn't paint Southern subjects. Horace Bradley, director of the Art Students League, art director for Harper's magazines, and art columnist for the *Atlanta Constitution.* Clara Weaver Parrish, who designed for Tiffany. Nell Choate Jones, raised in Brooklyn, who said, "I am a Southerner and that's all there is to it" (**745**). Robert Gwathmey, the only Southern painting instructor at North Carolina's avant-garde Black Mountain College, whose depictions of blacks led even some black critics to jump to the wrong conclusion about his race. Red Grooms, "the Walt Disney of the art world." We could go on.

SOUTHERN PAINTERS WHO (MOSTLY) STAYED

762. **Henrietta Johnston** (?–1728 or 1729) was born in Ireland and came to Charleston as the wife of an underpaid Anglican clergyman, whose income she supplemented with portraits. She was probably the first female American artist and definitely the first to work in pastels.

763. **Jeremiah Theus** (1719?–74) had a near monopoly on portrait painting in Charleston. His 1740 ad read: "Gentlemen and Ladies may have their Pictures drawn, likewise landskips of all sizes, crests and coats of Arms for Coaches or Chaises. Likewise for the convenience of those who live in the Country, he is willing to wait on them at their respective Plantations." He died rich, mourned as "a very ingenious and honest man." Over 170 of his paintings survive. (See **742.**)

764. **John Abbot** (1751–1840) came to America in 1776 and eventually settled in Burke County, Georgia, whence he sent specimens and watercolors of local insects and birds to England. (In

Mrs. Samuel Prioleau (1715), by Henrietta Johnston. Collection of the Museum of Early Southern Decorative Arts

1816 one collector had 4,000 specimens and 3,140 watercolors.) Lacking scientific training, Abbot couldn't publish his own work, so only about two hundred were published in his lifetime. U.S. ornithologists revere him as a pioneer, and he should be better known as an artist.

765. **Joshua Johnston** (or Johnson) seems to have been the first black portrait painter. For nearly thirty years (1796–1824) a "limner" of that name was listed at addresses in Baltimore. Beyond that and the twenty-one extant paintings attributed to him, we have little except his own 1798 ad: "As a self-taught genius, deriving from nature and industry his knowledge of Art: and having experienced many insurpassable obstacles in the pursuit of his studies; it is highly

Mrs. Benjamin Yoe and Daughter (c. 1810), by Joshua Johnston. Collection of the Museum of Early Southern Decorative Arts

John J. Audubon. Library of Congress USZ62-20210

gratifying to him to make assurances of his ability to execute all commands, with an effect, and in a style, which must give satisfaction."

766. **John James Audubon** (1785–1851) was born in Santo Domingo and raised in France. In 1804 he moved to Pennsylvania and became an avid hunter. After failed business ventures and more successful hunting in Kentucky, he set off down the Mississippi to do a book of life-size portraits of the birds of America, supporting himself (but not, it seems, his wife and children) by teaching music and drawing, painting portraits, and doing taxidermy. He sketched from life, then drew freshly killed birds wired into natural poses. His eye-level drawings, mostly in watercolor, range (like the birds) from delicate to austere to exotic.

767. **Maria Martin** (1796–1863), a Charlestonian, seems like your standard Southern maiden aunt—running her invalid sister's household, helping her blind brother-in-law, developing her talent for painting when she could, and getting very little credit when her work was published. But behind those dreary facts was a happy life. She was a valued partner to her brother-in-law (later, husband) John Bachman on the text of Audubon's *The Viviparous Quadrupeds of North America*. Audubon taught her to paint and used her backgrounds for *Birds of America*. (Audubon credits her with eleven, but stylistic evidence attributes thirty to her.)

WEEKS PICKING

Detail from *Hauling the Whole Week's Picking* (c. 1842), by William Henry Brown. Historic New Orleans Collection 1975.93.2

768. William Henry Brown (1808–83) stands out not because he was a silhouettist (there were others), but because of his ambitious subjects: "entire family groups, military companies, fire companies with their engines and horse-carriages, sporting scenes, race-courses and marine views" (his words). He was proudest of his silhouette of the first passenger train in New York State (1831)—the passengers are all clearly identifiable. His *Portrait Gallery of Distinguished American Citizens* (1845) has twice been reissued in facsimile. The illustration here is part of a larger work done to entertain the children in a house where he was a guest.

769. Richard Clague (1821–73) was born in Paris to parents from New Orleans, and studied in New Orleans, France, and Switzerland. He exhibited in Paris 1848–53, then returned to New Orleans to stay, except for service in the Confederate Army. Probably the first Southerner to earn his living painting landscapes, he was teacher and guide to other Louisiana landscape artists. A critic wrote, "There is no meretricious glare about these fine studies, no straining after effect, no clap-trap of any kind."

770. Nicola Marschall (1829–1917) was a Prussian who immigrated to Alabama as a young man and became a dyed-in-the-wool Southerner. He designed the Stars and Bars (**322**) and Confederate Army uniforms, enlisted in the army, serving as a draftsman, and stayed in the South after the War, painting portraits of Confederate leaders.

771. **William Aiken Walker** (1838–1921), a Charlestonian, was wounded in the Civil War and spent the rest of it drawing fortifications and maps. (He also painted a deck of playing cards with Davis, Lee, Jackson, and Beauregard as kings.) After the War he specialized in paintings of Southern blacks (**747**), small ones for tourists as well as larger, more sophisticated works. Two of the latter were reproduced by Currier and Ives. Today his work is attacked as politically incorrect, but it adds up to a remarkable record of black life, and it's very expensive.

772. **Alexander John Drysdale** (1870–1934) studied at the Art Students League, then returned to his native New Orleans. Painting with watercolor or with kerosene-thinned oils, he tried to capture "transitory effects of nature" and did so to the satisfaction of a great many tourists and locals, in some ten thousand paintings. (Estill Pennington says that "owning a Drysdale became a part of the local art consciousness.") His drinking was legendary and his facility is now scorned, but at its best his work is highly evocative.

773. **William and Ellsworth Woodward** (1859–1939, 1861–1939), brothers born in Massachusetts, were trained at the Rhode Island School of Design and settled in New Orleans. Busy and important as teachers and administrators, somehow they even found time to paint. William helped start Tulane's architecture school, and his paintings of dilapidated New Or-

leans buildings inspired the preservation movement (**882**). Ellsworth headed Newcomb College's art department and helped found Newcomb Art Pottery (**125**); he was also director of the Delgado Museum (now the New Orleans Museum of Art). Believing that "art must always begin at home," they nurtured Southern art.

774. **Alice Ravenel Huger Smith** (1876–1958) was a Charleston painter, printmaker, and illustrator as well as a writer, historian, and preservationist. Largely self-taught, she was strongly influenced by Japanese woodblock prints. Her books include a biography of miniaturist Charles Fraser; *The Dwelling Houses of Charleston* (1917, written with her father); *A Carolina Rice Plantation in the Fifties* (1936, with her own lovely watercolors); and *A Charlestonian's Recollections, 1846–1913* (1950). She was the first of several successful women painters in Charleston in the twenties.

775. **John McCrady** (1911–68), a skillful and innovative New Orleans painter working in the regionalist style, became nationally famous after a New York show in 1937: a five-page spread in *Life,* praise in *Time* and the *New Republic.* In 1939 he painted *The Shooting of Huey Long* (**424**) for *Life,* and his proposal to paint "The Life and Faith of the Southern Negro" won him a Guggenheim. In 1948 the *Daily Worker* called him a racist, which seems to have stunned him; he painted very little after that, though he continued to teach.

776. **We ought to mention** Walter Inglis Anderson, the Southern Thoreau, who used watercolor instead of words, whose "pond" was the Gulf of Mexico, and whose fame grows daily; Sam Gilliam, who had a one-man show at the Museum of Modern Art in 1961; Benny Andrews,

whose extraordinary family is a story in itself—his father, George, is a painter known as the Dot Man, and his brother Raymond was a novelist; and Gari Melchers, Lamar Dodd, Hale Woodruff . . . But this is only 1001 things, remember?

THE CONTEMPORARY SOUTHERN TRIUMVIRATE

YOU'RE PRETTY MUCH ON your own for living artists. The South has plenty of them. Some might as well be in Peoria, but many still use Southern subjects: the landscape, hunting, fishing, semis, hogs, Elvis. Some look pretty good, but we're waiting to see how they turn out. We've just *got* to mention these three, though.

777. **Jasper Johns** (b. 1930), South Carolinian, sculptor, painter, and erstwhile window dresser for Tiffany's, is credited with beginning pop art in his 1958 New York show. Critic Brian O'Doherty said his art about art "provided everything the New York critical intelligence requires to require its own narcissism"—banal subjects and heavy irony.

778. **Robert Rauschenberg** (b. 1925) wanted to preach but loved to dance—a sin in the Church of Christ. Dancing won, but now he preaches world peace through his Rauschenberg Overseas Culture Exchange, spending millions to reach millions with his own brand of collaborative art. His work uses collage, homely found objects, silk screen, photography, paint, and anything else that interests him on any surface that attracts him. It's technically skilled, often oversize, and always decorative. He's a one-man art industry. Surprised to hear he's a Texan?

779. **Cy Twombly** (b. 1928) was *the* art story in 1994. Critic Deborah Solomon called it

Twomblymania. The Museum of Modern Art mounted a big retrospective; two New York galleries had adjunct displays; and the Menil Collection in Houston has a new Twombly pavilion. Hostile critics have called him "a painter who has turned hesitation into a full-blown style" and his style "furtive," "gloriously weak," and a "neurotic scrawl," but Solomon says, "He is our Tiepolo, turning the past into airy puffs"—a typical Southern pastime.

PHOTOGRAPHY

THE SOUTH HAS INSPIRED documentary photographers since the days of Matthew Brady.

780. **Some distinguished outsiders** have recorded Southern life and landscape. Two who had the help of Southern writers were Walker Evans, who worked with James Agee (**453, 523**) on *Let Us Now Praise Famous Men* (1941), and Margaret Bourke-White, who worked with her

Tenant farmer Floyd Burroughs ("George Gudger" in *Let Us Now Praise Famous Men*), photographed by Walker Evans, 1936. Farm Security Administration/Library of Congress USF34-2101-8138

husband, Erskine Caldwell, on *You Have Seen Their Faces* (1937). The Farm Security Administration provided work for artists in the late 1930s by sending them out to document Depression conditions: Walker Evans, Dorothea Lange, Marion Post Wolcott, Ben Shahn, Russell Lee, Arthur Rothstein, and others took thousands of pictures all over the South, and some are great photographs.

AMONG THE MANY FINE homegrown photographers of the South:

781. Frances Benjamin Johnston (1864–1952). Trained as a painter at the Art Students League, she became a political photojournalist known for photos of industries and mines. She also did public-relations photos of Hampton Institute and Tuskegee and worked for the Carnegie Foundation's survey of Southern colonial architecture, which produced over six thousand images between 1933 and 1940, some of them used in *The Early Architecture of North Carolina* (1941) and *Plantations of the Carolina Low Country* (1938).

782. Clarence John Laughlin (1905–85). His work evokes a line from "Abide with Me": "Change and decay and all around I see." He shared a New York show in 1940 with the French photographer Eugène Atget, a kindred spirit. Speaking of spirits, his book *Ghosts along the Mississippi* (1948) was a big success. His manipulated, surrealist images are striking, but even the straightforward ones grab you (**727**).

783. William Eggleston (b. 1939). A relative youngster, born in Memphis, he had the first show of color photography ever mounted at the Museum of Modern Art. Place and time are his subjects, and his dye-transfer printing tech-

nique yields images of startling intensity. "I am at war with the obvious."

SELF-TAUGHT ARTISTS

IT'S HARD TO GENERALIZE, except to say that the South has a lot of them. Some create naive art with a documentary impulse because they "want our children to know what things were like" (Bernice Sims). But many more express personal visions that range from eccentric to downright weird. Why? And why are there so many of them? We don't know. Most are rural, many (not all) are illiterate or nearly so, most are religious. Many take up art late in life, and some clearly use it to deal with loneliness or to redefine themselves after retirement or disability or the death of a spouse. Many must feel like exiles in their own country, given the changes they've seen (**471**). Does the South still turn them out? The youngest ones we know of were born in the fifties, but since most start late, we'll have to wait and see.

Lonnie Holley says, "Just let it leak from your heart and soul through your eyes and hands and then it IS art." But here are some frequent characteristics.

784. Many work obsessively and don't mind repeating themselves. Annie Hooper, for instance, made about 2,500 sculptures of biblical figures. We mean no disrespect when we say these artists remind us of our six-year-old daughter happily drawing the same castle over and over (it was a good castle).

785. They rarely use canvas and paint: "Art is everything we have used, waiting to be used again" (Lonnie Holley). "Old life just makes new life. That's what recycle is all about. When God died, he rose again" (Thornton Dial, Sr.). "In the junkyard, the piece will tell me exactly what it is, what I want" (Charlie Lucas). "I paint with my finger 'cause that's why I got it and that brush don't wear out. When I die, the brush dies" (Jimmy Lee Sudduth).

786. **Many are inspired by dreams and visions.** They believe art is a "God-given job" (Edgar Tolson). "Just about everything I make in my art come to me through my dreams" (James Harold Jennings). "In a dream it was shown to me what I have to do" (Minnie Evans). "I looked up in the sky and right there in the noon day light He hung a tombstone for me to carve" (William Ed-

mondson). "When I started I prayed and I prayed and the Lord sunk a vision from the sun" (John "J. B." Murry). "I like to take nothing and make something of it. That's the way of the Lord" (Anderson Johnson). Lonnie Holley must be right: "It's not by luck that the South is holy."

787. **There's often an urge to witness.** Much of this art shares an impulse with roadside "GET RIGHT WITH GOD" signs. From the outside of a Mississippi grocery store that says "JESUS CHRIST OWNS THIS STORE WE WORK FOR HIM" it's an easy progression to Margaret's store, built by the Reverend H. D. Dennis near Vicksburg, which is covered with verses and ad-

Dream of Prophets in the Air, by Minnie Evans. North Carolina Museum of History, Raleigh

monitions, then to Howard Finster's paintings, covered with texts like: "ONLY 3 PLACES FOR SOULS: EARTH FOR MAKING A CHOICE HELL FOR PUNISHING AND JUSTICE HEAVEN FOR REST AND PEACE AND GLORY" or "HELL IS A HELL OF A PLACE."

788. This art often does include text— a lot of text. "In the beginning was the Word" and it's all over many of these works, often from Revelation, the Bible's most colorful book. Lisa Howorth calls it "visual glossolalia." Why are image and text so often combined? Perhaps it's the importance of print to the marginally literate; the ubiquitous ads and posters of small-town life; the habit of wallpapering with newspapers; German *Fraktur;* Revelation's frequent references to writing on things or people ("a scarlet coloured beast, full of names"); the Sears catalog, with "all that color and all that mystery and all that beauty" (Harry Crews). Who knows?

Swan Parade, by Clementine Hunter. Red Piano Too Art Gallery, St. Helena Island, S.C.

SOME NAMES TO KNOW:

789. A couple of early ones: 1. William Edmondson progressed from tombstones to handsome small stone sculptures. He was the first black to have an exhibit at the Museum of Modern Art (1937). 2. Clementine Hunter was a maid for the artists' colony at Melrose Plantation (**733**). In the 1940s she asked to use some leftover paints, and the results led to exhibitions, articles, and fame.

790. Some more recent ones: 1. Minnie Evans (1892–1987) painted lyrical, highly patterned, colorful images. "We talk of heaven, we think everything is going to be white. But I believe we're going to have the beautiful rainbow colors." 2. Sister Gertrude Morgan (1900–80) founded the Everlasting Gospel Mission in New Orleans, believed she was the bride of Christ, always wore white, and lived in a white house with white furniture and all-white piano keys (and a lawn of four-leaf clovers). She dropped street preaching to take up painting for God in a

A Howard Finster camel. Red Piano Too Art Gallery, St. Helena Island, S.C.

Throne of the Third Heaven of the Nations Millennium General Assembly (c. 1950–64), by James Hampton.
National Museum of American Art

Howard Finster, Man of Visions, with his portrait of Elvis.
DixiePix

storefront church. 3. In a rented garage, discovered at his death, James Hampton had a little sign saying, "Where there is no vision the people perish" (Proverbs 29:18), and his *Throne of the Third Heaven of the Nations Millenium General Assembly* (c. 1950–64), an amazing 177-piece construction of furniture and paperboard covered with gold and silver tinfoil, kraft paper, and plastic. It's now in the National Museum of American Art.

791. **Two living ones:** 1. Howard Finster was a preacher until 1976, when a tiny face appeared in a paint smudge on his finger and told him to "paint sacred art." He paints on anything from gourds to cars, his work is taught in art schools, and he has an 800 number. 2. Clyde Jones's fantastic, imaginative animals can be seen in his yard in Bynum, North Carolina, and in museums around the country. He does them mostly with a chain saw, and he won't sell them but gives them away when he feels like it. Quite a guy.

Clyde Jones and one of his critters. DixiePix

Ten

Preaching and Teaching

RELIGION AND HIGHER EDUCATION

While the South is hardly Christ-centered, it is most certainly Christ-haunted.

—FLANNERY O'CONNOR

A Seminary of learning is greatly necessary for the Instruction of our Youth, and ought to be one of the first objects of attention after the promotion of Religion.

—GEORGIA STATUTE, 1783

CHURCHES WERE FIRST, BUT schools came right behind. Those priorities may still obtain.

The Bible Belt

SOME STATISTICS TO PONDER

792. Protestant Christianity is the religion of the South. Even including Texas and Florida, only one out of six Southern Christians is a Roman Catholic. All told, seven out of ten residents of the South are Protestant, compared to four out of ten non-Southerners. And, since non-Protestants are geographically concentrated *within* the South, the Protestant ascendancy in most Southern communities is even greater than these figures would suggest.

Sunday Morning, 1939, by Virginia-born Thomas Hart Benton. Library of Congress USZ62-107758

Like it says. DixiePix

793. Baptists and other evangelical denominations account for the great majority of Southern Christians. Slightly over half the South's Protestants say they're Baptists, and most of the rest are Methodists, Campbellites, Pentecostals, or members of other low-church bodies with roots in the evangelical tradition and an emphasis on individual conversion. According to the Southern Focus Poll, 51 percent of all residents of the South say converting unbelievers is a "very important" thing for churches to do, compared to 32 percent of other Americans. ("The South" here is the eleven undisputed Confederate states plus Kentucky and Oklahoma.)

794. That old-time religion is good enough for most Southerners. The Southern Focus Poll reports that the Bible is found in 96 percent of Southern households, 47 percent of the South's residents claim to have read it in the past week, and 66 percent believe it's "scientifically, historically, and literally true." The Devil exists, say 84 percent of the South's residents, and 78 percent expect the Second Coming. Religion is "very important" in the lives of 65 percent; 67 percent say grace at meals and 45 percent claim to attend church at least weekly. (All those figures are higher in the Deep South, and lower for non-Southerners.)

VARIETIES OF SOUTHERN RELIGION

THERE ARE MANY *KINDS* of Baptists and even more kinds of Pentecostals. You can't tell the players without a program.

795. Baptists split with Congregationalists in the seventeenth century over infant baptism (they were against it), and they've been cantan-

River baptism near Morehead, Kentucky, 1940. Marion Post Wolcott, Farm Security Administration/Library of Congress USF34-55314-D

kerous ever since. Today in the South there are literally dozens of Baptist conventions, associations, and fellowships as well as innumerable "independent Baptist" congregations that aren't affiliated with anybody. Most are old-fashioned Bible-believing churches that don't mind being described that way; all hold out for adult baptism (by immersion) and a high degree of congregational independence. "Niche marketing" has been successful: the South is more Baptist now than it was at the turn of the century. Among the many varieties:

796. THE SOUTHERN BAPTIST CONVENTION, which split with the Northern Baptists in 1845 over slavery, is the biggest of all. Although still concentrated in the South, it's now the largest Protestant denomination in the country, with a membership approaching 15 million (of whom some 500,000 are black), in all fifty states. Troubled of late by controversy between conservatives and "moderates" over such issues as scriptural inerrancy,

the Southern Baptists are still the thousand-pound gorilla of Southern religious life.

797. THE FREE WILL BAPTISTS emerged in the eighteenth century. As the name implies, they reject strict Calvinism. They practice open communion and foot washing. With headquarters in Antioch, Tennessee, they claim a quarter million members, two-thirds of them in seven Southern states. Two similar but smaller groups are the General Baptists, strong in the upper South, and the Evangelical Baptists, with a few thousand members in North Carolina.

798. PRIMITIVE BAPTISTS, on the other hand, *are* strict Calvinists (a/k/a Old School, Regular, Anti-mission, or Hard Shell Baptists) who took a hike in the 1820s over the question of missions, which they reject as unscriptural. Most also reject instrumental music and have maintained the old shape-note (**538–39**) singing tradition. Strictly congregational, they have no headquarters but do support a publishing house in Arkansas. Something under a hundred thousand, mostly Southern, attend roughly a thousand churches.

Primitive Baptist church, Georgia. DixiePix

799. THE BAPTIST MISSIONARY ASSOCIATION OF AMERICA and THE AMERICAN BAPTIST ASSOCIATION originated in the "Landmark" movement of the 1850s, which emphasized the total autonomy of local churches, claimed an unbroken succession of Baptist congregations from the time of Christ, asserted that the church was for believers only, and refused to recognize "alien immersions." They claim a combined membership approaching a million, mostly in the South. Don't confuse them with the American Baptist Churches in the U.S.A., formerly the Northern Baptist Convention.

800. BLACK BAPTISTS formed their own churches when slavery ended, recapitulating in the process some of the divisions among their former masters. (The National Primitive Baptists, for example, share the theology and traditions of their white brethren.) In 1895 three good-sized associations merged to form the National Baptist Convention, from which the National Baptist Convention of the U.S.A., Inc., split in a 1915 organizational dispute. Today the two bodies have some 3 and 7 million members respectively. A 1961 disagreement with the "incorporated" convention produced the Progressive National Baptists, probably the largest of many

Free Will Baptist foot washing. North Carolina Collection, University of North Carolina Library, Chapel Hill

smaller black Baptist groups. In 1965 two-thirds of African-American Christians were Baptists, but that proportion has declined with the growth of Pentecostal groups.

801. OTHER BAPTIST GROUPS in the South (mostly white) include the Baptist Bible Fellowship, International; the Central Baptist Association; the Duck River Baptists (who come in two flavors, Missionary and Separate); Evangelical Baptists (formerly the Church of the Full Gospel); the Liberty Baptist Fellowship (independent churches associated with Jerry Falwell); Pentecostal Free Will Baptists; Reformed Baptists; Separate Baptists; Seventh Day Baptists; Sovereign Grace Baptists; United Baptists; United Free Will Baptists; and no doubt new ones this year. The Two-Seed-in-the-Spirit Predestinarian Baptists may have gone out of business now, but there were a few hundred of them in the 1950s.

802. **Methodists** in the South have lately played Avis to the Baptists' Hertz—and they've been losing market share. Once #1, they're still #2, but they can now claim only one out of six Southern Protestants. Southern evangelicalism began with their founder, John Wesley: although his only trip to America as a missionary in Georgia was brief and disastrous (he fled facing a civil lawsuit), the church he organized later, with its circuit riders and revival-style preaching, was the backbone of Southern religion until about 1890, when adherents of the Holiness movement began to split off. Some Southern bodies with Wesleyan roots:

803. THE UNITED METHODIST CHURCH, the largest Methodist body in the South, was formed by the 1939 reunion of the Methodist Episcopal Church and the Methodist Episcopal Church, South, which had split over slavery in 1845. In 1968 the

reunited Methodists merged with the Evangelical United Brethren, which brought in a few congregations of Shenandoah Valley Germans.

804. THE SOUTHERN METHODIST CHURCH is a small remnant of the Methodist Episcopal Church, South, with a few thousand members in a hundred-plus churches, all in the South. When the two sectional Methodist churches reunited, these folks held out, citing the "alarming infidelity and apostasy" of the Northern church.

Working on a building: Mount Zion Methodist Church, North Carolina. North Carolina Collection, University of North Carolina Library, Chapel Hill

805. BLACK METHODISTS are found primarily in three bodies: the African Methodist Episcopal Church, the African Methodist Episcopal Zion Church, and the Christian (before 1956: Colored) Methodist Episcopal Church. The first two were founded by Northern free blacks in 1816 and 1796 respectively; the CME Church was established in 1870 by black Methodists in the South, with the blessing of white Southern Methodists. The three groups' headquarters are in Washington, Charlotte, and Memphis. AME membership stands at about 2 million nationwide; AME Zion and CME each have about half that figure. Several smaller black Methodist bodies have a few thousand members each.

806. THE WESLEYAN CHURCH is one of the most interesting of several small white Methodist groups found in the South. It resulted from the 1968 merger of the Wesleyan Methodist Church, a splinter from the larger Methodist body in 1843 to protest slavery, and the Pilgrim Holiness Church, one of the many Pentecostal sects begun in the 1890s. Given its antislavery heritage, it may seem odd that the church has about a quarter of its 100,000 members in the South, especially in the Carolinas and Virginia, but it long ago turned its attention from social issues to sanctification.

807. THE CHRISTIAN CHURCH, also known as O'Kellyites (after founder James), arose from a 1792 intra-Methodist quarrel in North Carolina over hierarchical authority—hence its other name, Republican Methodists. In 1931 it merged with Yankee Congregationalists to form what, after some more mergers, became the United Church of Christ. Neither the original Christian Church nor the United Church of Christ is to be confused with any sort of Campbellite (**818**).

Presbyterian Church in Port Gibson, Mississippi, points the way to heaven. Deborah Purviance

808. Presbyterians were at Jamestown by 1620, but most came to the South with the great Scotch-Irish (**98**) migration. Calvinist in their origins and governed by "presbyteries," or councils of elders and clergy, the Presbyterians have been distinguished in the South for their commitment to learning, and they've been overrepresented among the region's elite. Although Southerners make up a slight majority of U.S. Presbyterians, only 5 to 6 percent of Southern Protestants say they're Presbyterian.

809. THE PRESBYTERIAN CHURCH (U.S.A.) claims the allegiance of most Southern Presbyterians these days. It was formed in 1983 by the reunion of the Northern and Southern churches that split at the outbreak of the Civil War. (Its headquarters, fittingly, are in Louisville.) Congregations of the former Southern Presbyterian church make up about 40 percent of its membership.

810. THE PRESBYTERIAN CHURCH IN AMERICA split in 1973 from the main body of Southern Presbyterians, alarmed at theological liberalism (and liberalism of other sorts) and opposed to the impending reunion with Northern Presbyterians. Headquartered in Atlanta, this is an uncharacteristically fast-growing species of Presbyterianism, with approximately 200,000 communicants in over one thousand churches, mostly in the South.

811. THE CUMBERLAND PRESBYTERIAN CHURCH was organized in Tennessee in 1810, following the Cane Ridge revival (**824–25**). Its founders rejected the thoroughgoing Calvinism of their parent church and sought to establish an evangelical church to work on the frontier. Today the church has about 100,000 members, mostly in the South, and headquarters in Memphis. There is a small, separate black Cumberland Presbyterian group.

812. ASSOCIATE REFORMED PRESBYTERIANS are strong in the Carolinas and Georgia and have been since the church was founded in 1822 as the result of a North-South split in an older group of Covenanter and Seceder origins—and don't worry, even most Presbyterians don't follow all this. Basically, these are hard-core Calvinists who hold to the Westminster Confession and the old ways. Only after 1946 was the singing of hymns (as opposed to psalms) allowed. Erskine Caldwell's father was an ARP minister.

Shaking a snake in eastern Kentucky. National Archives

813. Pentecostal and Holiness groups ("Holy Rollers" is an impolite label usually employed by those whose churches are growing less rapidly) mostly trace their origins either to religious ferment in east Tennessee beginning in the 1880s or to the Pentecostal movement begun around 1900 on the West Coast. Some denominations are black, some white, some strikingly both, but all believe in such gifts of the Holy Spirit as speaking in tongues. Most engage in faith healing, foot washing, and other practices found in scripture; a fringe takes up serpents and drinks poison on the same warrant. Pentecostals have experienced explosive growth, but they've carried the evangelical Protestant tendency to fragmentation about as far as it can go. Tiny groups litter the religious landscape, independent storefronts and tabernacles spring up like mushrooms, and accurate membership figures are hard to come by. Two of the largest denominations:

814. THE CHURCH OF GOD IN CHRIST (COGIC) was founded in 1897 by Charles Harrison Mason in Lexington, Mississippi, after black Baptists "disfellowshipped" him for his extreme emphasis on sanctification. After Mason attended the Azusa Street Revival (**829**) he converted COGIC into a Pentecostal body, working closely with white Pentecostals, many of whom he ordained. (In 1914, with his blessing, they formed their own denomination.) Jailed for his pacifist views in World War I, Mason continued to lead the church until his death at ninety-five. COGIC's Mason Temple in Memphis is the largest black-owned meeting place in the country; it was the site of Martin Luther King, Jr.'s last address. COGIC is growing rapidly: with nearly 4 million members and over ten thousand churches, it is the least-known major denomination in the United States.

815. THE ASSEMBLIES OF GOD are somewhat more visible, if only because their clergy includes such well-known televangelists (**832**) as Jimmy Swaggart and Jim Bakker. Formed in Hot Springs, Arkansas, in 1914, the Assemblies of God now have approximately 2 million members in over eleven thousand churches.

816. SMALLER GROUPS ABOUND. In the Church of God family is the original Church of God (Cleveland, Tennessee), but also the (Original) Church of God, the Church of God of Prophecy, the Church of God (Huntsville, Alabama), and the Church of God Mountain Assembly. Holiness groups include the Pentecostal Assemblies of the World (biracial when founded in 1907, now mostly black), the Pentecostal Holiness Church International, the United Holy Church of America, the Emmanuel Holiness Church, the Pentecostal Church of God, the International Pentecostal Church of Christ, the United Pentecostal

Church International—you get the idea. One group founded by "Mother Lewis" in 1903 has splintered into a dozen, with increasingly complex names: for instance, one such group is called the House of God, Holy Church of the Living God, the Pillar and Ground of the Truth House of Prayer for All People (Hebrew Pentecostal).

817. **Episcopalians,** like Presbyterians, have been around since Jamestown; in fact, the Anglican church was by law established in the colonies south of Maryland. Handicapped by onerous ordination requirements, however, and perhaps unsuited for the task anyway, Anglicans left the evangelization of the Southern frontier to other churches. Consequently, they're thickest on the ground not far from the coast in the older seaboard states, and they're even less numerous than Presbyterians (though just as classy). The University of the South (**836**), an Episcopal institution, was a great center for the cult of the Lost Cause (**332–43**).

818. **Campbellites** (after founder Alexander Campbell) come from an indigenous American religious movement originating in the Cane Ridge revival of 1801 (**824**). All its founders were Presbyterians, but Campbellites reject the concept of "denomination" and church polity is congregational. Three varieties each claim a million or so adherents spread through the lower Midwest and upper South to the Southwest. The Christian Church (Disciples of Christ) is the most liberal of the three; the Churches of Christ the most conservative (splitting in 1927 over admitting unimmersed believers to fellowship). The third variety, called the Christian Churches and Churches of Christ, describes itself as a "middle group."

819. **Smaller Protestant denominations** in the South have generally been ethnic churches, concentrated in areas settled by non-British immigrants (**99, 103–4**). Thus, the Church of the Brethren (or Dunkers, referring to their practice of threefold immersion) is mostly Germans in the Shenandoah Valley, as are the Mennonites. Moravians settled in and near Winston-Salem. Lutherans and a number of evangelical groups are found in Texas. Similarly, Quakers (though not exactly "ethnic") have long been in the North Carolina Piedmont, an area of surprising religious diversity. Recent migration is making Southern metropolitan areas centers for everything from Korean Presbyterians to Unitarians, but the numbers are still small.

820. **Roman Catholics** were found in colonial Maryland, thanks to (Catholic) Lord Baltimore, and there's a curious outpost in north-central Kentucky, where Marylanders settled. Elsewhere Catholicism, like off-brand Protestantism, is usually associated with non-British ethnicity: Mexicans and Germans in Texas, Cubans and other Latin Americans in south Florida, Cajuns and Creoles (of both races) in Louisiana, Irish and Italians and Yankee migrants in Southern cities. Still, in many Southern communities there are no known non-Protestants.

821. **Jews** have been in the South for a long time (**108–9**), but after 1800 most Jewish immigrants avoided the region. Enough came, however, to allow a social distinction in many older cities between Reform congregations (usually established by German Jews who came as early as the 1840s) and Conservative ones (serving Eastern European Jews who came later). Lately, Jewish communities in large Southern cities

Congregation Bnai-Sholom (1898), Huntsville, Alabama.
DixiePix

have been augmented by migration from the region's smaller towns as well as from the North.

822. **Other religions** are beginning to be represented in the South, though still in small numbers. Hindus and Buddhists are building temples in unlikely places, and there are mosques for both Sunni Muslims and the Nation of Islam. Louisiana's long-standing voodoo tradition (**128–31**) has lately been supplemented by Cuban Santeria in Florida and similar forms of religious expression in south Texas, while a few Northern black migrants to rural South Carolina have revived something resembling the original Yoruba strain. Devotees of Meher Baba have a center in Myrtle Beach, the Krishna Consciousness folks have one in West Virginia, and South

Carolina is now home to thousands of black Baha'is and American Indian Mormons. Strange things are happening.

REVIVALS

THE SOUTH'S EVANGELICAL PROTESTANTISM took its present shape thanks to revivals, and understanding the institution is still important for understanding the religion of most Southerners. Two episodes and two terms to know:

823. **The (First) Great Awakening,** as far as the South was concerned, began on the Virginia frontier in the 1740s and spread quickly and spontaneously to neighboring colonies. The Awakening's emphasis on human depravity and the need for individual salvation apparently struck a chord with many Southerners, especially those isolated from the steadying influence of the coastal settlements. This Southern version of a phenomenon more often associated with New England Congregationalism benefitted the Baptists, New Light Presbyterians, and especially Wesleyans, whose itinerant methods and soul-saving preachers were well suited to a frontier largely neglected by the rigid, establishment Church of England.

824. **The Second Great Awakening** was pretty much a rerun of the first, a spontaneous and fairly successful attempt in the early years of the nineteenth century to evangelize the Southern frontier, which by then had moved across the Appalachian Mountains. (This time the Presbyterians largely sat it out, leaving matters in Baptist and Methodist hands.) One innovation was the camp meeting: one of the first, attended by upwards of ten thousand souls, was at Cane Ridge, Kentucky, in 1801 (**537**).

Illustration from Gorham's *Camp Meeting Manual.* North Carolina Museum of History, Raleigh

825. Camp meetings began with "brush arbors," canopies of tree branches built for shelter. A "brush arbor revival" can still evoke powerful nostalgia in some circles, but camp meetings have now often moved into permanent campgrounds with large sheds surrounded by family-owned cabins. Talking of the old days, Lillian Smith said, "Guilt was then and is today the biggest crop raised in Dixie, harvested each summer just before cotton is picked." No doubt, but conviviality, music, and matchmaking are harvested, too.

A tent revival. Caufield & Shook Collection, Photographic Archives, University of Louisville

826. Revivals have largely replaced camp meetings these days. Usually in the summertime, a visiting evangelist will set up shop for a week or so, often sponsored by a local church, preaching every evening to reclaim the errant and refresh the commitments of the faithful. The classic setting is a tent, but more and more revivals these days seem to be held indoors, where it's air-conditioned.

SOME DRAMATIS PERSONAE OF SOUTHERN RELIGION

IN THE SOUTH, AS in this book, religious leaders pop up all over the place, from the Confederate Army (**294**) to the civil rights movement (**393, 395–97**). But here's an odd lot of interesting or colorful or important figures you won't find in other chapters. (We'll spare you David Koresh.)

827. **James Henley Thornwell** (1812–62) was the son of a South Carolina plantation overseer and a devout Baptist mother. He graduated at the top of his class from the state college and became a schoolteacher. Converted to Presbyterianism by a reading of the Westminster Confession, he went to New England for ministerial training but was put off by the prevailing liberalism and returned to South Carolina. There he became president of his alma mater, a powerful thinker and preacher, the Old South's leading theologian, and one of the leading defenders of slavery.

828. **Carry Nation** (1846–1911) was converted at age ten at a Kentucky camp meeting. Mysticism and bad luck (and possibly a touch of insanity inherited from her mother's family) governed her decisions thenceforth. She married an alcoholic Mason, so she hated both alcohol and fraternal orders. She left him, and when he died six months later, taught school to support herself, her insane child, and her mother-in-law. In 1877 she contracted another unhappy marriage, to David Nation, and ended up in Kansas, where she became a temperance activist. Visions led her to conclude that saloons, being illegal, could simply be destroyed, so she took her trusty hatchet and went to work. After more than thirty arrests, she hired a manager, went

An Atlanta cartoonist's view of Carry Nation, c. 1900.
Albert Volberg

on lecture tours (biting the hand that fed her, she denounced Harvard and Yale as "hellholes"), and sold souvenir hatchets (anticipating Lester Maddox [**429**]). Her second husband divorced her for desertion.

829. **William Joseph Seymour** (1870–1922) was born in Louisiana, the son of former slaves. He taught himself to read and studied with a Methodist evangelist in Cincinnati. Ordained in a small evangelical sect, he went to Houston to preach and to look for relatives lost in slavery times. There he studied at the segregated Houston Bible School, literally sitting outside the classroom door. He moved to Los Angeles and started a prayer meeting. On April 9–12, 1906, members of the group began to speak in tongues. Attracting huge crowds (mostly white), the congregation moved to larger quarters, the Azusa Street Mission, and the ensuing revival gave birth to the international Pentecostal movement.

830. **Father Divine** (1882–1965) was born George Baker in Savannah and began preaching as a young man in Georgia. After his arrest as a public nuisance, he moved north in 1914. In 1930 he adopted the name Father Divine, and his Harlem-based Peace Mission movement spread throughout New York City and elsewhere. It preached racial equality and attracted a following primarily (though not exclusively)

among his fellow blacks. Many of his followers thought Divine was exactly that, a belief he did not discourage.

831. **William Franklin "Billy" Graham** (b. 1918) went the opposite direction from James Henley Thornwell. Raised fundamentalist Presbyterian, he seems to have rebelled as a youth by becoming a fundamentalist Baptist. Converting at age sixteen, he was ordained at twenty-one and drifted awhile through several good causes (recruiting for Youth for Christ, running fundamentalist schools) before he found his true calling at thirty-one, when an eight-week revival in Los Angeles made him a household name. Since then he has preached salvation to millions around the world and has become our de facto clergyman laureate, spiritual adviser to presidents. He is a Southern evangelist with a television program, but he's not a televangelist.

The Reverend Billy Graham. *U.S. News & World Report*/Library of Congress U9-4620-10

832. **Televangelists** are, however, mostly a Southern thing. Several run vast business empires, broadcasting networks, colleges (Oral Roberts, Pat Robertson, Jerry Falwell). Most are aggressively conservative (Falwell: "We are in a holy war for the survival of families") and quite willing to mix religion and politics (Falwell again: "The idea [that] religion and politics don't mix was invented by the Devil to keep Christians from running their own country. If any place in the world we need Christianity, it's in Washington"). Several have succumbed to the world, the flesh, and the Devil: Jim Bakker, defending his opulent Heritage U.S.A. (before he went to jail), asked, "Why should I apologize because God throws in crystal chandeliers, mahogany floors, and the best construction in the world?" His wife, Tammy Faye, added, "You don't have to be dowdy to be a Christian." The Bakkers aren't native Southerners, but they assimilated.

Educational Institutions

THIS MAY SEEM LIKE anticlimax after religion. After all, the South isn't known for its *educational* institutions. But these fifteen strike us as Southern in interesting—and very different—ways.

833. **The College of William and Mary** was named for the reigning monarchs when it was founded in 1693. The second oldest college in the United States (after Harvard), it was the nation's first true university, opening colleges of law and medicine in 1781. Originally Church of England, it became nonsectarian after the Revolution, and state-supported a century later.

Closed twice by war and once (in the 1880s) by financial difficulties, it was eclipsed for years by the upstart University of Virginia, but it anchors Colonial Williamsburg (**885**), numbers distinguished politicians and jurists among its graduates, and gave birth to Phi Beta Kappa and the student honor code.

834. **The Citadel** and **Virginia Military Institute** have fierce individual identities and proud, distinctive traditions, but the two remaining state-supported military colleges have a great deal in common. VMI in Lexington, Virginia, is older (1839 vs. 1842), and The Citadel in Charleston, South Carolina, is bigger (approx. three thousand students vs. one thousand), but both offer college instruction combined with rigorous military discipline. Cadets from both schools fought in the Civil War (VMI's at the Battle of New Market, The Citadel's at Fort Sumter), both have distinguished military alumni, and each has an all-male tradition more or less constantly under attack in the courts and the press.

The old Citadel, Charleston. DixiePix

835. Berea College, opened in the Kentucky foothills in 1855 with the help of Cassius Clay (**269**), offered biracial and coeducational education from grade school through college. Closed briefly by proslavery mobs and the Civil War, it has operated on that basis from 1866 until the present, save for a period when state law required it to operate a separate institute for black students. Largely financed by Northern philanthropy, Berea has been notable for its service to the Appalachian South. Nearly all its students are from the Southern mountains and pay tuition by working in the college's work-study program.

836. The University of the South, in Sewanee, Tennessee, was meant to be just that, the national university of the South, but the timing was wrong. Founded in 1857, largely at the instigation of Leonidas Polk (**294**), it lost both its endowment and its original mission in the Civil War. It has survived as a small, elite college for men (coed after 1969), with an Anglican connection and a Tory ambience. Its seminary prepares Episcopal clergy, and the *Sewanee Review,* founded in 1892, upholds high literary standards.

837. Atlanta University Center has been an important educational institution for the black South. It incorporates a half dozen historic schools. Clark Atlanta University was formed by the 1988 merger of Atlanta University (the oldest component, founded in 1865) and Clark College (founded 1869). Spelman was established in 1881 in some old Union Army barracks as the first college for black women in the United States. Morehouse, a men's college, was already in business, founded in 1867. Morris Brown, a coed college, was founded in 1881. The Interdenominational Theological Center completes the picture. Altogether, some eleven thousand undergraduates and over a thousand graduate students are enrolled in these institutions. Martin

Luther King, Jr., was a Morehouse man, and W. E. B. Du Bois taught at Atlanta University.

838. Fisk University and **Meharry Medical College** are neighbors in Nashville. Fisk was begun immediately after the Civil War, for the education of newly freed slaves. Jubilee Hall (1875) was paid for by the Jubilee Singers (**541**) (still in existence). Its library has an extensive collection of papers and manuscripts by noted black Americans, including the university's famous president Charles S. Johnson. Meharry was founded in 1876 to educate black health professionals. Nearly 40 percent of all black doctors and dentists practicing today are Meharry graduates.

839. Tuskegee Institute was founded in 1881 by Booker T. Washington (**390**), helped by a $2,000

Tomb of Lee at Washington and Lee. *Library of Southern Literature* (1907)

loan from the state of Alabama. Tuskegee specialized in vocational training, following the example of Washington's alma mater, Hampton Institute. With agricultural scientist George Washington Carver on its faculty for many years, and Washington as president, Tuskegee gained national prominence. (See **738.**)

840. Washington and Lee University has been through several name changes since it was founded in 1749, acquiring the "Washington" after a generous gift from George, then "Lee" after the death of president Robert E. (**287**). Located in Lexington, Virginia, W&L has long been a small liberal-arts college with a student body mostly from the South. Its proud Virginia heritage seems to have survived desegregation and coeducation just fine. Lee's tomb is in the college chapel named for him, and the national headquarters of the Kappa Alpha Order (**346**) are located nearby.

841. Sweet Briar College, founded in 1901, is typical of a number of small, mostly private colleges that started as glorified finishing schools for young Southern ladies and have turned into pretty good—or even better—women's liberal-

Booker T. Washington lifts the veil of ignorance from his people, on the campus at Tuskegee. DixiePix

arts colleges. (We picked it rather than some other because we like its name.) Some five hundred mostly Southern students and a good many horses inhabit Sweet Briar's lovely 3,300-acre campus in Virginia's Blue Ridge foothills, a safe distance from the distractions of Charlottesville and Lexington.

842. **The University of North Carolina,** opened in 1795, calls itself "the First State University" (ignoring the claims of the University of Georgia, which was chartered first, in 1785, but opened later). By 1861 only Yale had a larger student body. At first a school primarily for the planter elite, "Chapel Hill" has served in this century as a major regional university, attracting students from across the South (like Walker Percy and Shelby Foote from Mississippi) and nurturing regional scholarship and creative activity with graduate programs in history, literature, and the social sciences, its journals, its press, and its library (especially the incomparable Southern Historical Collection).

843. **The University of Virginia** was founded in 1819 by Thomas Jefferson (**729**), who designed its original "academic village" and curriculum, served as its first rector, and put the fact on his tombstone. Jefferson wanted the Charlottesville school to serve a natural aristocracy of talent, not just planters' sons like those enrolled at Chapel Hill—which makes it ironic that "Mr. Jefferson's university" became the most self-consciously gentlemanly state college in the nation. It's coed now and has some twenty thousand students.

844. **The University of Mississippi** ("Ole Miss") would be just your generic Southeastern Conference football-and-party school if not for its association with Oxford boy William Faulkner, the segregationist riots attending the admission of James Meredith (**377**), the continuing attachment of many students and alumni to the Confederate battle flag as a school symbol, and its recent emergence as a major center for scholarship on the South, with the Center for the Study of Southern Culture and related enterprises. The chancellor once candidly observed, "If this university isn't Southern . . . it's not anything." No problem.

Mr. Jefferson's University, Charlottesville. Office of War Information/Library of Congress USW3-33767-C

Colonel Rebel, the Ole Miss mascot, on a tire cover. DixiePix

845. The North Carolina School of the Arts, founded in 1965, offers professional training from middle school through college (and some graduate degrees) in dance, music, art, drama (including design and production), and filmmaking. Helen Hayes called it "infinitely the best school in America" for the arts. Its graduates are ubiquitous: few orchestras or dance companies are without NCSA alumni. Disney's Broadway production of *Beauty and the Beast* had nine in its cast and crew, including the Beast, Lumière, the assistant concertmistress, and someone with the delightful title of chief pyrotechnician.

THESE NEXT TWO AREN'T colleges, but each has contributed in its way to the South's intellectual and cultural life—and we don't know where else to put them.

846. The Penn Center was founded in 1862 on St. Helena Island by Laura Towne and Ellen Murray, two classic unpaid Yankee schoolmarms. It was part of an effort to help newly freed slaves on the South Carolina Sea Islands (**28**), which had been occupied by Union troops. When the Philadelphia Freedmen's Relief Association sent a prefab schoolhouse by boat, the school was named after William Penn. In 1953 Penn Center closed its school and became a conference center, especially useful as a place for integrated gatherings. (Martin Luther King and SCLC held meetings there in the sixties.) It is now engaged in an effort to preserve Gullah (**95**) culture and the local community and is raising funds for restoration and a museum.

847. The Rosenwald Foundation (1917–48) was founded in Chicago by Julius Rosenwald, president of Sears, Roebuck (a major influence in the South in other ways [**788**]). It "concentrated on equalization of opportunities among the various groups in America, contributing substantial sums to Negro education, Negro health, fellowships for Negroes and white Southerners." Fellowships went to social scientists, writers, artists, dancers, musicians, and folklorists, including at least thirty-five people mentioned in this book.

Sea Island School No. 1, St. Helena Island, South Carolina, for the education of freed slaves, 1862. Library of Congress USZ62-107754

Eleven

Kicking Back

SPORTS AND TOURISM

I know why we lost the Civil War. We must have had the same officials.

—COACH BUM PHILLIPS

Some native Southerners still operate on the theory that a Yankee is worth more than a bale of cotton and twice as easy to pick.

—JONATHAN DANIELS

The Japanese like the American South.
—JACK SODEN, PRESIDENT OF ELVIS PRESLEY ENTERPRISES

Sports

How Southerners relate to some major sports:

848. Fishing is something Southerners do a lot of. They have lots of water (one-half of the contiguous U.S. coastline, huge bays and sounds, natural and man-made lakes) and lots of fish, crab, oysters, and shrimp. They do it with cane poles, dry flies, and bass boats loaded with accessories. They do it to relax and they do it professionally—in tournaments, no less (they even do it on TV). They do it alone, and they do it in

Kentucky hunter and hound, 1940. Marion Post Wolcott, Farm Security Administration/Library of Congress USF33-31161

groups. They do it for food and they do it just for fun. Eighty percent of Southerners were taken fishing as children. It's sort of like—

849. Hunting, which Southerners also go in for. These days they do it more for sport than for sustenance, though they eat what they kill. They do it alone, with man's best friend, and in groups ad hoc (a dove shoot with the guys) and permanent (a posh hunt club). They're not as likely to hunt as to fish, but 42 percent of Southerners, male and female, were taken hunting as children.

850. Horse racing used to be a Southern thing. Once, it was legal only for gentlemen—in 1674 a Virginia "Labourer" (a tailor) was arrested for the crime of racing a mare. By 1865 the South (including D.C.) had eighty-three major race courses, while the North had only twenty-two. The Christians got down on it because of the gambling, but thanks to Kentucky, the South still has the Big One: the Derby is not just part

Fishing on the bayou, 1940. Marion Post Wolcott, Farm Security Administration/Library of Congress USF34-54247-D

The Kentucky Derby. Caufield & Shook Collection, Photographic Archives, University of Louisville

of the Triple Crown, it's an excuse for Southerners around the world to indulge in another favorite leisure-time activity—julep (**662**) parties.

851. **Stock car racing** combines the thrills and excitement of horse racing with the Southern cult of the car ("Nobody with a good car needs to be justified," says Hazel Motes in Flannery O'Connor's *Wise Blood*). Some early heroes like Junior Johnson developed their fearless driving style and their improved automobiles evading revenooers on mountain roads. Since then racing has become big business. A lot of good old boys have become rich and famous, tickets are more expensive, and audiences are more upscale: posh new condos overlooking Atlanta Speedway are named Tara Place. Forty-nine percent of Southerners have been to the races, and most drivers still come from North Carolina, Tennessee, and Alabama. (See **36, 874**.)

852. **Basketball** is mostly an enthusiasm of the upper South, with winning college traditions in Kentucky, North Carolina, and (lately) Arkansas. Professional basketball came late to the region, and geographer John F. Rooney, Jr., has shown that only Kentucky and Tennessee are as much as 20 percent above the national average in per capita production of major-college players, while most Southern states are well below average.

853. **Baseball** players are even less likely than basketball players to be from the South. Only Florida and Alabama are above average in producing major leaguers, and Alabama's just barely. Still, the South produces some of the best (Fred Hobson notes that "the South served

A car fit for the King. North Carolina Museum of History, Raleigh

Cedar Grove baseball team, North Carolina, 1939. Southern Historical Collection, University of North Carolina Library, Chapel Hill

the same function in baseball that it served in the nation's economy: It was a colony producing the raw materials"). Lately, the region has taken the Atlanta Braves (**879**) to its heart, even if most of them are carpetbaggers.

854. **Soccer, swimming, gymnastics, wrestling, track, and women's sports of all kinds**—forget it.

855. **Football** is the South's sport. Where else would a house-and-garden magazine like *Southern Living* pick an all-star football team every fall? Yet it makes sense in the South: much of the region's social life does center around tailgate parties. Every Southern state is above (and most of them well above) the national average in per capita production of major-college and professional football players: Mississippi, Louisiana, and Texas lead the nation. Willie Morris: "It is no doubt a cliche, yet true, that Southern football is a religion, and many Southern football heroes have achieved a sort of civil sainthood." Which makes it ironic that the sport was imported from New England.

SOUTHERN SPORTS HALL OF FAME

OUR OWN SELECTIONS, OBVIOUSLY. We could argue about it.

856. **Expatriate Southerners** have been as conspicuous in American sports as in American music, and mostly for the same reason: the great migration of blacks from the South before 1970. Consider baseball's Jackie Robinson, grandchild of a slave and son of a sharecropper, born in Cairo, Georgia, but raised in California. Or Joe Louis, boxing's Brown Bomber, born a share-

TODAY'S POPULAR HERO.

An Atlanta cartoonist salutes the South's new hero, c. 1900. Albert Volberg

cropper's child in Chambers County, Alabama, who moved to Detroit when he was twelve. Or Jesse Owens, hero of the 1936 Olympics, whose father moved his family from the Alabama cotton fields to Cleveland, where he found work in a steel mill. Or Jim Brown, perhaps football's greatest runner, raised by his great-grandmother on Saint Simons Island, Georgia, until he was seven, when he joined his mother in

Manhasset, New York. Dozens of other champions and All-Americans have similar biographies.

BUT WE'LL STICK TO athletes born and bred in the South.

857. **Ty Cobb** (1886–1961) was born to respectable parents in Banks County, Georgia. Against his father's wishes, he played minor-league ball for Augusta, then joined the Detroit Tigers in 1905, where he set a score of records that still stand, including a lifetime batting average of .367 and thirty-five stolen home plates. By all accounts "the Georgia Peach" was an unpleasant character: a racist, brawler, and bully, he alienated two wives and all of his children, and he died rich but friendless. But he was one heck of a ballplayer. His teammate Sam Crawford said of him, "He came up from the South, you know, and he was still fighting the Civil War. He was always trying to prove he was the best."

858. **Hank Aaron** (b. 1934) was born in Mobile, Alabama. As a boy he delivered ice, which he said gave him the wrists that made Sandy Koufax call him "the last guy I ever want to see coming up to the plate." After playing amateur and semipro ball in Mobile, Aaron joined the Indianapolis Clowns of the Negro American League, but was quickly picked up by the Braves organization and started in the big leagues in 1954. His play (and his salary) with Atlanta broke many records, but he will always be remembered for his 715th home run, which beat Babe Ruth's career total. Acknowledged by Mickey Mantle as "the best ballplayer of my era," Aaron ranks with Ruth and Ty Cobb among the greatest of all time.

859. **Honorable mention (baseball)** to Tris Speaker, Rogers Hornsby, and Nolan Ryan of Texas, Pepper Martin and Mickey Mantle of Oklahoma, and Willie Mays of Alabama. And Babe Ruth of Baltimore: there's no doubt about him, just about Baltimore. Shoeless Joe Jackson of South Carolina deserves some sort of mention, although maybe not honorable, given his implication in the Black Sox scandal. Separate but equally honorable mention to Rube Foster of Texas, founder of organized Negro baseball, and to some of the great Negro League players: Satchel Paige of Alabama; Pop Lloyd, "the Black Honus Wagner," from Florida; and Josh Gibson, "the Babe Ruth of Negro baseball," from Buena Vista, Georgia.

860. **Jack Johnson** (1878–1946) was the first black heavyweight champion, and his impenetrable defense made him arguably the best fighter ever. Johnson began boxing as a dockworker in his hometown of Galveston, Texas, and lost only 7 of his 114 fights (he knocked out four men in one night). He won the world title in 1908, setting off the search for a "great white hope" who could beat him. Former champion Jim Jeffries tried, but Johnson knocked him out in 1910. Johnson went into vaudeville, enjoyed his fame, and outraged white opinion by marrying not just one white woman but (eventually) three. He fled the country to avoid imprisonment on a morals charge, fought bulls in Spain, produced a revue in London, boxed and wrestled in Europe and Mexico, and lost his title to Jess Willard in Havana in 1915. (He claimed he threw the fight.) Returning to the United States in 1920, he served his time in prison, then boxed exhibitions and lectured for a living.

861. **Muhammad Ali** (b. 1942) was born Cassius Marcellus Clay to a black working-class family in Louisville, Kentucky. He took up boxing (at a police officer's urging) when he was twelve and

The Greatest. Connie Ives—Hot Shot Photos

won the light-heavyweight gold medal at the 1960 Olympics. After nineteen professional victories, he applied his credo "Float like a butterfly, sting like a bee" to defeat Sonny Liston for the heavyweight championship in 1963. Then he beat Liston again, by a knockdown in the first round, to silence any doubters. He became a Black Muslim, changed his name, and had his title taken away when he was indicted for draft evasion (he won on appeal). By the 1970s he had lost his lightning speed, but he regained the championship, lost it, then got it back again in 1978. At his peak his self-assessment as "the greatest" wasn't far off the mark, but it took his insouciant, taunting style to make him a hero throughout the world.

862. **Honorable mention (boxing):** Tom Molineaux, born a slave, a great fighter robbed of the championship in a thirty-three-round bare-knuckle bout with Englishman Tom Cribb in 1810; Hammering Henry Armstrong of Mississippi, simultaneous featherweight, welterweight, and lightweight champion in the 1930s; and Joe Frazier of South Carolina, just because

he's a good man. Frazier was thrown out of school when he beat up a boy who called his mama names; when he won the heavyweight championship, he bought her a plantation. Yet he once said, "I'm not the kind of guy who enjoys knocking people down. I'd rather help them up."

863. **Jim Thorpe** (1888–1953) was an Oklahoman of French, Irish, and American Indian ancestry. At Carlisle Indian School in Pennsylvania he was a triple-threat All-American halfback and also played baseball and lacrosse. He played both baseball and football professionally, but his greatest moment was his decisive victory in both the pentathlon and decathlon at the 1912 Olympics. Although his medals were taken away when his earlier pro baseball career was discovered, and his declining years were marred by alcoholism and a variety of unsuccessful schemes to capitalize on his fame, he was without question the most talented and versatile athlete of his era.

864. **Babe Didrikson Zaharias** (1914–56), from Port Arthur, Texas, was the greatest woman athlete of her time, the female counterpart to Jim Thorpe. She broke the world javelin record at age sixteen, then set U.S. records in the high jump, broad jump, eighty-meter hurdles, eight-pound shot put, and baseball throw. She won gold medals in the hurdles and javelin at the 1932 Olympics and would have won in the high jump except that the judges disallowed her headfirst style. After that, she concentrated on golf, winning the U.S. Open three times. Her last words to her husband were "I'll never die, honey."

865. **Wilma Rudolph** (b. 1940) was born to a poor black Tennessee farming family with many

children. Crippled by childhood polio, she wore a leg brace for years, but she persevered to become a high school basketball star, then joined the remarkable track and field program at Tennessee State University. In 1960 she became the first American woman to win three Olympic gold medals in track.

866. **William R. Johnson** (1782–1849), famous horse-race promoter from North Carolina, specialized in head-to-head matchups between Northern and Southern horses. In one of his races the backers of the Southern horse reportedly won $2 million. But Johnson's best-known promotion came in 1823, when his syndicate challenged the great Northern champion American Eclipse to a three-heat race at Union Course, Long Island. Recognizing that their horse, Sir Henry, was outclassed, Johnson and his Southern partners ran him all out in the first heat and won it, while the Northern jockey prudently saved his horse for the last two heats, which he won from the exhausted Sir Henry. The Southerners lost the $10,000 stake, but won far more from heavy side bets on the first heat. There's a metaphor there somewhere.

867. **Man o' War** (1917–47) came from distinguished lineage (his sire was the great stallion Fair Play). "Big Red" won twenty of his twenty-one races, just about every major race except the Kentucky Derby, which he never entered. He brought record prize money to his owner, August Belmont (who didn't need it), and retired to Faraway Stud Farm. His descendants have included Never Say Die and Seabiscuit.

868. **Secretariat** (1970–89) was born at the Meadow in Doswell, Virginia, to Somethingroyal by Bold Ruler. The first two-year-old to be voted Horse of the Year, he was sold for a record $6.08

million. As a three-year-old, he came from behind to win the Kentucky Derby, then came from behind to win the Preakness, then won the Belmont by thirty-one lengths to capture racing's Triple Crown. His Derby and Belmont times are still records. He retired to stud at Claiborne Farms in Paris, Kentucky. This horse had a lot of heart. Literally. At autopsy his ticker was found to be twice the normal size.

869. **Joe Namath** (b. 1943) was a working-class boy from Beaver Falls, Pennsylvania, who played his most memorable football for the New York Jets in the Super Bowl of 1969. So why's he on this list? Because he played first for the Crimson Tide of Alabama, that's why. Because he was Joe Willie Namath before he was Broadway Joe. Because he got kicked off the team in his junior year for partying and came back to take the Tide to a national championship in 1964. Because Bear Bryant (**872**) called him "the greatest athlete I have ever coached." Because he was the Elvis of sports, a white guy who absorbed and popularized black style. We'll even forgive him his movie role as a Confederate veteran in *The Last Rebel*.

870. **Michael Jordan** (b. 1963), a self-described "country boy from Wilmington, North Carolina," is also the best basketball player of all time. Although he showed early athletic talent in Little League baseball, he was too small at first to make the high school basketball team. When he finally did, in his junior year, there was no looking back. He won every honor and broke nearly every record at the University of North Carolina, and went on to do the same with the Chicago Bulls of the NBA, as an unstoppable "big guard" who routinely slam-dunked from the foul line. His talent for spectacular shots was matched by his talent for spectacular endorsement deals:

Michael Jordan as a Tar Heel. University of North Carolina

with Nike, McDonald's, Coca-Cola, Chevrolet, and a dozen other sponsors. He "retired" in 1993 to become the richest AA baseball player in the United States but returned to the hardwood after one season.

871. **Ray Wilson Scott** (b. 1933) founded the Bass Anglers Sportsman Society (BASS) in 1967 and three years later sponsored the first Bassmasters Classic tournament. His Montgomery-based empire now includes syndicated television programs and *Bassmaster* magazine, with over 2.5 million readers (including George Bush, a personal friend). Scott didn't invent competitive bass fishing, but he made the South's favorite water sport a big business—and we mean *big.* "I knew there was this subculture out there," he said. "All I had to do was roll away the rock and let that guy out!" Wearing his

trademark Stetson hat, Scott still leads the morning prayer at the annual Classic, but lately he has turned his promotional energies to deer hunting.

872. **Paul "Bear" Bryant** (1913–83) walked on water—and a poster still for sale in Alabama shows him doing it. "In Alabama," Senator Jeremiah Denton explained, "Coach Bryant is second only to God. We believe that on the eighth day the Lord created the Crimson Tide." In thirty-eight years as a college football coach Bryant had one losing season, twenty-nine bowl games, and a record 323 victories. Six of his Alabama teams were national champions. The youngest of an Arkansas sharecropping family's eleven children, he got his nickname at age twelve by wrestling a bear. He played for Alabama's 1935 Rose Bowl team and came back to coach in 1958: "Mama called," he explained. He drove his players, but they loved him. So did the sportswriters, who made him a near-mythical figure. He retired after the 1982 season and died four weeks later.

Bear Bryant of 'Bama. University of Alabama

873. Arthur Ashe (1943–93) was a talented young tennis player, but he was black, so he left Jim Crow Virginia to play at UCLA. After a distinguished professional career, he came home. When he died, thousands of his fellow Virginians, black and white, stood in the cold to view his body, lying in state in the Virginia governor's mansion. Now his statue will stand with those of the Confederacy's heroes on Richmond's Monument Avenue. Ashe was a great player, who won major tournaments—the first black man to win the U.S. Open, the first to win Wimbledon—but there have been, and are, greater players. Ashe is *known* for playing tennis, but he's *honored* because he may have been the last gentleman to play what was once a gentleman's sport. How fitting that he was a Virginian.

874. Richard Petty (b. 1937) was far and away the most popular driver during the years that saw stock car racing transformed from dirt-track obscurity to a multimillion-dollar enterprise. Driving his famous "Petty blue" Plymouth, he won twice as many NASCAR races as anyone else ever has—two hundred of them between 1960 and 1984. Son of one race driver and father of another, Petty grew up in rural North Carolina and has never lost an endearing common touch. He's legendary for signing autographs as long as fans want him to, and he has lent his popularity to everything from antilitter campaigns to Goody's headache powders (**712**). Since his retirement in 1992 he has pursued a number of interests, including a dip in the waters of North Carolina Republican politics, but as one of three figures known in the South as the King—the others are Jesus and Elvis—why would he be interested in a demotion?

875. Paul Charles Morphy (1837–84), taught to play chess by his father (a Louisiana Supreme

Richard Petty in uncharacteristic garb. Connie Ives—Hot Shot Photos

Court judge of Irish-Spanish descent), displayed as a child the talent and prodigious memory that allowed him to win simultaneous games, blindfolded. After a European tour in 1859, he was generally acknowledged as the chess cham-

Paul Morphy. Library of Congress USZ62-49178

pion of the world. But his career was short: soon after that triumph, mental instability put an end to it. (Chess may not be a sport, exactly, but we'll take our champions where we find them.)

876. Grantland Rice (1880–1954) graduated from Vanderbilt as captain of the baseball team. Unsure whether to be a poet or a professional athlete, he became a sportswriter, eventually for the *New York Tribune,* then as a syndicated columnist. A tireless traveler, he was present at nearly every major sports event and coined such memorable labels as the Mannassa Mauler (Jack Dempsey) and the Four Horsemen (the 1924–25 Notre Dame backfield). And he wrote some poetry after all, notably the lines about "the Last Great Scorer" marking "not 'won' or 'lost' / But how you played the game."

877. Walter Lanier "Red" Barber (1908–92) was distant kin to poet Sidney Lanier, and it showed in this great baseball announcer's style. Born in Columbus, Mississippi, he started his radio career (after a series of odder jobs) in college, and broadcast (for the Cincinnati Reds) the first major-league game he ever saw. In 1939 he went to the Dodgers, where he introduced New Yorkers to expressions like "rhubarb," "tall cotton," "the catbird seat," and "tearing up the pea patch." In 1953 he moved to the Yankees but was fired in 1966 when he reported that only 413 fans were present at one game. He was inducted into the Hall of Fame in 1978 and enjoyed a late second career as a popular sports commentator for National Public Radio. For listeners across the country Barber was a model of the Southern gentleman, a sports enthusiast who could get excited about camellias.

878. Bobby Jones (1902–71) got a New York ticker-tape parade when he won the four major

U.S. and British golf tournaments at age twenty-eight. That sweep capped a golfing career that began in his Atlanta childhood; shortly after, he retired from tournament play and returned to his Atlanta law practice, turning his energies toward popularizing his sport. Jones was a gracious and soft-spoken Southern gentleman, a great representative for the game of golf. He conceived and will always be identified with the Augusta National Golf Course, home of the Masters Tournament.

879. The Atlanta Braves were the South's first major-league baseball team. Bought by Ted Turner (**249**) in 1976, they acquired a national—and especially, it appears, a regional—following by appearing regularly on WTBS, Turner's cable "superstation." Even before the Braves were contenders, the Southern Focus Poll reported that they were the favorite team of half of Southerners who had a favorite team. Turner no longer personally sweeps the bases after the fifth inning, and Chief Nockahoma, who used to pitch his teepee in the outfield, is gone, but the "tomahawk chop" remains to annoy the sensitive. And you've got to love a team that has promotions like Wedlock and Headlock Night (a mass wedding before the game and professional wrestling afterward).

Tourist Attractions and Resorts

SOME OF THESE ARE for local consumption, but a good many were developed with Yankees in mind. As the motto of one of Flannery O'Connor's fictional towns puts it, "Beauty Is Our Money Crop"—that and history.

Sarah Greene Reed

Place in South Carolina may be the oldest: one hundred slaves worked for a decade, beginning in 1741, to lay out its 110 acres of symmetrical terraces and lakes (and it's where the camellia was introduced to America). Callaway Gardens in Georgia is one of the biggest: 2,500 acres, with a famous butterfly center. Others to note are Bellingrath (Alabama), Biltmore (**896**), and Brookgreen (South Carolina), where sculpture is a bonus.

882. **Historic preservation** may be one of the modern South's great successes. It has saved urban neighborhoods that now offer living on a comfortable human scale, has increased property values and tourism revenues (Charleston has 5 million tourists a year), and has helped keep a regional identity alive. In 1856 groups organized to save both Mount Vernon and Nashville's Hermitage (Andrew Jackson's house). The New South wasn't too worried about

The Vieux Carré. DixiePix

880. **Grand old resort hotels** dot the Southern beaches and mountains: for example, the Grove Park, an arts and crafts masterpiece in Asheville; the Jekyll Island Club, where millionaires once disported themselves; the Greenbriar, more high-society R&R. Other resort areas dependent on Mother Nature include the whole town of Hot Springs, Arkansas, and the sandhills of North Carolina (golfers' heaven in Southern Pines and Pinehurst).

881. **Famous gardens** have *improved* on Mother Nature, and for a long time. Middleton

preservation until the 1920s, when Northern museums and collectors began removing whole rooms of paneling and such, and prosperity threatened sites that had survived war and poverty. The imminent destruction of Charleston's Manigault House (**889**) led to the creation of the Society for the Preservation of Old Dwellings and the passing of America's first historic district zoning ordinance in 1931. A threat to New Orleans's French Quarter led to the first public commission that could protect buildings and offer local tax exemption.

HISTORIC SITES

883. **St. Augustine, Florida** (**82**), offers the Old City, with its narrow streets, Spanish buildings, cathedral, and the Castillo de San Marcos (the fort, begun in 1672). It owes much of its later development to Henry Flagler, whose railroad down the east coast of Florida in the 1880s brought tourists to his elaborate hotels, like the Ponce de Leon, which cost $1.25 million, had 540 rooms and an artists' colony (**749**) out back, and was one of the first buildings in the United States made of poured concrete.

884. **Jamestown** (**84**), part of the heavy-duty historic area around Williamsburg, is confusing: In 1607 the English settled Jamestown *Island,* which now contains archaeological ruins (only the church tower still stands). Jamestown *Settlement* offers a re-created palisaded fort, an Indian village, a museum, and three full-size (but tiny) sailing ships like those that brought the colonists.

885. **Colonial Williamsburg,** the South's biggest and most famous preservation project, was begun in the 1920s, funded mostly by John D.

Rockefeller. Critics have carped at everything from whether 440 later buildings should have been left in situ to why town life and social relations had been so neatened up and sanitized, and Williamsburg has responded by broadening its treatment of the lives of blacks and women. It attracts more than a million tourists a year. The Abby Aldrich Rockefeller Folk Art Center is there, too.

886. **The James River plantations,** a string of architectural jewels between Williamsburg and Richmond, display the remains of the life that established Virginia's reputation for gentility, tastefulness, and hospitality. Our favorite is Shirley, still owned by the family that built it, but Evelynton, Berkeley, Carter's Grove, and

Replicas of *Susan Constant, Discovery,* and *Godspeed* at Jamestown. Courtesy the Jamestown-Yorktown Foundation

Westover (1730), estate of William Byrd, II (see **443**). (Gardens open to the public.) Virginia Division of Tourism

Sherwood Forest are all treasures, and all are open to the public.

887. **Savannah** was planned by Georgia's founder, James Edward Oglethorpe, around a series of squares, with houses facing the squares, creating an open cityscape with a strong feeling of community. In 1854 Frederick Law Olmsted praised Savannah's "rural and modest aspect for a place of its population and commerce." General Sherman must also have seen its charms—on December 21 he sent word to Lincoln: "I beg to present you as a Christmas gift the city of Savannah." Despite having one of the largest historic districts in the United States (2.2 square miles), Savannah has so far escaped being overly gussied up for tourists.

888. **Beaufort, South Carolina,** was founded by rice and indigo planters and prospered after the introduction of long-fibered Sea Island cotton in the 1790s. "Beaufort [is] a picturesque town composed of villas, the summer residences of numerous planters who retire here during the hot season, when the interior of South Carolina is unhealthy. . . . Each villa is shaded by a verandah, surrounded by beautiful live oaks and orange trees laden with fruit," wrote an Englishman in 1849. Beaufort and nearby islands have provided the backdrop for recent movies like *The Great Santini, The Big Chill, The Prince of Tides, Forrest Gump,* and *The Jungle Book.*

889. **Charleston, South Carolina (630, 724, 882),** is a stunning city on a narrow point at the confluence of two rivers. An eighteenth-century visitor, J. Hector St. John Crèvecoeur, was impressed: "An European at his first arrival must be greatly surprised when he sees the elegance of their houses, their sumptuous furniture, as well as the magnificence of their tables." The city he saw was largely destroyed by three major fires and a devastating hurricane, but postbellum poverty kept the surviving structures from being replaced by more stylish ones. Now, alas, the city's charm is endangered by the tourism that is its economic lifeblood.

Manigault House, Charleston, South Carolina (see **882**). DixiePix

890. **New Orleans** offers antiquarians the French Quarter, the Garden District (an elegant nineteenth-century American suburb), Jackson Square with its old Spanish cathedral, and historic houses galore. It offers *everyone* gluttony and wickedness (**46**), most famously at Carnival (from Latin *carne vale*—"o flesh, farewell"), which begins with Epiphany and ends with Mardi Gras (Fat Tuesday, or Shrove Tuesday in more sedate circles), the day before Lent. Mobile claims the first Mardi Gras celebration, but New Orleans gets most of the attention and the visitors. Rachel (Mrs. Andrew) Jackson: "It is the finest country to the eye of a stranger, but a little while tires one of the dissipations of this place." Walker Percy: "The tourist is apt to see more nuns and naked women than he ever saw before."

Micajah Burnett, Shaker architect. Courtesy Shaker Village of Pleasant Hill

Mardi Gras ball in the 1870s. *The Great South*

891. **Old Salem,** in Winston-Salem, North Carolina, founded in 1766, was for Moravians only. Each family had its own house, yard, and garden, but communal virtues were stressed. Old Salem was incorporated in 1950, when destruction threatened. Buildings are preserved as they evolved; there has been no attempt to represent only one historical period, as at Williamsburg (**885**). (See **122, 899.**)

892. **Pleasant Hill, Kentucky,** founded in 1805 by the Shakers, was a community of five hundred residents and four thousand acres by midcentury but was closed in 1910, the result of the sect's celibacy. The buildings are models of elegant simplicity, restored and open to the public. Twenty-three were designed by Micajah Burnett, the community's master carpenter, architect, and town planner from 1813 to 1840.

893. **Battlefields** are everywhere. Many are federal or state parks, with guides, videos, maps, exhibits, gift shops, etc. Check out the Cyclorama of the Battle of Atlanta. Remember the Alamo.

894. **Other historic preservation sites** worth a visit are: Westville, near Lumpkin, Georgia, a re-

The Alamo, San Antonio. *The Great South* (1875)

Confederate heroes in stone. Georgia's Stone Mountain Park

creation of a mid-nineteenth-century village; Rugby, Tennessee, a utopian community founded in 1880 by the Englishman who wrote *Tom Brown's School Days;* Natchez, Mississippi, with five hundred antebellum buildings that take turns starring in the Garden Club's famous pilgrimages; New Bern, North Carolina's colonial capital, with its reconstructed Tryon Palace and English-style gardens; and Miami's art deco district, "where neon goes to die."

SOMEWHAT LESS HISTORIC SITES

895. **Stone Mountain,** outside Atlanta, is a geological oddity, a Confederate monument, and a tourist complex. The mountain itself is a unique 825-foot-tall granite dome. The monument, a carving of Davis (**283**), Lee (**287**), and Jackson (**288**), is bigger than a football field: Lee is nine stories tall (two legendary luncheons were held on his head and his shoulder). Carving was begun in 1923 but languished until the state of Georgia took over, hiring sculptors whose thermo-jet torches finished the job in 1972. The tourist complex includes a glamorized antebellum plantation (the "overseer's house" was ac-

tually a planter's house), a sound and light show, etc.

896. **Biltmore,** the French Renaissance chateau begun in 1889 by George Washington Vanderbilt outside Asheville, North Carolina, is the largest private house ever built in America—250 rooms (three times the size of the White House). A thousand workers took five years to build it, using Indiana limestone brought in on a special railroad line. Architect Richard Morris Hunt helped Vanderbilt loot Europe to fill it: seventy thousand art works and antiques, thousands of books, and Napoleon's chess table. Frederick Law Olmsted (who did Central Park) landscaped the 125,000-acre estate, which includes farms and game preserves. Vanderbilt's forester, Gifford Pinchot, thought the contrast to "the one-room cabins of the Appalachian mountaineers . . . was a devastating commentary on the injustice of concentrated wealth." The estate now grosses $30 million a year from tourists.

897. **Orlando,** the South's new tourist Mecca, claims to draw 13.5 million people a year to an odd assortment of attractions (some not really in Orlando), including (need we say?) the Dis-

ney World complex (Disney–MGM Studios Theme Park, Epcot Center, Magic Kingdom, and Pleasure Island), Universal Studios Florida, the Kennedy Space Center (at Cape Canaveral), Busch Gardens (in Tampa), Cypress Gardens, Silver Springs, Sea World, and Gatorland (which plans to embalm the old Florida with a Cracker village).

898. **Memphis** attracts over 3.5 million tourists a year, and only 650,000 of those go to Graceland (**606, 908**). So what do the others do? They go for the Church of God in Christ (**814**) Annual Holy Convocation (22,500 delegates spent over $20 million in 1993); barbecue at over one hundred BBQ (**645**) restaurants; the Memphis in May International Festival, which includes the World Championship Barbecue Cooking Contest; Beale Street (**45**); the old Sun Records studio (**564**); the National Civil Rights Museum; the Center for Southern Folklore; that bizarre stainless-steel pyramid; and an assortment of smaller attractions, like watching five mallard ducks at the Peabody Hotel march single file from the elevator and down a red carpet to the strains of the "King Cotton March," jump in the lobby's marble fountain, and swim around. Honest.

Sun Records studios, birthplace of rock and roll. DixiePix

MUSEUMS

THE CHARLESTON MUSEUM (1773) was the first museum in America, and Southerners have been busy building new ones ever since. A few unusual ones:

899. **The Museum of Early Southern Decorative Arts,** part of Old Salem (**891**), has fifteen period rooms arranged in chronological order from 1690 to 1820, four galleries, and a huge collection of artifacts. It sponsors research and scholarly publications.

900. **The Morris Museum of Art** in Augusta, Georgia, devoted entirely to Southern art, was founded in 1992. In temporary but elegant quarters overlooking the Savannah River, its ten galleries house a large permanent collection and special exhibits. The museum has a research library and archives in its Center for the Study of Southern Painting and already boasts an impressive list of publications, many of them by art historian Estill Curtis Pennington.

901. **Other museums for enthusiasts** include the Museum of the Confederacy (Richmond), the Museum of the Southern Jewish Experience (Utica, Mississippi), the World of Coca-Cola (Atlanta), the civil rights museums in Memphis and Birmingham, the Delta Blues Museum (Clarksdale, Mississippi), the U.S. Space and Rocket Center (Huntsville, Alabama [**37**]), the Atlanta History Center (sounds unlikely, we know), the Museum of the New South (Charlotte, of course), and, coming in 1998, the Roger Ogden Museum of Southern Art (New Orleans). (And see **907**.)

LEGITIMATE THEATER

EASY TO FIND, FROM the Carolina Playmakers, founded in 1918 and still going strong, to the newish Alabama Shakespeare Festival. Two odd ones:

902. Barter Theater, founded in the Depression by Robert Porterfield, an out-of-work actor. Seeing plenty of food at home (Abingdon, Virginia), he started a theater there where actors worked for food: "With vegetables you cannot sell, you can buy a good laugh." The first year, they cleared $4.35 and two barrels of jelly. Taking "ham for Hamlet," they used the hams to pay royalties to playwrights like Noël Coward, Tennessee Williams, and Thornton Wilder, but not vegetarian G. B. Shaw, who took spinach (his loss). Many Barter actors have gone on to fame, like Jim "Ernest" Varney, and even to glory: Gregory Peck, Patricia Neal, Hume Cronyn, Ernest Borgnine. Barter's the oldest professional equity theater in the nation and seems to be going strong: it plays five matinees and five evenings a week.

903. Outdoor historical drama may be peculiarly Southern. Or maybe it's just peculiar. Paul Green (1894–1981) won a Pulitzer as a Broadway playwright for *In Abraham's Bosom,* but he found immortality back home in North Carolina with his "symphonic dramas": the first, *The Lost Colony* (1937) (**83**), is still going, as are four more. The sincerest form of flattery has inspired dozens of others, most recently *Pathway to Freedom,* in Snow Camp, North Carolina, about local Quakers and the Underground Railroad (**266**).

Tourist cabins near Bardstown, Kentucky, 1940. Marion Post Wolcott, Farm Security Administration/Library of Congress USF34-55218-D

TACKY TOURIST TRAPS

FORGET DISNEY WORLD. FORGET Six Flags and King's Dominion. Here are some real tourist traps—not the kind like Ludowici, Georgia, that used to make the AAA blacklist, but the kind you pay for voluntarily and remember for a lifetime. A half dozen classics and a couple of promising up-and-comers:

904. Gatlinburg, Tennessee, likes to brag about its mountain scenery and crafts, but discerning visitors head straight for the wax museum (always a good sign). There's also the Guinness World Records Museum, the World of Illusions, the Mysterious Mansion haunted house, and Christus Gardens, offering dioramas of the life of Jesus. Just over the mountain is Cherokee, North Carolina, where you'll find Saunoke's Bear Land, the World's Largest Bingo Game, and Chief Henry, "the World's Most Photographed Indian"—and soon, on the Cherokee reservation (**90**), a $100-million "casino megaparlor," run by Harrah's of Memphis. Twenty minutes in the opposite direction is Pigeon Forge, Tennessee, with outlet shopping, country-music shows, water slides, simulated skydiving, Hee Haw Village, an Elvis museum, the car in which

Sheriff Buford Pusser (of *Walking Tall*) was killed, and the Dixie Stampede, a rodeo *cum* dinner-theater experience that includes "friendly competition between Confederate and Yankee performers." (There's another Dixie Stampede in Myrtle Beach, South Carolina.) Dolly Parton's Dollywood is in Pigeon Forge, too, but it's a rip-off.

905. Eureka Springs, Arkansas, is another mountain resort that got out of hand. The tone was set by right-wing radio preacher Gerald L. K. Smith with his seven-story-tall thousand-ton "Christ of the Ozarks." It anchors a sort of Christian theme park offering a four-hour Passion play, the Christ Only Art Gallery, and other wonders. Nearby you'll find Dinosaur World, the Wonderful World of Tiny Horses, and Dogpatch, U.S.A.; down the road is Booger Hollow, where you can buy a Boogerburger and check out the Double Decker Outhouse. Hardly fifty miles north is Branson, Missouri, once just the site of the Ozark Music Hall of Fame, but now, in a truly weird development, the second most popular tourist destination in the United States, as country-music biggies flock to build music halls and theaters there. Our advice is to stick with Eureka Springs and the tiny horses.

906. San Marcos, Texas, is no Eureka Springs, but it makes up in quality what it lacks in quantity. At Aquarena Springs you'll find glass-bottomed boats, a replica Spanish mission, a bird show, and something called the Sky Spiral, but what put San Marcos on this list is Ralph the Diving Pig, who appears with a supporting cast of Indian braves and mermaids in a goofy historical pageant viewed, in part, from an underwater theater. Round out your day with a visit to nearby Wonder World, where you can tour a large cave formed by an earthquake and one of

Ralph the Diving Pig in action. Aquarena Springs Resort

those houses where the laws of gravity are mysteriously suspended.

907. Nashville isn't known as the Athens of the South—home of Vanderbilt University and a

Ryman Auditorium, Nashville, original home of the Grand Ole Opry. DixiePix

replica of the Parthenon—but, to the dismay of some genteel citizens, as Music City, U.S.A. It has two (you might say *dueling)* country-music wax museums. There are also two car museums and two Elvis Cadillacs (one, gold, is in the Country Music Hall of Fame and Museum). So many museums, so little time. Check out the ones devoted to Hank Williams (Jr. and Sr.), Jim Reeves, Kitty Wells, and Barbara Mandrell. Take in the lavish new Opryland if you must, but don't miss historic sites like the old Ryman Auditorium, home of the Opry before it moved, Tootsie's Orchid Lounge, where performers went after the show, and Ernest Tubb's record shop across the street.

908. **Memphis** has a lot going for it **(898)**, but it's on this list for one thing only: Graceland. Home and grave of the King of Rock and Roll. Look at the jumpsuits on display. Look at the furnishings Elvis selected himself for the Jungle Room. Look at America's most visited grave, in the Meditation Garden. Look at the tasteful souvenirs for sale in the authorized shops. Look at what's for sale in the *un*authorized shops. Try

not to look at the other pilgrims. Go during Death Week, if you can. Visit the old Sun Records studio, Humes High School, and the other sacred sites. Be sure to swing down to Tupelo, Mississippi, where you can see the Birthplace, the adjoining meditation chapel (available for weddings), and the Elvis-theme McDonald's, and whatever you do, don't miss Graceland Too, a remarkable museum run by two fans in Holly Springs.

909. **South of the Border** is south of the *South Carolina/North Carolina* border, on Interstate 95, and began in 1949 as a beer stand serving dry counties across the state line. SOB is now 350 acres of motel, campground, miniature golf course, amusement park, video-game arcade, bingo parlor, five eating places, fourteen tacky gift shops, two fireworks stands, a Blenheim ginger ale **(708)** bottling plant, and who knows what else this month, offering everything from cherry bombs to kosher grits, in a setting that pays bizarre homage to our Good Neighbors to the South. Approximately 250 billboards, a ninety-seven-foot-tall statue of Pedro, and a two-hundred-foot-high sombrero-shaped viewing tower (with a view of nothing much) do a bang-up job of catching Florida-bound Yankees.

Store window, Memphis, 1995. DixiePix

Yankee bait on I-95. Ace-Hi Advertising

910. **Kissimee, Florida,** represents the wonderful world of Florida tourism, beating out Cypress Gardens (waterskiing and hoopskirted belles) and Weeki Wachee (mermaids and trained birds) by its sheer variety. Within a couple of miles you'll find everything from gator wrestling to a dinner-theater musical based on the antics of Al Capone. Horse lovers can choose chariot races at Arabian Nights, jousting at Medieval Times, or rodeo at Wild Bill's Wild West Dinner Extravaganza. You want culture, there's a miniature Great Wall at Splendid China. Or check out the Tupperware Dream House in the Tupperware Awareness Center at the Tupperware World Headquarters. And of course there's an Elvis Presley museum, which houses (for some reason) Herbie the Love Bug.

911. **Rock City** was created by the inventor of miniature golf and his wife. "See Rock City" signs on innumerable barns and birdhouses once meant that every American motorist knew about this remarkable rock garden on Lookout Mountain, near Chattanooga. By now hundreds of thousands have walked the Enchanted Flagstone Trail to Fairyland Caverns, where, thanks to black-light technology—well, let *The New Roadside America* tell us: "Demonically grinning and glowing elves perched on simulated rock shelves greet you as you descend a long series of underground rooms. The walls, ceilings, and floors are completely covered with fake crystals, stalactites, and stalagmites, all painstakingly glued in place." In one grotto, "fluorescent Barbie Dolls wearing wings and glowing tutus" float overhead. It all winds up in Mother Goose Village. This sounds like a bad trip from the 1960s, but Rock City has actually been in business since 1932.

Twelve

The Mythic South

THE SOUTH OF THE MIND

We Southerners are a mythological people, created half out of dream and half out of slander, who live in a still legendary land.

—JONATHAN DANIELS

One of the main ways the South is different from the rest of the country is that it's more thickly overlaid with mythologies, all these competing mythologies.

—JAMES APPLEWHITE

WHATEVER IT MAY BE on the ground, the South exists in people's minds, and it has ever since Jefferson wrote in 1785 that Southerners are "fiery, voluptuary, indolent, unsteady, independent, jealous for their own liberties, but trampling on those of others, generous, candid, without attachment or pretensions to any religion but that of the heart." (Northerners were pretty much the opposite.)

Observers have always been quick on the draw with generalizations about Southern life and character, and the natives have usually been ready to help. In fact, the South may have grown more myths than cotton. Here's some of what they've said about Dixie. Some of it may even be true.

The Plantation Myth

MANY PERCEPTIONS OF THE South grew out of the sectional conflict leading up to the Civil War. Plantation life was glamorized by slavery's defenders (**260–65**) and also by Yankees like Stephen Foster (**610**). Even the most hated and effective piece of abolitionist propaganda, Harriet Beecher Stowe's *Uncle Tom's Cabin* (1852), bought into Southern ideals of gentility (Simon Legree is a Yankee) and saw the South as a gracious, romantic society, albeit with a tragic flaw. Losing the War didn't make Southerners *less* fond of the Old South, in fact just the opposite—Thomas Nelson Page (**465**) gushed that its life "was one of singular sweetness and freedom from vice, . . . replete with happiness and content"—and Tin Pan Alley (**573**) and the movies picked up where the plantation novel (**462–65**) left off.

912. **Chivalry** was part of the medieval feudalism that many Southern gentry saw as the ancestor of their society, and they claimed that ideal for themselves. "Chivalrous C.S.A." was actually the title of a popular Confederate song; the chorus went "Chivalrous, chivalrous people are! / Chivalrous, chivalrous people are! / In C.S.A.! In C.S.A.! / Aye, in chivalrous C.S.A.!" Mark Twain (**461**) blamed Sir Walter Scott for making Southerners fall in love with the "sham chivalries of a brainless and worthless long-vanished society" and went on to blame Scott for the Civil War. Certainly, Scott's novels were found leather-bound in every cultured household, houses have names like Rotherwood and Waverley (**722**), and his influence even extended to architecture: the library in the Tennessee state capitol is an imitation of Scott's library at Abbotsford.

The Plantation Myth can be hazardous. DixiePix

913. **Aristocratic descent** often was (and still is) part of white Southerners' self-image. Antebellum Virginians especially talked about their "Cavalier" heritage, from the younger sons of

English noble families, and today the University of Virginia Cavaliers play in the Atlantic Coast Conference. Some sprigs of the aristocracy did come to Virginia, but they couldn't have been *that* prolific.

914. Southern honor was part of the chivalric code, a principle to live by and to die for. Robert E. Lee exemplifies the best of it: "I wish to live under no other government and there is no sacrifice I am not ready to make for the preservation of the Union save that of honor." Duels are probably the worst of it. Mary Boykin Chesnut (**447**), in her diary: "For us, soon as one defamatory word is [uttered] pistols come at once to the fore. That is South Carolina ethics."

915. A martial tradition was one result of Southern honor. Alexis de Tocqueville wrote in 1835 that white Southerners were "passionately fond of hunting and war." General Sherman wrote of "the young bloods of the South": "War

Sergeant Alvin York at the Tennessee state capitol. DixiePix

suits them. . . . They are splendid riders, first-rate shots, and utterly reckless." (He added, "These men must all be killed or employed by us before we can hope for peace.") This ideal was embodied in military schools (**834**) and military careers. In 1910, 93 percent of the nation's generals were connected to the South by birth, schooling, or marriage. The region has also produced more than its share of heroes, including Medal of Honor winners Alvin York and Audie Murphy.

THE SOUTH WAS SURPRISINGLY successful at exporting this view of itself.

916. Even foreigners held this image. Richard Monckton Milnes, Lord Houghton, a real aristocrat, observed during the Civil War that the Southerner "is much braver and cunninger and daringer than the cultivated shopkeeper of the North. It is just as if the younger sons of the Irish and Scotch nobility were turned loose against the bourgeoise of Leeds."

917. A half century after Appomattox H. L. Mencken, no friend of the modern South, showed the power of the myth: "In the south there were men of delicate fancy, urbane instinct and aristocratic manner—in brief, superior men—in brief, gentry. . . . It was a civilization of manifold excellences—perhaps the best that the western hemisphere has ever seen—undoubtedly the best that these states have ever seen."

Agrarianism

918. The agrarian ideal was Southern before there was a self-conscious South. You hear it from John Smith (**442**) and William Byrd (**443**) and, famously, from Jefferson: "Those who labour in the earth are the chosen people of God." Thomas Heyward, Jr., president of the Agricultural Society of South Carolina, observed in 1785 that farming "is one of the most innocent and at the same time the most pleasing and beneficial of any [occupations]. By its variety it keeps the mind amused; . . . by its exercise and regularity it conduces to give vigor and health to the body; and in the end it is productive of every other necessary and convenience of life. . . . It becomes the duty, therefore, as well as the interest of every citizen to encourage and promote it."

919. Agriculture was good for the nation, in the agrarian view, not just for farmers themselves. Jefferson again: "Cultivators of the earth are the most valuable citizens. They are the most vigorous, the most independent, the most virtuous, and they are tied to their country and wedded to its liberty and interests by the most lasting bonds."

920. Love of the land is closely related to the importance of agriculture, and many have seen land and its ownership as a Southern obsession. "Land keeps the family intact," Andrew Lytle wrote; "all serve it and are kept by it." And from the painter Carroll Cloar: "There is a joy in the sense of belonging, of possessing and being possessed, by the land where you were born."

921. Scorn for commerce and industry is the other side of the agrarian coin. Thus Jefferson called a nation's industrial class "a canker which soon eats to the heart of its laws and constitution," and Sidney Lanier lamented "that universal killing ague of modern life—the fever of the unrest of trade."

922. The Nashville Agrarians produced an eloquent defense of Southern agrarianism in 1930—just as the South was turning its back on farming for good. *I'll Take My Stand: The South and the Agrarian Tradition* argued that Southern culture (1) was rural, (2) was threatened by (Yankee) industrialism, and (3) was worth saving. This complaint, from Andrew Lytle, was typical: "The good-road programs drive like a flying wedge and split the heart of this provincialism—which prefers religion to science, handcrafts to technology, the inertia of the fields to the acceleration of industry, and leisure to nervous prostration." The Agrarians were literary men (**487**), not farmers, and critic Lewis Simpson has observed that "no American writers ever worked harder at inheriting their inheritance." But historian Richard King calls their manifesto "the closest thing to an authentic conservative vision which America has seen."

Sidney Lanier. *Library of Southern Literature* (1907)

Other Time-Honored "Southern Characteristics"

MANY TRAITS THAT HAVE been attributed to Southerners are part of both the plantation and the agrarian myths.

923. **Individualism**—in the sense of independence and self-reliance—has been tied to self-respect since the days of the frontier, at least for white men. W. J. Cash (**445**) told how it worked in the Old South, portraying the planter "wholly content with his autonomy and jealously guardful that nothing should encroach upon it," poorer whites "as fiercely careful of their prerogatives of ownership, as jealous of their sway over their puny domains, as the grandest lord," and the whole crowd displaying "intense distrust of, and, indeed, downright aversion to, any actual exercise of authority beyond the barest minimum essential to the existence of the social organism."

924. THE AGRARIANS agreed with Cash that individualism was a Southern trait (although they thought it was a good thing). "The greatest of all privileges," Donald Davidson wrote, "is the privilege of being let alone—of being neither promoted, nor subsidized, nor regulated, nor suppressed, nor interfered with in any way. Perhaps this is one of the great unchartered American rights and underlies those that are specifically chartered in the United States Constitution. Whether privilege or right, it is something that the South of tradition has always understood very well and has warmly defended."

925. THIS MOONSHINER ETHIC is still alive and well, at least in the small-town and rural South. Roy Reed observes that Southerners still "carry in their hearts or genes or livers or lights an ancient, God-credited belief that a man has a right to do as he pleases. . . . A right to go to hell or climb to the stars or sit still and do nothing, just as he damn well pleases, without restraint from anybody else and most assuredly without interference from any government anywhere." The lyrics of country music celebrate this attitude: Hank Williams, Jr. (**602**), brags that "a country boy can survive," and Charlie Daniels adds that if you don't like the way he's living, "just leave this long-haired country boy alone."

Andrew Lytle, the last Agrarian. Photograph by Curt Richter

926. **Southern hospitality** is legendary, and mostly real (certainly if you come with the right connections). It grew out of rural life: people came a long way to visit, so they stayed. Hugh Jones wrote, in *The Present State of Virginia* (1721), "No people can entertain their friends with better cheer and welcome; and strangers and travellers are here treated in the most free, plentiful and hospitable manner." Architect Samuel Sloan (**728**), comparing Southern houses to Northern, said that "the laws of hospitality, observed there, require a larger number of sleeping apartments for a family of the same number of persons, since, at many seasons of the year, the Southern householder takes pride in converting his mansion into a sort of honorary hotel."

927. **Southern manners** have inspired a good deal of comment, usually favorable. "The Southern Negro has the most beautiful manners in the world," William Alexander Percy wrote, "and the Southern white, learning from him, I suspect, is a close second." Percy obviously thought a lot about the subject; he concluded that "manners are essential and are essentially morals." Not everyone takes them at face value, however. Hodding Carter once wrote that Southerners will be polite until they're angry enough to kill you, and a character in a Gail Godwin novel observes that politeness itself "is a very effective form of aggression." But everyone agrees that Southern manners are *different* and that they largely define the Southern lady and gentleman (**933, 944**).

928. **A taste for leisure** (laziness, if you disapprove) has also been part of the image of the South since before there was a South. This was an equal-opportunity image: the gentry had leisure, poor whites and slaves were lazy—

nobody worked any harder than he had to. William Byrd (**443**) called North Carolina Lubberland: " 'Tis a thorough aversion to labor that makes people file off to North Carolina, where plenty and a warm sun confirm them in their disposition to laziness for their whole lives." Edward King put a less disapproving spin on it: "This is the South, slumbrous, voluptuous, round and graceful. Here beauty peeps from every door-yard. Mere existence is pleasure; exertion is a bore."

929. THE STAYING POWER OF THIS IMAGE is remarkable. It was never easy to reconcile with the lives of many Southerners who had to work hard to get by, but studies of regional stereotypes have always shown that *all* Americans, North and South alike, thought of Southerners as people who took life easy. Harper Lee: "We work hard, of course, but we do it in a different way. We work hard in order not to work. Any time spent on business is more or less wasted, but you have to do it in order to be able to hunt and fish and gossip." Ben Robertson: "We sit on the piazza and rock and we talk in the kitchen, and the days and the years go by and we get old. Rocking, fishing, talking—all in the midst of leisure. We take our time in our country."

930. THIS IMAGE MAY BE CHANGING. Recent studies find that Southerners of all ages no longer see any regional difference in pace, laziness, or willingness to work hard. Outside the South, older people still see Southerners as slower than average, but young people do not. Maybe it's air-conditioning.

931. **Ignorance, provincialism, and lack of culture** have been the usual complaints about the South (mostly—but not only—from outsiders). Hugh Jones wrote in 1721 that Virginians were

"for the most part only desirous of learning what is absolutely necessary, in the shortest and best method." J. Gordon Coogler said, in a purely original rhyme from *Purely Original Verse* (1897), "Alas, for the South! Her books have grown fewer— / She never was much given to literature." And H. L. Mencken said it most scathingly in "The Sahara of the Bozart" (**8**).

932. The benighted South. Add violence to ignorance, and you get this persisting image. Historian George Tindall traces it to the 1920s, when the old abolitionist view of the South "was reinforced by a variety of images in that decade and after: the Scopes Trial, the Ku Klux Klan, lynchings, chain gangs, the Fundamentalist movement, hookworm and pellagra, the Scottsboro trials, labor violence." Events of the civil rights era gave it new life in the 1950s and 1960s. But there's an appetite for it, too: Harriette Simpson Arnow put a feud in her first novel, *Mountain Path* (1936), only when her New York editor insisted.

Convict labor. Jack Delano, Farm Security Administration/Library of Congress USF33-20861-MS

Southern Social Types

THESE MYTHS ARE POPULATED by a relatively small number of Southern *types* who wander through American popular culture. More than that, we suggest: when Southerners are seen as *Southerners* (not just as Americans who happen to be in the South), they're usually seen as representatives of one or another of these types.

Most of the white male types have been around since before the War. Daniel Hundley, a Harvard-trained lawyer from Alabama, working in Chicago, described several of them in *Social Relations in Our Southern States* (1860).

933. The Southern gentleman, said Hundley, has "a natural dignity of manner" and "the utmost self-possession—that much coveted *savoir faire,* which causes a man to appear perfectly at home, whether it be in a hut or a palace." He is "remarkably easy and natural, never haughty in appearance, or loud of voice— even when angry rarely raising his voice above the ordinary tone of gentlemanly conversation." And so forth. Robert E. Lee, after his death, became the model of the gentleman for generations of Southern boys (**287, 346**).

934. The evil aristocrat came from the underside of the plantation myth, propagated in the rhetoric of Yankee abolitionists and antislavery Southerners like Hinton Helper (**270**). Oddly, the proslavery Hundley allowed that this figure existed, although he called him the Southern Yankee, insisting that his ruthlessness and greed were un-Southern: "The crack of his whip is heard early, and the crack of the same is heard late . . . , and yet his heart is still unsatisfied; for he grasps after more and more, and cries to the fainting slave: 'Another pound of money, dog, or I take a pound of flesh!' " Today this figure survives mostly in historical settings—in lurid novels and movies like *Mandingo* (**979**), for instance—but a modern version may be emerging in characters like tycoon J. R. Ewing of TV's *Dallas* (**995**).

935. The comic gentleman Hundley called the Cotton Snob, writing that by "displays of arrogance and ill-breeding, [he] renders himself both ridiculous and contemptible." He's still around, usually identifiable by his white suit: Boss Hogg on *The Dukes of Hazzard,* Senator Phogbound in *Li'l Abner,* Colonel Sanders peddling fried chicken.

936. The yeoman was Hundley's highfalutin label for the admirable version of the Southern common man. Yeomen had little in the way of worldly goods; their only "inheritance [was] the ability and the will to earn an honest livelihood . . . by the toilsome sweat of their own brows." This Jeffersonian figure exhibited "a manly independence of character" and wouldn't "under any circumstances humiliate himself to curry favor with the rich or those in authority," but he wasn't all tedious nobility: Hundley observed that he liked sports, barbecue, and home-brewed spirits.

937. The good old boy was the yeoman's 1970s equivalent. Long an expression among rural and working-class white Southerners for someone with virtues like reliability, independence, good-fellowship, some physical courage, and self-deprecating humor, "good old boy" went national after Tom Wolfe defined it in a 1965 *Esquire* article on stock car racing. Soon celebrated in

Definitely a good old boy. Photo by Allen Johnson

Burt Reynolds movies and country songs, the type lost its precision when it started to be applied to middle-class Southerners, as when Rebel Yell billed itself as "the whiskey of the Good Ole Boys." The phrase was often used in analysis of the Carter White House, at first approvingly but increasingly with scorn. Its present disreputable connotations, dating from that period, can include anything from cronyism to dim-wittedness.

938. Bubba as a label rather than a common name (**146**) became a near synonym for "good old boy" during the 1992 campaign (**417**) of another Southern presidential candidate, Bill Clinton of Arkansas. Unlike "good old boy," however, "Bubba" was never used admiringly. Even South-

Bubba now serves Coney Island hot dogs on the interstate. DixiePix

erners had fun maligning Bubba (Maryln Schwartz said there was no "Bubba vote": "Bubba thinks a primary is the first coat of paint you put on when you're painting the pickup"), but Bubba got even in the 1994 congressional elections.

939. The redneck villain is the scary version of the white Southern common man—Mr. Hyde to the yeoman's Dr. Jekyll. Hundley called him the Southern Bully, noting his propensity for gambling, drinking, swearing, chewing tobacco, and fighting. Especially fighting, because aggression is this character's principal distinguishing characteristic. Billy Carter put his finger on it: "A good ole boy is somebody that rides around in a pickup truck . . . and drinks beer and puts 'em in a litter bag. A redneck rides around in a pickup truck and drinks beer and throws 'em out the window."

940. THE WORD "REDNECK" was originally just a synonym for "yeoman," referring to an attribute white nongentlemen acquired by working in the sun. Robert Love Taylor, governor of Tennessee

in the 1880s, used to refer to his supporters as "my beloved rednecks"—and they called him "Our Bob." But by the 1960s "redneck" had become an epithet for what F. N. Boney called "the pale beast of Dixie, who stalks Negroes, Yankees, Federal officials, United Nations representatives, and all the other good guys." Vicious rednecks figured in movies from *Easy Rider* to *In the Heat of the Night* and, of course, on television news programs, too. C. Vann Woodward has rightly observed that people who would choke on the "n-word" speak of rednecks without hesitation, but like other ethnic epithets, "redneck" should be used with care and precision (if at all). Preacher Will Campbell says, "I can use redneck because I am one." That criterion seems to work for the n-word as well.

941. Poor white trash refers to a different sort of low-class white Southerner—not mean, just trashy. Antebellum blacks probably coined the phrase; certainly they employed it. Hundley used it to describe "about the laziest two-legged animals that walk erect on the face of the Earth. Even their motions are slow, and their

Brother Dave Gardner, Southern hipster and founder of the NAAWT. Candace Gardner Hare

speech is a sickening drawl . . . ; while their thoughts and ideas seem likewise to creep along at a snail's pace." All p.w.t. do is drink and hunt (if it isn't much trouble) and lie around in the yard with the dogs. Too lazy to be dangerous, these aren't heroes like yeomen or villains like rednecks; they're just comic figures—as Hundley put it, "a very pitiable sight to the truly benevolent," but "a ludicrous one to those who are more mirthfully disposed." Comedian Brother Dave Gardner once proposed a National Association for the Advancement of White Trash.

A pair of Georgia crackers. *The Great South* (1875)

942. **Hillbilly** is an approximate synonym for "white trash" these days, especially outside the South, where poor  Southern whites get put down with this label whether they come from the mountains or not. Hillbilly fools are stock comic figures in America's mass media. Part of the humor is sex-role reversal: from Dogpatch to Booger Holler, the men are lazy and/or incompetent, while the women do the work (another notion going back to William Byrd, II) and are proficient with guns and chewing tobacco. In *Li'l Abner* Sadie Hawkins Day institutionalizes this topsy-turvy arrangement.

THERE ARE OTHER WAYS to dump on Southern working-class or poor whites.

943. **Cracker** was originally a nickname for those who lived in the piney woods of south Georgia and north Florida. The word's etymology is disputed: some connect it with cracking corn (grits, etc.); others say it applies to mule skinners or farmers who cracked whips to con-

trol their cattle. Although the name of Atlanta's minor-league baseball team used to be the Crackers, the word is now almost always pejorative, and blacks have long used it as a racial epithet. "Peckerwood" has pretty much the same connotations. Local favorites have included "mudheads," "whelps," and "bigbenders" for Tennesseans (the Tennessee River was known to Indians as River with the Big Bend); "buzzards" for Georgians (state law protected buzzards as essential scavengers); "corncrackers" for Kentucky mountaineers; "fly-up-the-creeks" for rural Floridians (after a local bird); "goobergrabbers" for Alabamians and Georgians (from a local word for peanuts); "sandlappers" (i.e., clay-eaters [**713**]) for South Carolinians; "sandhillers" in Georgia and the Carolinas (from those states' infertile sandhills regions); and "ridgerunners" throughout the mountain and piedmont South.

THERE ARE SOME WELL-KNOWN white female types as well, notably:

944. The Southern lady. She's been around since plantation days, too. Wilbur Fisk Tillett wrote in 1891 that "American civilization has nowhere produced a purer and loftier type of refined and cultured womanhood than existed in the South before the war. . . . In native womanly modesty, in neatness, grace, and beauty of person, in ease and freedom without boldness of manner, in refined and cultivated minds, in gifts and qualities that shone brilliantly in the social circle, in spotless purity of thought and character, in laudable pride of family and devotion to home, kindred, and loved ones—these were the qualities for which Southern women were noted and in which they excelled." She comes in several varieties, from fluttery and helpless to—

945. The Steel Magnolia. A fairly recent label for an old type, this refers to the iron-willed, determined, competent figure that sometimes resides beneath the fluff and charm of the Southern lady. Though never universal, this character is more widespread than many Yankees realize. Novelist Reynolds Price: "Southern women are Mack trucks disguised as powder puffs." "The Steel Magnolias" is now the name of a women's Harley-Davidson club in Houston.

946. The Southern belle, the Southern lady's larval form, has been particularly celebrated. "Beautiful, graceful, accomplished in social charm, bewitching in coquetry, yet strangely steadfast in soul," wrote Francis Pendleton Gaines, "she is perhaps the most winsome figure in the whole field of our fancy." Carl Carmer recorded a toast offered at an Alabama fraternity dance in the 1930s: "To Woman, lovely woman of the Southland, as pure and chaste as this sparkling water, as cold as this gleaming ice, we lift this cup, and pledge our hearts and lives to the protection of her virtue and chastity." (Florence King remarked, "Anything can happen in a land where men drink toasts to frigidity.") The belle, all too aware that she has to turn into a Southern lady, is known for her frivolity, which may or may not be a put-on, and which has often been deplored, grudgingly admired, or eagerly imitated.

PART OF BEING A Southern lady is displaying Southern manners and dispensing Southern

Juliette Gordon Low, founder of the Girl Scouts, as a budding Steel Magnolia.
Juliette Gordon Low Birthplace, Savannah

hospitality. Three outstanding examples from history:

947. Dolly Madison (1768–1849), wife of James Madison, was a model Southern hostess, legendary for never forgetting a name. At home in Virginia, "the care and entertainment of visitors, the government of servants, the whole policy of the interior, was admirably managed with equal grace and efficiency," wrote one visitor. Dolly had few critics, but she told one "that to her, abundance was preferable to elegance; that . . . she did not hesitate to sacrifice the delicacy of European taste for the less elegant, but more liberal, fashion of Virginia." When President Madison died, she answered all condolence letters herself.

948. Emily Post (1873–1960) was born in Baltimore, but we'll claim her because manners were her thing. A standard-issue aristocrat (travel, private schools, debut) forced by divorce to write for money, she produced *Etiquette: The Blue Book of Social Usage* (1922), which sold over a million copies in her lifetime and generated a newspaper advice column that inspired 250,000 letters. "Etiquette is the science of living. It embraces everything. It is the code of sportsmanship and of honor. It is ethics." Very Southern indeed.

949. Perle Mesta (Pearl Reid Skirvin Mesta, 1889–1975) was a rich Texan who married a steel magnate and spent her money on parties both political and social (also philanthropy, but that's not why she's legendary). When she was rewarded with the post of "envoy extraordinary and minister plenipotentiary" to Luxembourg, she entertained even more, supposedly including 25,000 American servicemen. Her story inspired Irving Berlin's 1950 musical *Call Me Madam,* which starred Ethel Merman and included the song "The Hostess with the Mostes' on the Ball."

ALTHOUGH THE SOUTHERN LADY has been widely acknowledged to be an admirable creature, there have been dissenters (mostly female). Three examples, one English, one Yankee, one Southern:

950. Fanny Kemble (451) found antebellum Southern ladies "extremely sickly in their appearance [and] languid in their deportment and speech" and thought they needed a good workout: "[The climate requires] energetic and invigorating habits both of body and mind. Of

Emily Post. Library of Congress USZ62-101761

these, however, the Southern ladies appear to have, at present, no very positive idea."

951. Helen Brown Norden resented what she saw as Southern women's superior ability to manipulate men, complaining that they "are all Scarlett O'Haras under their skins. That fair, false, fatal lady was no peculiarity of Civil War days. She flowered long before Grant took Richmond, and she has been avenging the Confederacy on Northern manhood ever since."

952. Ellen Glasgow (498) said of one of her heroines: "The chief object of her upbringing, which differed in no essential particular from that of every other well-bred and well-born Southern woman of her day, was to paralyze her reasoning faculties so completely that all danger of mental unsettling, or even movement, was eliminated from her future."

WORKING-CLASS SOUTHERN WOMEN haven't been as thoroughly typologized (Hundley said almost nothing about them), but they can be included with some of the male types, by implication—as redneck women or hillbilly gals, for instance. One type to keep an eye on is:

953. The Good Woman. With her origins in the nineteenth-century farm woman (the yeoman's wife), the Good Woman has emerged in the lyrics of country music (especially those of Loretta Lynn) as a major role model for Southern women who aren't ladies. Michael Hicks describes her: "The Good Woman should appear competent, wholesome, patient, but have a wild streak that's hidden most of the time." She can "bake pies, raise three children, and keep the house clean while working, singing, being a great lover, and saving coupons for the grocery store." Unlike the lady, she never even *pretends*

to be helpless, and she treats her man as an equal.

AS FOR THE OTHER inhabitants of the Old South myth:

954. Black Southern types flourished in American popular culture well into this century, a whole menagerie of happy darkies like Sambo and Rastus, Amos and Andy and Kingfish, Aunt-this and Uncle-that, mammies, bucks, wenches, pickaninnies . . . For the most part they're now gone with the wind—and good riddance. Maybe we'll do a sequel to this book and call it *1001 Things Everyone Should Forget About the South.*

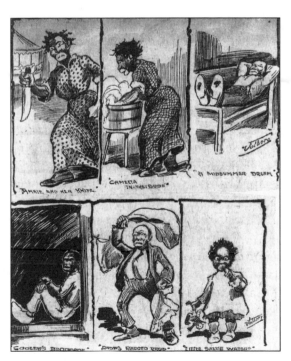

Turn-of-the-century cartoon stereotypes. DixiePix

The Mass-Media South

THE SOUTH HAS ALWAYS been a favorite setting and topic for American popular culture, which has both reflected and shaped how the world thinks about Dixie. We've already looked at literature and popular music; here are some movies and television shows worth pondering.

THREE MILESTONES OF MOVIE HISTORY

955. *The Birth of a Nation* (1915) was the masterwork of D. W. Griffith, Kentucky-born son of a Confederate colonel. Griffith's adaptation of Thomas Dixon's (**496**) *The Clansman* tells a distinctly unreconstructed story: its glorification of the Ku Klux Klan got it banned in several Northern cities, its portrayal of blacks offended many viewers (and more since), but it was a great popular success and introduced such techniques as the close-up, the long shot, and the moving shot. James Agee called its depiction of a Confederate charge "the most beautiful shot I have seen in any movie"; President Wilson (**438**) said it was "like writing history with lightning" and "all so terribly true." (See **367**.)

956. *Gone with the Wind* (1939)—well, what is there to say about David O. Selznick's epic? "Frankly, my dear, I don't give a damn"? Not likely. Vivien Leigh, Clark Gable, Leslie Howard, Olivia de Havilland, Hattie McDaniel, and Butterfly McQueen—all delivered memorable performances in this four-hour, $4-million adaptation of Margaret Mitchell's novel (**521**). The movie won eight Oscars, set box-office records, and garnered an unprecedented television audi-

One of the original boys in the hood. Dixie Pix

Miss Scarlett. © 1939 Turner Entertainment Co./All Rights Reserved

ence in 1976. Dismiss it as bad history, a period soap opera, insufferably condescending to its black characters, or join the millions of viewers who have been swept up in the story; it's hard to be indifferent to the saga that put the whole world on a first-name basis with Scarlett and Rhett.

957. ***The Southerner*** (1945) stars Zachary Scott and Betty Field as a tenant-farming couple struggling against adversity (while Miss Field's hair stays perfectly in place). William Faulkner had a hand in the screen adaptation of G. S. Perry's *Hold Autumn in Your Hand* and once said that the catfish-catching scene was his best Hollywood work, which is odd because the scene has no dialogue. Directed by Jean Renoir and greatly admired by cineastes, this film is perhaps best seen as being in the 1930s documentary tradition embodied in the photographs of the Farm Security Administration (**780**).

BEST IN GENRE

THERE IS NO SINGLE "Southern" like the American "Western"—too many competing myths. But there are definitely several *kinds* of Southern movies. Here are a few, with our favorite examples.

958. **Best Heartwarming Farm Family Movie:** *Places in the Heart* (1984) is basically *The Southerner* redivivus: a Texas family conquers adversity in the 1930s. Sally Field won an Oscar as the widowed mother. Mel Gibson and Sissy Spacek appeared in *The River,* pretty much the same movie, at just about the same time.

959. **Best Heartwarming Farm Family Movie, Separate but Equal Division:** *Sounder* (1972)

is also pretty much the same movie, with a twist: this is about a *black* sharecropping family in the 1930s. And they're in *Louisiana.* An adaptation of William Armstrong's novel, this offers Kevin Hooks as a sort of Negro John Boy Walton (**993**), an outstanding performance by Cecily Tyson, and a score by Taj Mahal. Miss Tyson also acted up a storm in the award-winning TV movie *The Autobiography of Miss Jane Pittman* (1974), adapted from Ernest Gaines's (**517**) novel. Either of these offers a more edifying picture of black Southern rural life than Steven Spielberg's adaptation of Alice Walker's overrated *The Color Purple* (1985) (**530**).

960. **Best Aristocratic Depravity Film:** *Cat on a Hot Tin Roof* (1958), Tennessee Williams's (**511**) tale of patriarchy and mendacity in the Mississippi Delta, with classic performances by Paul Newman as the obligatory damaged Williams hero, Elizabeth Taylor as his wife, Cat, and Burl Ives as Big Daddy. This is arguably the best of many not-bad film adaptations of Williams plays, rivaled only by *A Streetcar Named Desire* (1951).

Big Daddy and family. ©1958 Turner Entertainment Co./All Rights Reserved

961. Best Dumb Southerner Movie: We're still undecided about *Forrest Gump* (1994), so we'll play it safe with *No Time for Sergeants* (1958). Adapted from Mac Hyman's book, this may be the best of the many, mostly bad movies about how a white Southerner's naiveté creates havoc and/or carries the day. Here Andy Griffith plays a Georgia draftee. This hook seems especially well suited to the TV sitcom format (**989–96**).

962. Best Vicious Redneck Movie: *Deliverance* (1972). This could easily have been really *bad.* Four Atlanta business guys (Burt Reynolds, Ned Beatty, Jon Voight, Ronny Cox) go on a canoe trip and run into some seriously depraved country boys—but somehow it works. This movie must have set the Georgia tourism industry back fifty years. James Dickey (**515**) adapted his own novel for the screen and makes a brief appearance as a sheriff.

James Dickey wrote *Deliverance* and plays a sheriff.
Photograph by Curt Richter

963. Best Good Old Boy Movie: Well, *Smokey and the Bandit* (1977) is as good as any. Burt Reynolds stars as a trucker with the hammer down and a load of illegal Coors beer. All the traditional roles are there: the sidekick (Jerry Reed), the girlfriend (Sally Field), the comic lawman (Jackie Gleason as Sheriff Buford T. Justice). This comic reworking of such fifties drive-in classics as *Thunder Road* (1958) was part of the pop-culture rehabilitation of the South roughly coincident with Jimmy Carter's election. If your video store doesn't have this one, almost any Burt Reynolds movie will do.

964. Best Deep South Race Relations Movie: *To Kill a Mockingbird* (1962), with Gregory Peck in an Oscar-winning performance as a small-town white lawyer raising two children and defending a black man accused of rape. Horton Foote's adaptation of Harper Lee's novel (**524**) won an Oscar, too. Honorable mention: *In the Heat of the Night* (1967), with Sidney Poitier and Rod Steiger. Too many movies in this category—for example, *Mississippi Summer* (1968), *The Heart of Dixie* (1989), *Mississippi Burning* (1988)—are simplistic melodrama, but check out the fair-to-middling movie version of Faulkner's *Intruder in the Dust* (1949).

965. Best Prison Brutality Film: *I Am a Fugitive from a Chain Gang* (1932) established the genre and, with Paul Muni heading a fine cast, is still the greatest. But runner-up *Cool Hand Luke* (1967), with Paul Newman and George Kennedy, gives it a run for its money, and is funnier. Funnier still is *Swamp Women* (1955), a B movie about four female convicts: director Roger Corman got the first Lifetime Achievement Award given by drive-in movie critic Joe Bob Briggs.

966. Best Cartoon: Just about got to be Disney's *Song of the South* (1946), based on Joel Chandler Harris's **(467)** version of the Uncle Remus stories, which made Br'er Rabbit and them other bro's world-famous. ("Zip a Dee Doo Dah" won an Oscar.) But a less saccharine cartoon treatment of the South (if you can find it) is *Southern Fried Rabbit,* which combines most midcentury clichés about Dixie in one tongue-in-cheeky Bugs Bunny feature.

967. Best Country-Music Movie: *Coal Miner's Daughter* (1980), starring Sissy Spacek. The biography of Loretta Lynn offers good music and a gritty, gripping story (mostly true). Honorable mention: Robert Altman's sprawling, star-studded *Nashville* (1975) and *Tender Mercies* (1983), a little gem that won Oscars for actor Robert Duvall and screenwriter Horton Foote. Special citation for unlikely casting: the surprisingly good *Your Cheatin' Heart* (1964), with George Hamilton as Hank Williams **(602)**.

Loretta Lynn, coal miner's daughter. Connie Ives—Hot Shot Photos

968. Best Elvis Movie: Probably *King Creole* (1958), if only because Elvis plays a singer. This adaptation of Harold Robbins's *A Stone for Danny Fisher* (moved from Chicago to New Orleans) is marginally less lame than most Presley vehicles, and some of the songs ("Trouble," "Hard Headed Woman") are better than okay. Movies *about* the King are better: Kurt Russell as *Elvis* (made-for-TV, 1979), *Heartbreak Hotel* (1988—an Ohio lad kidnaps Elvis as a present for his mom), and Jim Jarmusch's weird *Mystery Train* (1989), with a great performance by Screamin' Jay Hawkins. Better still is the Vegas concert documentary *Elvis: That's the Way It Is* (1970), but we're getting pretty far from Memphis here.

969. Best Southern Teen Flick: Not a lot of competition, but we like a pleasantly unassuming film about four high school girls' 1963 Myrtle Beach fling, *Shag* (1989). It offers a painless introduction to the odd Carolina dance of that name **(582)**, some good performances by a cast including Bridget Fonda and Phoebe Cates, and a Confederate-flag bikini in one scene.

970. Best "Woman's Picture": *Come Back to the Five and Dime, Jimmy Dean, Jimmy Dean* (1982), Robert Altman's adaptation of the Broadway play, starring Sandy Dennis, Cher, Karen Black, and Kathy Bates as the girlfriends who gather for a reunion of their James Dean fan club. The critics didn't care for this one, but we think it's a much better vehicle for strong female performances than the disappointing *Steel Magnolias* (1989) and *Fried Green Tomatoes* (1991). The accents are better, too.

971. Best Picture Set in New Orleans: *The Big Easy* (1987) is basically a crime movie with a love story between detective Dennis Quaid and

Assistant D.A. Ellen Barkin, but the real star is funky present-day New Orleans, which provides great Cajun music and lots of atmosphere. Quaid deserves an award for his fine Cajun accent alone, quite different from his generic Southern as an over-the-top Jerry Lee Lewis in *Great Balls of Fire!* (1989) or as hero of the—

972. **Best Southern Sports Movie:** *Everybody's All-American* (1988), an adaptation of Frank Deford's novel about what happens to an LSU football star and his homecoming queen when they grow up. Superb performances by Quaid, Jessica Lange, and John Goodman make this even better than runners-up *North Dallas Forty* (1979—Nick Nolte in an adaptation of Peter Gent's novel) and *Semi-Tough* (1977—Burt Reynolds in an adaptation of Dan Jenkins's novel).

973. **Best Recent Civil War Picture:** No award. They don't make 'em like *The Birth of a Nation*

Red Skelton in *A Southern Yankee.* © 1948 Turner Entertainment Co./All Rights Reserved

anymore. But honorable mention to Ted Turner's (**249**) *Gettysburg* (1993) for a nice try and some impressive battle scenes (over five thousand reenactors participated) (**312**). It's fun spotting famous faces—Turner himself dies in Pickett's Charge—but Martin Sheen's face is attached to Robert E. Lee, and it's just not . . . right. For comic relief, check out Red Skelton's *A Southern Yankee* (1948).

974. **Best Movie about Southern Politics:** *All the King's Men* (1949), based on Robert Penn Warren's (**508**) novel, a thinly disguised account of the life of Huey Long (**424**). Broderick Crawford's unforgettable performance, backed by a fine cast, won this the Oscar for best picture. For a lighter look at Louisiana politics, check out Paul Newman as Huey's brother Earl, in *Blaze* (1989).

THERE HAVE BEEN SO many good documentaries about the South that we decided to split this category.

975. **Best Documentary That's Good for You:** *Eyes on the Prize* (1992), a first-rate, six-hour account of the entire course of the civil rights movement from 1954 to 1965, offers just about all you need to know about this remarkable period in Southern, and American, history. First runner-up: *Louisiana Story* (1948), a look at the oil industry in southern Louisiana, courtesy of Standard Oil. Sounds like a yawner from sixth-grade social studies, but it's actually an accomplished and influential piece of filmmaking, with score by Virgil Thomson. Second runner-up: *Harlan County, U.S.A.* (1977), an Academy Award–winning portrayal of a Kentucky coal-mine strike. If your taste runs to labor-relations morality plays, this is far better than the fictional *Norma Rae* (1979).

Bill Monroe, by Kata Billups. Red Piano Too Art Gallery, St. Helena Island, S.C.

976. Best Documentary That You'll Enjoy: *High Lonesome* (1994), the story of bluegrass music (**558**), with special attention to its patriarch, Bill Monroe. If you're a fan, you must see this. If you're not, it may make you one. Honorable mention: *Grits* (1980), an amusing compendium of gritslore; *Vernon, Florida* (1988), an off-center look at a very peculiar town; *Mississippi Blues* (1983), by two filmmakers, one American and one French.

THE FIVE WORST MOVIES
ABOUT THE SOUTH

WE'RE TALKING *REALLY BAD,* not just banal and pointless (like many of the later works of Elvis). We mean movies that make you say, "I can't believe I'm seeing this!" The South has in-

spired a great many, and they're bad in so many different ways: some pretentious, some blatantly exploitative, some silly to the point of imbecility, some—well, you'll see. We'll do this Letterman-style, in reverse order.

977. *Hillbillys in a Haunted House* (1967) tells a story about ghosts and espionage that critic Leonard Maltin accurately describes as "moronic." It stars Ferlin Husky, Merle Haggard, and some other country singers who should have known better. This was Basil Rathbone's last movie, and it may have killed him. *Las Vegas Hillbillys* (1966), to which this is a sequel, had Jayne Mansfield and Mamie Van Doren instead of Rathbone, but it's not appreciably better.

978. *Southern Comfort* (1981) shows what happens when some clean-cut National Guardsmen get crossways with some chinless swamp rats. Let's just say it makes *Deliverance* look like a day in the park and speaks eloquently to the need for a Cajun Anti-Defamation League.

979. *Mandingo* (1975) is a trashy sado-historical epic based on Kyle Onstott's trashy novel, starring James Mason as the evil owner of a Louisiana slave-breeding plantation, Susan George as his slutty daughter, Ken Norton as a hunky black fighter—all stereotypes present and accounted for. This movie and its sequel, *Drum* (1976), make the slavery episodes of TV's *Roots* look like an artistic and historical tour de force. It's even worse than *Slaves* (1969), which gets at least a little credit for good intentions.

980. *Two Thousand Maniacs* looks in loving detail at the gruesome deaths and dismemberment of several Northern tourists who innocently stumble on the town of Pleasant Valley, which was wiped out by Union troops but reappears every hundred years looking for revenge. This 1964 film is the reductio ad absurdum of the genre based on Yankee fears of the creepy folk who live in the rural South.

FINALLY (FANFARE, PLEASE), the single worst picture ever made about the South:

981. ***Hurry Sundown***'s ad campaign asked the question "Will the South Overcome the Bigotry of the Hate-Laden White Aristocrats?" Set in the 1940s and based on a best-selling but deservedly forgotten novel, Otto Preminger's 1967 film is about a conniving real estate speculator (Michael Caine, with possibly the worst Southern accent ever recorded) who tries to take the land of two families, a simple spiritual-singing black one and a noble common-white one. A bigoted judge and a lynch mob complete the picture. This turkey had to be Walker Percy's (**513**) model for the ridiculous movie in *Lancelot*. The kindest word applied to it by the critics was "ludicrous" (Judith Crist).

Josephine Humphreys wrote the novel *Rich in Love*. Photograph by Curt Richter

FOUR GOOD RECENT MOVIES ABOUT THE SOUTH

ONE GOOD THING ABOUT these is that they don't fit any of the hackneyed old categories.

982. ***Driving Miss Daisy*** (1989) portrays the complex relationship between an old Jewish lady and her black chauffeur. Jessica Tandy and Morgan Freeman are superb in Alfred Uhry's adaptation of his Pulitzer-winning play. Predictably, some critics scoffed at the idea that white employer and black servant could develop mutual respect and affection, but moviegoers didn't care: *Miss Daisy* was a box-office success and won a clutch of Oscars.

983. ***Rich in Love*** (1992) adapts Josephine Humphreys's novel about a family abandoned by its wife and mother, with luminous performances by young Kathryn Erbe and veteran Albert Finney (whose accent is impeccable). Writer Alfred Uhry and director Bruce Beresford show that *Driving Miss Daisy* was no accident. Like Pat Conroy's *Prince of Tides*, Humphreys's novel is about a dysfunctional family in the South Carolina Low Country, but the similarity stops there: there's no New York psychiatrist played by Barbra Streisand, and the tone is wry and affectionate.

984. ***Mississippi Masala*** (1992) stars Denzel Washington and Sarita Choudhury in a Romeo

and Juliet story set in Greenwood, Mississippi. The daughter of a refugee Indian couple from Uganda falls in love with a black Mississippian, and complications ensue. With fine performances all around and lots of irony (who *is* more African?), director Mira Nair's charming and often amusing movie deals sensitively with what could have been a delicate topic and is only rarely preachy about it.

985. *My Cousin Vinny* (1992) was called a "dopey comedy" by *Variety,* which shows how much they know. The funniest picture yet about interregional misunderstanding, it puts a twist on the dumb hillbilly gimmick: the comic fish out of water here are lawyer Joe Pesci and girlfriend Marisa Tomei, working-class New York Italian-Americans in the Deep South. Fred Gwynne gives a fine performance as a judge, and for once the Southern legal system comes off as something other than brutal and corrupt.

THREE RECENT SLEEPERS

MAYBE YOU'LL LIKE THESE, maybe you won't, but they're not the South you're used to seeing.

986. *sex, lies, and videotape* (1989) stars South Carolina–born model Andie MacDowell as the frigid wife of an impotent but kinky Louisiana lawyer who is carrying on, in his fashion, with her sexpot sister—when an old college friend comes to visit. (MacDowell says, "Daddy went by himself to see it and was embarrassed.") They loved Steven Soderbergh's film at Cannes, and if you like the idea of Eric Rohmer in Baton Rouge, you might like it, too.

987. *Sherman's March* (1986) is more like

Woody Allen in North Carolina. Ross McElwee filmed this tale, and he's its principal character. Setting out to retrace the path of Sherman's army, McElwee winds up in a feckless quest for the ideal Southern woman. The movie's Southernness is enhanced by a quirky subplot involving Burt Reynolds.

Burt Reynolds, who became an icon in *Sherman's March.* Connie Ives—Hot Shot Photos

988. *Miss Firecracker* (1989), Beth Henley's reworking of her off-Broadway play, stars Holly Hunter in a marvelous re-creation of her stage role as a sweet and funny Mississippi girl. Miss Henley said of Miss Hunter, "Holly and I share a Southern sensibility: that joyous-despairing view of life."

PRIME-TIME DIXIE

AS IT OFTEN DOES, television has taken Hollywood's already simplistic genres and dumbed them down. Here are some of the results.

989. Kountry Komedies. *The Real McCoys,* starring Walter Brennan, an exploitation of the comic consequences of a hillbilly family's moving to the San Fernando Valley, aired on ABC in 1957. An immediate hit, it ran for six years and started a trend. CBS aired five countrified sitcoms in the early sixties, roughly divided into those featuring Southerners who were smarter than they looked *(The Andy Griffith Show* and its spin-offs) and those featuring Southerners who were every bit as dumb as *they* looked *(The Beverly Hillbillies* and its relations). They drew enormous audiences, but by 1971 CBS had canceled them all, seeking younger, hipper, urban viewers.

990. THE ANDY GRIFFITH SHOW was the continuing saga of Mayberry, North Carolina, home of Sheriff Andy Taylor, son Opie, Deputy Barney, and Aunt Bee, enlivened by occasional characters like the mad hillbilly, Ernest T. Bass. Andy solved little problems weekly from 1960 until 1968, when Griffith left the show. This sympathetic treatment of small-town Southern life still attracts a large audience: the Andy Griffith Show Rerun Watchers Club has scores of chapters (political consultant James Carville co-founded the one in D.C.). Spin-offs included *Mayberry, R.F.D.,* the post-Griffith version of the show, and *Gomer Pyle, U.S.M.C.,* with Jim Nabors. Some years later Griffith returned to prime time as *Matlock,* a lawyer seemingly modeled after Senator Sam Ervin of Watergate fame, another font of homespun wisdom.

991. THE BEVERLY HILLBILLIES was *The Real McCoys* without the subtlety. The Clampetts—Jed and Granny and sexy Elly May and big, dumb cousin Jethro Bodine—moved to California after oil appeared in their Ozark front yard. This slim premise fueled nine years' worth of

episodes and a 1994 movie version. Spin-offs included two sitcoms set in Hooterville, which the Clampetts used to visit: *Petticoat Junction,* about the owner of the Shady Rest Hotel and her daughters Billie Jo, Bobbie Jo, and Betty Jo, and *Green Acres,* about a Manhattan lawyer seeking the simple life, with Eva Gabor as his socialite wife and a remarkably intelligent pig named Arnold.

992. Hee Haw joined the CBS lineup in 1969, offering a mix of cornpone humor, farmer's-daughter pulchritude, and musical numbers. Critics saw it as a down-home version of *Rowan and Martin's Laugh-In,* but it was also in the old minstrel-show tradition **(572)**, albeit with white faces. High points were the humor of the Reverend Grady Nutt and Junior Samples. Caught in CBS's 1971 purge of country programming, it promptly moved into syndication and survived for another generation. A mercifully short-lived spin-off was the sitcom *Hee Haw Honeys.*

993. The Waltons, John Boy and his warm, wholesome, close-knit Virginia mountain family, were CBS's big Southern hit for the 1970s, coming into American households one Thursday night in 1972 and staying for nearly a decade. Earl Hamner, Jr., creator and narrator, based his stories on his own childhood. This heartwarming alternative to both the nasty redneck and comic hillbilly versions of Southern rural life may even have contributed to the 1976 election of Jimmy Carter. After the program was established, however, the Waltons lost their accents—that is, they stopped being Southern.

994. The Dukes of Hazzard was an obvious CBS knockoff of Burt Reynolds's popular good-old-boy movies. Starting in 1979, Bo and Luke Duke drove weekly at high speeds through Hazzard County's improbable combination of mountains and swamps in their indestructible car, the General Lee. (Over two hundred Dodge Chargers were sacrificed to film the series.) Their nemesis was blustering, white-suited Boss Hogg, aided by incompetent Sheriff Roscoe P. Coltrane and his deputies, Enos and Cletus. With the help of good-old-girl cousin Daisy, wise old Uncle Jesse, and hillbilly buddy Cooter, the Dukes invariably prevailed. (Ben Jones, who played Cooter, later served a brief but amusing term as a Georgia congressman.) Spin-offs included a Saturday morning cartoon and a series starring Deputy Enos. NBC countered with *B. J. and the Bear,* about a good-old-boy truck driver, which spun off *The Misadventures of Sheriff Lobo,* about a g.o.b. sheriff's department. ABC already had the g.o.b. *Carter Country.* All these programs were set in Jimmy Carter's home state, and only *The Dukes of Hazzard* long survived his administration.

995. **Dallas** was set in a very different South. First aired in 1978, the depravity it portrayed wasn't the low-rent, *Tobacco Road* version of midcentury. J. R. Ewing (Larry Hagman) was a Sunbelt tycoon straight out of Kirkpatrick Sale's book *Power Shift* (**12**). This "human oil slick" (as *Time* magazine called him) was the sort of lying, cheating, scheming Southern potentate who hadn't figured in American mythology since the days of the Slave Power. By 1980 this prime-time soap opera was the most popular show in the entire world. Imitations included *Flamingo Road,* with Stella Stevens as Lute-Mae Sanders, owner of a Florida casino and brothel.

996. **Designing Women,** introduced by CBS in 1986, seemed to break new ground with its story of four modern women who ran an Atlanta decorating firm. But three— a lady, a comic belle,

and a good old girl—were familiar Southern types; only one, a middle-class "single parent," was not. A critical success, the program was saved from cancellation in 1987 by a carefully orchestrated public protest. When some called the show preachy, producer Linda Bloodworth-Thomason replied, "The show is preachy by design. The women are Southern, and Southern is being preachy." She and her husband later gave us *Evening Shade,* set back in the classic small town, with Burt Reynolds as a high school football coach and a marvelous supporting cast. Even with Southern producers, however, the program faithfully conformed to Roy Blount's Law: the stronger the accent, the dumber the character.

The Myth of the New South

WHAT IS THE SOUTH becoming? One of the most potent myths for at least the last century has been that of "the New South." Nobody agrees what it will look like, but it'll be something.

997. **The first New South** was largely the creature of Henry Grady (1850–89), longtime editor of the *Atlanta Constitution* (**7**). His speech with that title, delivered to the New England Club of New York in 1886, popularized the phrase and argued that the South was an ideal area for industrial investment, with a pool of cheap American-born labor, no unions, and boundless raw materials. Not all Southerners liked the idea. The Agrarians (**487, 922**) thought a "New South" on Grady's terms meant *no* South, and W. J. Cash mocked the idea of salvation through new industry as "a chicken-pox

Henry Grady, prophet of the New South. Library of Congress USZ62-93459

of factories on the Watch-Us-Grow maps." But that's pretty much what happened (**207–33**).

998. **Subsequent New Souths** have come and gone, as Ed Yoder put it, "like French constitutions and theories of the decline of Rome." Joel Garreau counts "at least six major, widely hailed New Souths since Lee's surrender to Grant, not to mention the minor, trial-balloon New Souths that the sad surplus of New Southern journalists float from time to time (everybody's got to eat)." Walker Percy chimed in with, "My definition of a New South would be a South in which it never occurred to anybody to mention the New South."

ALTHOUGH FEW SOUTHERNERS ARE nostalgic about sharecropping and Jim Crow, not everybody's wild about the direction the South seems to be going. Three skeptics, to close:

999. **Walker Percy**'s character Will Barrett, in *The Last Gentleman*: "He had noticed this about the South since he returned. Along the Tidewater everything was pickled and preserved and decorous. Backcountry everything was being torn down and built anew. The earth itself was transformed overnight, gouged and filled, flattened and hilled, like a big sandpile. The whole South throbbed like a diesel. . . . The South . . . was happy, victorious, Christian, rich, patriotic and Republican. . . . The happiness of the South was very formidable. It was an almost invincible happiness. It defied you to call it anything else. Everyone was in fact happy. The women were beautiful and charming. The men were healthy and successful and funny; they knew how to tell stories. They had everything the North had and more. They had a history, they had a place redolent with memories, they had good conversation, they believed in God and defended the Constitution, and they were getting rich in the bargain. They had the best of victory and defeat. Their happiness was aggressive and irresistible. . . . Oh, they were formidable, born winners (how did they lose?)."

1000. **Nicholas Lemann:** "When white people talk about 'the southern way of life,' it actually isn't any longer a code phrase for white supremacy; it connotes the 'totally planned community' around a golf course, cheese grits and honey-baked ham at the pre-game brunch, a five-year subscription to *Southern Living.*"

1001. **Flannery O'Connor:** "The anguish that most of us have observed for some time now has been caused not by the fact that the South is alienated from the rest of the country, but by the fact that it is not alienated enough, that every day we are getting more and more like the rest of the country, that we are being forced out, not only of our many sins, but of our few virtues."

Acknowledgments

We owe very special thanks to our agent, Gordon Kato, who thought we should write this book, and our editor, Rob Robertson, who agreed (and helped us to do it). We also thank the staff of the University of North Carolina library: our task would have been much harder without access to that great library's collections. For poll data we're indebted to Bev Wiggins and the staff of the Southern Focus Poll at UNC's Institute for Research in Social Science; and for cartographic assistance, to Martin Levin of Mississippi State University. William Betts, copy editor at Doubleday, went beyond the call of duty to double as fact checker, and saved us from altogether too many errors.

For helpful suggestions, consultation, moral support, or just writing books we found extraordinarily useful, we thank our friends Jim Auchmutey, Bill Bamberger and Alice Boyle, Tommy and Cindy Edwards, John Egerton, Elizabeth Fox-Genovese, Lisa Howorth, Anne Goodwyn Jones, Michael Lance, Jessie Poesch, Wayne Pond, Charles Reagan Wilson, David Moltke-Hansen and others too numerous to name (but you know who you are). Also Phyllis Volberg and our daughters Elisabeth and Sarah (Dale wants it on the record that she couldn't have stuck it out without them). Hugh McGraw of the Sacred Harp Publishing Co. and Susanne Pelt of South of the Border aren't personal friends, but they helped us anyway. Ted Teague and Susan Beal provided valuable research assistance.

Writing the book was almost easier than locating illustrations and getting permission to use them. A pox on those who made those chores difficult, but they make us thankful for the gracious folk who actually helped us. Many are acknowledged alongside the pictures they provided, but particular thanks to the staff of the Library of Congress Photographs and Prints Division; James C. Anderson, Delinda Stephens Buie, and Bill Carner of the University of Louisville Photographic Archives; Catherine Wahl of the Morris Museum of Art; Elayne Scott of Red Piano Too Art Gallery; John Coski and his colleagues at the Museum of the Confederacy; Eric Blevins of the North Carolina Museum of History; Jerry Cotten, photographic archivist at UNC's Wilson Library; Jon Kukla and John T. Magill of the Historic New Orleans Collection; Sharron Sarthou and Lisa Speer of the University of Mississippi Library; and Alecia Holland Harper of the journal *Southern Cultures*. We're especially grateful to four individual photographers: Curt Richter, who obligingly let us use some of his striking photographs of Southern authors; Bill Ferris, better known as the director of the Center for the Study of Southern Culture at the University of Mississippi; Connie Ives of Hot Shot Photos; and Jack Moebes, formerly of the Greensboro *News and Record.*

Index

[NOTE: References are to entry numbers, not pages. "912b" means the reference is found in material *before* entry 912.]

Aaron, Hank, 858
Abbot, John, 764
Abby Aldrich Rockefeller Folk Art Center, 885
abolitionism, 267, 353, 389, 448, 457, 464, 912b, 932, 934
Acadians (see Cajuns)
Acuff, Roy, 540, 565, 601, 712
Africans, early importation of, 85, 92, 156, 171, 348, 349; preservation of culture, 95, 126–30, 133, 135, 156, 467, 541, 575, 619, 667, 670, 674, 697, 713, 723
Agee, James, 453, 523, 720, 780, 955
agrarianism, 419, 443, 446, 918–21
Agrarians, 32, 196, 487, 491, 922, 924, 997
agribusiness, 196
agriculture, 72, 111, 168–77, 183–87, 196, 918–19
Ailey, Alvin, 523, 628
"ain't," 151
Alabama Shakespeare Festival, 902b
Alamo, 87, 460, 893
Albany Movement, 376
Albert, Carl, 29
Algonquin Books, 493, 494
Ali, Muhammad, 861
alligators, 55, 63
Allman Brothers Band, 567
Allston, Washington, 751
American Airlines, 207, 213
American Colonization Society, 268
American Dance Festival, 631
American Tobacco Company, 241
"American Trilogy," 616
Ammons, A. R., 516
Amos and Andy, 954
Anderson, Robert, 306
Anderson, Walter Inglis, 776
Andersonville Prison, 316

andouille, 692
Andrews, Benny, 776
Andrews, George, 776
Andrews, Raymond, 776
Andy Griffith Show, The, 989–90
Ansa, Tina, 132, 483
Appalachian Trail, 49
Appalachians, 16, 23, 200, 543, 835, 896
Applewhite, James, 492, 912b
Appomattox, 30, 320, 335
Aquarena Springs, 906
archaisms, 150–51
"Are You from Dixie?", 612
armadillo, 65
Armstrong, "Hammering Henry," 862
Armstrong, Louis, 589, 592, 593
Arnow, Harriette Simpson, 932
Arrested Development, 619
art deco, 894
Art Students League, 754, 757, 758, 760, 761, 772, 781
Ash, Mary Kay, 248
Ashe, Arthur, 873
Ashland Oil, 209
Asian Anthropologist in the South, An, 454
Asian-Americans, 112–14, 118, 346
Assemblies of God, 815
Atkins, Chet, 561
Atlanta: 7, 319, 366, 393, 396, 397, 429, 588, 619, 662, 683, 737, 810, 878, 893, 895, 901, 943, 962, 996; businesses, 207, 212, 220, 233, 242, 249, 705; capital of emerging Southeast, 13, 15, 51, 220; and Southern folkways, 163, 165–67, 652
Atlanta Braves, 249, 853, 858, 879
Atlanta Compromise, 364
Atlanta *Constitution,* 467, 669, 761, 997

Atlanta Hawks, 249
Atlanta History Center, 901
Atlanta Olympic Committee, 397
Atlanta Speedway, 851
Atlanta University, 391, 837
Atwater, Lee, 645
Audubon, 766, 767
August House, 494
Augusta National, 38, 878, 900
Aunt Jemima, 693
Austin, 65, 548, 562
azaleas, 81
Azusa Street, 829

Bachman, John, 767
bacon, 259, 633, 637, 667, 669, 698
Baha'i, 609, 822
Bailey, Guy, 159
Bakker, Jim, 815, 832
Balfa Brothers, 568
Ball, Marcia, 548
Baltimore, Lord, 820
banks, 215, 227
Baptists, 9, 89, 90, 112, 793, 795–801, 823–24, 831
barbecue, 640–47, 898
Barber, Walter Lanier "Red," 877
Barnett, Ross, 377, 427
barrelhouse, 549
Barry, Marion, 374
Barter Theater, 902
Barth, John, 493
Barton, Lou Ann, 548
baseball, 258, 711, 853, 856–59, 870, 877, 879
basketball, 258, 852, 870
baskets, 127
Bass Anglers Sportsman Society, 871
Bassett, John Spencer, 390

battle flag, 322–23, 345, 844, 969
Battle of New Orleans, 236, 433
battlefields, 893
bayous, 59, 101
BC, 712
beach music, 566, 582
Beale Street, 45, 590, 608, 898
Bearden, Romare, 760
beaten biscuits, 675
Beauregard, Pierre Gustave Toutant, 290, 771
Beauvoir, 283, 726
bebop, 570, 609
beer, 702, 909, 963
beignets, 696
Bell, John, 410
Bell, Madison Smartt, 533
belle, 946
Bellingrath Gardens, 881
Ben Ali, 115
benighted South, 932
Benjamin, Judah P., 285
benne (sesame), 156, 697
Bennett, Joe, and the Sparkletones, 612
Berea College, 835
Beresford, Bruce, 983
Berry, Chuck, 565
Berry, Wendell, 533
Bessinger, Maurice, 643
Betts, Doris, 483, 486, 533
Beverly Hillbillies, The, 989, 991
bi- or tri-racial isolate groups (see "little races")
Bible, 9, 224, 481, 788, 794
Big and Little (in names), 141
Big Apple, 578
Big Easy, The, 971
big mules, 407, 425
Bilali Mohomet, 115
Bilbo, Theodore, 423
Biltmore, 881, 896
Birdwhistell, Ray L., 163
Birmingham, 15, 375, 378, 901
Birth of a Nation, 367, 496, 955
birth rate, 191, 197
biscuits, 675–76
black and tans, 404
Black Belt, 20
Black Bottom, 577
black codes, 356
black elected officials, 388
black-eyed peas, 667
black lung, 194

black-widow spiders, 70
Blackburn, William, 492
blackened redfish, 693
Blackwood Brothers, 540
Blair, John, 494
Blake, Blind, 547, 588
Blake, Eubie, 574, 624
Bland, Bobby "Blue," 565
Bland, James, 611
Blaze, 974
Blease, Coleman, 421
Blenheim ginger ale, 708, 909
Blockbuster Entertainment, 231
Bloodworth-Thomason, Linda, 996
Blount, Roy, 633b, 996
Blue Ridge Parkway, 49
Bluegrass, 21
bluegrass music, 558, 594, 599, 976
blues, 45, 46, 132, 546–54, 586–90, 593, 608, 901, 976
Blues Archives, 608
blues shouting, 552
BMW, 205
boiled peanuts, 686
Bolden, Charles "Buddy," 584
boll weevil, 6, 72, 220
boll weevils (political label), 409
Bolton, Ruthie, 446
Boney, F. N., 940
Bonnie Blue Flag, 321
"Bonnie Blue Flag" (song), 326, 340
boogie-woogie, 156, 549, 587
Boone, Daniel, 41
Booth, John Wilkes, 301
bottle tree, 134
boudin, 692
bourbon, 216, 331, 660–62
Bourbon Street, 46
Bourbons (see Redeemers)
Bourke-White, Margaret, 780
Bradley, Horace, 761
Bragg, Braxton, 292, 294, 295, 315
"branch," 153
Branson, Missouri, 24, 905
Brass Ankles, 91
Breckinridge, John C., 410
Brenner family (painters), 749
Br'er Rabbit, 467, 966
Briggs, Joe Bob, 965
"brook," 153
Brookgreen Gardens, 881
Brooks, Cleanth, 490, 492
Brooks, Garth, 563

Brown, Albert Gallatin, 275
Brown, Clarence "Gatemouth," 548
Brown, James, 566
Brown, John, 301, 353
Brown, Larry, 533
Brown, Mary Ward, 482
Brown, Ruth, 553
Brown, William Henry, 768
Brown, William Wells, 457
Brown-Forman, 211, 216
Brownlow, William Gannaway "Parson," 281
brown lung, 194
Brown v. Board of Education, 369, 392, 425
brunch, 695, 1000
Brunswick stew, 641, 666
brush arbors, 825
Bryant, Paul "Bear," 869, 872
Bubba, 146, 417, 938
Buddhists, 822
Bull Run (see Manassas)
Bunker, Eng and Chang, 118
burgoo, 666
"Burial of Latané, The," 334, 337
burial practices, 133
Burke, James Lee, 534
Burlington Industries, 210
Burnett, Micajah, 892
Bush, George, 441, 871
Butler, Pierce, 446, 451
buttermilk, 657, 676, 701
butternuts, 330
Byrd, Harry Flood, 372, 431
Byrd, William, 53, 443, 637, 918, 928, 942

Cabell, James Branch, 462, 499, 519
Cable, George Washington, 100
Caesar, Shirley, 542
Café du Monde, 696
cafeterias, 219, 633
Cajans, 91
Cajuns, 19, 59, 74, 86, 101, 469, 534, 554, 568, 633, 692, 693, 820, 971, 978
Caldwell, Erskine, 780, 812
Calhoun, John C., 260, 433
call and response, 541
Callaway Gardens, 881
Calvinists, 135, 797–98, 808, 811–12
Camel cigarettes, 241
camellias, 81, 253, 878, 881
camp meetings, 541, 824–26, 828
Campbell, Will, 940

Campbellites, 793, 807, 818

Candler, Asa, 242

Cane Ridge, 811, 818, 824

Caribbean, 92, 100, 172, 349

Carmer, Carl, 946

Carmichael, Hoagy, 613

Carnival (holiday), 890

carnivorous plants, 79

Carolina Playmakers, 902b

carpetbaggers, 402

"Carry Me Back to Old Virginny," 611

Carter, Billy, 702, 939

Carter, Hodding, 927

Carter, James Earl "Jimmy," 39, 142–44, 416, 440

Carter Family, 557, 594

Carter's Grove, 886

Carver, George Washington, 839

Carville, James, 990

Cash, Johnny, 564, 594, 907

Cash, W. J., 445, 479, 742b, 749, 923, 997

Castilians, 101

Cat on a Hot Tin Roof, 511, 960

Catawbas, 90

catfish, 22, 664, 957

Catholics, 96, 99–101, 104–6, 109, 128, 367, 792, 820

Cato's rebellion, 350

cavalier, 913

caves, 24, 62, 313, 906, 911

Celtic, 98, 546

Census South, 2, 198, 387

Center for Southern Folklore, 898

Center for the Study of Southern Culture, 47, 844

Chancellorsville, 288, 311, 335

Chaney, James, 381

Chapel Hill, 842–43

Chapman, Conrad Wise, 756

Chappell, Fred, 492

Charles, Ray, 566, 607, 609, 613

Charleston: 120, 306, 350–51, 834, 899b; architecture, 714b, 724, 731, 882; arts and crafts, 121, 127, 620, 630, 739, 742, 763, 774; early settlement, 85, 103, 108; food, 651–52, 671, 697

"Charleston," 574, 576

Charleston Museum, 899b

Chenier, Clifton, 569

Cherokee, North Carolina, 904

Cherokees, 3, 42, 88, 90, 279, 297

Chesapeake, 84

Chesnut, Mary Boykin, 272, 447, 914

Chesnutt, Charles Waddell, 468, 470

chess pie, 681

chewing tobacco, 169, 211, 241, 711, 939, 942

Chicago blues, 550

Chickamauga, 303

Chickasaws, 88

chicken-fried steak, 699

chickory, 696

Chief Henry, "the World's Most Photographed Indian," 904

Chief Nockahoma, 879

chiggers, 68

child labor, 189

chili, 699

Chincoteague, 175

Chinese, 112

chitlin circuit, 553

Chitlin Strut, 639

chitterlings, 639

"Chivalrous C.S.A.," 912

chivalry, 167, 912

Choctaws, 88, 90, 690

Chopin, Kate, 100, 469, 732

Christ of the Ozarks, 905

Christ Only Art Gallery, 905

Christian Church, 807

Christus Gardens, 904

Church of God, 816

Church of God in Christ, 814, 898

Church of the Brethren, 103, 819

Churches of Christ, 618

cigarettes, 169, 211, 241, 259

Citadel, 351, 834

Citizens' Council, 427

Civil Rights Act of 1964, 382, 414

civil-rights movement, 331, 367, 369–84, 389–97, 413–14, 426–29, 439, 544, 901, 932, 975

Clague, Richard, 769

Claiborne Farms, 868

Clark Atlanta University, 837

classical music and dance, 620–32

Claxton Fruitcake Co., 684

clay, 60, 122, 633b, 713, 944

Clay, Cassius Marcellus (1810–1903), 269, 835

Clay, Cassius Marcellus (1942–   ), 861

Clay, Clement C., 286

Clay, Henry, 268, 434–35

Cleburne, Patrick, 295

Cliburn, Van, 627, 629

Cline, Patsy, 603

Clinton, Bill, 39, 417, 441

Cloar, Carroll, 920

clogging, 581

coal, 23, 34, 195, 200

Coal Miner's Daughter, 967

Cobb, Ty, 857–58

Coca-Cola, 155, 212, 242, 705, 901

cocktails, 695

coffee, 258, 670, 696

Coffin, Levi, 266

COGIC (see Church of God in Christ)

Coincoin, Marie Therese, 733

Cole family (potters), 122

Coleman, Ornette, 571

collards, 219, 668

Collins, Floyd, 62

Color Purple, The, 530, 959

Coltrane, John, 571

Columbia/HCA Healthcare, 229

Come Back to the Five and Dime, Jimmy Dean, Jimmy Dean, 970

Commission on the Future of the South, 200

Compaq Computers, 208, 232

Compromise of 1850, 278

Compromise of 1877, 359, 411

concurrent majority, 260

condiments, 677b, 677–78

Confederate Air Force, 347

Confederate Memorial Day, 341

Confederate States, 3

Congregationalists, 795, 807

Congress of Racial Equality, 395

Conner, Eugene "Bull," 378

Conquered Banner, 339

Conroy, Pat, 530, 533, 983

consumer patterns, 251–59

convict-lease system, 420

Coogler, J. Gordon, 931

Cooke, George, 744

Cooke, Philip St. George, 305

Cooke, Sam, 566

Cooley, Spade, 559

coon songs, 573, 615

Copperheads, 44, 401

CORE (see Congress of Racial Equality)

corn, 168, 211, 221, 633, 634, 648, 650, 701, 943

corn cribs, 716

corn whiskey, 660–61

cornbread, 657–59, 669

corndog, 685

cornpone, 655

Cornwell, Patricia D., 536

cotton, 6, 72, 94, 173, 186, 196, 210, 235, 238, 245, 745

Cotton Kingdom, 6

Cotton Snob, 935

country dancing, 583

country ham, 633, 635, 638, 675

country music, 24, 557–63, 593–94, 599–603, 617, 904–5, 907, 967

Country Music Hall of Fame, 593, 601, 907

Cracker Barrel Old Country Stores, 226, 633

crackers, 467, 897, 943

crackling cornbread, 634, 658

Crater, The, 318

Craven family (potters), 122

crawfish, 691–92

creasy greens, 668

Creeks, 88

Creole Jazz Band, 592

Creoles, 91, 96, 100, 236, 469, 622, 820

Crews, Harry, 137, 176, 446, 515, 533, 788

Crimson Tide, 869, 872

Crisis, The, 391, 489

Croatans (see Lumbees)

Crockett, Davy, 460

Crow, Dr. James, 661

Crump, Edward Hull "Boss," 430

CSS Virginia, 308

Cubans, 110, 346, 820, 822

Cumberland Gap, 41

Cumberland Plateau, 15, 23

Cumberlands, 23

Currier and Ives, 748, 771

Cyclorama, 893

cypress, 75, 744

Cypress Gardens, 897, 910

Czechs, 105

Dabbs, James, Jr., 167

Daingerfield, Elliot, 757

Dallas, 207, 222, 230, 248, 647, 706

"Dallas" (television program), 145, 934, 995

Daniels, Charlie, 51, 567, 925

Daniels, Jonathan, 848b, 912b

Daniels, Josephus, 31

Dare, Virginia, 83

Darlington, South Carolina, 36

Darrow, Clarence, 32

Dave (potter), 123

Davenport, "Cow Cow," 549

Davenport, Guy, 492

Davidson, Donald, 487, 924

Davis, Jefferson, 273–75, 283–86, 295, 320, 329, 333, 341, 895

Davis, Rev. Blind Gary, 547

Davis, Varina Howell, 283

Day, Thomas, 734

Dayton, Tennessee, 32

Daytona, 18, 36

De Soto, Hernando, 43, 54

Deep South, 5, 6, 14, 20, 73, 94, 103, 384, 410, 412–15, 964

Delaware, 2, 4, 26, 354, 714

Deliverance, 962

Delmarva Peninsula, 26

Delta Air Lines, 220

Delta blues, 546, 550, 567, 586, 593

Delta Blues Museum, 608, 901

demagogues, 418–29

Dennis, Rev. H. D., 787

Denton, Jeremiah, 872

derby pie, 698

Designing Women, 996

"Detroit City," 617

Devil, the, 587, 794, 832

Dew, Thomas Roderick, 261

Dial, Thornton, Sr., 785

diaries, 271–72, 443, 446, 447, 452, 469, 914

Dickey, James, 80, 460, 508, 515, 530, 962

Diddley, Bo, 554

Dillard, Annie, 493

diminutives, 142

dinner, 157, 539, 665

dirt, 633b, 713, 944

Disciples of Christ, 818

disfranchisement, 357, 360b–63, 381, 402, 404–5, 418, 431

Disney, Walt, 220, 460, 522, 761, 845, 897, 966

District of Columbia, 2, 354

Dixie, 5, 29, 573

"Dixie" (song), 325–26, 566

Dixie Hummingbirds, 542

Dixiecrats, 11, 408, 413, 425

Dixieland jazz, 46, 555–56, 559

Dixon, Thomas, Jr., 470, 496, 530, 955

Dixon, Willie, 550

Dr Pepper, 212, 706

Dodd, Lamar, 776

dogtrot, 714, 722

dogwood, 76

Domino, Fats, 553

Dorsey, Thomas A., 595

double names, 139, 143–44

double negative, 151

doublewide, 152

Douglas, Ellen, 533, 587

Douglas, Stephen, 410

Douglass, Frederick, 115, 389, 448, 541

Driving Miss Daisy, 982

Drysdale, Alexander John, 772

DuBois, W. E. B., 132, 364, 391, 489, 519, 837

duelling, 276, 914

Duke, James "Buck," 241

Duke University, 492, 532, 631

"Dukes of Hazzard, The," 935, 994

Dunkers, 103, 819

E. M. Todd Co., 637

Eastern Shore, 26, 84

Edgefield, South Carolina, 122–23

Edgerton, Clyde, 533

Edmondson, William, 786, 789

Eggleston, William, 783

election of 1860, 273, 410

election of 1876, 11, 411

election of 1928, 404, 412

election of 1948, 408, 413

election of 1964, 414, 439, 609

election of 1968, 415, 428

election of 1976, 12, 394, 416, 440

election of 1992, 417, 441, 938

Elizabethan English, 161

Ellison, Ralph, 505, 509, 512

Elvis, 45, 540, 564, 606, 616, 692, 701, 723, 908, 968

Elvis (movie), 968

Elvis: That's the Way It Is, 968

Elvis Presley Enterprises, 848b

emancipation, 92, 178, 285, 349, 354

Emmett, Dan, 325, 572

Emory University, 242, 459

Encyclopedia of Southern Culture, 495

Encyclopedia of Southern History, 495

English (settlers), 83–85, 97, 730, 884, 894, 913

Enterprise, Alabama, 72

Episcopalians, 294, 817, 836

Ervin, Sam, 990

Eureka Springs, Arkansas, 905

evangelical Protestantism, 793, 802, 811, 813, 823–26, 831, 832

Evangelical United Brethren, 803

Evans, Eli, 348b

Evans, Minnie, 786, 790

Evans, Walker, 453, 780
Evening Shade, 996
Everglades, 55
Everly Brothers, 564
Evers, Medgar, 379
Everybody's All-American, 972
Ewing, J. R., 145, 934, 995
Exxon, 209
Eyes on the Prize, 975

Fabulous Thunderbirds, 548
faith-healing, 137, 813
family, 16, 478
family names, 138–39
Farm Security Administration, 780
Farmers Alliance, 418
Farragut, David Glasgow, 304
fasola, 538
Father Divine, 830
Faubus, Orval, 373, 426
Faulkner, Dean, 518
Faulkner, William: 485, 494, 503, 505, 510,
     513, 519b, 521, 844, 957, 964; quoted,
     133, 176, 260b, 370, 475
Federal Express, 213
Federal Writers' Project, 449
Ferris, William, 47
feuds, 16, 932
filé, 690
Finster, Howard, 787, 791
fire ants, 71
fire-eaters, 273–77, 400
First Union (bank), 215
fishing, 28, 58, 114, 848, 871
Fisk University, 497, 541, 838
Fitzhugh, George, 262
Five Blind Boys of Mississippi, 542
Five Civilized Tribes, 42, 88
"fixing to," 159
Flagg, Fannie, 672
Flagler, Henry, 749, 883
Flatt, Lester, 558
Florida: 54, 55, 77, 82, 198–200, 535, 682,
     943, 976; ethnic and racial groups, 88,
     90, 98, 106–11, 114; relation to South,
     4, 12, 18; and tourism, 25, 883, 897,
     910
flush toilets, 192
folk medicine, 136–37
folk music, 258, 537, 541, 543, 544, 540–48
Folsom, James Elisha "Big Jim," 425
Food Lion, 225
foot washing, 797, 813

football, 258, 855, 856, 869, 872, 972
Foote, Horton, 964, 967
Foote, Shelby, 181, 260b, 306b, 842
foreign investment, 204, 206
Forrest, Nathan Bedford, 293
Forrest Gump, 888, 961
Fort Pillow, 293
Fort Sumter, 276, 290, 306, 834
Fortune 500, 206–15, 232
"forty acres and a mule," 176, 355
Foster, Rube, 859
Foster, Stephen, 572, 610, 912b
Fountain, Pete, 556
Fox, John, 23
fox hunting, 175
Frank, Leo, 419
Franklin, 295
Fraser, Charles, 774
Frazier, Joe, 862
Fredericksburg, Texas, 104
free jazz, 571
Freedom Riders, 375
French, 56, 59, 85, 86, 96, 99–101, 568–69,
     662, 690–96
French Quarter, 46, 882, 890
fried chicken, 246, 634, 665
fried fish, 656, 664
Fried Green Tomatoes, 970
fried pies, 633, 683
fried tomatoes, 672, 970
Frito-Lay, 221
Frizzell, Lefty, 560, 565
fruitcake, 684
fugitive slaves, 54, 91
Fugitives, the, 487–88, 491, 500
Fuller, Blind Boy, 547
furniture, 206, 211, 714b, 734, 739b–41, 889

Gaines, Ernest J., 175, 176, 517, 959
Gaineswood, 732
gambling, 25, 175, 850, 939
game, 663, 690, 745, 746
Garden District, 890
gardening, 253, 494
gardens, 81, 121, 881, 894, 897, 904, 908,
     910
Gardner, Angela Davis, 492
Gardner, Dave, 168b, 941
Garner, John Nance, 439b
Garreau, Joel, 908
Garrett, George, 515, 533
Gastonia, 33
Gatlinburg, 904

Gatling, Richard, 239
Gatorade, 708
Genovese, Eugene, 527
gentleman, Southern, 346, 843, 873, 877,
     878, 927, 933, 935
Georgetown, South Carolina, 171
Georgia-Pacific, 211
Germans, 40, 86, 103, 104, 204, 698, 714,
     803, 819–21
Gettysburg (battle), 289, 291, 312
Gettysburg (movie), 973
Gibbons, Kaye, 493, 533
Gibson, Josh, 859
gifts of the Holy Spirit, 813
Gilchrist, Ellen, 533
Gildersleeve, Basil Lanneau, 343
Gillespie, Dizzy, 570, 609
Gilliam, Sam, 776
Gilman, Caroline, 263
gin, cotton, 173, 235
ginseng, 78
Glasgow, Ellen, 442b, 470, 498, 519b, 952
Glorieta, New Mexico, 309
Godwin, Gail, 533, 927
Goldthwaite, Anne, 758
golf, 38, 258, 864, 878, 880, 1000
"Gomer Pyle, U.S.M.C.," 990
Gone with the Wind, 260b, 521, 956
Goo Goo Cluster, 688
goober (peanut), 156, 686, 943
good old boy, 937–38, 963
good woman, 953
Goodman, Andrew, 381
Goody's, 712, 874
goofer dust, 128
Gordon, Caroline, 504
Gore, Albert, Jr., 417
Gore, Albert, Sr., 372
gospel music, 259, 540, 542, 595, 601,
     605
Gothic (in architecture), 728
Gothic (in literature), 455, 461
Gottschalk, Louis Moreau, 622
grace (at meals), 148, 794
Graceland, 898, 908
Grady, Henry, 7, 168b, 178, 997
Graham, Billy, 536, 831
Grand Ole Opry, 557, 599, 601, 602, 688,
     712
grandfather clauses, 362
Graniteville, South Carolina, 238
Grau, Shirley Ann, 525
Great Alibi, 178b

Great Awakenings, First and Second, 823–24
Great Dismal Swamp, 53
Great Migration, 47, 368, 856
Great Seal of the Confederacy, 329
Great South, The, 450
Great Wagon Road, 40, 98
Greek Revival (in architecture), 727, 729, 731
Greeks, 107
Green, Al, 537b
Green, Paul, 903
Green Acres, 991
Greenberg, Reuben, 120
Greenbriar, the, 880
greens, 149, 219, 634, 636, 648, 667–69
Gregg, William, 238
Greyhound, 207, 213
Griffin, John Howard, 454
Griffith, Andy, 961, 989, 990
Griffith, D. W., 955
Grimké, Archibald, 117
Grimké, Sarah and Angelina, 267
grist, 651, 716
grits, 71, 106, 636, 638, 649–54, 657, 909, 976, 1000
Grits (movie), 976
Grizzard, Lewis, 162, 494
Grooms, Red, 761
Guillaume, Louis, 335
guitar boogie, 549
Gujeratis, 113
Gulf Coast, 25, 65, 77, 114
Gullah, 28, 95, 519, 686, 846
gumbo, 156, 670, 690
Gurganus, Allan, 475, 478, 483, 485, 533
Guthrie, Woody, 594, 597, 598
Gwathmey, Robert, 761

Hadas, Moses, 332b
Haggard, Merle, 977
Haiti, 128, 389, 723
Haitians, 96, 100, 110
Haley, Alex, 219, 484
Haliwa, 91
Hamilton, George, 967
Hammond, James Henry, 6
Hamner, Earl, Jr., 993
Hampton, James, 790
Hampton Institute, 390, 781, 839
Hampton plantation, 716
Handy, W. C., 45, 551, 589, 590, 624
Hannah, Barry, 533

Harington, Donald, 533
Harlan, John Marshall, 280, 365
Harlan, Kentucky, 34, 975
Harlan County, U.S.A., 975
Harlem Renaissance, 483, 489, 507, 590
Harpers Ferry, 353
Harpo, Slim, 554
Harris, Eddy L., 454
Harris, Joel Chandler, 467, 966
Harris, Phil, 615
Harris, Wynonie, 553
Harrison, William Henry, 434
Hawkins, Ronnie, 564
Hayes, Roland, 541
head cheese, 639
headache powders, 712, 874
health, 67, 136–37, 194, 229
Heam, Lafcadio, 1b
Heartbreak Hotel, 968
Hee Haw, 992
Helper, Hinton Rowan, 270, 934
helpfulness, 166
hemp, 174, 239
Henderson, William McCranor, 533
Henley, Beth, 988
Henry, Marguerite, 175
Hentz, Caroline Lee, 263, 464
herbalists, 136
Hermitage, 741, 882
Heyward, DuBose, 488
Hiaasen, Carl, 535
Hickenlooper, Olga, 623
high blood, 136
High Lonesome, 976
High Point, North Carolina, 211
Highland Games, 102
Highway 61, 47
hillbilly, 543, 942, 953b, 977, 985, 989–91, 994
Hillbillys in a Haunted House, 977
Hilton Head, 28
Hindu, 113, 822
Hines, Duncan, 243, 246
Hirsch, Sidney Mttron, 487, 500
Hirt, Al, 556
Hispanics, 110–11
historic preservation, 773, 774, 882–94
Hobson, Fred, 853
hoecake, 655
hog jowl, 639
Hogg, Boss, 935, 994
hogs, 98, 168, 177, 178, 637–45, 658, 777b
Holiday Inns, 224, 233

holidays, 341, 354, 667
holiness churches, 802, 806, 813, 816
Holley, Lonnie, 784b, 785–86
Holly, Buddy, 564
holy rollers, 813
homicide, 10
hominy, 649
hominy grits, 649, 651
honky-tonk music, 560
honor, 17, 914
hoodoo, 128–32, 136, 156
Hooker, John Lee, 550, 553
hookworm, 67, 194, 932
Hooper, Annie, 784
Hope, Arkansas, 39, 674
Hopkins, Lightnin', 548
hoppin' john, 667
Hornsby, Rogers, 859
horses, 21, 175, 254, 850, 866–68, 905, 910
hospitality, 886, 926, 947–49
hot brown, 698
Hot Springs, Arkansas, 39, 644, 815, 880
House, Son, 546
housing, 152, 192, 194
Houston, Sam, 279
Houston, Texas, 105, 112–14, 165, 232, 394, 779, 945
Howlin' Wolf, 550
Howorth, Lisa, 788
Hughes, Langston, 489
Huguenots, 85, 99
Huizenga, Wayne, 231
Hull, Cordell, 150
Humphreys, Josephine, 477, 492, 533, 983
Hundley, Daniel, 156, 933–36, 939, 941
Hunt, Richard Morris, 896
Hunt, William Morris, 749
Hunter, Clementine, 733, 789
Hunter, Holly, 988
hunting, 63, 64, 252, 745, 849, 915
Huntsville, Alabama, 37, 816, 901
Hurry Sundown, 981
Hurston, Zora Neale, 129–31, 483, 489, 507, 720
hushpuppies, 656
Hyman, Mac, 492, 961
hymns, 537–42, 812

I Am a Fugitive from a Chain Gang, 965
ice houses, 718
ice tea, 633, 700
I'll Take My Stand, 32, 922

immersion, baptism by, 795, 799, 818, 819

In the Heat of the Night, 940, 964

income, 182–84, 188, 199

Indians (American), 40, 43, 74, 116, 119, 200, 297, 822, 863; folkways, 59, 64, 74, 78, 126b, 168, 169, 640, 649, 654, 655, 680, 690, 709; major groups in South, 55, 88–90

Indians (Asian), 113, 346, 984

indigo, 170, 234, 888

Indigo Girls, 617

individualism, 445, 581, 923

industrial wages, 188, 203

industrialization, 7, 15, 168b, 196, 922, 997

infant baptism, 795

Inherit the Wind, 32

initials (as name), 145

instant grits, 653

Interdenominational Theological Center, 837

International Ballet Competition, 632

International Home Furnishings Market, 211

Irish Catholics, 106, 820

Issues (racial group), 91

Italianate architecture, 728

Italians, 106, 694, 820, 985

J. C. Penney, 207, 214

Jack Daniel's, 216, 661

Jackson, Andrew, 236, 278, 399, 433, 741, 882, 890

Jackson, Jesse, 395

Jackson, Mahalia, 589, 595, 605

Jackson, Mississippi, 178, 220, 375, 379, 632

Jackson, Rachel (Mrs. Andrew), 433, 890

Jackson, Shoeless Joe, 859

Jackson, Thomas "Stonewall," 288, 310, 311, 332, 333, 335, 771, 895

Jackson, Tony, 575

Jacobs, Harriet, 448

jambalaya, 671, 691

James, Elmore, 550

James, Frank and Jesse, 300

James Beam Distilling Co., 661

Jamestown, 84, 177, 348, 660, 808, 817, 884

Jargon Society, 494

Jax, 702

Jay, William, 730, 731

jazz, 555–56, 570–71, 592, 609

jazz funeral, 555, 609

Jefferson, Blind Lemon, 548

Jefferson, Thomas, 398, 432, 457, 727, 729, 843, 912b, 918–19, 921

Jekyll Island, 28, 880

Jennings, James Harold, 786

Jennings, Waylon, 562, 600

Jesus, 157, 332, 346, 595, 605, 787, 790, 792b, 874, 904, 905

Jews, 108–9, 119, 120, 285, 346, 500, 821, 901, 982

Jim Crow, 572

Jim Crow era, 112, 360–84, 873

jitterbug, 555, 579

jogging, 258

John Boy, 993

John the Conqueror root, 130, 132

Johnny Reb, 330, 677

Johns, Jasper, 777

Johns Hopkins, 343, 496

Johnson, Anderson, 786

Johnson, Andrew, 282, 357, 437

Johnson, Bushrod, 287b

Johnson, Charles S., 489, 838

Johnson, Jack, 860

Johnson, James P., 574, 576

Johnson, James Weldon, 489, 497

Johnson, Junior, 851

Johnson, Lyndon B., 372, 382, 414, 435, 439

Johnson, Robert, 546, 587

Johnson, William B., 233

Johnson, William H., 759

Johnson, William R., 866

Johnston, Frances Benjamin, 781

Johnston, Henrietta, 762

Johnston, Joshua, 765

Jones, Anne Goodwyn, 493

Jones, Bobby, 38, 878

Jones, Clyde, 791

Jones, George, 560

Jones, Hugh, 926, 931

Jones, Nell Choate, 745, 761

Joplin, Scott, 585

Jordan, Barbara, 394

Jordan, Michael, 870

Jordan, Terry, 20b

Jordanaires, 540

Jr., II, III, etc., 140

Jubilee Singers, 541, 838

juke joints, 553, 575, 577

julep, 347, 662, 698, 850

Juneteenth, 354

K-Paul's Restaurant, 693

Kansas City, 229, 552, 644

Kant, Immanuel, 633

Kappa Alpha Order, 346, 840

Kaufman, Wallace, 492

Kefauver, Estes, 372

Kelly, Walt, 64

Kemble, Fanny, 17, 451, 950

Kenan, Randall, 483, 533

Kendall, John S., 448

Kennedy, John Pendleton, 452, 463

Kennedy, Robert, 375

Kennedy Center, 736

Kennedy Space Center, 897

Kentucky Derby, 610, 662, 698, 850, 867, 868

key lime pie, 682

Keyes, Frances Parkinson, 100

KFC (Kentucky Fried Chicken), 246

King, B. B., 45, 608

King, Coretta Scott, 393

King, Edward, 450, 749, 928

King, Florence, 486, 946

King, Grace, 100

King, Martin Luther, 142, 371, 376, 378, 380, 393, 595, 605, 814, 837, 846

King, Richard, 922

King, Susan Petigru, 264

King Creole, 692, 968

Kingfish (Huey Long), 424

Kingfish (radio character), 954

Kirk, Samuel, and Son, 740

Kissimee, Florida, 910

kitchens, 221, 715–17, 721, 728

Knights of the White Camellia, 81

Korean Presbyterians, 819

Koreans, 114, 819

Kress Stores, 217

Ku Klux Klan, 81, 293, 358, 367, 378, 419, 496, 634, 942, 955

kudzu, 80

La Rocca, Nick, 556

LaBeef, Sleepy, 564

labor, 189, 262, 364, 425, 544, 928, 932; agricultural, 170–72, 183, 196; unions, 33–34, 203, 220, 223, 225, 392, 598, 975, 997

lady, 73, 498, 927, 944–53, 996

Lafitte, Jean, 236

Lake Okeechobee, 55, 172

Lake Pontchartrain, 56

Landmark, 799

landscape painting, 744, 749, 757, 763, 769, 777b, 780

Lanier, Sidney, 470, 877, 921

lard, 177, 637, 658

Latané, Bibb, 167

Laughlin, Clarence John, 782

Laveau, Marie, 131

laziness, 67, 928, 930, 941–42

Leadbetter, Huddie (Leadbelly), 594, 596, 597

Lee, Harper, 66, 524, 929, 964

Lee, Robert E., 30, 283b, 287, 288, 291, 310–13, 317, 319–20, 353, 390, 840, 973; as icon, 333, 335–36, 341, 346, 438, 753, 771, 895, 933, 994; quoted, 283b, 291, 336, 914

Lee's birthday, 341

leisure, 480, 848b–911, 922, 928–29

Lemann, Nancy, 479, 704

Lemann, Nicholas, 1000

Leslie, Miriam Florence Folline (Frank), 240

Lester, Jeeter, 48, 77

Lester, Lazy, 554

levees, 52, 55, 61

Levine, Robert V., 165–66

Lewis, Jerry Lee, 144, 455, 564, 971

Lewis, John, 396

liberalism, 258, 412, 414–17, 425, 428, 429, 439, 441, 810, 827

Liggett and Myers, 211

Light Crust Doughboys, 600

Li'l Abner, 935, 942

Lily-whites, 404

Lincoln, Abraham, 282, 283, 286, 301, 306, 353, 354, 410, 437

Lincoln, Mrs. Abraham, 305

Lindy Hop, 579, 582

line dances, 583

lining out, 537

Lisitzky, Ephraim E., 119

literacy tests, 360, 362–63

Little Dixie, 29

"little races," 91, 96

Little Richard, 553

Little Rock, Arkansas, 230, 373, 426

live oak, 75

Lloyd, Pop, 859

local colorists, 467b, 467–69

log cabin, 714

Logan, Rayford, 366

Lomax, Alan, 591, 598

Lomax, John, 596

Lone Star, 206, 702

Lonesome Sundown, 554

Long, Huey Pierce, 424, 669, 974

Longstreet, Augustus Baldwin, 458, 459

Longstreet, James, 289

Longstreet Press, 494

Lonzo and Oscar, 689

Lookout Mountain, 315, 911

Lost Cause, 283, 287, 332b, 332–43, 817

Lost Cause, 332

Lost Colony, 83, 89

Lost Colony, The (movie), 903

lottery, 258

Louis, Joe, 856

Louisiana State University, 495, 529

Louisiana Story, 975

Low, Juliette Gordon, 332

Low Country, 85, 161, 697, 717, 724, 983

L.S.U. (see Louisiana State University)

Lucas, Charlie, 785

Lumbees, 89

Lumpkin, Katharine Du Pre, 332

Lutherans, 103, 104, 819

lynching, 366, 370, 419–21, 614

Lynn, Loretta, 603, 953, 967

Lynyrd Skynyrd, 567, 618

Lytle, Andrew, 531, 920, 922

M1 carbine, 244

"ma'am," 148

McCarthy, Cormac, 533

McClard's (restaurant), 644

McClinton, Delbert, 548

McColl, Hugh, Jr., 227

McCord, Louisa S., 265

McCorkle, Jill, 533

McCormick, Cyrus, 237

McCrady, John, 775

MacDowell, Andie, 986

McFee, Michael, 533

McGhee, Brownie, 547

MacKethan, Lucinda, 493

Macon, Nathaniel, 398

McTell, Blind Willie, 547

Maddox, Lester, 429

Madison, Dolly, 947

Madison, James, 398, 432

magazines, 251–59

magnolia, 73, 321

malaria, 69, 194

Mallard, Prudent, 741

"Mamaw," 154

Mammoth Cave, 62

Man o' War, 867

Manassas, 288, 290, 307, 331

Mandingo, 934, 979

Manigault house, 882

manners, 484, 531, 633b, 927, 948

manufacturing, 201, 203

March on Washington, 380, 393

Mardi Gras, 890

Margaret's store, 787

Marlette, Doug, 80, 494

Marschall, Nicola, 770

Marshall Tucker Band, 567

martial tradition, 915

Martin, Maria, 767

Martineau, Harriet, 450

"Maryland, My Maryland," 327, 340

Mason, Bobbie Ann, 533

Mason, Charles Harrison, 814

Mason-Dixon Line, 1, 331

Masters Tournament, 38, 878

Mays, Willie, 859

Meeker, Joseph Rusling, 749

Meharry Medical College, 838

Melchers, Gari, 776

Melrose plantation, 733, 789

Melungeons, 91

Memphis, 22, 45, 47, 293, 356, 393, 430, 645, 811, 814, 898; businesses, 213, 217, 218, 224; music, 564, 566, 608, 908

Memphis Slim, 550

Mencken, H. L., 8, 9, 32, 445, 487, 714b, 917, 931

Menil Collection, 779

Mennonites, 103, 819

Mercedes, 202, 205

Mercer, Johnny, 604

Meredith, James, 377, 844

"mess," 149

Mesta, Perle, 949

Methodists, 9, 281, 332, 793, 802–7, 823–24

Metoyer, Louis, 733

Mexican War, 392, 435, 436

Mexican-Americans, 111, 200, 820

Miami, 109, 110, 535, 894

Middle Passage, 348

Middleton Place, 881

"might could," 159

Mignot, Louis Remy, 755

migration, 193, 198, 368, 387

Military Order of the Stars and Bars, 345

Miller, Caroline, 520

Mills, Robert, 727, 729, 731

Milnes, Richard Monckton, Lord Houghton, 916

miniature golf, 909, 911
minstrel-show tradition, 325, 545, 572, 573, 574, 610, 611, 992
mint julep, 347, 662, 698, 850
Miss Firecracker, 988
Mississippi Delta, 22, 47, 112, 546, 550, 960
Mississippi Masala, 984
Mississippi Summer Project, 381
Missouri, 2–4, 24, 29, 62, 174, 300, 545, 905
Missouri Compromise, 268
Mitchell, Margaret, 260b, 521, 956
Mobil, 209
Mobile, Alabama, 219, 304, 890
mobile home, 152
mockingbird, 66
mojos, 128, 132, 156
Molineaux, Tom, 862
Monitor and *Merrimack,* 308
Monk, Thelonius, 570
Monk, Wayne "Honey," 642
Monroe, Bill, 558, 599, 976
Monroe, James, 432
Montgomery, Alabama, 322, 371, 375, 383, 393, 602, 871
Montgomery, Michael, 161–62
Monticello, 680, 729
Monument Avenue (Richmond), 873
monuments, 338, 341, 731, 746, 873, 895
Moon Pie, 689
Moonlight Bar-B-Que Inn, 646
Moravians, 103, 122, 621, 819, 891
Mordecai, Henry, 732
Morehouse College, 837
Morgan, Sister Gertrude, 790
Mormons, 90, 97, 822
Morphy, Paul Charles, 875
Morris, Willie, 446, 472–73, 855
Morris Brown College, 837
Morris Museum of Art, 900
Morrison's Cafeterias, 219
Morton, Jelly Roll, 591
Mosby, John Singleton, 298
mosquitoes, 55, 69
Mount Vernon, 640, 680, 727, 882
Mountain Dew, 36, 707
Moyers, Billy Don, 144
muffuleta, 694
mules, 44, 168, 176, 355, 407, 485, 716
Murphy, Audie, 915
Murray, Albert, 446
Murry, John "J.B.," 786
Muscle Shoals, 566

Museum of Early Southern Decorative Arts, 899
Museum of the Confederacy, 329, 901
Museum of the New South, 901
Museum of the Southern Jewish Experience, 901
Muslims, 115, 822, 861
mutton, 646
My Cousin Vinny, 985
My Old Kentucky Home, 610
Myrtle Beach, 109, 822, 904, 969
mystery writers, 534b–36

NAACP (see National Association for the Advancement of Colored People)
Nabors, Jim, 990
"nadir, the," 366
Namath, Joe, 144, 869
NASCAR, 36, 712, 874
Nashville, 967
Nashville Network, 583
Nashville Sound, 561–63
Natchez, 43, 743, 753, 894
Natchez Trace, 43
Nation, Carry, 828
Nation of Islam, 822, 861
National Association for the Advancement of Colored People, 117, 225, 323, 379, 391, 489, 497
National Civil Rights Museum, 898, 901
National Road, 44
National Textile Workers Union, 33
NationsBank, 215, 227
natural resources, 195
Neal, Bill, 636
Nehi, 708
Nelson, Willie, 562, 613
New Bern, North Carolina, 894
New Critics, 490, 491
New Madrid earthquake, 57
New Market (battle), 834
New Mexico, 3
New Orleans, 19, 31, 43, 46, 56, 69, 86, 100, 106, 119, 129, 131, 236, 304, 356, 433, 890, 968, 971; arts and architecture, 725, 741, 743, 749, 773, 882; ethnic groups, 100, 106, 119; food, 652, 687, 690–96, 702; music and nightlife, 31, 46, 549, 555–56, 584, 591, 592, 605, 622
New Roadside America, 911
New Smyrna, Florida, 107
New South, 7, 15, 210, 470, 901, 997–98

"new Southern cuisine," 636, 668, 672
New Traditionalists, 560, 563
Newcomb pottery, 125, 770
Newman, Frances, 488, 502
nicknames, 143, 146
Nisbett, Richard, 164
Nissan, 205
Norden, Lewis, 533
North Carolina A&T University, 374, 395
North Carolina School of the Arts, 845
Norton, Ken, 979
No Time for Sergeants, 961

O'Connor, Flannery, 484–86, 514, 792b, 851, 880b, 1001
Oglethorpe, James Edward, 887
O'Hara, Scarlett, 260b, 956
Ohr, George, 124
oil, 101, 195, 209, 975
Okefenokee Swamp, 54
O'Kellyites, 807
Oklahoma, 2–4, 17, 29, 42, 88
okra, 156, 670, 690
Old Salem, North Carolina, 621, 891, 899
Old South Ball, 346
Old South myth, 748, 912–17, 923
Ole Miss (see University of Mississippi)
Oliver, King, 592
Olmsted, Frederick Law, 450, 715, 887, 896
opera, 256, 585, 620
Opryland, 907
Orbison, Roy, 564
Order of the Confederate Rose, 345
Original Dixieland Jazz Band, 556
Orlando, Florida, 897
Ory, Kid, 592
Osborne Brothers, 558
Osceola, 116
outbuildings, 716
outdoor drama, 903
Outer Banks, 27
outlaws, 300
Outlaws (country music), 562
Owens, Jesse, 856
Owensboro, Kentucky, 646
Oxmoor House, 494
Ozarks, 16, 24, 905

Page, Thomas Nelson, 465, 912b
Page, Walter Hines, 470, 633
Paige, Satchel, 859
Pakistanis, 113

palm trees, 77
Palmer, Fanny, 748
palmetto, 77
"Papaw," 154
Park Sausage Company, 639
Parker, Charlie, 570
Parks, Rosa, 371
Parris Island, 28
Parrish, Clara Weaver, 761
Parthenon, 907
Parton, Dolly, 603, 904
Patton, Charley, 546, 586
Peachtree Publishers, 494
Peachtree Street, 51
Peale family (painters), 750
pecan pie, 680, 698
Peer, Ralph, 557, 593, 594
pellagra, 194, 615, 932
Pemberton, John Clifford, 296, 313
Pemberton, John S., 705
Penn Center, 846
Penney's, 207, 214
Pennington, Estill Curtis, 900
Pentecostals, 793, 806, 813–16, 829
Pepsi, 212, 607, 705
Pepsico, 221, 246, 707
Percy, Walker, 474, 480, 504, 513, 529, 890, 981, 998, 999
Percy, William Alexander, 61, 518, 927
Perelli, Achille, 746
Perkins, Carl, 564
Perot, Ross, 441
Peterkin, Julia, 132, 519
Petersburg, Virginia, 290, 318
Petigru, James L., 278
Petty, Richard, 712, 874
Pharr, Robert Deane, 483
Phi Beta Kappa, 833
Phillips, Bum, 848
Phillips, Sam, 564
Phillips, Ulrich, 348b, 448
phosphates, 195
piazzas, 715, 724
Pickett, Wilson, 566
Pickett's Charge, 312, 973
pickles, 677
Piedmont, 15, 103, 122, 819
Piedmont blues, 547, 588
Pigeon Forge, Tennessee, 904
Piggly-Wiggly, 218
Pinckney family, 234
Pine Mountain Settlement School, 580

Pinehurst, North Carolina, 880
Pinkerton Tobacco Co., 211
pirates, 27, 236
"piss-ant," 150
pitcher plants, 79
Plains, Georgia, 39
plantation houses, 715, 726
plantation myth, 445, 463, 467b, 912b, 912–17, 934
plantation novel, 462–65
Pleasant Hill, 892
Plessy v. *Ferguson,* 280, 365, 369
po' boy, 694
Pocahontas, 442
Poe, Edgar Allan, 455, 491
Poesch, Jessie, 751
Poet Laureate, Confederacy, 338, 339
Poet Laureate, USA, 508
Pogo, 54, 64
poke sallet, 668
Polk, James Knox, 435
Polk, Leonidas, 294, 836
poll tax, 361, 425, 615
Ponce de Leon (hotel), 883
Populist, 361, 399, 419
porches, 720, 722, 724–26
pork, 177, 633, 635, 637–44, 648, 691
pork rind, 639
Port Royal, 85
Porte Crayon (see Strother, David Hunter)
Porter, Katherine Anne, 472, 526
portico, 726, 727
Portis, Charles, 533
Portman, John, 737
possum, 64, 65, 663
Post, Emily, 948
post-vocalic *r,* 160
pot likker, 657, 668, 669
potters, 122–25
poultry processing, 26, 111, 211, 223
poverty, 22, 190, 200, 386
pralines, 687
Presbyterians, 288, 808–12, 823, 827
Presley, Elvis (see Elvis)
Price, Byron, 17
Price, Leontyne, 626
Price, Reynolds, 162, 348b, 492, 533, 538, 633b, 633, 945
privy, 67, 70, 192, 716
Prohibition, 216, 367, 412
proslavery thought, 260–65, 285, 456, 827
Prosser, Gabriel, 350

protest songs, 544
Prudhomme, Paul, 693
public health, 194
publishing, 250, 470, 494–95
Pulitzer Prize, 498, 505, 508, 510, 511, 519–32, 903, 982
Pusser, Buford, 904

Quaker Products, 653
Quakers, 266, 267, 819, 903
Quantrill, William Clarke, 300
quilts, 126

R&B (see rhythm-and-blues)
race riots, 356, 366, 377, 427
ragtime, 545, 585, 588, 591
railroads, 112, 178, 883
Rainey, Ma, 551, 589
raised cottage, 726
Raleigh, Sir Walter, 83
Ralph the Diving Pig, 906
Ramos gin fizz, 695
Ramsay, David, 82b
Randolph, A. Philip, 392, 489
Randolph, John, 398
Ransom, John Crowe, 487, 490
Rauschenberg, Robert, 778
Ravenel, Shannon, 493
Rawlings, Marjorie Kinnan, 522
Reagan, Ronald, 416
Real McCoys, 989
rebel yell, 331
Rebel Yell (whiskey), 331, 937
Reconstruction, 81, 355–59, 402–5, 411, 437
red beans, 671
Red Bones, 91
Red Clay Ramblers, 60
Red Clay Reader, 60
Red Man, 211, 711
Redding, Otis, 566, 617
Redeemers, 359, 405
red-eye gravy, 638, 650
redneck, 567, 939–40, 962
Redneck Riviera, 25
Redstone Arsenal, 37
Reed, Ishmael, 530
Reed, Jerry, 963
Reed, Jimmy, 550
Reed, Roy, 480, 925
Reelfoot Lake, 57
Reeves, Jim, 561, 907
relishes, 677

Rendezvous, 645
Report on Economic Conditions of the South, 182–95
Republicans, 11, 16, 356–59, 402–4, 410–17
Research Triangle Park, North Carolina, 228, 738
resort hotels, 880
revivals, 537, 802, 823–26, 829, 831
revues, 551, 574
Reynolds, Burt, 962, 963, 972, 987, 996
Reynolds, R. J., 241
Reynolds Metals, 211
Rhett, Robert Barnwell, 274
rhythm-and-blues, 553, 565
ribs, 645
rice, 171, 239, 643, 667, 671, 690, 691, 697
Rice, Grantland, 876
Rich in Love, 983
Richards, T. Addison, 69, 744, 745, 754
Richardson, Henry Hobson, 735
Richmond, 15, 320, 341, 350, 499, 536, 637, 746, 873, 901
ring shout, 135
ring tournaments, 175
Ritz-Carlton Hotels, 233
Rivers, Rosetta Raulston, 745
Roanoke Island, 83
Roberts, Elizabeth Madox, 501
Roberts, Oral, 832
Robertson, Ben, 446, 478, 633b, 929
Robertson, Pat, 832
Robertson, Robbie, 537b
rock and roll, 553, 555, 564–67, 606
Rock City, 911
rockabilly, 564
Rockefeller, John D., 67, 885
Rockin' Dopsie, 569
Rocky Mountain spotted fever, 70
Rodgers, Jimmie, 557, 599
Roger Ogden Museum of Southern Art, 901
Rooney, John F., Jr., 852
Roosevelt, Franklin D., 182b, 601, 654
Rosenwald Foundation, 847
Rubin, Louis D., Jr., 471, 477, 493, 498
Rudolph, Paul, 738
Rudolph, Wilma, 865
Ruffin, Edmund, 277
Rugby, Tennessee, 894
Rushing, Jimmy, 552
Ruth, Babe, 601, 858, 859
Ryan, Abram Joseph, 332, 339
Ryan, Nolan, 859
Ryman Auditorium, 907

Sabine Pass (battle), 314
Sacred Harp, 538
Sahara of the Bozart, 8, 931
St. Augustine, Florida, 82, 883
St. Helena Island (see Sea Islands)
Sale, Kirkpatrick, 995
Sam and Dave, 566
Samples, Junior, 992
Sanders, Colonel Harland, 246, 665, 935
Sanders, John, 494
sanitation, 194
Santeria, 822
Sapelo Island, Georgia, 115
SAS Institute, 228
Saturn (automobile), 205
saw-mill gravy, 676
Sawyier, Paul, 749
Sazerac, 695
scalawags, 298, 403
Schwartz, Maryln, 938
Schwerner, Michael, 381
SCLC (see Southern Christian Leadership Conference)
Scopes, John, 32, 932
Scotch-Irish, 40, 98, 660, 808
Scott, Evelyn, 503
Scott, Ray Wilson, 871
Scott, Sir Walter, 912
Scott, Winfield, 302
Scottish, 102
Scottsboro, Alabama, 35, 597, 932
scriptural inerrancy, 794, 796
Scruggs, Earl, 558, 599
sculpture, 746, 777, 784, 789, 895
scuppernong wine, 703
Sea Islands, 28, 95, 127, 173, 355, 541, 846
Second Coming, 794
second line, 555
Secretariat, 868
segregation, 364–66, 369, 372–82, 385, 426–29
Seignouret, François, 741
self-taught artists, 784–91
Selma, Alabama, 383
Seminoles, 55, 88, 90, 116
sense of place, 476
separate but equal, 365
Settle, Mary Lee, 533
7-Eleven, 222
Seven-Up, 212, 706
Sewanee (see University of the South)
sex, lies, and videotape, 986

Seymour, William Joseph, 829
shag (dance), 582
Shag (movie), 969
shape-note music, 537–39, 798
sharecroppers, 178, 184, 366, 453
Sharp, Cecil, 543, 580
she-crab soup, 697
Shell Oil, 209
Shenandoah Valley, 40, 49, 103, 310, 714, 819
Sherman, William T., 303, 887, 915
Sherman's March, 178, 319
Sherman's March (movie), 987
Shiloh (battle), 290, 518
shimmy, 574–79
Shirley plantation, 886
Shore, Dinah, 500
shotgun house, 723
Siamese Twins, 118
silverware, 714b, 739–40
Simmons, Philip, 121
Simmons, William J., 367
Simms, William Gilmore, 456, 491, 714b
Simpson, Lewis, 922
Sims, Bernice, 784b
"sir," 148
sit-ins, 374
Skaggs, Ricky, 563
slave insurrections, 349–53
slave narratives, 389, 448–49, 457
slave quarters, 175, 717
slavery, 92–95, 178, 260–72, 343, 348–54, 443
Sledge, Percy, 566
Slim, Lightnin', 554
Sloan, Samuel, 728, 926
slow speech, 162
smiling, 163
Smith, Alice Ravenel Huger, 774
Smith, Bessie, 551, 574, 589
Smith, Gerald L. K., 905
Smith, John, 64, 442, 460, 654, 918
Smith, Lee, 138–39, 483, 493, 533
Smith, Lillian, 614, 825
Smith, "Pine Top," 549
Smithfield ham, 635, 638
smokehouses, 716
smokeless tobacco, 710
Smokey and the Bandit, 963
snake-handling, 813
Snow, Hank, 565
snuff, 169, 211, 709–10
soft drinks, 155, 212, 242, 704–8, 712

soil erosion, 80, 187

Solid South, 11, 406, 412–13, 439

Song of the South, 966

Sonny Bryan's Smokehouse, 647

Sons of Confederate Veterans, 345

soul food, 634, 639, 679

soul music, 537b, 566–67, 573, 607, 617

Sounder, 959

sour-mash, 661

souse, 639

south Florida, 18, 106, 109–10, 535, 820

south Louisiana, 59, 568–69

South of the Border, 909

Southeast, 13, 15, 89–90, 103, 225

Southern bully (social type), 939

Southern Christian Leadership
    Conference, 371, 395, 397, 846

Southern Comfort, 216

Southern Comfort (movie), 978

Southern Focus Poll, 148, 155, 157, 159,
    662, 793–94, 879

Southern Fried Rabbit, 966

Southern Gothic, 455, 461

Southern grotesque, 484

Southern Historical Collection, 842

Southern lady, 73, 498, 927, 944–53, 996

Southern Living, 206, 494, 635, 776, 855,
    1000

Southern Manifesto, 372

Southern Partisan, 403

Southern Pines, 880

Southern Regional Council, 396

Southern Renaissance, 8, 488, 502

Southern rock, 65, 323, 567, 580, 618

Southern Students Organizing Committee,
    331

Southern Style, 250

Southern Yankee (social type), 934

Southern Yankee (movie), 973

Southerner, The, 957

Southland Corporation, 222

"Southland in the Springtime," 617

Southwest, 17, 560, 583

Southwest Airlines, 229

Southwestern humor, 458–61

Spalding, Phinizy, 737

Spanish, 82, 85, 86, 87, 100, 101, 883, 890

Spanish moss, 74–75

Speaker, Tris, 859

speaking in tongues, 813, 829

Spelman College, 837

Spencer, Elizabeth, 533

spirituals, 537, 541, 543–44

Spivey, Victoria, 551

Spoleto Festival, 630

sponge-diving, 107

spoonbread, 659

Spotsylvania (battle), 317

springhouses, 716

Springs Industries, 210, 245

square dance, 580

Stainless Banner, 324

Stanback headache powder, 712

Standard Oil, 975

Stanley Brothers, 558

Stars and Bars, 322, 344, 770

state flags, 323

states' rights, 372, 400

States' Rights Democratic Party (see
    Dixiecrats)

Statesmen Quartet, 540

Statler Brothers, 540

steamboats, 43, 741, 748

steel magnolia (social type), 73, 945

Steel Magnolias (movie), 970

Stephens, Alexander Hamilton, 284

Still, William Grant, 624

stockcar racing, 16, 36, 660, 851, 874, 937

Stone, Edward Durell, 736

Stone Mountain, 895

Stono Creek, 350

storytelling, 479, 515

Storyville, 31, 592

Stowe, Harriet Beecher, 912b

Strait, George, 563

"Strange Fruit," 614

Stribling, T. S., 488, 519b

Strother, David Hunter, 53, 452

Stuart, J. E. B., 291

Stuckey's, 687

Student Nonviolent Coordinating
    Committee, 374, 396

Styron, William, 492, 527

subsidies, industrial, 202

Sudduth, Jimmy Lee, 785

sugarcane, 55, 172

Suggs, Simon, 458

Sullivan, Walter, 531

Sully, Thomas, 752

Sun Records, 564, 898, 908

Sunbelt, 12, 995

Sunni Muslims, 822

"supper," 157

Swaggart, Jimmy, 815

swamp blues, 554

Swamp Women, 965

swamps, 53–55, 75

Sweet Briar College, 841

sweet potato pie, 679, 683

swimming, 854

Tabasco sauce, 678

tailgate parties, 855

taking it easy, 165, 928

Tallchief, Maria, 625

Talmadge, Eugene, 422

tamales, 644

Tarpon Springs, Florida, 107

tasso, 692

Tate, Allen, 480, 482, 487, 504, 531

Taulbert, Clifton, 483

taxes, 181, 190–91, 361

Taylor, John, 398

Taylor, Koko, 550

Taylor, Peter, 531

Taylor, Rex, 140

Taylor, Robert Love, 940

Taylor, Zachary, 283, 436

"TCBY," 230

televangelists, 815, 832

tenant farmers, 184, 453, 957

Tennessee capitol, 735b

Tennessee State University, 865

Tennessee Valley Authority, 58

Terry, Sonny, 547

tertium quids, 398

Tex, Joe, 566

Texas barbecue, 647

Texas blues, 548

Texas Instruments, 208, 232

Texas Pete hot sauce, 678

Texas Playboys (see Wills, Bob)

Texas two-step, 583

textiles, 33, 188, 194, 210, 238, 245

Tharpe, Rosetta, 542

"That's What I Like About the South," 615

Theus, Jeremiah, 763

Thomas, Ella Gertrude Clanton, 271, 446

Thomas, George Henry, 303

Thompson, Hunter S., 474

Thompson, John R., 337

Thornton, Big Mama, 553

Thornwell, James Henley, 332, 827

Thorpe, Jim, 863

Thunder Road, 50

ticks, 70

Tidewater, Virginia, 160–61

Tilden, Samuel, 359, 411

Till, Emmett, 370

Tillett, Wilbur Fisk, 944
Tillis, Mel, 617
Tillman, Benjamin R., 418
Timrod, Henry, 338
Tin Pan Alley, 545, 573, 612, 615
Tindall, George, 97, 932
Tindley, C. A., 544
tobacco, 111, 169, 188, 211, 241, 283b,
    709–11
tobacco barn, 714, 719
Tobacco Road, 48, 51, 77
de Tocqueville, Alexis, 450, 915
Tolson, Edgar, 786
tomahawk chop, 879
Tompkins, Sally Louisa, 299
Toole, John Kennedy, 529
Toomer, Jean, 483
Tootsie's Orchid Lounge, 907
touchiness, 164
tourism, 16, 18, 24–26, 43, 45–46, 55, 62,
    81, 535, 661, 747, 880–911, 980
Toyota, 205
Trail of Tears, 42, 88
travel writing, 450
Travis, Merle, 588
Travis, Randy, 563
Trollope, Frances, 450
Tubb, Ernest, 560, 907
Tulane University, 125, 773
Tupelo, Mississippi, 908
Tupperware, 910
Turks, 91
Turner, Big Joe, 552–53
Turner, Nat, 352, 527
Turner, Robert Edward "Ted," 249, 879, 973
turnip greens, 219, 668
Turpin, Tom, 545
Tuskegee Institute, 390, 738, 781, 839
TVA (see Tennessee Valley Authority)
Twain, Mark, 160, 162, 461, 912
Twitty, Conway, 564, 907
Two Thousand Maniacs, 980
Twombly, Cy, 779
Tyler, Anne, 492, 532
Tyler, John, 434
Tyson Foods, 211, 223

UDC (see United Daughters of the
    Confederacy)
Uhry, Alfred, 082 83
Uncle Ben, 671
Uncle Julius, 468
Uncle Remus, 467, 966

Uncle Tom's Cabin, 464, 912b
Underground Atlanta, 429, 696
Underground Railroad, 266, 903
Unionists, 278–82, 410, 433, 437
Unitarians, 819
United Church of Christ, 807
United Confederate Veterans, 342, 345
United Daughters of the Confederacy, 158,
    344
United Mine Workers, 34
University of Alabama, 378, 428
University of Arkansas, 177
University of Florida, 346, 708
University of Georgia, 842
University of Mississippi, 323, 377, 427,
    608, 844
University of North Carolina, 734, 842, 870
University of South Carolina, 418, 827
University of Southwestern Louisiana, 19
University of the South, 294, 817, 836, 843
University of Virginia, 729, 913
university presses, 495
UPS, 207, 213
Urban League, 489
U.S. Space and Rocket Center, 901
U.S. Tobacco, 211, 710

Valentine, Edward Virginius, 746
Valley Campaign, 310
Vance, Rupert B., 10
Vanderbilt, George Washington, 896
Vanderbilt University, 487, 490, 922
Vandiver, Frank, 17
Vardaman, James K., 420
Varney, Jim "Ernest," 902
Vaudechamp, Jean Joseph, 741, 743
vaudeville blues, 551, 589
Vaughan, Stevie Ray, 548
Venus flytrap, 79
Vernon, Florida, 976
Vesey, Denmark, 350–51
veterans, Confederate, 181, 323, 342, 345,
    362
Vicksburg, Mississippi, 22, 296, 313, 787
Vidalia onions, 673, 677
Vietnamese, 114
Vieux Carré (see French Quarter)
Vincent, Gene, 564
Virginia Dynasty, 432
Virginia Military Institute, 288, 834
Vlach, John Michael, 723
VMI (see Virginia Military Institute)
von Braun, Werner, 37

voodoo (see hoodoo)
Voting Rights Act of 1965, 360, 384

Wachovia (bank), 215
Wal-Mart, 214, 229, 247
Walker, Alice, 483, 507, 530, 959
Walker, Jerry Jeff, 144
Walker, T-Bone, 548
Walker, William Aiken, 747, 771
Wallace, George C., 378, 415, 425, 428, 609
Walton, Sam, 247
Waltons, The, 993
"War Between the States," 158
Ward, Clara, 542
Warner, Anne Bradford, 493
Warren, Robert Penn, 178b, 472, 475, 479,
    487, 490, 508, 974
Washington, Booker T., 364, 390, 449, 470,
    839
Washington, George, 53, 329, 432, 444, 640,
    727, 750, 752
Washington, William D., 334, 337
Washington and Lee, 287, 346, 840
watermelon, 39, 674, 677
Waters, Muddy, 550, 553, 596
Watie, Stand, 297
Watson, Thomas Edward, 419
"We Shall Overcome," 544
Webster, Daniel, 436
Webster, Katie, 554
Weems, Mason Locke "Parson," 444
Wells, Junior, 550
Wells, Kitty, 603, 907
Welty, Eudora, 134, 466, 476, 481, 485, 510,
    526
Wesley, John, 802
Wesleyans (see Methodists)
West, William Edward, 753
West Virginia, 2, 3
Western swing, 559, 600
Westville, Georgia, 894
Whigs, 302, 403–4, 434, 436
whiskey, 16, 50, 660–62, 937
Whistler, James McNeill, 76
White, John, 83
White, Josh, 547, 588, 614
White, Martha, 653
white lightning, 660
white primary, 363
white trash, 941
Whitney, Eli, 235
Whittle, Chris, 250
Wigfall, Louis Trezevant, 276

Wilber's, 641
Wilderness Road, 40–41
Wilkinson, Sylvia, 493
William and Mary, College of, 261, 833
Williams, Big Joe, 546
Williams, David Marshall, 244
Williams, Evan, 660
Williams, Hank, 565, 593, 602, 691, 907, 967
Williams, Hank, Jr., 148, 907, 925
Williams, Jonathan, 494
Williams, Tennessee, 511, 530, 960
Williamsburg, Virginia, 833, 884–85
Williamson, Sonny Boy, 550
Wills, Bob, 559, 600
Wilson, Augusta Jane Evans, 466
Wilson, Charles Reagan, 73
Wilson, Clyde, 501, 522

Wilson, Woodrow, 438, 440, 465, 955
wine, 674, 703
Wirz, Henry, 316
Wister, Owen, 17
WLAC, 553
Wolfe, Thomas, 506
Wolfe, Tom, 937
Woodruff, Hale, 776
Woodward, C. Vann, 447, 449, 527, 714b, 940
Woodward, William and Ellsworth, 773
wool hats, 399
Wright, Charles, 518
Wright, Richard, 509
wrought iron, 121
WTBS, 249, 879
Wynette, Tammy, 603

Yancey, William Lowndes, 273
yellow fever, 69
"Yellow Rose of Texas," 328, 340
yellow-dog Democrats, 406
yeoman, 936–37, 940, 953
Yoder, Ed, 998
Yoknapatawpha Press, 494
York, Alvin, 915
"you-all," 147
Young, Andrew, 196b, 394, 397

Zaharias, Babe Didrickson, 864
Zelinsky, Wilbur, 44, 143, 251–57
zydeco, 96, 554, 569
Zydeco, Buckwheat, 569